Love Hina

赤松 健

by Ken Akamatsu **Vol.5**

ALSO AVAILABLE FROM TOKYOPOP®

MANGA

.HACK//LEGEND OF THE TWILIGHT
@LARGE (October 2003)
ANGELIC LAYER*
BABY BIRTH*
BATTLE ROYALE*
BRAIN POWERED*
BRIGADOON*
CARDCAPTOR SAKURA
CARDCAPTOR SAKURA: MASTER OF THE CLOW*
CHOBITS*
CHRONICLES OF THE CURSED SWORD
CLAMP SCHOOL DETECTIVES*
CLOVER
CONFIDENTIAL CONFESSIONS*
CORRECTOR YUI
COWBOY BEBOP*
COWBOY BEBOP: SHOOTING STAR*
CYBORG 009*
DEMON DIARY
DIGIMON*
DRAGON HUNTER
DRAGON KNIGHTS*
DUKLYON: CLAMP SCHOOL DEFENDERS*
ERICA SAKURAZAWA*
FAKE*
FLCL*
FORBIDDEN DANCE*
GATE KEEPERS*
G GUNDAM*
GRAVITATION*
GTO*
GUNDAM WING
GUNDAM WING: BATTLEFIELD OF PACIFISTS
GUNDAM WING: ENDLESS WALTZ*
GUNDAM WING: THE LAST OUTPOST*
HAPPY MANIA*
HARLEM BEAT
I.N.V.U.
INITIAL D*
ISLAND
JING: KING OF BANDITS*
JULINE
KARE KANO*
KINDAICHI CASE FILES, THE*
KING OF HELL
KODOCHA: SANA'S STAGE*
LOVE HINA*
LUPIN III*
MAGIC KNIGHT RAYEARTH*

MAGIC KNIGHT RAYEARTH II* (COMING SOON)
MAN OF MANY FACES*
MARMALADE BOY*
MARS*
MIRACLE GIRLS
MIYUKI-CHAN IN WONDERLAND* (October 2003)
MONSTERS, INC.
PARADISE KISS*
PARASYTE
PEACH GIRL
PEACH GIRL: CHANGE OF HEART*
PET SHOP OF HORRORS*
PLANET LADDER*
PLANETES* (October 2003)
PRIEST
RAGNAROK
RAVE MASTER*
REALITY CHECK
REBIRTH
REBOUND*
RISING STARS OF MANGA
SABER MARIONETTE J*
SAILOR MOON
SAINT TAIL
SAMURAI DEEPER KYO*
SAMURAI GIRL: REAL BOUT HIGH SCHOOL*
SCRYED*
SHAOLIN SISTERS*
SHIRAHIME-SYO: SNOW GODDESS TALES* (Dec. 2003)
SHUTTERBOX (November 2003)
SORCERER HUNTERS
THE SKULL MAN*
THE VISION OF ESCAFLOWNE
TOKYO MEW MEW*
UNDER THE GLASS MOON
VAMPIRE GAME*
WILD ACT*
WISH*
WORLD OF HARTZ (COMING SOON)
X-DAY*
ZODIAC P.I. *

For more information visit www.TOKYOPOP.com

*INDICATES 100% AUTHENTIC MANGA (RIGHT-TO-LEFT FORMAT)

CINE-MANGA™

CARDCAPTORS
JACKIE CHAN ADVENTURES (November 2003)
JIMMY NEUTRON
KIM POSSIBLE
LIZZIE MCGUIRE
POWER RANGERS: NINJA STORM
SPONGEBOB SQUAREPANTS
SPY KIDS 2

NOVELS

KARMA CLUB (April 2004)
SAILOR MOON

TOKYOPOP KIDS

STRAY SHEEP

ART BOOKS

CARDCAPTOR SAKURA*
MAGIC KNIGHT RAYEARTH*

ANIME GUIDES

COWBOY BEBOP ANIME GUIDES
GUNDAM TECHNICAL MANUALS
SAILOR MOON SCOUT GUIDES

062703

Love Hina

By

Ken Akamatsu

Volume 5

Los Angeles • Tokyo • London

Translator - Nan Rymer
English Adaptation - Adam Arnold
Retouch and Lettering - Jeremy Canceko
Cover Layout - Anna Kernbaum

Editor - Luis Reyes
Managing Editor - Jill Freshney
Production Coordinator - Antonio DePietro
Production Manager - Jennifer Miller & Mario M. Rodriguez
Art Director - Matt Alford
Editorial Director - Jeremy Ross
VP of Production - Ron Klamert
President & C.O.O. - John Parker
Publisher & C.E.O. - Stuart Levy

Email: editor@TOKYOPOP.com
Come visit us online at www.TOKYOPOP.com

A  Manga

TOKYOPOP Inc.
5900 Wilshire Blvd. Suite 2000
Los Angeles, CA 90036

ISBN: 1-59182-016-2

First TOKYOPOP printing: August 2002

10 9 8 7 6 5 4 3

Printed in the USA

Love Hina

The Story Thus Far ...

Fifteen years ago, Keitaro Urashima made a promise to a girl that they would go to Tokyo University together. Now at the age of twenty, he's finding it more and more difficult to keep that promise, much less find that girl again.

He's inherited from his globetrotting grandmother the Hinata House, a quiet residential dorm where he can work as the landlord and prepare for his upcoming exams in peace... if it wasn't for the fact that Hinata House is actually a girls dormitory with a clientele none too pleased that its new, live-in landlord is a man – or as close to a man as poor Keitaro can be. The lanky loser incessantly (and accidentally) crashes their sessions in the hot springs, walks in on them changing... and pokes his nose pretty much everywhere it can get broken, if not by the hot-headed Naru, then by one of the other Hinata inmates – Kitsune, a late-teen alcoholic with a diesel libido; Motoko, a swordswoman who struggles with feminine issues; Shinobu, a pre-teen princess with a colossal crush on Keitaro; and Su, a foreign girl with a big appetite.

Having both failed the Tokyo U exam, Keitaro and Naru, after a bit of soul searching, have decided to give it another go. But Keitaro still hasn't voiced his romantic feelings for his study mate. To make matters worse, Keitaro gets a part time job with Seta, a college professor at Tokyo U who is also the object of Naru's crush. Seta represents Keitaro's rival and boss in one, though the absent-minded professor hasn't a clue about any of it. His concerns are for his young ward Sarah, for whom Seta has assumed responsibility.

CONTENTS

LOVE♡HINA

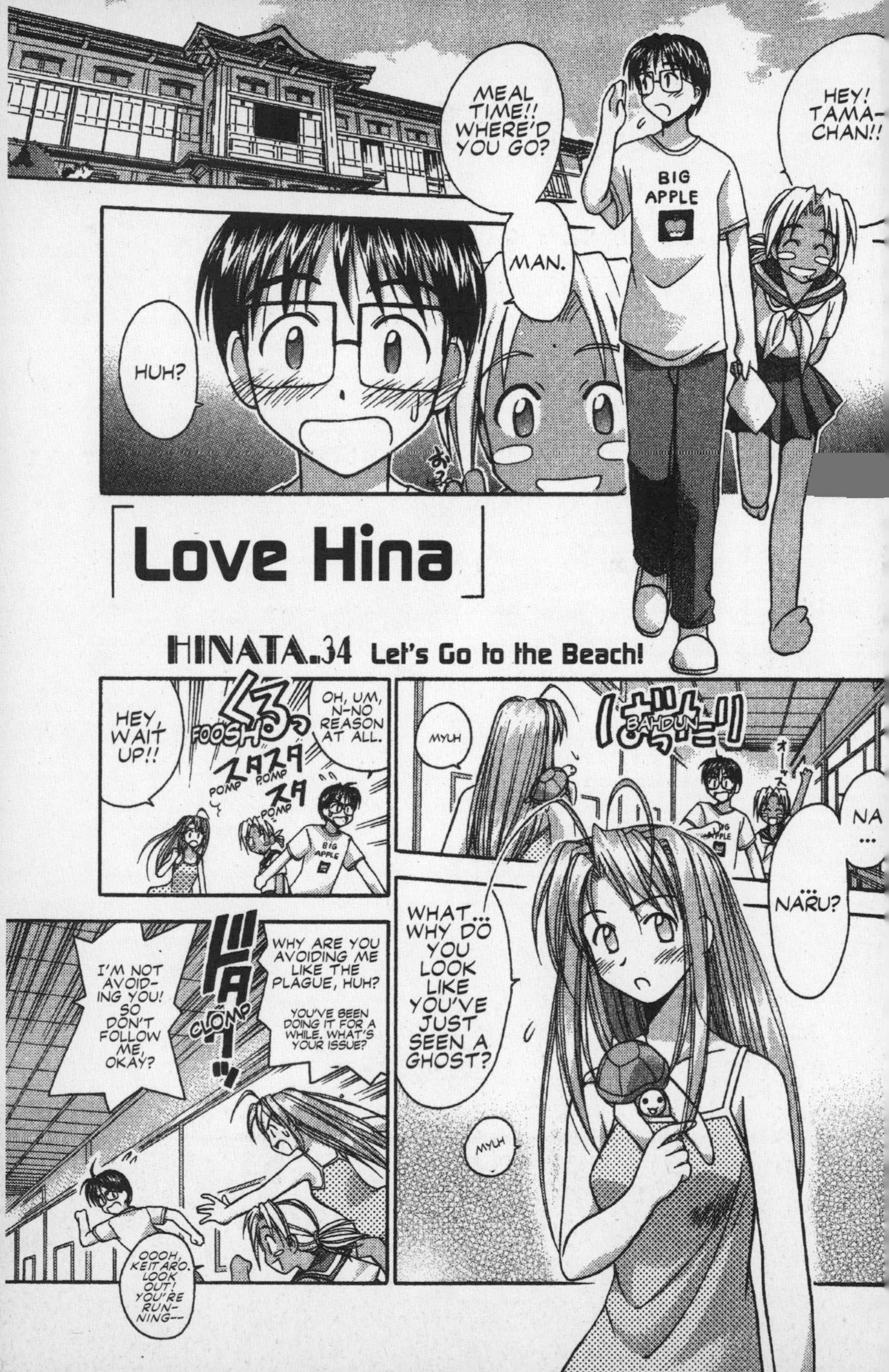
HEY! TAMA-CHAN!!
MEAL TIME!! WHERE'D YOU GO?
MAN.
HUH?
Love Hina
HINATA..34 Let's Go to the Beach!
BAHDUN
MYUH
NA...
NARU?
WHAT... WHY DÖ YOU LOOK LIKE YOU'VE JUST SEEN A GHOST?
MYUH
HEY, WAIT UP!!
くるっ
FOOSH
OH, UM, N-NO REASON AT ALL.
スタスタ
POMP POMP
スタ
POMP
WHY ARE YOU AVOIDING ME LIKE THE PLAGUE, HUH?
YOU'VE BEEN DOING IT FOR A WHILE. WHAT'S YOUR ISSUE?
I'M NOT AVOIDING YOU! SO DON'T FOLLOW ME, OKAY?
ドタ
CLOMP
OOOH, KEITARO. LOOK OUT! YOU'RE RUNNING--

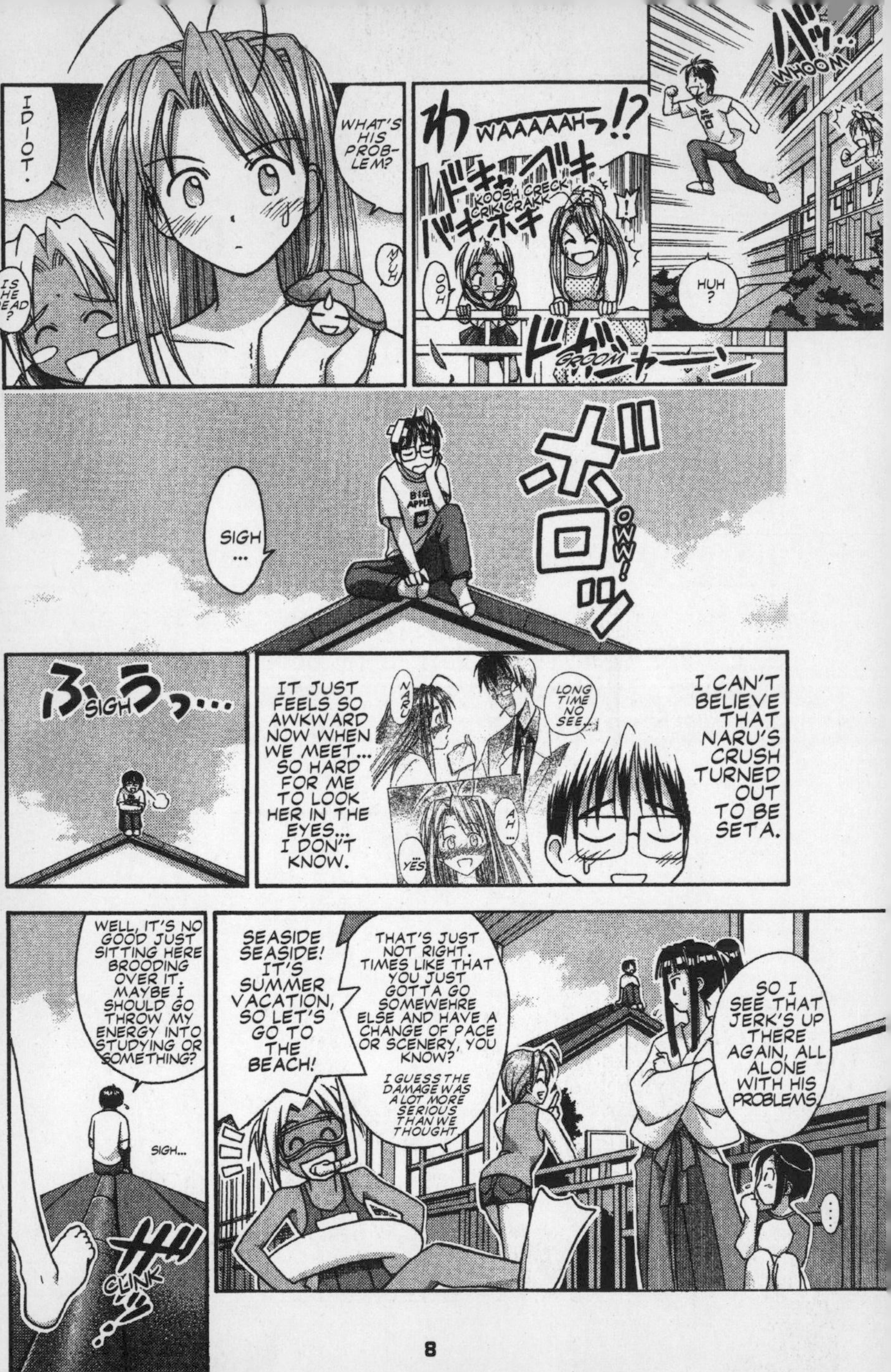
WHOOM
HUH?
WAAAAAH!?
KOOSH CRECK CRIK CRAKK
!
OOH
GROOM
WHAT'S HIS PROB-LEM?
MUH
IDIOT.
IS HE DEAD?
OWW!
SIGH...
I CAN'T BELIEVE THAT NARU'S CRUSH TURNED OUT TO BE SETA.
LONG TIME NO SEE...
NARU
IT JUST FEELS SO AWKWARD NOW WHEN WE MEET... SO HARD FOR ME TO LOOK HER IN THE EYES... I DON'T KNOW.
AH...
...YES
SIGH
SO I SEE THAT JERK'S UP THERE AGAIN, ALL ALONE WITH HIS PROBLEMS.
...
THAT'S JUST NOT RIGHT. TIMES LIKE THAT YOU JUST GOTTA GO SOMEWEHRE ELSE AND HAVE A CHANGE OF PACE OR SCENERY, YOU KNOW?
I GUESS THE DAMAGE WAS A LOT MORE SERIOUS THAN WE THOUGHT.
SEASIDE SEASIDE! IT'S SUMMER VACATION, SO LET'S GO TO THE BEACH!
WELL, IT'S NO GOOD JUST SITTING HERE BROODING OVER IT. MAYBE I SHOULD GO THROW MY ENERGY INTO STUDYING OR SOMETHING?
SIGH...
CLINK

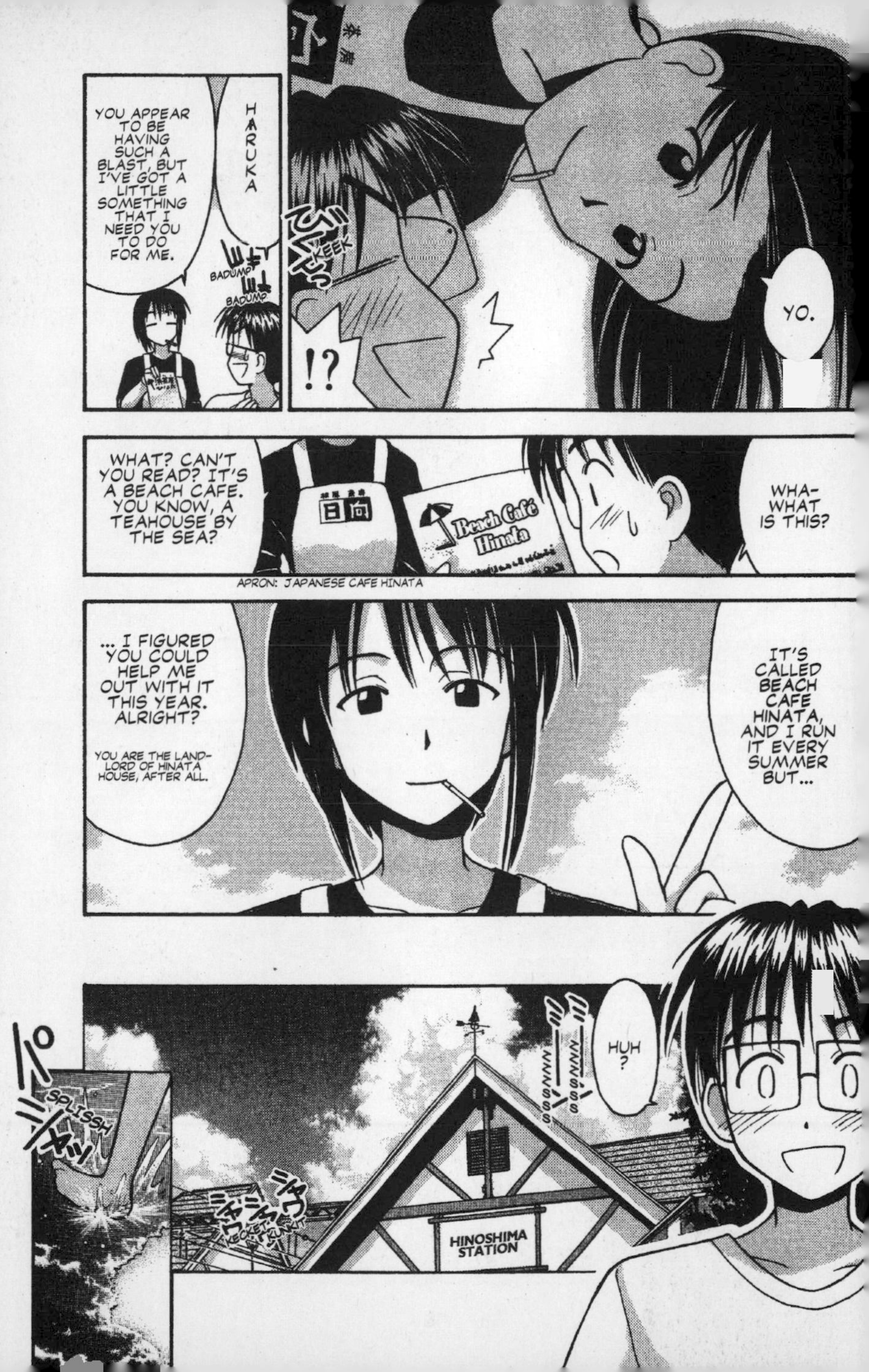
YO.
!?
KEEK
HARUKA
YOU APPEAR TO BE HAVING SUCH A BLAST, BUT I'VE GOT A LITTLE SOMETHING THAT I NEED YOU TO DO FOR ME.
BADUMP
BADUMP
WHA-WHAT IS THIS?
Beach Café Hinata
WHAT? CAN'T YOU READ? IT'S A BEACH CAFE. YOU KNOW, A TEAHOUSE BY THE SEA?
APRON: JAPANESE CAFE HINATA
IT'S CALLED BEACH CAFE HINATA, AND I RUN IT EVERY SUMMER BUT...
... I FIGURED YOU COULD HELP ME OUT WITH IT THIS YEAR. ALRIGHT?
YOU ARE THE LANDLORD OF HINATA HOUSE, AFTER ALL.
HUH?
NNNSSS
NNNSSS
HINOSHIMA STATION
SPLISSH

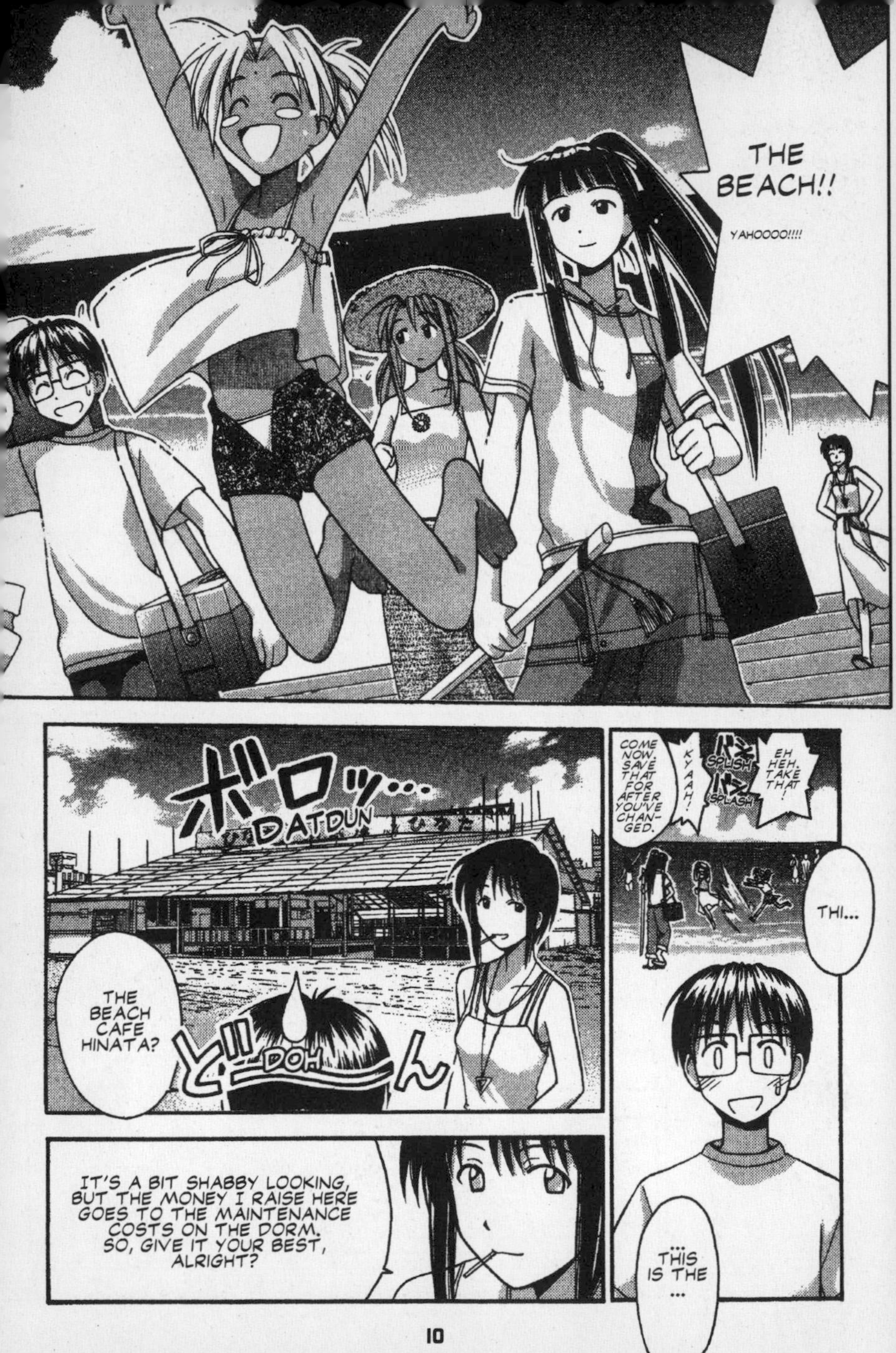
THE BEACH!!
YAHOOOO!!!!
EH HEH. TAKE THAT!
SPLISH
SPLASH
KYAAH!
COME NOW. SAVE THAT FOR AFTER YOU'VE CHANGED.
THI...
...THIS IS THE ...
DATDUN
THE BEACH CAFE HINATA?
DOH
IT'S A BIT SHABBY LOOKING, BUT THE MONEY I RAISE HERE GOES TO THE MAINTENANCE COSTS ON THE DORM. SO, GIVE IT YOUR BEST, ALRIGHT?

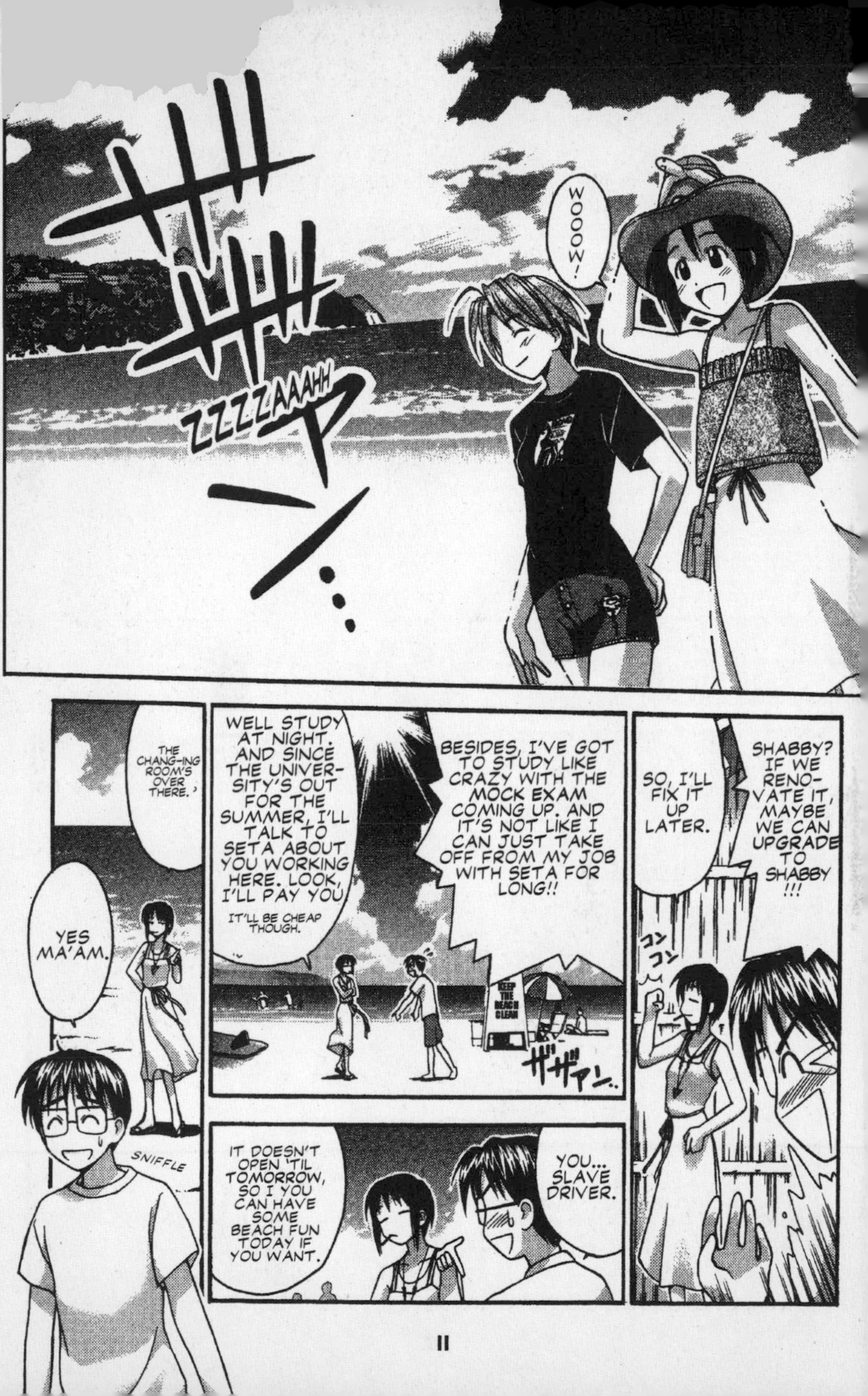
WOOOW!
ZZZZAAAHH
...
SHABBY? IF WE RENO-VATE IT, MAYBE WE CAN UPGRADE TO SHABBY!!!
SO, I'LL FIX IT UP LATER.
コン コン
BESIDES, I'VE GOT TO STUDY LIKE CRAZY WITH THE MOCK EXAM COMING UP. AND IT'S NOT LIKE I CAN JUST TAKE OFF FROM MY JOB WITH SETA FOR LONG!!
WELL STUDY AT NIGHT. AND SINCE THE UNIVER-SITY'S OUT FOR THE SUMMER, I'LL TALK TO SETA ABOUT YOU WORKING HERE. LOOK, I'LL PAY YOU.
IT'LL BE CHEAP THOUGH.
KEEP THE BEACH CLEAN
ザザァン..
YOU... SLAVE DRIVER.
IT DOESN'T OPEN 'TIL TOMORROW, SO I YOU CAN HAVE SOME BEACH FUN TODAY IF YOU WANT.
THE CHANG-ING ROOM'S OVER THERE.
YES MA'AM.
SNIFFLE

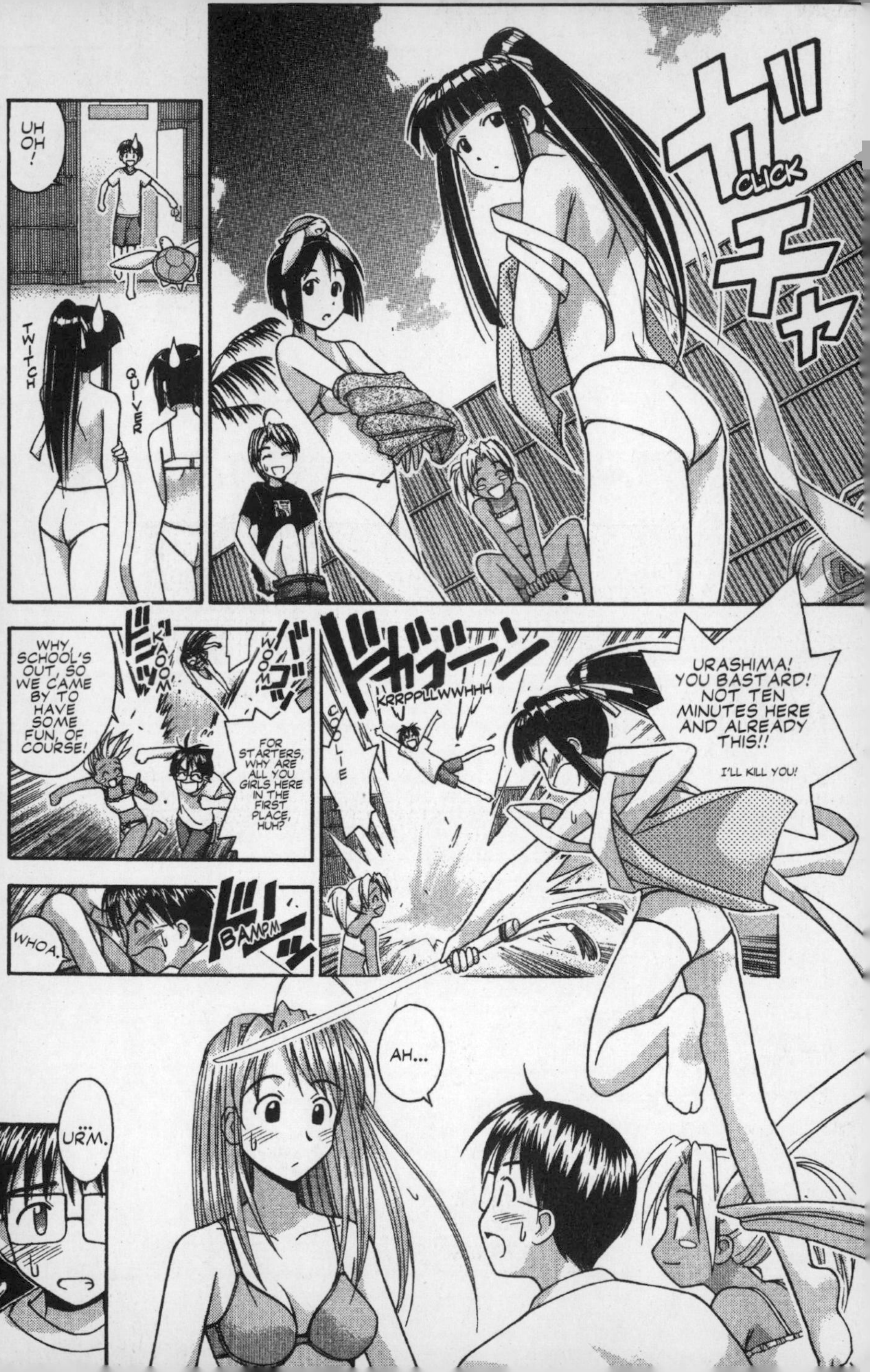
ガチャ
CLICK
UH OH!
TWITCH
QUIVER
URASHIMA! YOU BASTARD! NOT TEN MINUTES HERE AND ALREADY THIS!!
I'LL KILL YOU!
ドガゴーン
KRRPPLLWWHHH
W
COOLIE
バゴッ
WOOM
FOR STARTERS, WHY ARE ALL YOU GIRLS HERE IN THE FIRST PLACE, HUH?
ドミッ
KAOOM
WHY, SCHOOL'S OUT, SO WE CAME BY TO HAVE SOME FUN, OF COURSE!
ドーッ
BAMPM
WHOA.
AH...
...URM.

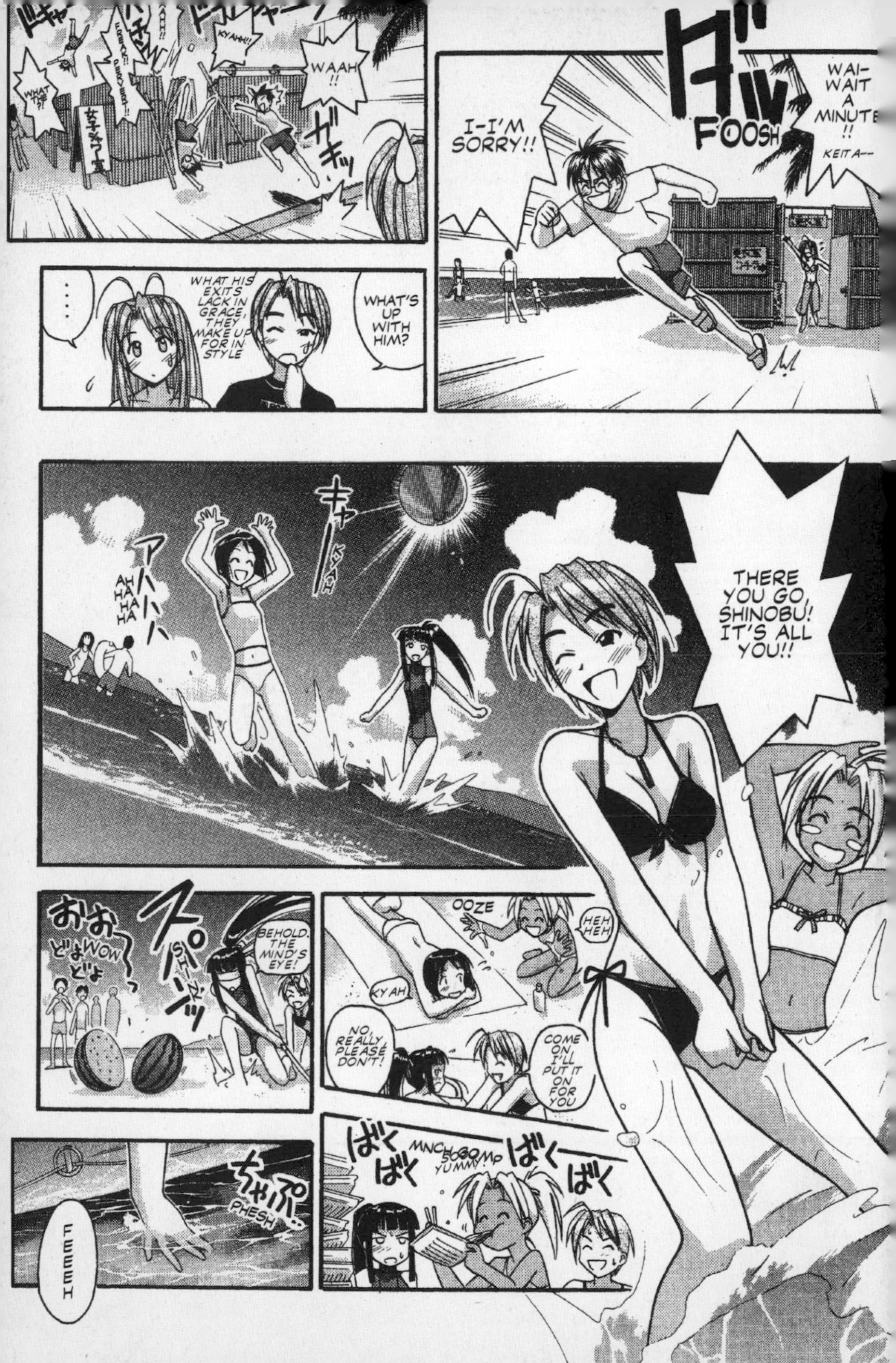
ダッ
FOOSH
WAI-WAIT A MINUTE!!
KEITA--
I-I'M SORRY!!
KYAHH!!
WAAH!!
FREAK!! PERVERT!!
WHAT THE?!
ガキッ
WHAT'S UP WITH HIM?
WHAT HIS EXITS LACK IN GRACE, THEY MAKE UP FOR IN STYLE
....
THERE YOU GO SHINOBU! IT'S ALL YOU!!
キャー
KYAH
アハハハ
AH HA HA HA
OOZE
HEH HEH
KYAH
COME ON I'LL PUT IT ON FOR YOU
NO, REALLY, PLEASE DON'T!
BEHOLD. THE MIND'S EYE!
スパーンッ
SHING
おお〜っ
どよ WOW どよ
ばくばく
MNCH GOMP
SO YUMMY
ばくばく
ちゃぷ
PHESH
FEEEH

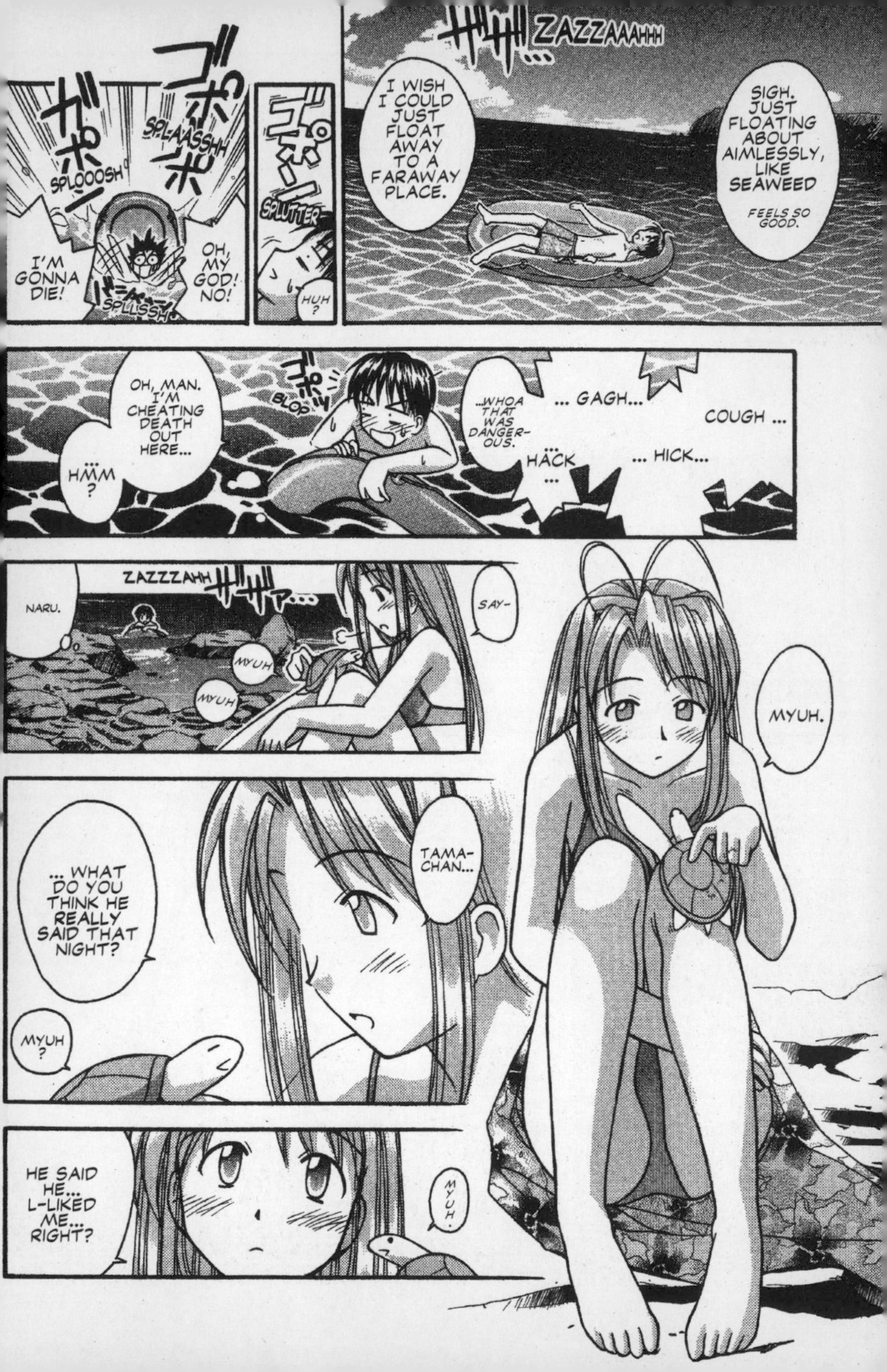
ZAZZAAAHHH
SIGH. JUST FLOATING ABOUT AIMLESSLY, LIKE SEAWEED
FEELS SO GOOD.
I WISH I COULD JUST FLOAT AWAY TO A FARAWAY PLACE.
SPLUTTER
HUH?
OH, MY GOD! NO!
SPLAASSHH
SPLOOOSH
I'M GONNA DIE!
SPLLSSH
COUGH ...
... HICK...
... GAGH...
... HÄCK ...
...WHOA THAT WAS DANGER-OUS.
BLOP
OH, MAN. I'M CHEATING DEATH OUT HERE...
... HMM?
SAY-
MYUH.
ZAZZZAHH
NARU.
MYUH
MYUH
TAMA-CHAN...
... WHAT DO YOU THINK HE REALLY SAID THAT NIGHT?
MYUH?
HE SAID HE... L-LIKED ME... RIGHT?
MYUH.

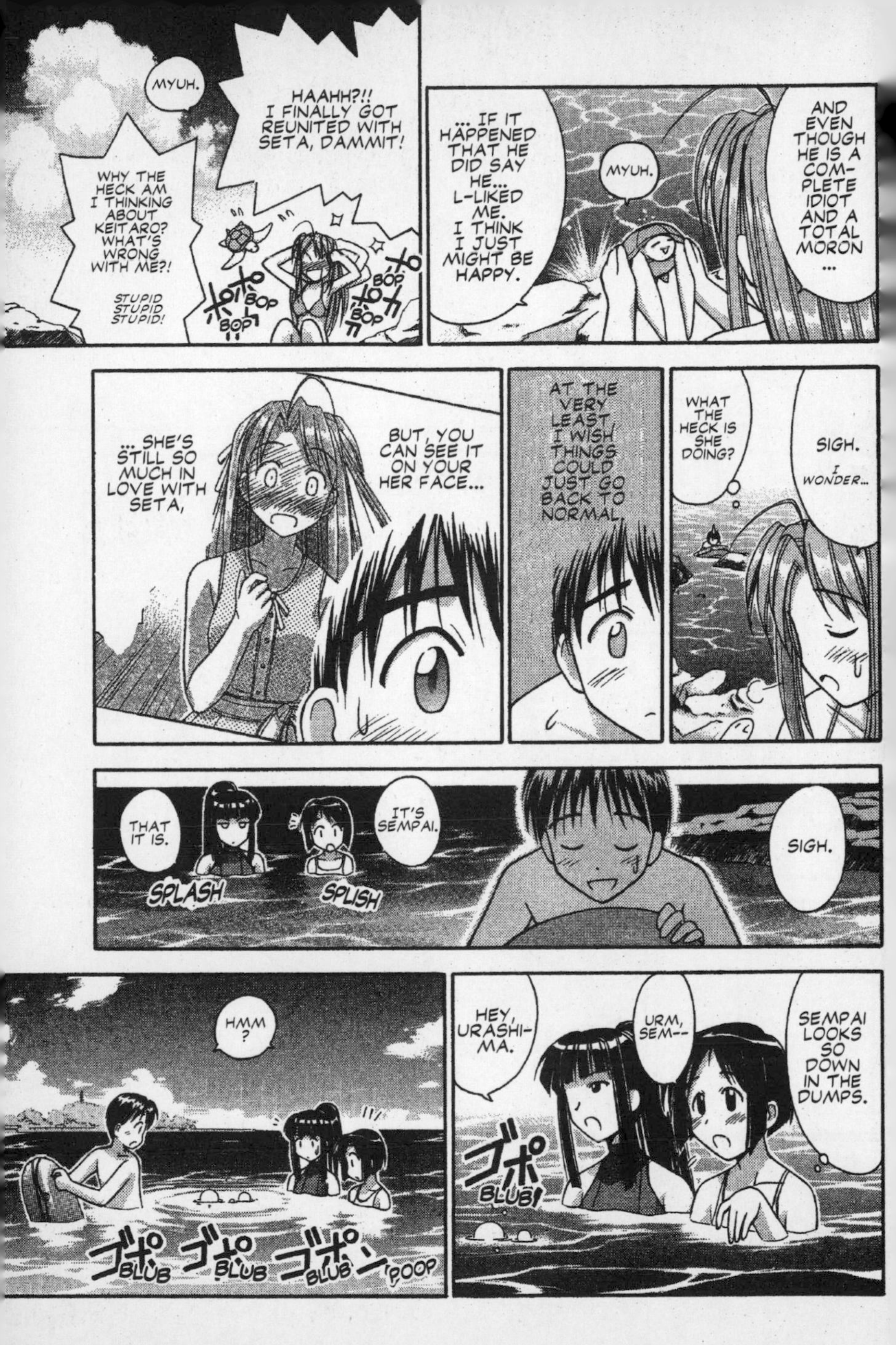
AND EVEN THOUGH HE IS A COMPLETE IDIOT AND A TOTAL MORON ...
MYUH.
... IF IT HAPPENED THAT HE DID SAY HE... L-LIKED ME. I THINK I JUST MIGHT BE HAPPY.
HAAHH?!! I FINALLY GOT REUNITED WITH SETA, DAMMIT!
MYUH.
WHY THE HECK AM I THINKING ABOUT KEITARO? WHAT'S WRONG WITH ME?!
BOP BOP BOP BOP
STUPID STUPID STUPID!
SIGH.
I WONDER...
WHAT THE HECK IS SHE DOING?
AT THE VERY LEAST, I WISH THINGS COULD JUST GO BACK TO NORMAL.
BUT, YOU CAN SEE IT ON YOUR HER FACE...
... SHE'S STILL SO MUCH IN LOVE WITH SETA,
SIGH.
IT'S SEMPAI.
THAT IT IS.
SPLISH
SPLASH
SEMPAI LOOKS SO DOWN IN THE DUMPS.
URM, SEM--
HEY, URASHIMA.
ゴポ BLUB!
HMM?
ゴポ BLUB ゴポ BLUB ゴポン BLUB POOP

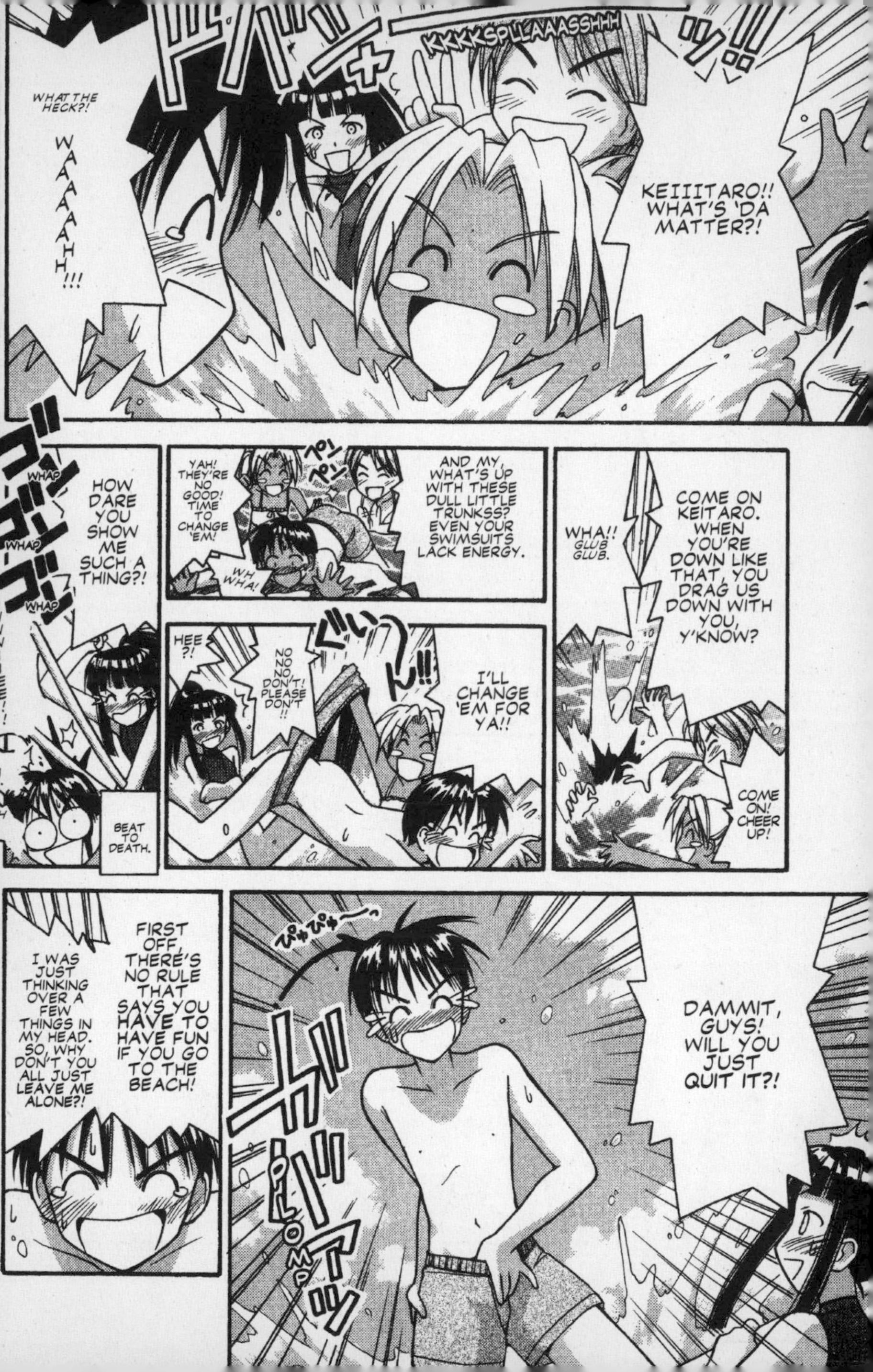
KKKKSPLLAAASSHHH
KEIIITARO!! WHAT'S 'DA MATTER?!
WHAT THE HECK?!
WAAAAAAAH!!!
COME ON KEITARO. WHEN YOU'RE DOWN LIKE THAT, YOU DRAG US DOWN WITH YOU, Y'KNOW?
WHA!! GLUB GLUB.
COME ON! CHEER UP!
AND MY, WHAT'S UP WITH THESE DULL LITTLE TRUNKSS? EVEN YOUR SWIMSUITS LACK ENERGY.
YAH! THEY'RE NO GOOD! TIME TO CHANGE 'EM!
WH WHA!
I'LL CHANGE 'EM FOR YA!!
NO NO NO, DON'T! PLEASE DON'T!!
HEE?!
HOW DARE YOU SHOW ME SUCH A THING?!
WHAP
WHAP
WHAP
BEAT TO DEATH.
DAMMIT, GUYS! WILL YOU JUST QUIT IT?!
PLOMP
FIRST OFF, THERE'S NO RULE THAT SAYS YOU HAVE TO HAVE FUN IF YOU GO TO THE BEACH!
I WAS JUST THINKING OVER A FEW THINGS IN MY HEAD. SO, WHY DON'T YOU ALL JUST LEAVE ME ALONE?!

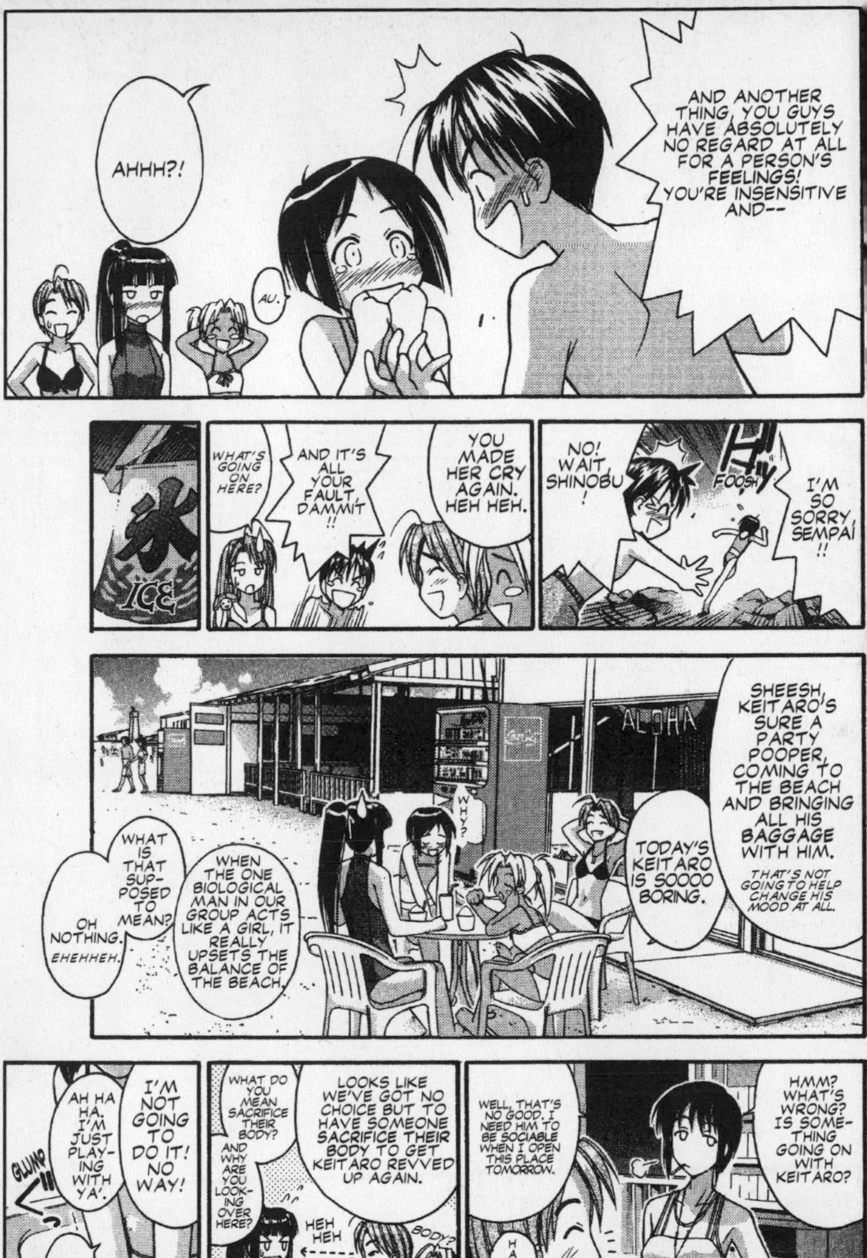
AND ANOTHER THING, YOU GUYS HAVE ABSOLUTELY NO REGARD AT ALL FOR A PERSON'S FEELINGS! YOU'RE INSENSITIVE AND--
AHHH?!
AU.
I'M SO SORRY, SEMPAI!!
FOOSH
NO! WAIT SHINOBU!
YOU MADE HER CRY AGAIN. HEH HEH.
AND IT'S ALL YOUR FAULT, DAMMIT!!
WHAT'S GOING ON HERE?
氷
ICE
ALOHA
SHEESH, KEITARO'S SURE A PARTY POOPER, COMING TO THE BEACH AND BRINGING ALL HIS BAGGAGE WITH HIM.
THAT'S NOT GOING TO HELP CHANGE HIS MOOD AT ALL.
TODAY'S KEITARO IS SOOOO BORING.
WHY?
WHEN THE ONE BIOLOGICAL MAN IN OUR GROUP ACTS LIKE A GIRL, IT REALLY UPSETS THE BALANCE OF THE BEACH.
WHAT IS THAT SUPPOSED TO MEAN?
OH NOTHING. EHEHHEH.
HMM? WHAT'S WRONG? IS SOMETHING GOING ON WITH KEITARO?
WELL, THAT'S NO GOOD. I NEED HIM TO BE SOCIABLE WHEN I OPEN THIS PLACE TOMORROW.
HARUKA
LOOKS LIKE WE'VE GOT NO CHOICE BUT TO HAVE SOMEONE SACRIFICE THEIR BODY TO GET KEITARO REVVED UP AGAIN.
WHAT DO YOU MEAN SACRIFICE THEIR BODY? AND WHY ARE YOU LOOKING OVER HERE?
BODY?
HEH HEH
I'M NOT GOING TO DO IT! NO WAY!
AH HA HA. I'M JUST PLAYING WITH YA'.
GLUMP
I...

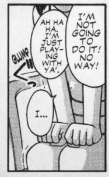

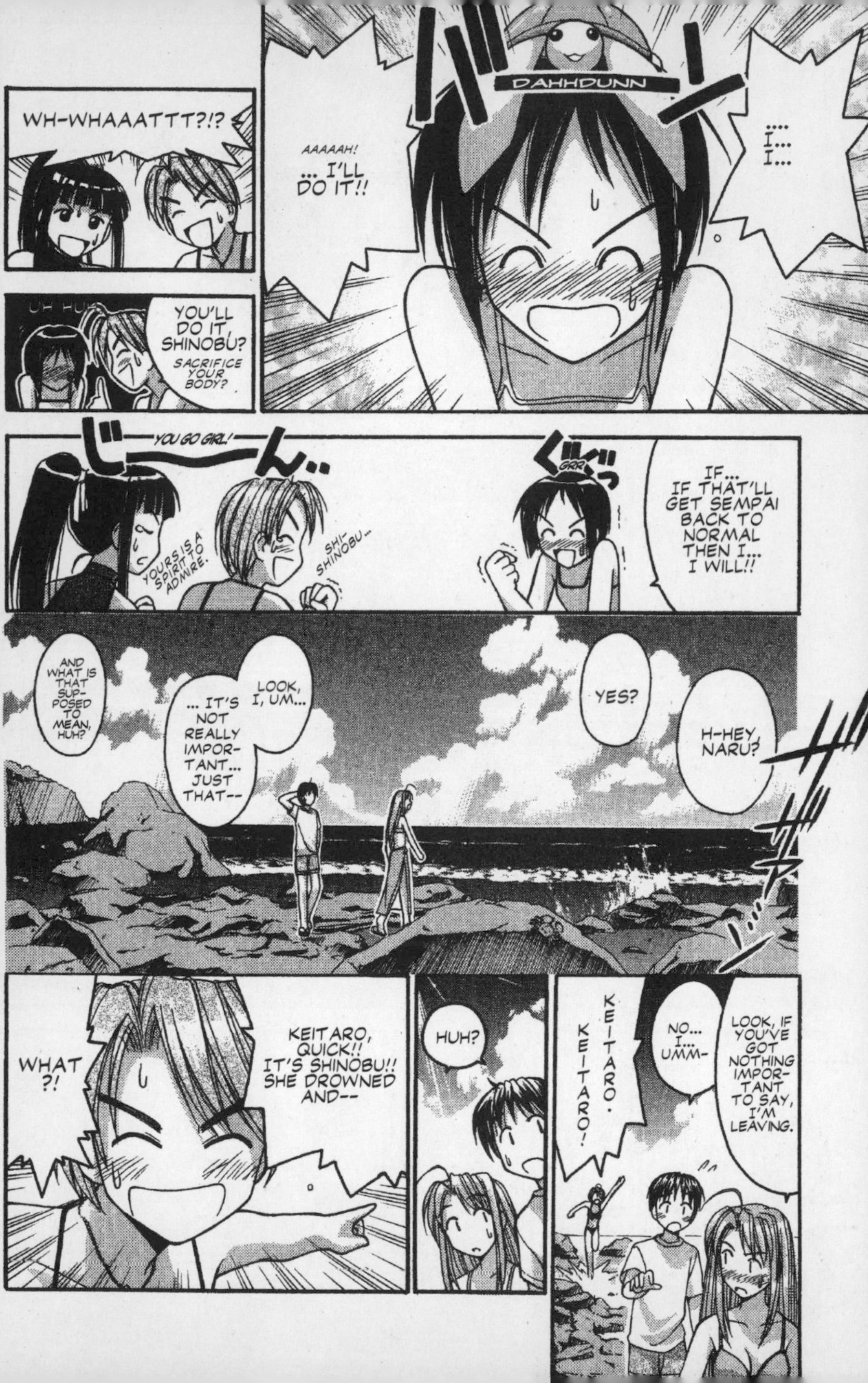
DAHHDUNN
... I... I...
AAAAAH! ... I'LL DO IT!!
WH-WHAAATTT?!?
UH HUH
YOU'LL DO IT, SHINOBU?
SACRIFICE YOUR BODY?
IF... IF THAT'LL GET SEMPAI BACK TO NORMAL THEN I... I WILL!!
GRR
SHI-SHINOBU...
YOU GO GIRL!
YOURS IS A SPIRIT TO ADMIRE.
H-HEY, NARU?
YES?
LOOK, I, UM...
... IT'S NOT REALLY IMPORTANT... JUST THAT--
AND WHAT IS THAT SUPPOSED TO MEAN, HUH?
LOOK, IF YOU'VE GOT NOTHING IMPORTANT TO SAY, I'M LEAVING.
NO... I... UMM-
KEITARO. KEITARO!
HUH?
KEITARO, QUICK!! IT'S SHINOBU!! SHE DROWNED AND--
WHAT ?!

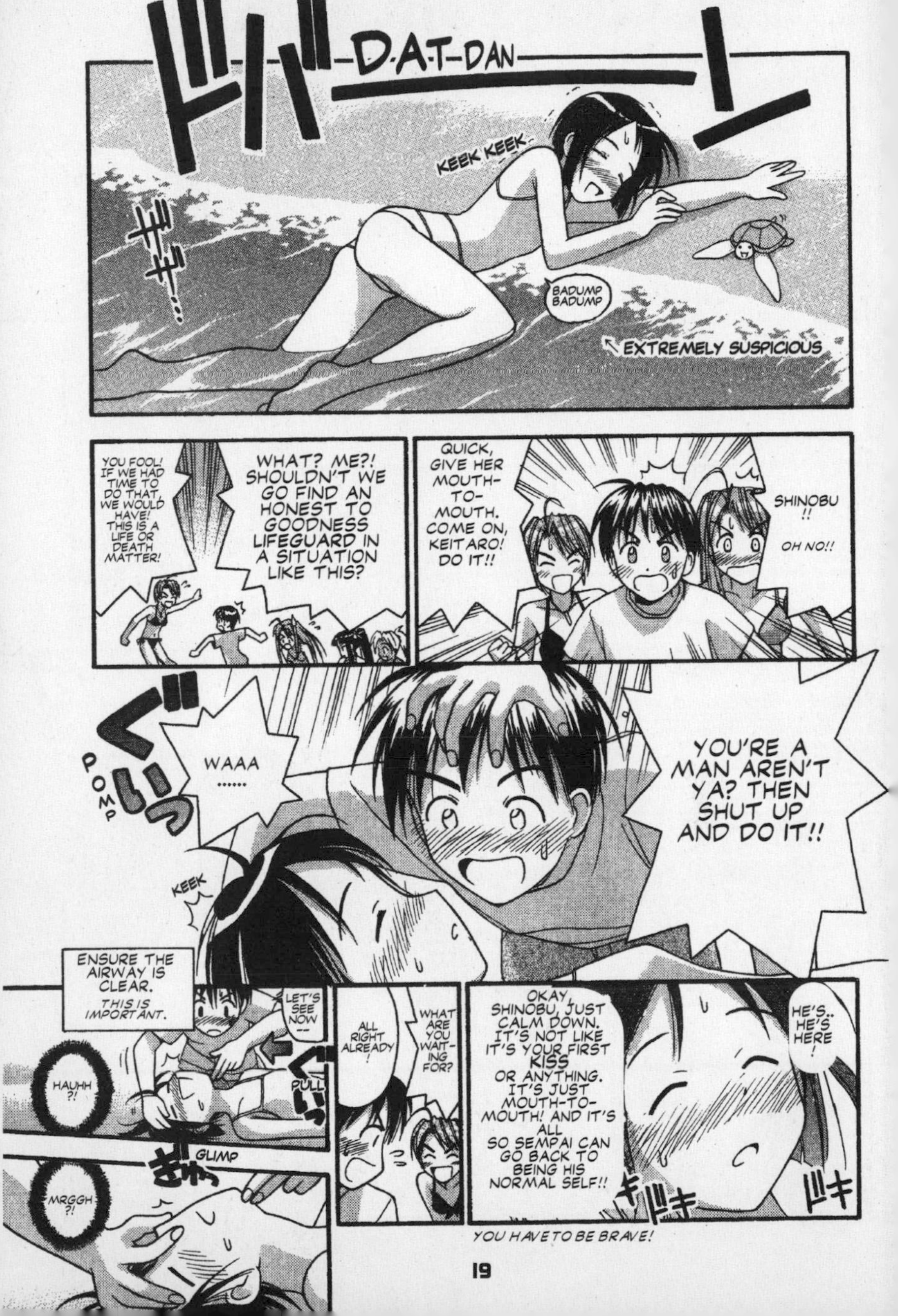
D-A-T-DAN
KEEK KEEK
BADUMP BADUMP
EXTREMELY SUSPICIOUS
QUICK, GIVE HER MOUTH-TO-MOUTH. COME ON, KEITARO! DO IT!!
SHINOBU !!
OH NO!!
WHAT? ME?! SHOULDN'T WE GO FIND AN HONEST TO GOODNESS LIFEGUARD IN A SITUATION LIKE THIS?
YOU FOOL! IF WE HAD TIME TO DO THAT, WE WOULD HAVE! THIS IS A LIFE OR DEATH MATTER!
YOU'RE A MAN AREN'T YA? THEN SHUT UP AND DO IT!!
WAAA ......
POMP
KEEK
HE'S.. HE'S HERE!
OKAY, SHINOBU, JUST CALM DOWN. IT'S NOT LIKE IT'S YOUR FIRST KISS OR ANYTHING. IT'S JUST MOUTH-TO-MOUTH! AND IT'S ALL SO SEMPAI CAN GO BACK TO BEING HIS NORMAL SELF!!
WHAT ARE YOU WAIT-ING FOR?
ALL RIGHT ALREADY!
ENSURE THE AIRWAY IS CLEAR.
THIS IS IMPORTANT.
LET'S SEE NOW --
HAUHH ?!
PULL
GLIMP
MRGGH ?!
YOU HAVE TO BE BRAVE!

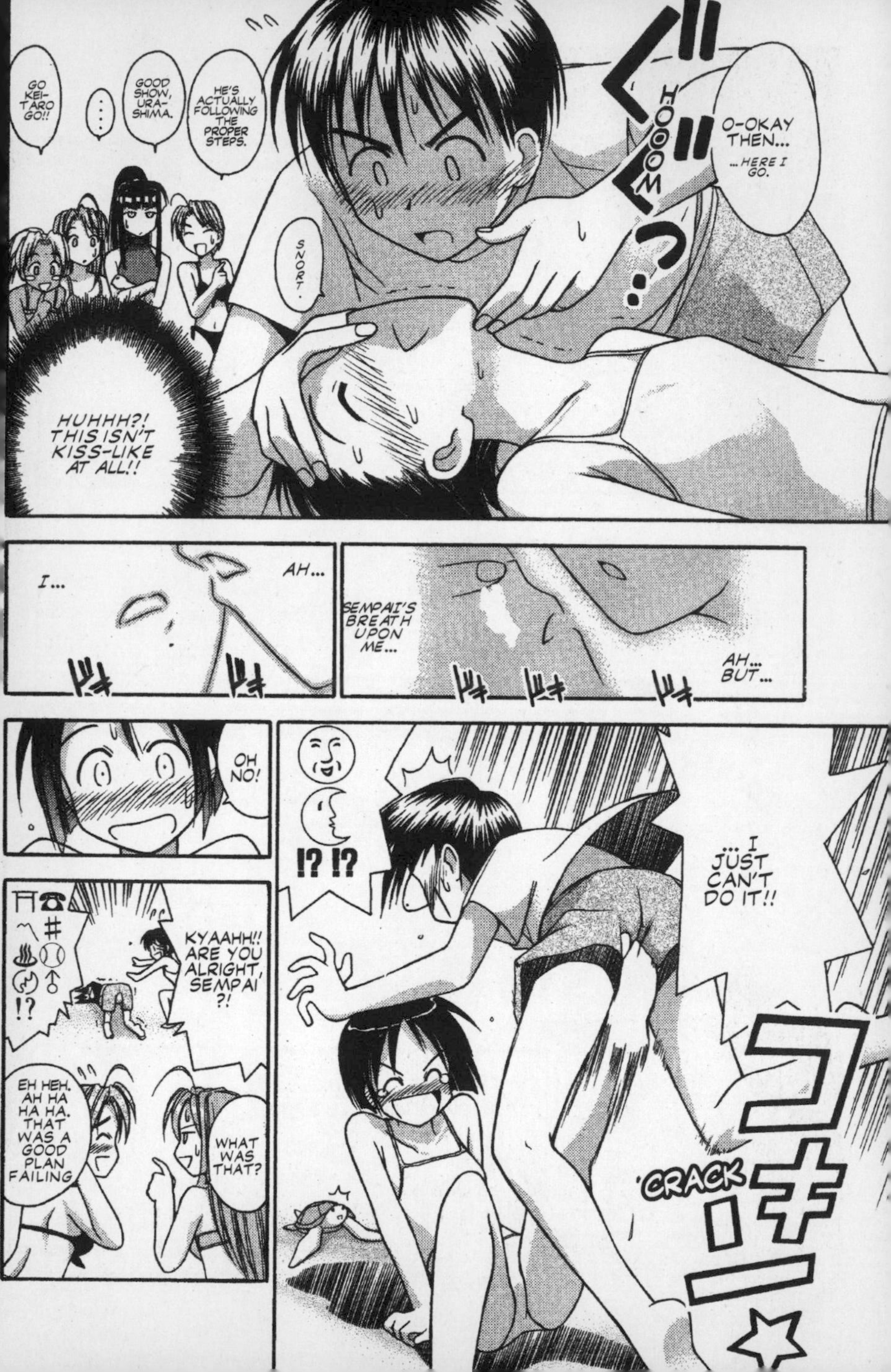
O-OKAY THEN...
...HERE I GO.
HOOOOM
HE'S ACTUALLY FOLLOWING THE PROPER STEPS.
GOOD SHOW, URA-SHIMA.
...
GO KEI-TARO GO!!
SNORT.
HUHHH?! THIS ISN'T KISS-LIKE AT ALL!!
AH... BUT...
SEMPAI'S BREATH UPON ME...
AH...
I...
!? !?
...I JUST CAN'T DO IT!!
CRACK
OH NO!
KYAAHH!! ARE YOU ALRIGHT, SEMPAI?!
!?
WHAT WAS THAT?
EH HEH. AH HA HA HA. THAT WAS A GOOD PLAN FAILING

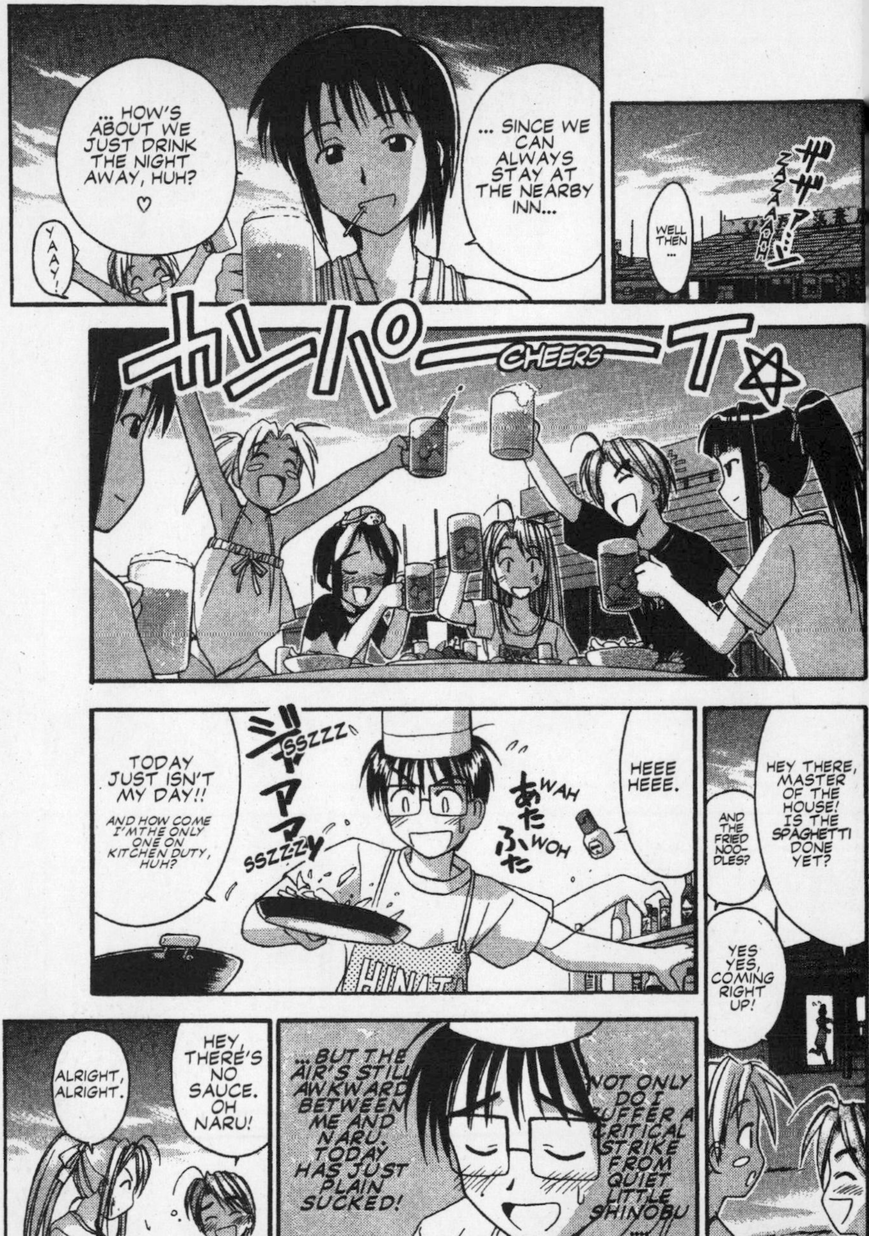
ザザァ…
ZAZAAAH
WELL THEN …
... SINCE WE CAN ALWAYS STAY AT THE NEARBY INN...
... HOW'S ABOUT WE JUST DRINK THE NIGHT AWAY, HUH? ♡
YAAAY!
カンパーイ
CHEERS
HEY THERE, MASTER OF THE HOUSE! IS THE SPAGHETTI DONE YET?
AND THE FRIED NOO-DLES?
YES YES, COMING RIGHT UP!
HEEE HEEE.
あたふた
WAH WOH
ジャアア
SSZZZ
SSZZZZ
TODAY JUST ISN'T MY DAY!!
AND HOW COME I'M THE ONLY ONE ON KITCHEN DUTY, HUH?
NOT ONLY DO I SUFFER A CRITICAL STRIKE FROM QUIET LITTLE SHINOBU ....
... BUT THE AIR'S STILL AWKWARD BETWEEN ME AND NARU. TODAY HAS JUST PLAIN SUCKED!
HEY, THERE'S NO SAUCE. OH NARU!
ALRIGHT, ALRIGHT.

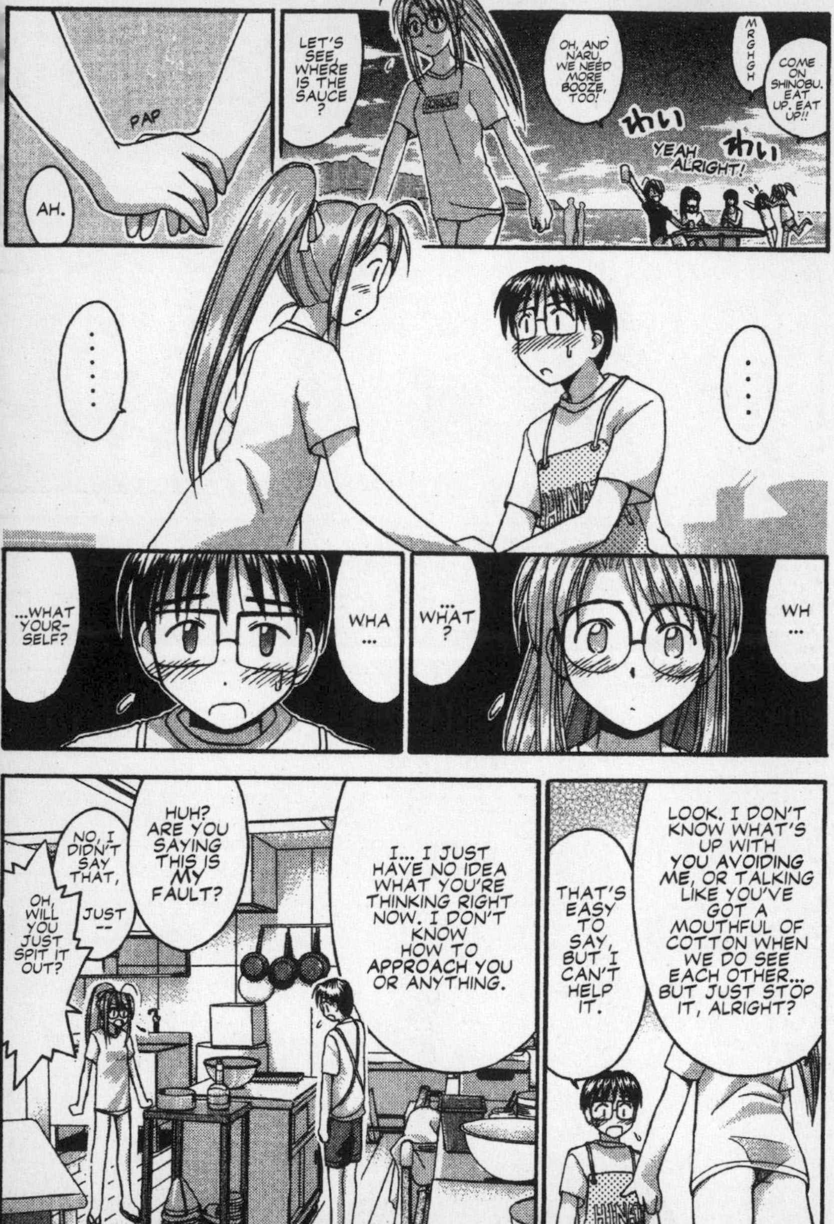
COME ON SHINOBU. EAT UP. EAT UP!!
MRGHGH
OH, AND NARU, WE NEED MORE BOOZE, TOO!
わい
わい
YEAH ALRIGHT!
LET'S SEE, WHERE IS THE SAUCE?
PAP
AH.
....
......
WH ...
... WHAT ?
WHA ...
...WHAT YOURSELF?
LOOK. I DON'T KNOW WHAT'S UP WITH YOU AVOIDING ME, OR TALKING LIKE YOU'VE GOT A MOUTHFUL OF COTTON WHEN WE DO SEE EACH OTHER... BUT JUST STOP IT, ALRIGHT?
THAT'S EASY TO SAY, BUT I CAN'T HELP IT.
I... I JUST HAVE NO IDEA WHAT YOU'RE THINKING RIGHT NOW. I DON'T KNOW HOW TO APPROACH YOU OR ANYTHING.
HUH? ARE YOU SAYING THIS IS MY FAULT?
NO, I DIDN'T SAY THAT,
JUST --
OH, WILL YOU JUST SPIT IT OUT?

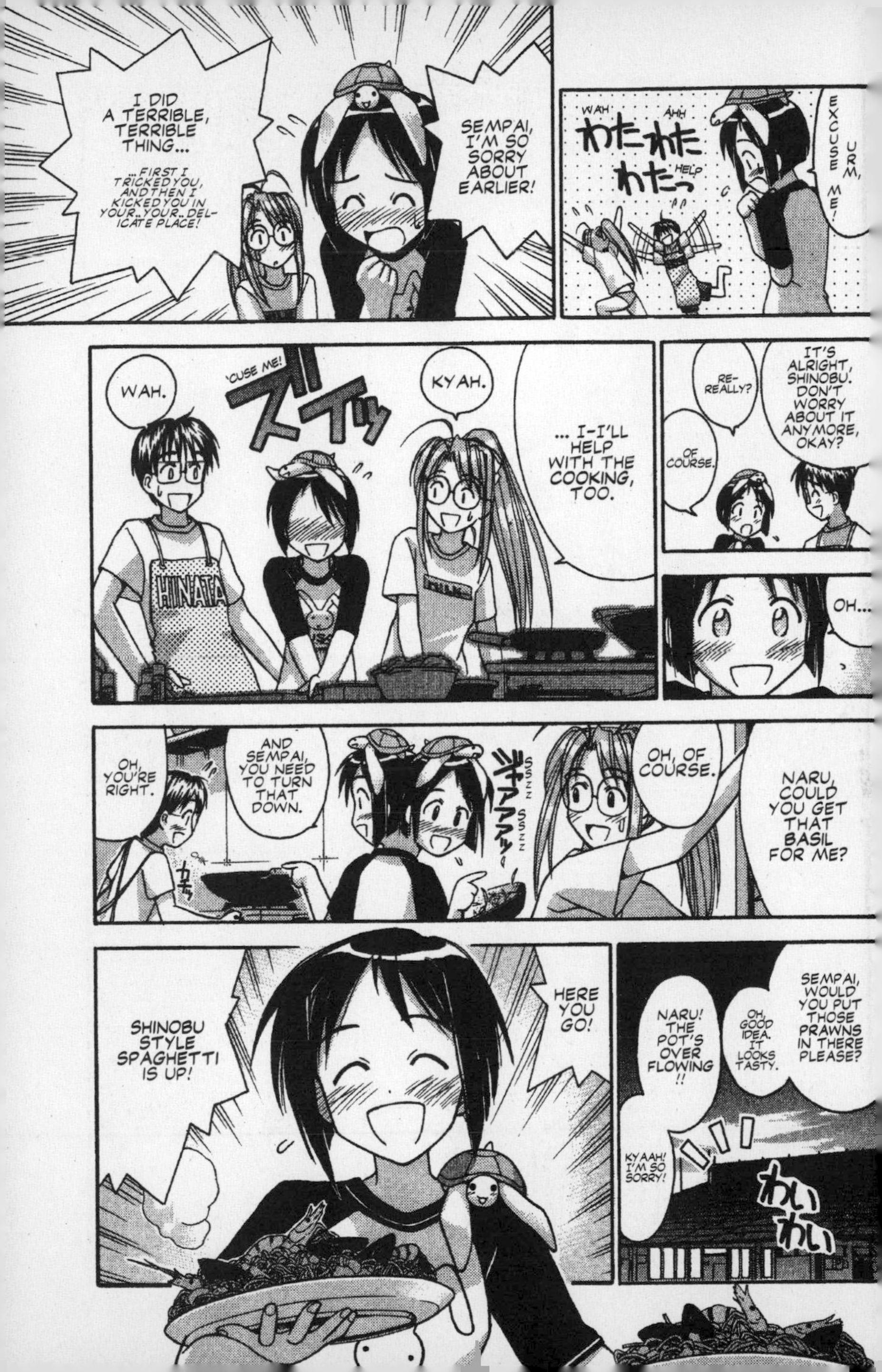
URM, EXCUSE ME!
WAH わたわた AHH わたわたっ HELP
SEMPAI, I'M SO SORRY ABOUT EARLIER!
I DID A TERRIBLE, TERRIBLE THING...
...FIRST I TRICKED YOU, AND THEN I KICKED YOU IN YOUR.. YOUR.. DELICATE PLACE!
IT'S ALRIGHT, SHINOBU. DON'T WORRY ABOUT IT ANYMORE, OKAY?
RE-REALLY?
OF COURSE.
OH...
... I-I'LL HELP WITH THE COOKING, TOO.
KYAH.
ズイッ 'CUSE ME!
WAH.
HINATA
NARU, COULD YOU GET THAT BASIL FOR ME?
OH, OF COURSE.
ジュアアッ SSZZ SSZZ
AND SEMPAI, YOU NEED TO TURN THAT DOWN.
OH, YOU'RE RIGHT.
カチッ CHIK
SEMPAI, WOULD YOU PUT THOSE PRAWNS IN THERE PLEASE?
OH, GOOD IDEA. IT LOOKS TASTY.
NARU! THE POT'S OVER FLOWING!!
KYAAH! I'M SO SORRY!
わいわい
HERE YOU GO!
SHINOBU STYLE SPAGHETTI IS UP!

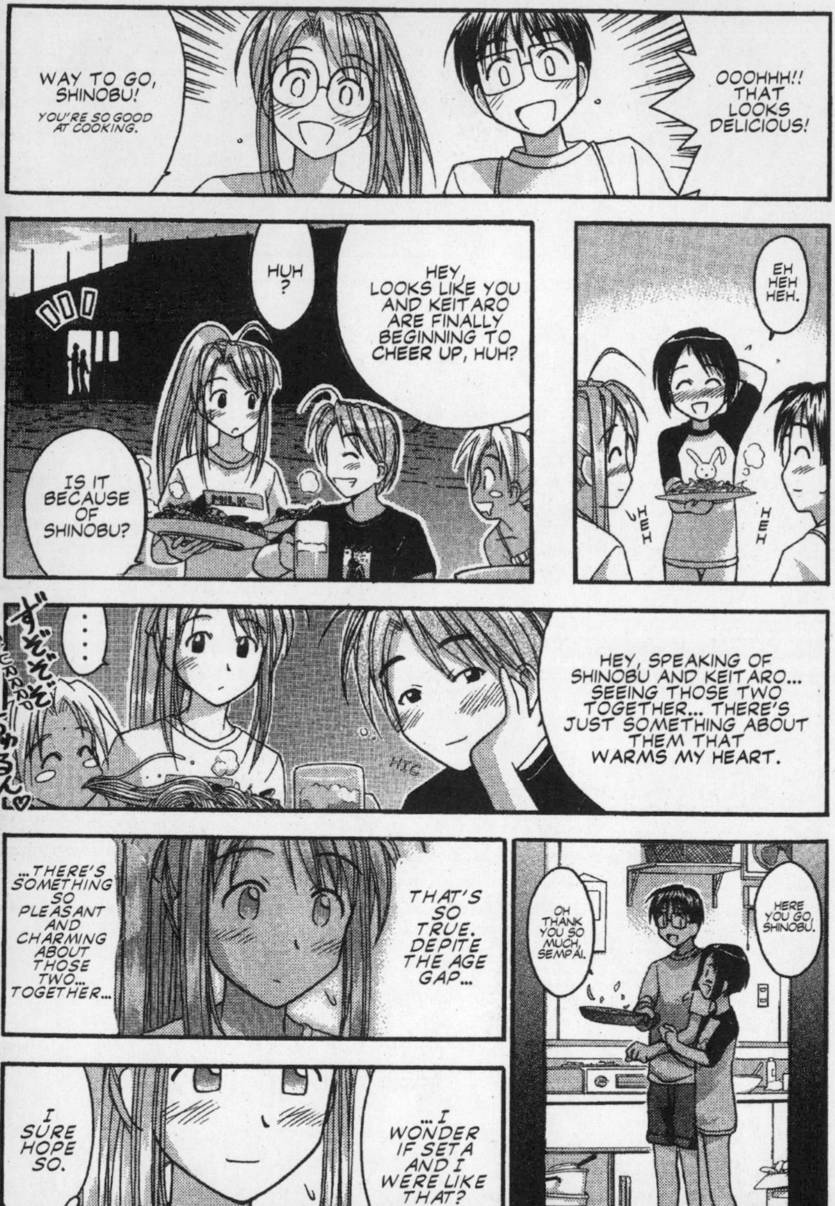

OOOHHH!! THAT LOOKS DELICIOUS!
WAY TO GO, SHINOBU!
YOU'RE SO GOOD AT COOKING.
EH HEH HEH.
HEH
HEH
HEY, LOOKS LIKE YOU AND KEITARO ARE FINALLY BEGINNING TO CHEER UP, HUH?
HUH?
IS IT BECAUSE OF SHINOBU?
HEY, SPEAKING OF SHINOBU AND KEITARO... SEEING THOSE TWO TOGETHER... THERE'S JUST SOMETHING ABOUT THEM THAT WARMS MY HEART.
HIC
....
ずぞぞ
SURRRP
HERE YOU GO, SHINOBU.
OH THANK YOU SO MUCH, SEMPAI.
THAT'S SO TRUE. DEPITE THE AGE GAP...
...THERE'S SOMETHING SO PLEASANT AND CHARMING ABOUT THOSE TWO... TOGETHER...
...I WONDER IF SETA AND I WERE LIKE THAT?
I SURE HOPE SO.

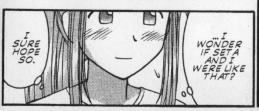

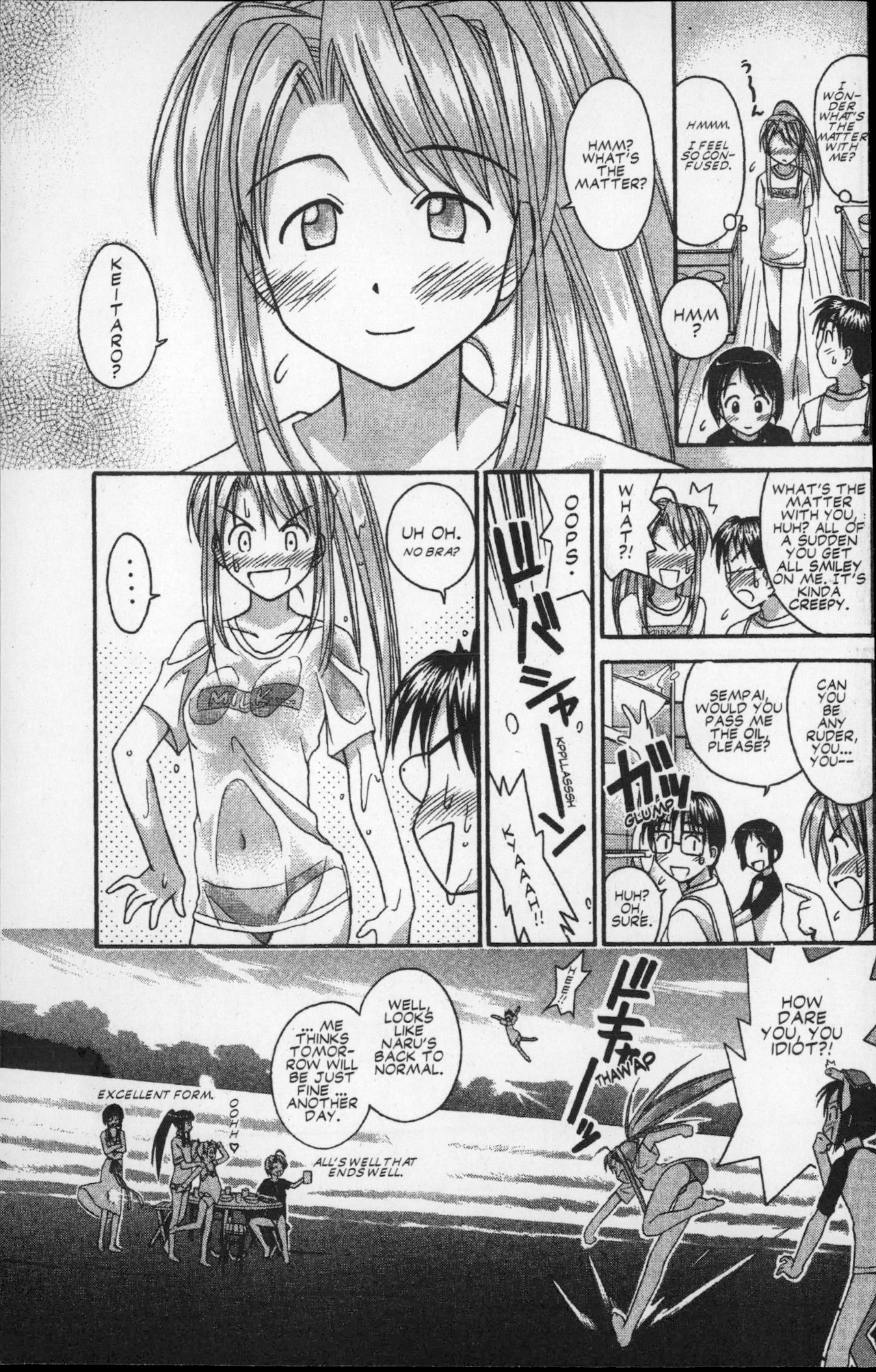
I WONDER WHAT'S THE MATTER WITH ME?
HMMM. I FEEL SO CONFUSED.
HMM?
HMM? WHAT'S THE MATTER?
KEITARO?
WHAT'S THE MATTER WITH YOU, HUH? ALL OF A SUDDEN YOU GET ALL SMILEY ON ME. IT'S KINDA CREEPY.
WHAT?!
CAN YOU BE ANY RUDER, YOU... YOU--
SEMPAI, WOULD YOU PASS ME THE OIL, PLEASE?
GLUMP
HUH? OH, SURE.
OOPS.
KPPLASSSH
KYAAAAH!!
UH OH. NO BRA?
....
HOW DARE YOU, YOU IDIOT?!
THAWAP
HEE!!
WELL, LOOKS LIKE NARU'S BACK TO NORMAL.
... ME THINKS TOMORROW WILL BE JUST FINE ... ANOTHER DAY.
OOHH ♡
EXCELLENT FORM.
ALL'S WELL THAT ENDS WELL.

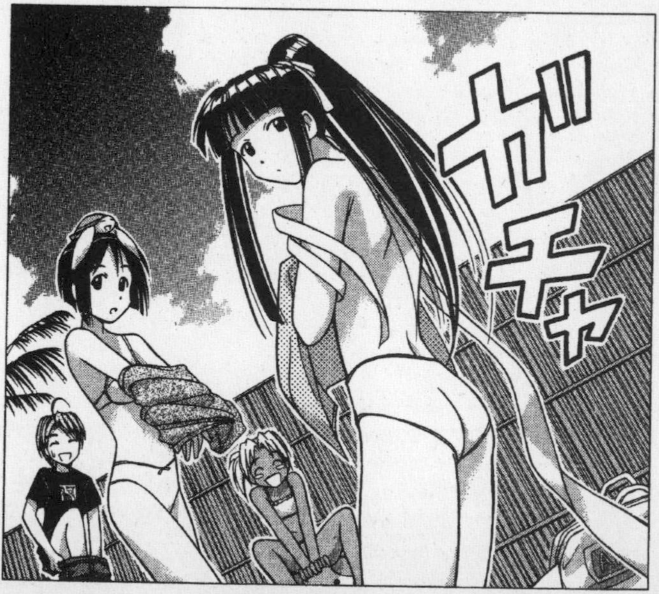
ガチャ

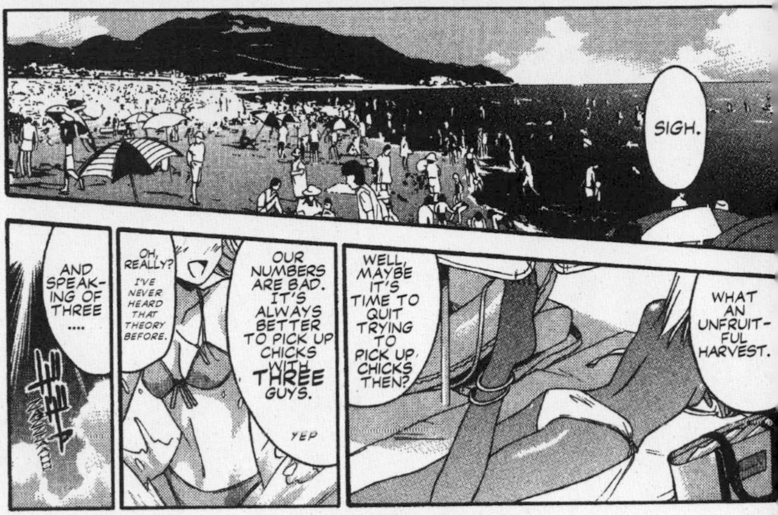
SIGH.
WHAT AN UNFRUIT-FUL HARVEST.
WELL, MAYBE IT'S TIME TO QUIT TRYING TO PICK UP CHICKS THEN?
OUR NUMBERS ARE BAD. IT'S ALWAYS BETTER TO PICK UP CHICKS WITH THREE GUYS.
YEP
OH, REALLY? I'VE NEVER HEARD THAT THEORY BEFORE.
AND SPEAK-ING OF THREE ....

Love Hina

HINATA.35 A Passionate Midsummer's Night

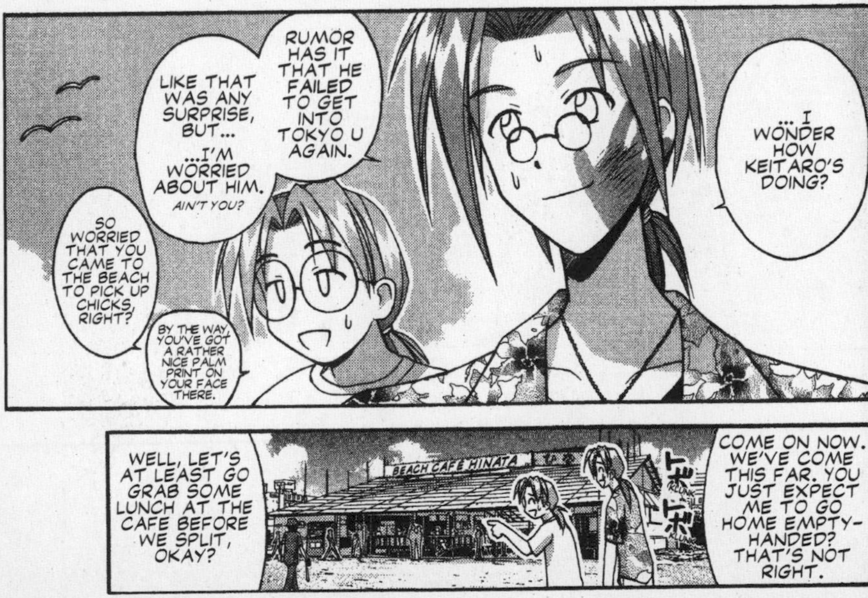
... I WONDER HOW KEITARO'S DOING?
RUMOR HAS IT THAT HE FAILED TO GET INTO TOKYO U AGAIN.
LIKE THAT WAS ANY SURPRISE, BUT... ...I'M WORRIED ABOUT HIM. AIN'T YOU?
SO WORRIED THAT YOU CAME TO THE BEACH TO PICK UP CHICKS, RIGHT?
BY THE WAY, YOU'VE GOT A RATHER NICE PALM PRINT ON YOUR FACE THERE.
COME ON NOW. WE'VE COME THIS FAR. YOU JUST EXPECT ME TO GO HOME EMPTY-HANDED? THAT'S NOT RIGHT.
KLUNK
KLUNK
BEACH CAFE HINATA
WELL, LET'S AT LEAST GO GRAB SOME LUNCH AT THE CAFE BEFORE WE SPLIT, OKAY?

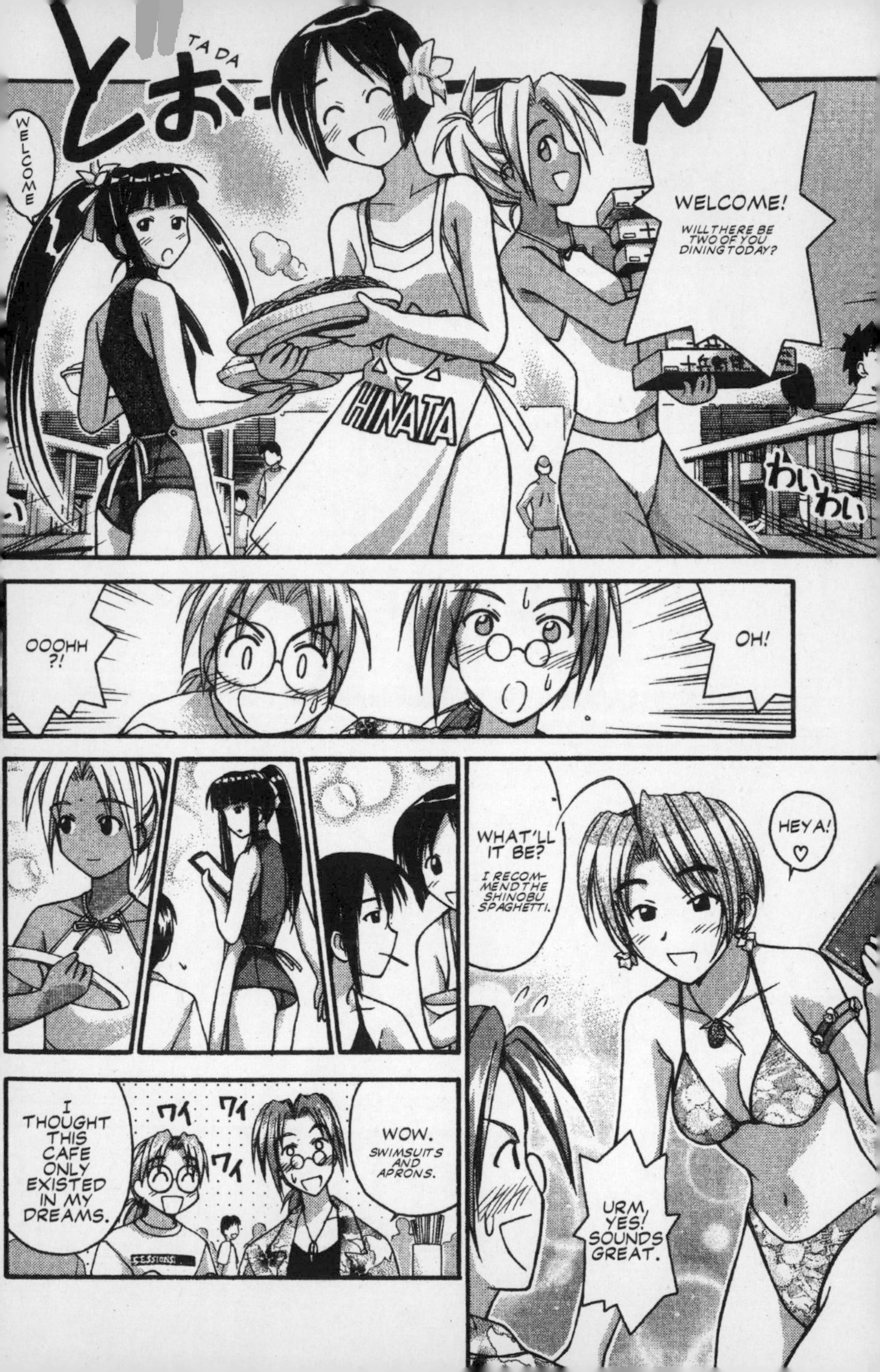
とぉーーーん
TA DA
WELCOME!
WILL THERE BE TWO OF YOU DINING TODAY?
WELCOME
わいわい
OH!
OOOHH ?!
HEYA! ♡
WHAT'LL IT BE?
I RECOMMEND THE SHINOBU SPAGHETTI.
URM, YES! SOUNDS GREAT.
WOW.
SWIMSUITS AND APRONS.
ワイワイ
ワイ
I THOUGHT THIS CAFE ONLY EXISTED IN MY DREAMS.

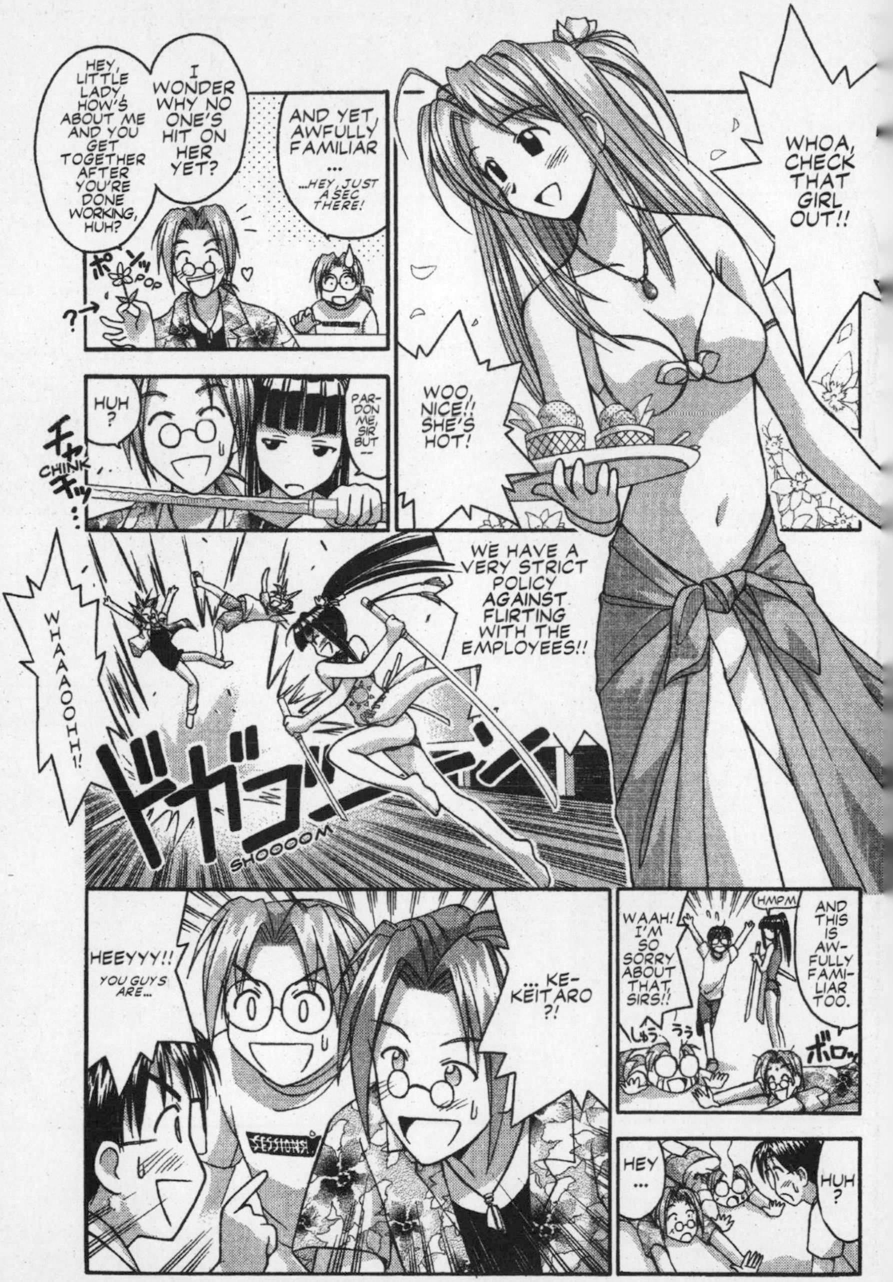
WHOA, CHECK THAT GIRL OUT!!
WOO NICE!! SHE'S HOT!
AND YET, AWFULLY FAMILIAR ...
...HEY JUST A SEC THERE!
I WONDER WHY NO ONE'S HIT ON HER YET?
HEY, LITTLE LADY, HOW'S ABOUT ME AND YOU GET TOGETHER AFTER YOU'RE DONE WORKING, HUH?
POP
PARDON ME, SIR BUT --
HUH ?
CHINK
WE HAVE A VERY STRICT POLICY AGAINST FLIRTING WITH THE EMPLOYEES!!
WHAAAAOOHH!
SHOOOOM
AND THIS IS AWFULLY FAMILIAR TOO.
HMPM
WAAH! I'M SO SORRY ABOUT THAT, SIRS!!
HUH ?
HEY ...
... KE-KEITARO ?!
HEEYYY!!
YOU GUYS ARE...

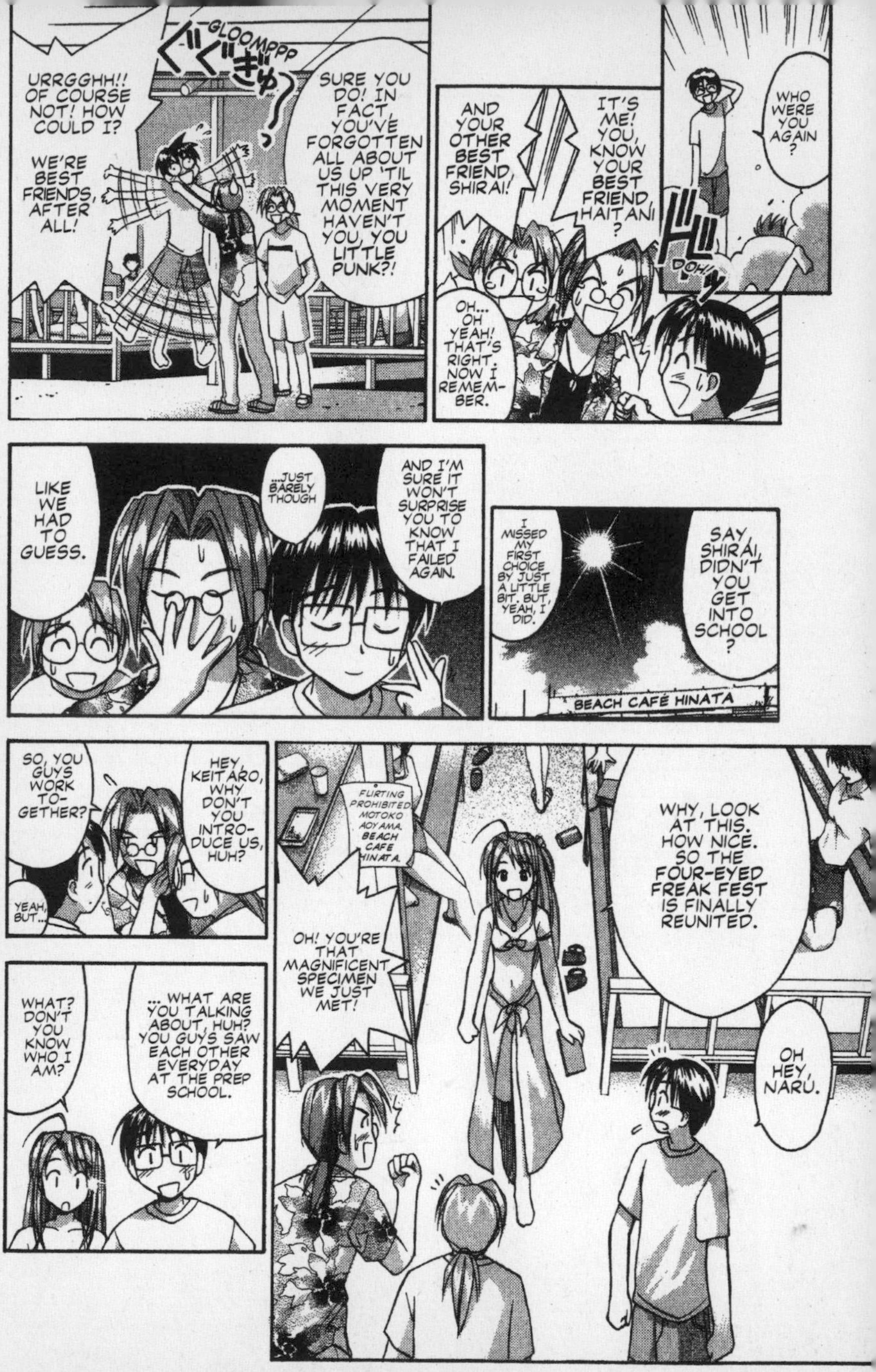
WHO WERE YOU AGAIN?
DOH!!
IT'S ME! YOU, KNOW YOUR BEST FRIEND, HAITANI?
AND YOUR OTHER BEST FRIEND, SHIRAI!
OH... OH YEAH! THAT'S RIGHT. NOW I REMEMBER.
GLOOMPPP
SURE YOU DO! IN FACT, YOU'VE FORGOTTEN ALL ABOUT US UP 'TIL THIS VERY MOMENT HAVEN'T YOU, YOU LITTLE PUNK?!
URRGGHH!! OF COURSE NOT! HOW COULD I?
WE'RE BEST FRIENDS, AFTER ALL!
SAY, SHIRAI, DIDN'T YOU GET INTO SCHOOL?
I MISSED MY FIRST CHOICE BY JUST A LITTLE BIT. BUT, YEAH, I DID.
BEACH CAFÉ HINATA
AND I'M SURE IT WON'T SURPRISE YOU TO KNOW THAT I FAILED AGAIN.
...JUST BARELY THOUGH
LIKE WE HAD TO GUESS.
WHY, LOOK AT THIS. HOW NICE. SO THE FOUR-EYED FREAK FEST IS FINALLY REUNITED.
OH HEY, NARU.
FLIRTING PROHIBITED MOTOKO AOYAMA. BEACH CAFE HINATA.
OH! YOU'RE THAT MAGNIFICENT SPECIMEN WE JUST MET!
HEY, KEITARO, WHY DON'T YOU INTRODUCE US, HUH?
SO, YOU GUYS WORK TOGETHER?
YEAH, BUT...
... WHAT ARE YOU TALKING ABOUT, HUH? YOU GUYS SAW EACH OTHER EVERYDAY AT THE PREP SCHOOL.
WHAT? DON'T YOU KNOW WHO I AM?

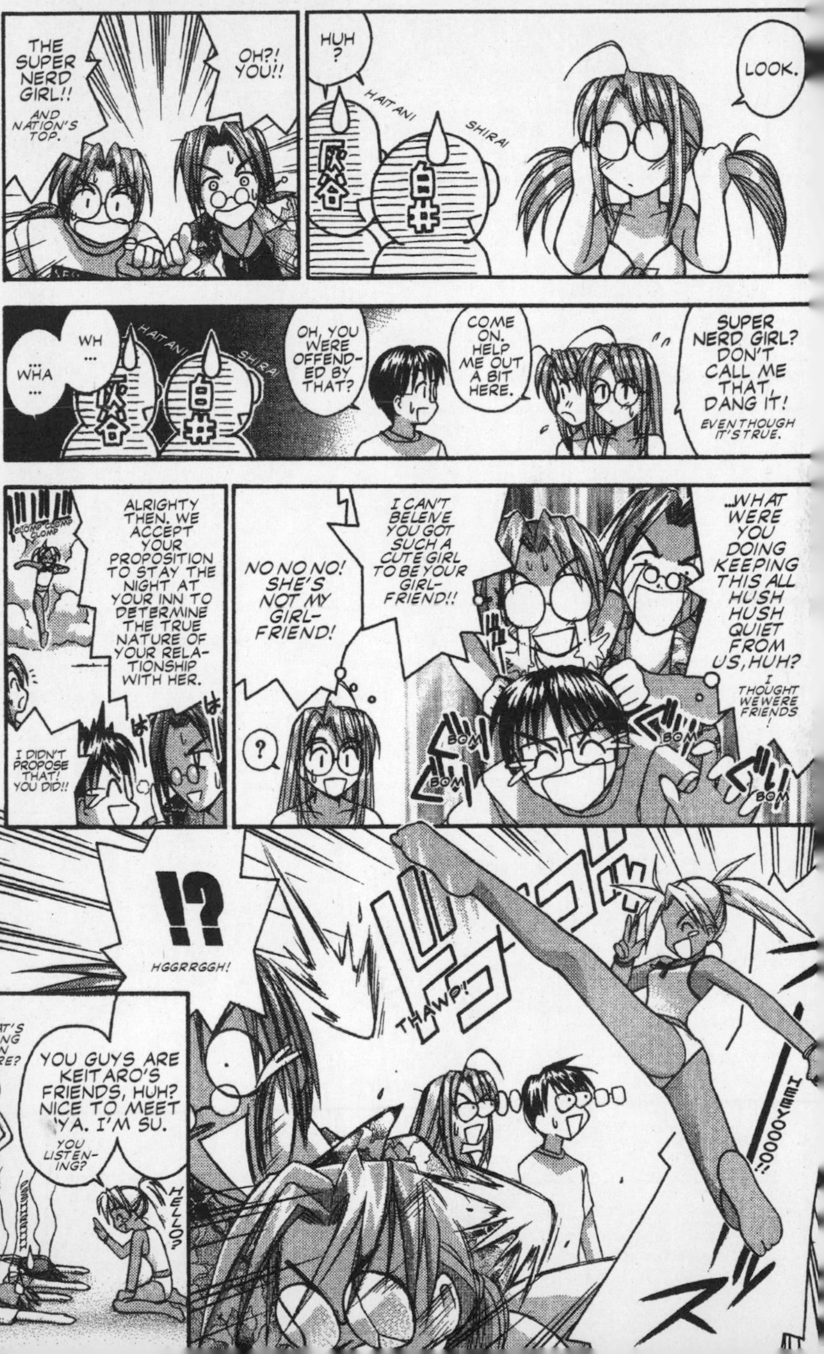
LOOK.
SHIRAI
白井
HAITANI
灰谷
HUH ?
OH?! YOU!!
THE SUPER NERD GIRL!!
AND NATION'S TOP.
SUPER NERD GIRL? DON'T CALL ME THAT, DANG IT!
EVEN THOUGH IT'S TRUE.
COME ON. HELP ME OUT A BIT HERE.
OH, YOU WERE OFFENDED BY THAT?
SHIRAI
白井
HAITANI
灰谷
WH ...
... WHA ...
...WHAT WERE YOU DOING KEEPING THIS ALL HUSH HUSH QUIET FROM US, HUH?
I THOUGHT WE WERE FRIENDS!
BOM
BOM
BOM
BOM
I CAN'T BELEIVE YOU GOT SUCH A CUTE GIRL TO BE YOUR GIRL-FRIEND!!
NO NO NO! SHE'S NOT MY GIRL-FRIEND!
?
ALRIGHTY THEN. WE ACCEPT YOUR PROPOSITION TO STAY THE NIGHT AT YOUR INN TO DETERMINE THE TRUE NATURE OF YOUR RELA-TIONSHIP WITH HER.
CLOMP CLOMP CLOMP
I DIDN'T PROPOSE THAT! YOU DID!!
HEYOOOOO!!
THAWP!!
!?
HGGRRGGH!
WHAT'S GOING ON HERE?
YOU GUYS ARE KEITARO'S FRIENDS, HUH? NICE TO MEET 'YA. I'M SU.
YOU LISTEN-ING?
HELLO?

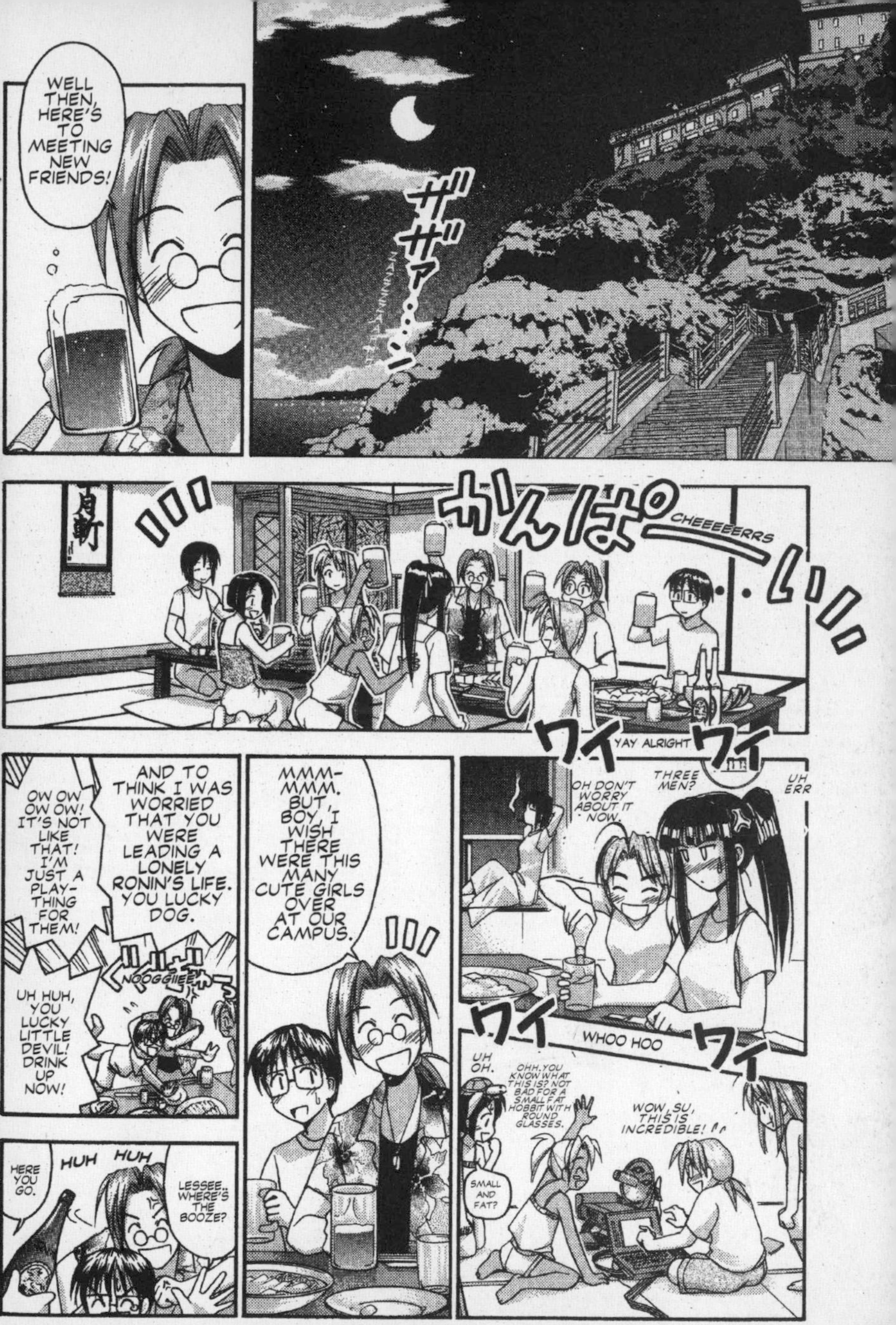

ザザァ…
WELL THEN, HERE'S TO MEETING NEW FRIENDS!
かんぱーい
CHEEEEERRS
ワイ YAY ALRIGHT ワイ
THREE MEN?
UH ERR
OH DON'T WORRY ABOUT IT NOW.
ワイ WHOO HOO ワイ
UH OH.
OHH, YOU KNOW WHAT THIS IS? NOT BAD FOR A SMALL FAT HOBBIT WITH ROUND GLASSES.
WOW, SU, THIS IS INCREDIBLE!
SMALL AND FAT?
MMM-MMM. BUT, BOY, I WISH THERE WERE THIS MANY CUTE GIRLS OVER AT OUR CAMPUS.
AND TO THINK I WAS WORRIED THAT YOU WERE LEADING A LONELY RONIN'S LIFE. YOU LUCKY DOG.
OW OW OW OW! IT'S NOT LIKE THAT! I'M JUST A PLAYTHING FOR THEM!
NOOGGIIEE
UH HUH, YOU LUCKY LITTLE DEVIL! DRINK UP NOW!
HUH HUH
LESSEE.. WHERE'S THE BOOZE?
HERE YOU GO.

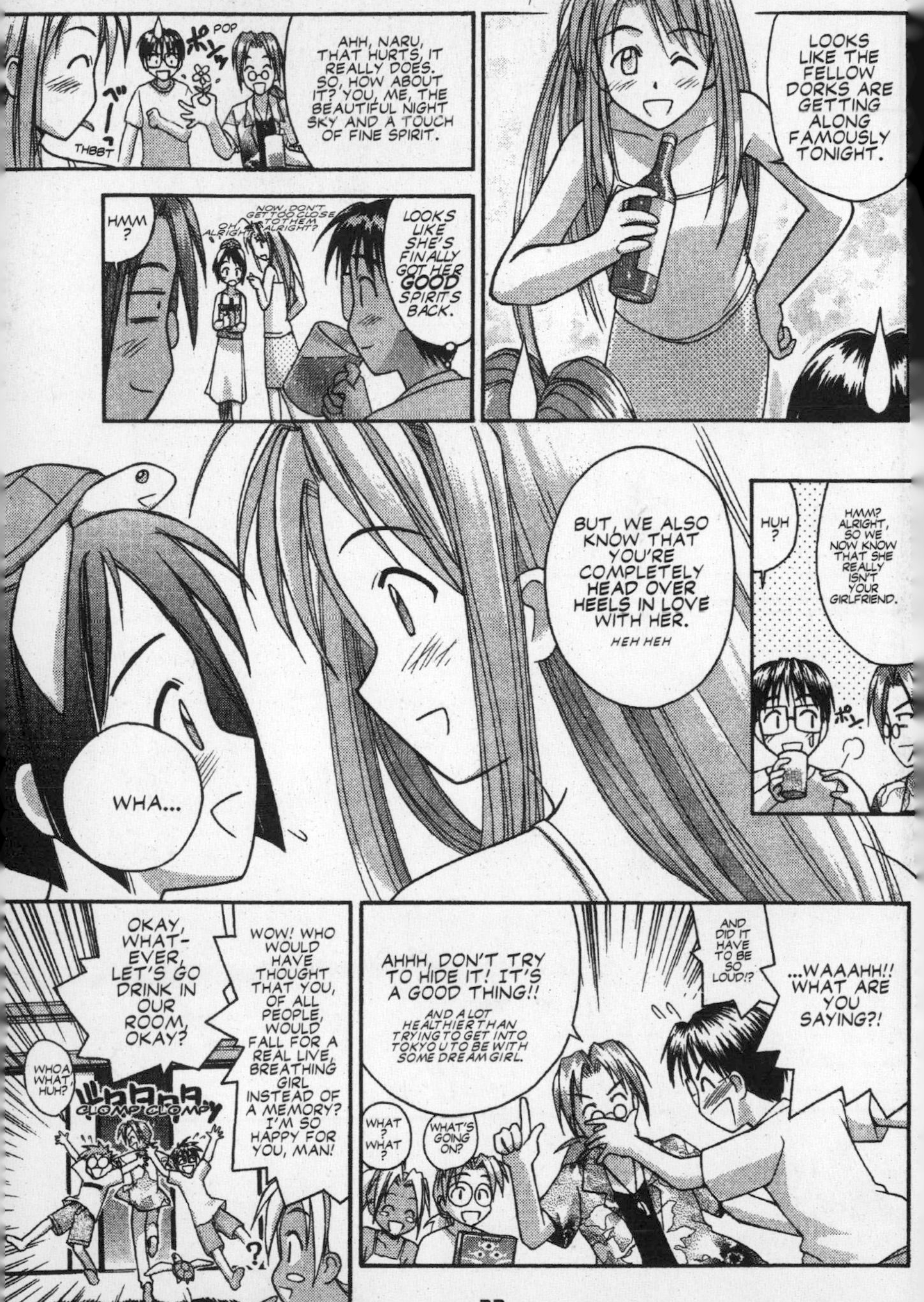
LOOKS LIKE THE FELLOW DORKS ARE GETTING ALONG FAMOUSLY TONIGHT.
AHH, NARU, THAT HURTS, IT REALLY DOES. SO, HOW ABOUT IT? YOU, ME, THE BEAUTIFUL NIGHT SKY AND A TOUCH OF FINE SPIRIT.
POP
THBBT
LOOKS LIKE SHE'S FINALLY GOT HER GOOD SPIRITS BACK.
NOW, DON'T GET TOO CLOSE TO THEM ALRIGHT?
OH ALRIGHT
HMM ?
HMM? ALRIGHT, SO WE NOW KNOW THAT SHE REALLY ISN'T YOUR GIRLFRIEND.
HUH ?
BUT, WE ALSO KNOW THAT YOU'RE COMPLETELY HEAD OVER HEELS IN LOVE WITH HER.
HEH HEH
WHA...
...WAAAHH!! WHAT ARE YOU SAYING?!
AND DID IT HAVE TO BE SO LOUD!?
AHHH, DON'T TRY TO HIDE IT! IT'S A GOOD THING!!
AND A LOT HEALTHIER THAN TRYING TO GET INTO TOKYO U TO BE WITH SOME DREAM GIRL.
WHAT'S GOING ON?
WHAT ? WHAT ?
WOW! WHO WOULD HAVE THOUGHT THAT YOU, OF ALL PEOPLE, WOULD FALL FOR A REAL LIVE, BREATHING GIRL INSTEAD OF A MEMORY? I'M SO HAPPY FOR YOU, MAN!
OKAY, WHAT-EVER, LET'S GO DRINK IN OUR ROOM, OKAY?
WHOA WHAT, HUH?
CLOMP CLOMP

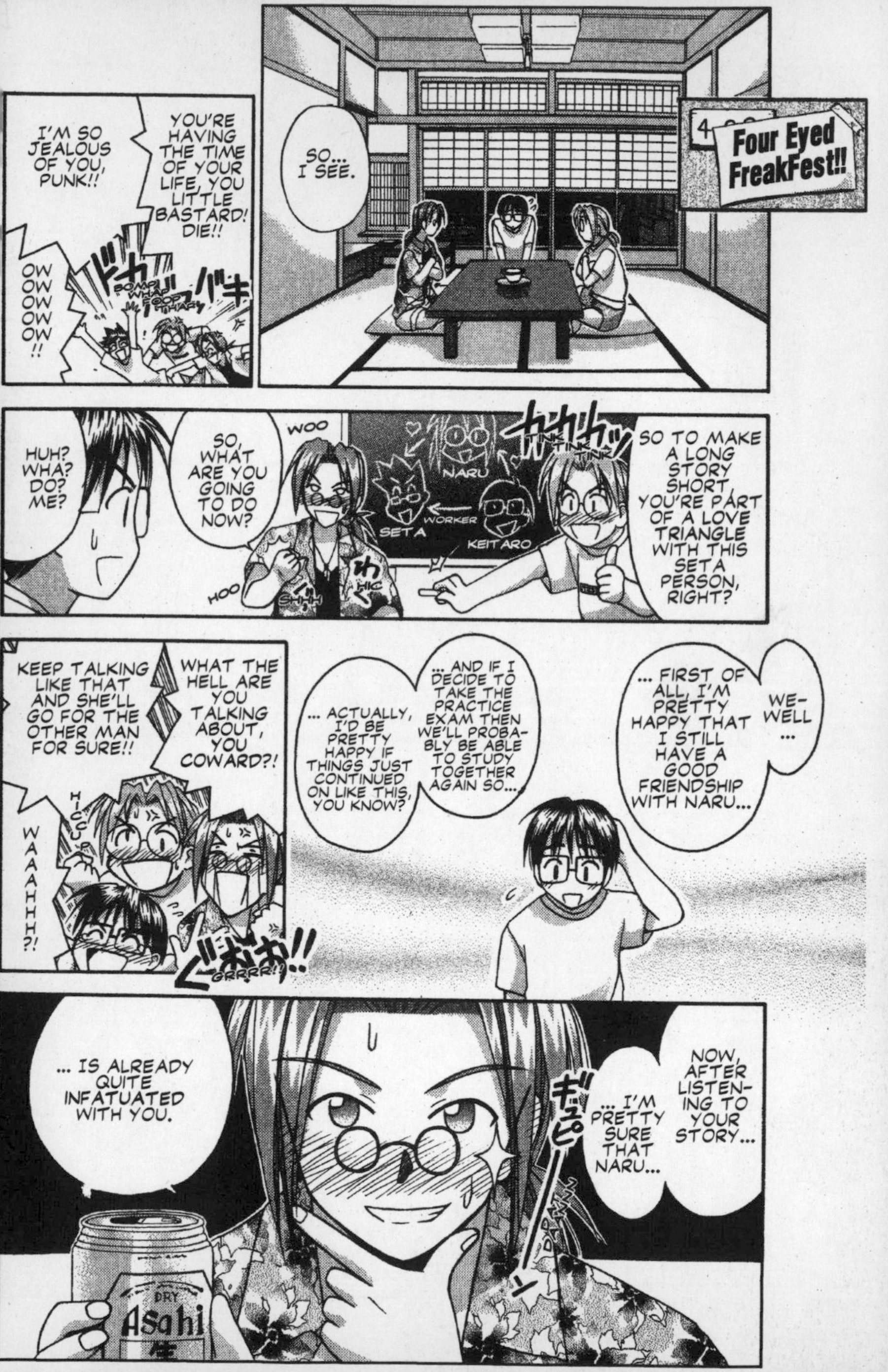
Four Eyed FreakFest!!
SO... I SEE.
YOU'RE HAVING THE TIME OF YOUR LIFE, YOU LITTLE BASTARD! DIE!!
I'M SO JEALOUS OF YOU, PUNK!!
OW OW OW OW OW !!
BOMP! WHAP! FOOP! THAP!
SO TO MAKE A LONG STORY SHORT, YOU'RE PART OF A LOVE TRIANGLE WITH THIS SETA PERSON, RIGHT?
TINK TINK TINK
NARU
SETA
WORKER
KEITARO
WOO
SO, WHAT ARE YOU GOING TO DO NOW?
HOO
SHHH
HIC
HUH? WHA? DO? ME?
WE-WELL ...
... FIRST OF ALL, I'M PRETTY HAPPY THAT I STILL HAVE A GOOD FRIENDSHIP WITH NARU...
... AND IF I DECIDE TO TAKE THE PRACTICE EXAM THEN WE'LL PROBABLY BE ABLE TO STUDY TOGETHER AGAIN SO...
... ACTUALLY, I'D BE PRETTY HAPPY IF THINGS JUST CONTINUED ON LIKE THIS, YOU KNOW?
WHAT THE HELL ARE YOU TALKING ABOUT, YOU COWARD?!
KEEP TALKING LIKE THAT AND SHE'LL GO FOR THE OTHER MAN FOR SURE!!
HICCUP
WAAAAHHH?!
GRRRR!!
NOW, AFTER LISTENING TO YOUR STORY...
... I'M PRETTY SURE THAT NARU...
... IS ALREADY QUITE INFATUATED WITH YOU.
DRY
Asahi

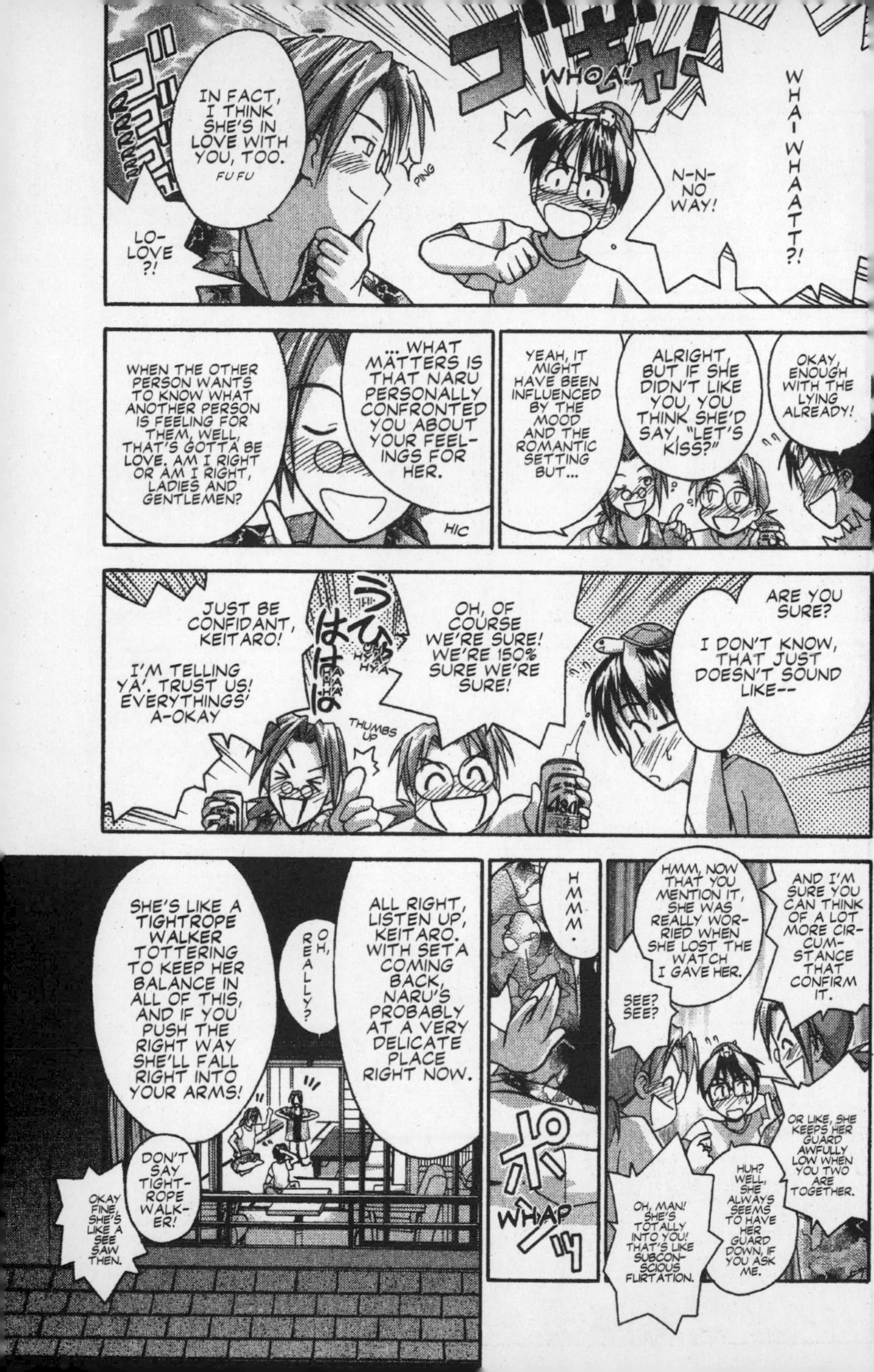
WHOA!
WHAI-WHHAATT?!
N-N-NO WAY!
PING
IN FACT, I THINK SHE'S IN LOVE WITH YOU, TOO.
FU FU
LO-LOVE?!
OKAY, ENOUGH WITH THE LYING ALREADY!
ALRIGHT, BUT IF SHE DIDN'T LIKE YOU, YOU THINK SHE'D SAY, "LET'S KISS?"
YEAH, IT MIGHT HAVE BEEN INFLUENCED BY THE MOOD AND THE ROMANTIC SETTING BUT...
... WHAT MATTERS IS THAT NARU PERSONALLY CONFRONTED YOU ABOUT YOUR FEEL-INGS FOR HER.
HIC
WHEN THE OTHER PERSON WANTS TO KNOW WHAT ANOTHER PERSON IS FEELING FOR THEM, WELL, THAT'S GOTTA BE LOVE. AM I RIGHT OR AM I RIGHT, LADIES AND GENTLEMEN?
ARE YOU SURE?
I DON'T KNOW, THAT JUST DOESN'T SOUND LIKE--
OH, OF COURSE WE'RE SURE! WE'RE 150% SURE WE'RE SURE!
THUMBS UP
JUST BE CONFIDANT, KEITARO!
I'M TELLING YA'. TRUST US! EVERYTHINGS' A-OKAY
AND I'M SURE YOU CAN THINK OF A LOT MORE CIR-CUM-STANCE THAT CONFIRM IT.
HMM, NOW THAT YOU MENTION IT, SHE WAS REALLY WOR-RIED WHEN SHE LOST THE WATCH I GAVE HER.
SEE? SEE?
OR LIKE, SHE KEEPS HER GUARD AWFULLY LOW WHEN YOU TWO ARE TOGETHER.
HUH? WELL, SHE ALWAYS SEEMS TO HAVE HER GUARD DOWN, IF YOU ASK ME.
OH, MAN! SHE'S TOTALLY INTO YOU! THAT'S LIKE SUBCON-SCIOUS FLIRTATION.
HMMM.
WHAP
ALL RIGHT, LISTEN UP, KEITARO. WITH SETA COMING BACK, NARU'S PROBABLY AT A VERY DELICATE PLACE RIGHT NOW.
OH, REALLY?
SHE'S LIKE A TIGHTROPE WALKER TOTTERING TO KEEP HER BALANCE IN ALL OF THIS, AND IF YOU PUSH THE RIGHT WAY SHE'LL FALL RIGHT INTO YOUR ARMS!
DON'T SAY TIGHT-ROPE WALKER!
OKAY FINE, SHE'S LIKE A SEE SAW THEN.

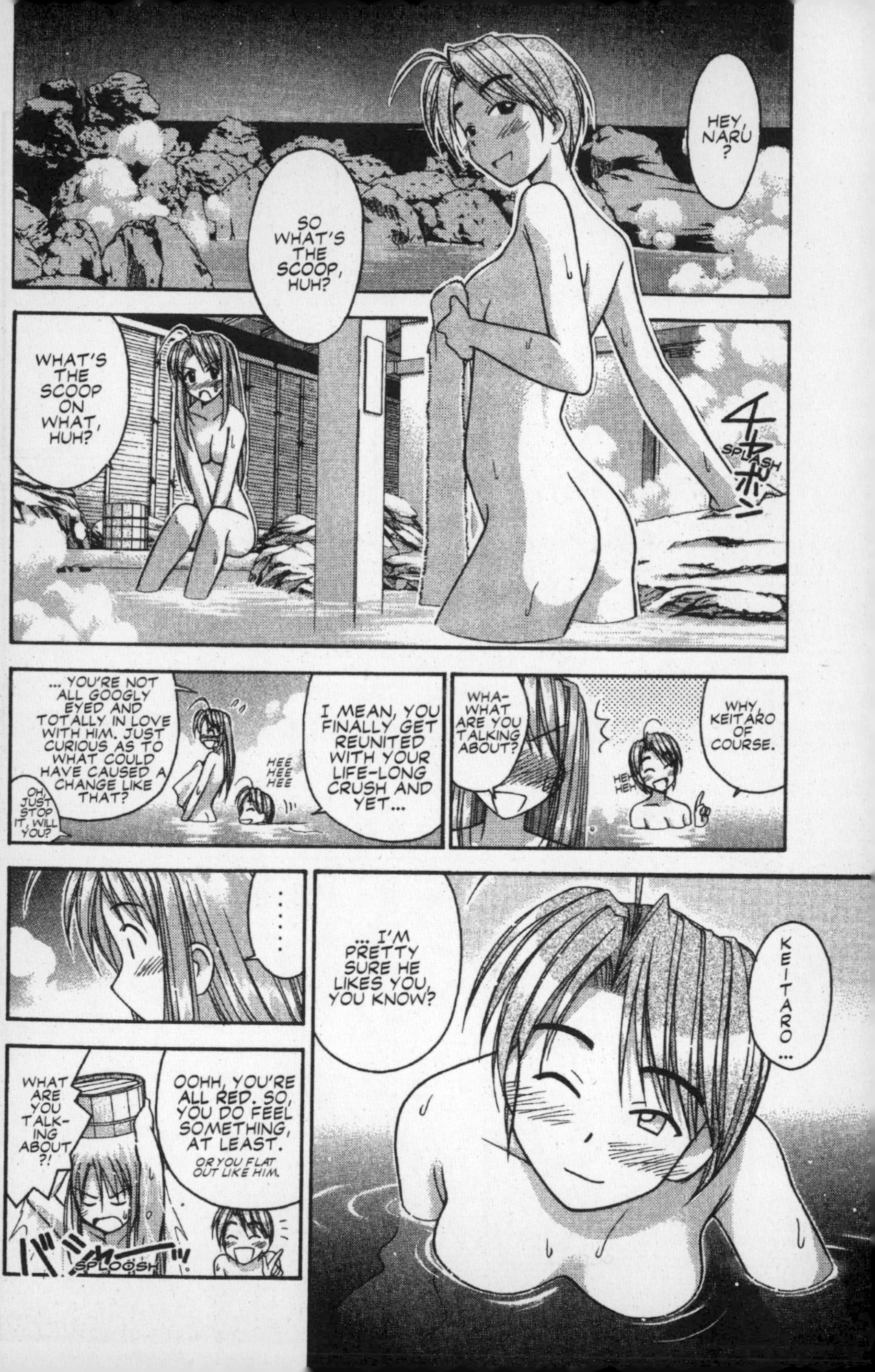
HEY, NARU?
SO WHAT'S THE SCOOP, HUH?
SPLASH
WHAT'S THE SCOOP ON WHAT, HUH?
WHY, KEITARO OF COURSE.
HEH HEH
WHA-WHAT ARE YOU TALKING ABOUT?
I MEAN, YOU FINALLY GET REUNITED WITH YOUR LIFE-LONG CRUSH AND YET...
... YOU'RE NOT ALL GOOGLY EYED AND TOTALLY IN LOVE WITH HIM. JUST CURIOUS AS TO WHAT COULD HAVE CAUSED A CHANGE LIKE THAT?
HEE HEE HEE
OH, JUST STOP IT, WILL YOU?
KEITARO...
... I'M PRETTY SURE HE LIKES YOU, YOU KNOW?
......
OOHH, YOU'RE ALL RED. SO, YOU DO FEEL SOMETHING, AT LEAST.
OR YOU FLAT OUT LIKE HIM.
WHAT ARE YOU TALKING ABOUT?!
SPLOOSH

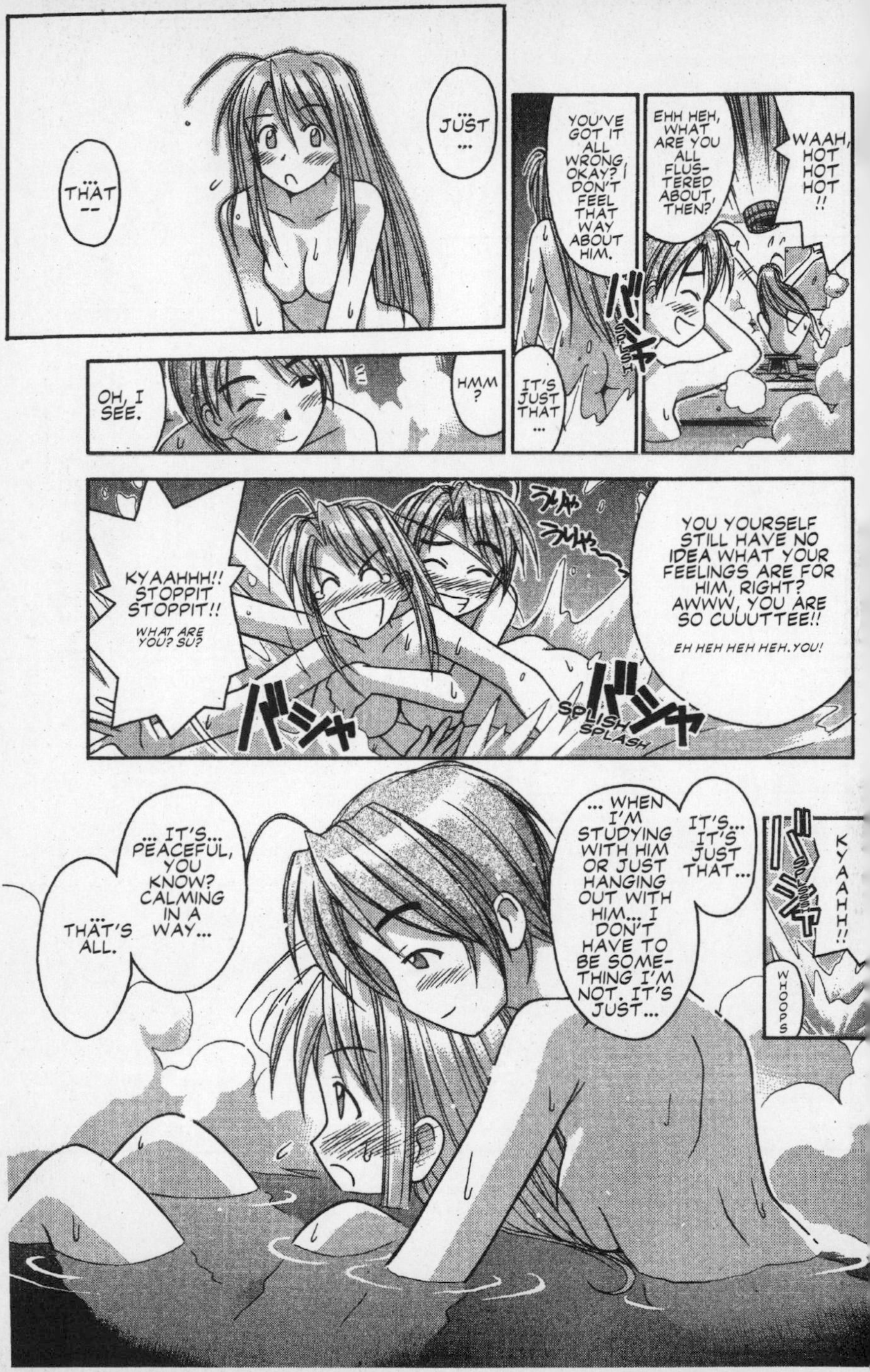
WAAH, HOT HOT HOT!!
EHH HEH, WHAT ARE YOU ALL FLUSTERED ABOUT, THEN?
YOU'VE GOT IT ALL WRONG, OKAY? I DON'T FEEL THAT WAY ABOUT HIM.
SPLASH
IT'S JUST THAT ...
... JUST ...
... THAT --
HMM?
OH, I SEE.
YOU YOURSELF STILL HAVE NO IDEA WHAT YOUR FEELINGS ARE FOR HIM, RIGHT? AWWW, YOU ARE SO CUUUTTEE!!
EH HEH HEH HEH. YOU!
KYAAHHH!! STOPPIT STOPPIT!!
WHAT ARE YOU? SU?
SPLISH SPLASH
KYAAHH!!
SPLASH
WHOOPS
IT'S... IT'S JUST THAT...
... WHEN I'M STUDYING WITH HIM OR JUST HANGING OUT WITH HIM... I DON'T HAVE TO BE SOMETHING I'M NOT. IT'S JUST...
... IT'S... PEACEFUL, YOU KNOW? CALMING IN A WAY...
... THAT'S ALL.

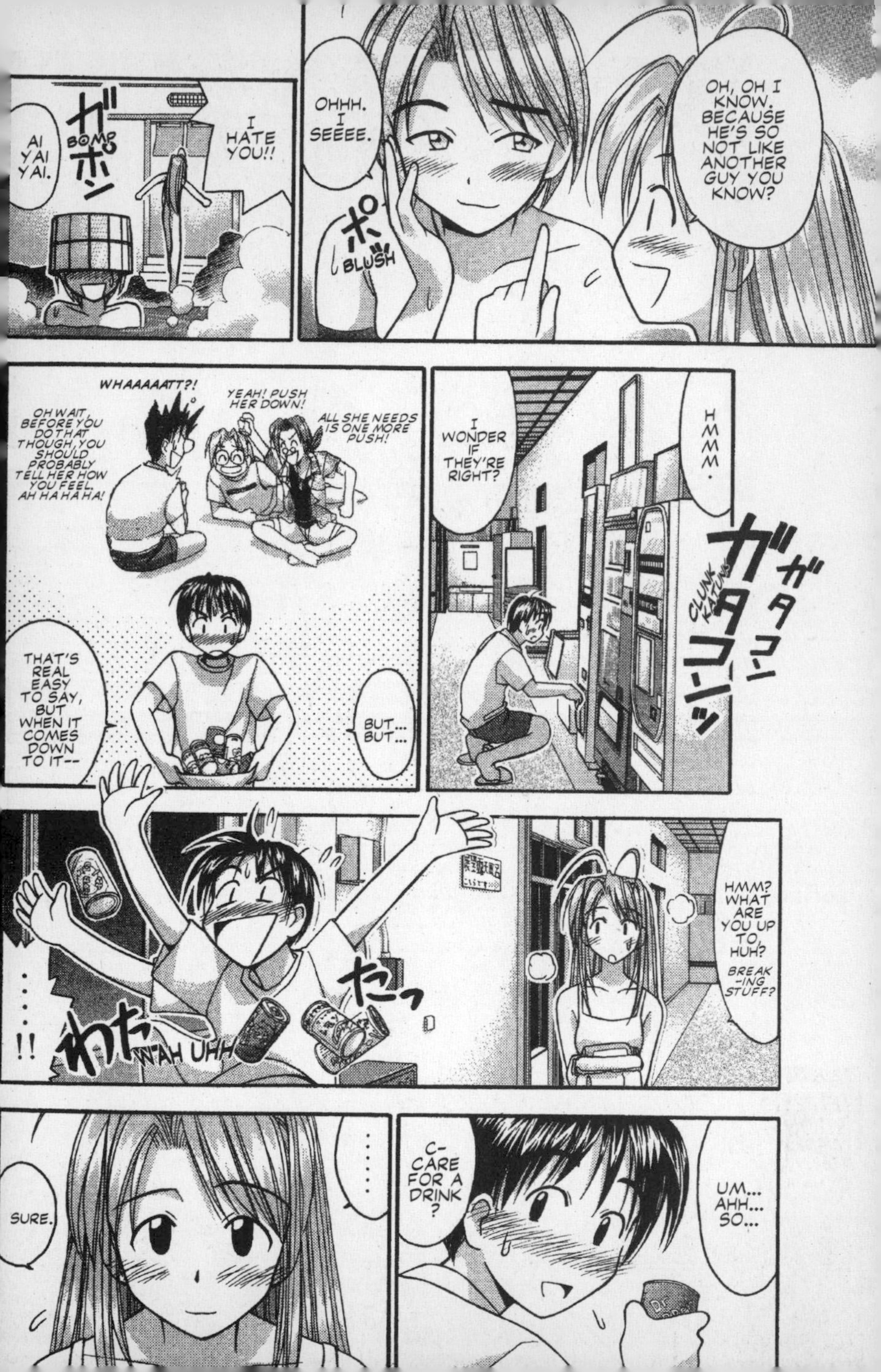
OH, OH I KNOW. BECAUSE HE'S SO NOT LIKE ANOTHER GUY YOU KNOW?
OHHH. I SEEEE.
ポ
BLUSH
I HATE YOU!!
ガボン
BOMP
AI YAI YAI.
HMMM.
I WONDER IF THEY'RE RIGHT?
ガタコン ガタコンッ
CLUNK KATUNK
WHAAAAATT?!
YEAH! PUSH HER DOWN!
ALL SHE NEEDS IS ONE MORE PUSH!
OH WAIT, BEFORE YOU DO THAT THOUGH, YOU SHOULD PROBABLY TELL HER HOW YOU FEEL. AH HA HA HA!
BUT... BUT...
THAT'S REAL EASY TO SAY, BUT WHEN IT COMES DOWN TO IT--
HMM? WHAT ARE YOU UP TO, HUH?
BREAK-ING STUFF?
たっ
わた
WAH UHH
.....!!
UM... AHH... SO...
C-CARE FOR A DRINK?
......
SURE.

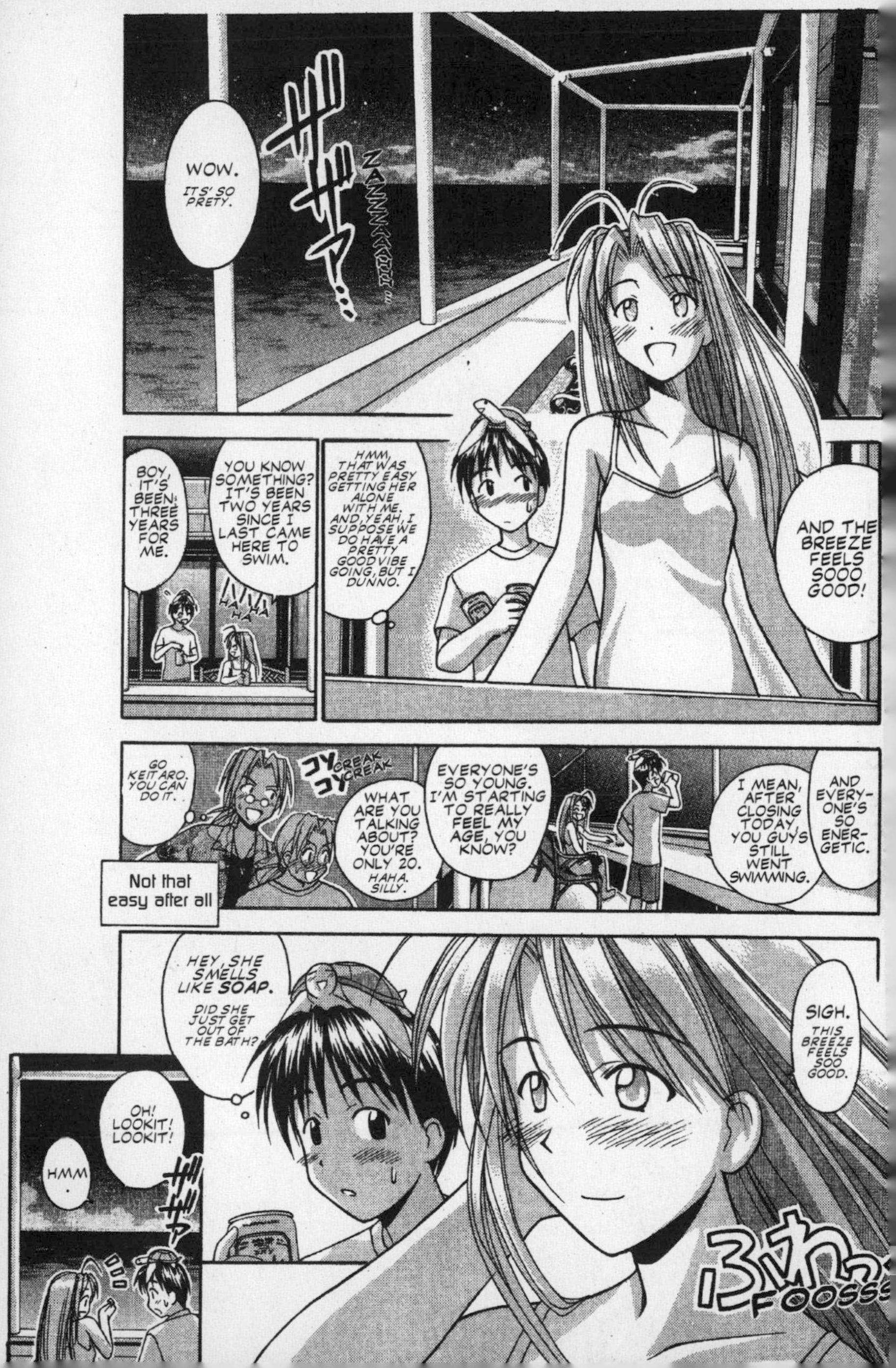
WOW.
IT'S' SO PRETTY.
AND THE BREEZE FEELS SOOO GOOD!
HMM, THAT WAS PRETTY EASY GETTING HER ALONE WITH ME. AND, YEAH, I SUPPOSE WE DO HAVE A PRETTY GOOD VIBE GOING, BUT I DUNNO.
YOU KNOW SOMETHING? IT'S BEEN TWO YEARS SINCE I LAST CAME HERE TO SWIM.
BOY, IT'S BEEN THREE YEARS FOR ME.
HA HA HA
AND EVERYONE'S SO ENERGETIC.
I MEAN, AFTER CLOSING TODAY, YOU GUYS STILL WENT SWIMMING.
EVERYONE'S SO YOUNG. I'M STARTING TO REALLY FEEL MY AGE, YOU KNOW?
WHAT ARE YOU TALKING ABOUT? YOU'RE ONLY 20. HAHA. SILLY.
CREAK CREAK
GO KEITARO. YOU CAN DO IT.
Not that easy after all
SIGH. THIS BREEZE FEELS SOO GOOD.
FOOSSS
HEY, SHE SMELLS LIKE SOAP. DID SHE JUST GET OUT OF THE BATH?
OH! LOOKIT! LOOKIT!
HMM.

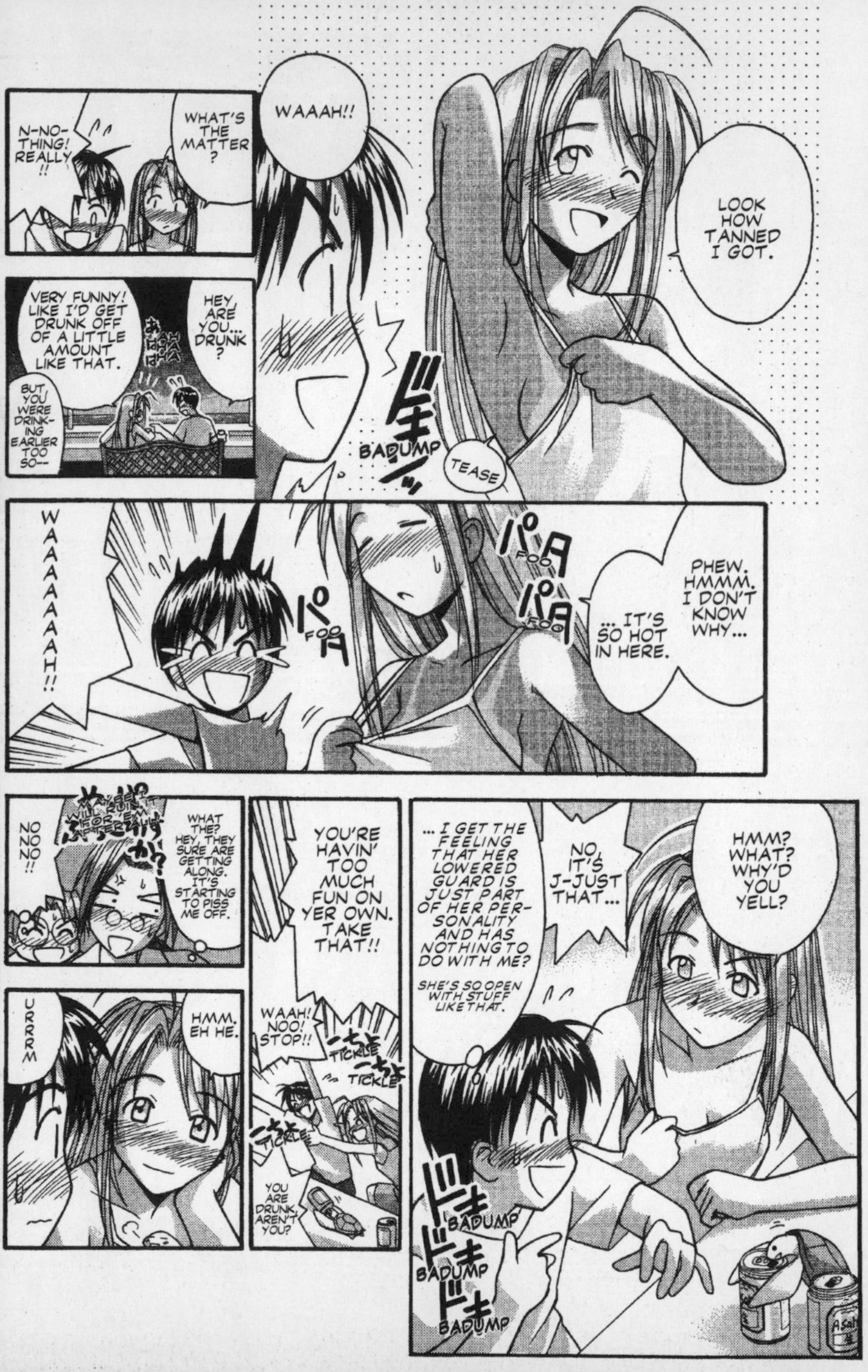
LOOK HOW TANNED I GOT.
WAAAH!!
BADUMP
TEASE
WHAT'S THE MATTER?
N-NOTHING! REALLY!!
HEY, ARE YOU... DRUNK?
AHAHA
VERY FUNNY! LIKE I'D GET DRUNK OFF OF A LITTLE AMOUNT LIKE THAT.
BUT YOU WERE DRINKING EARLIER TOO SO--
PHEW. HMMM. I DON'T KNOW WHY...
... IT'S SO HOT IN HERE.
FOO
FOO
FOO
WAAAAAAAAAAH!!
HMM? WHAT? WHY'D YOU YELL?
NO, IT'S J-JUST THAT...
... I GET THE FEELING THAT HER LOWERED GUARD IS JUST PART OF HER PERSONALITY AND HAS NOTHING TO DO WITH ME?
SHE'S SO OPEN WITH STUFF LIKE THAT.
BADUMP
BADUMP
BADUMP
YOU'RE HAVIN' TOO MUCH FUN ON YER OWN. TAKE THAT!!
WAAH! NOO! STOP!!
TICKLE
TICKLE
TICKLE
YOU ARE DRUNK, AREN'T YOU?
MAYBE IT WILL RUIN IT FOR 'EM AFTER ALL?
WHAT THE? HEY, THEY SURE ARE GETTING ALONG. IT'S STARTING TO PISS ME OFF.
NO NO NO!!
HMM. EH HE.
URRRM

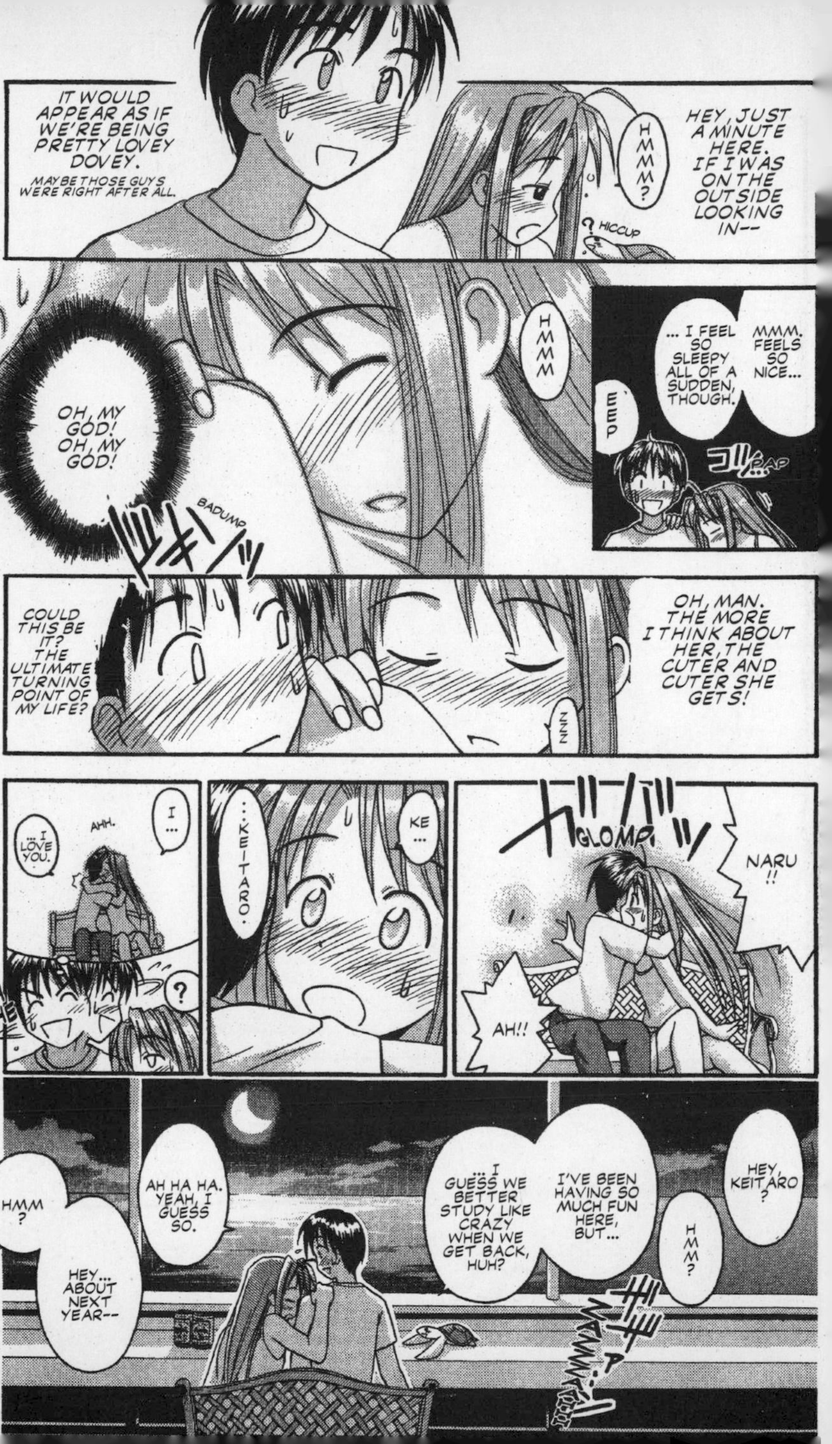
HEY, JUST A MINUTE HERE. IF I WAS ON THE OUTSIDE LOOKING IN--
HMMMM?
HICCUP
IT WOULD APPEAR AS IF WE'RE BEING PRETTY LOVEY DOVEY.
MAYBE THOSE GUYS WERE RIGHT AFTER ALL.
MMM. FEELS SO NICE...
... I FEEL SO SLEEPY ALL OF A SUDDEN, THOUGH.
EEP
PAP
HMMM
OH, MY GOD! OH, MY GOD!
BADUMP
OH, MAN. THE MORE I THINK ABOUT HER, THE CUTER AND CUTER SHE GETS!
ZZZ
COULD THIS BE IT? THE ULTIMATE TURNING POINT OF MY LIFE?
NARU!!
GLOMP
AH!!
KE...
...KEITARO.
I...
AHH.
... I LOVE YOU.
?
HEH HEHE
HEY, KEITARO?
HMM?
I'VE BEEN HAVING SO MUCH FUN HERE, BUT...
... I GUESS WE BETTER STUDY LIKE CRAZY WHEN WE GET BACK, HUH?
AH HA HA. YEAH, I GUESS SO.
HMM?
HEY... ABOUT NEXT YEAR--

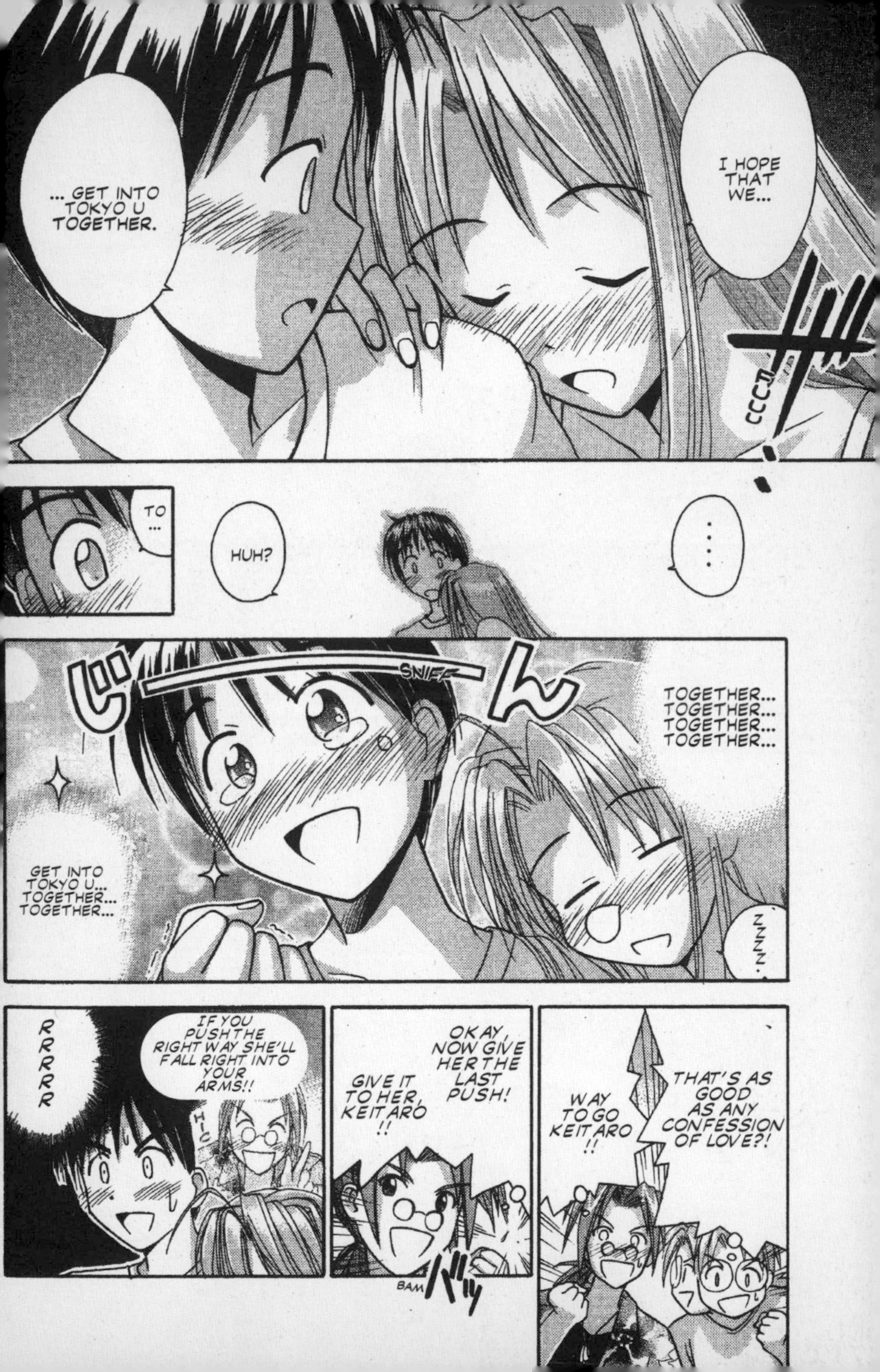
I HOPE THAT WE...
... GET INTO TOKYO U TOGETHER.
....
HUH?
TO ...
TOGETHER... TOGETHER... TOGETHER... TOGETHER...
SNIFF
ZZZ.
GET INTO TOKYO U... TOGETHER... TOGETHER...
THAT'S AS GOOD AS ANY CONFESSION OF LOVE?!
WAY TO GO KEITARO !!
OKAY, NOW GIVE HER THE LAST PUSH!
GIVE IT TO HER, KEITARO !!
BAM
IF YOU PUSH THE RIGHT WAY SHE'LL FALL RIGHT INTO YOUR ARMS!!
HIC
RRRRR

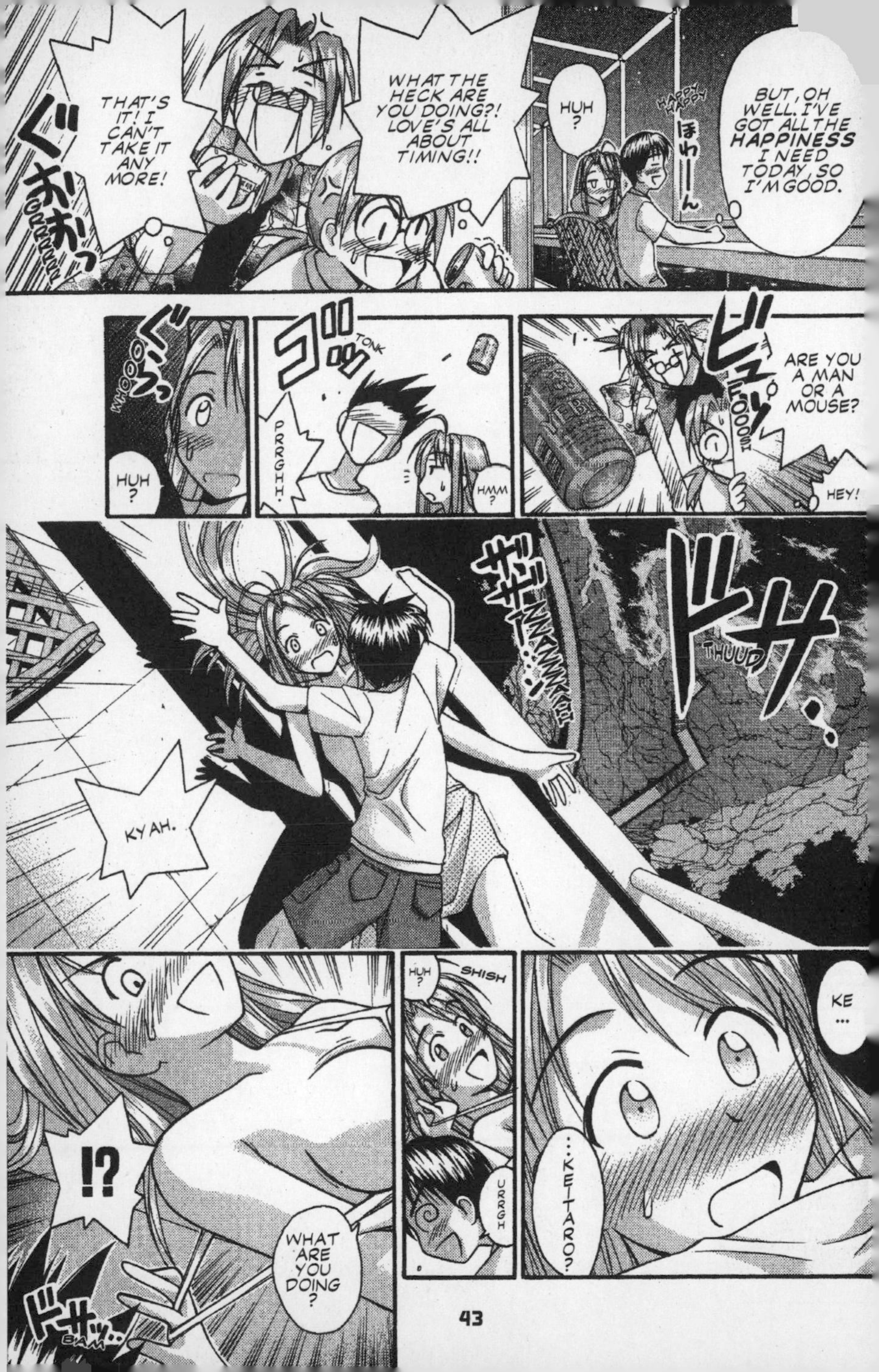
BUT, OH WELL. I'VE GOT ALL THE HAPPINESS I NEED TODAY, SO I'M GOOD.
HAPPY HAPPY
ほわーん
HUH?
WHAT THE HECK ARE YOU DOING?! LOVE'S ALL ABOUT TIMING!!
THAT'S IT! I CAN'T TAKE IT ANY MORE!
ぐおおっ
GRRRRR
ビュッ
FOOOSH
ARE YOU A MAN OR A MOUSE?
HEY!
ゴッ
TONK
PRRGHH.
HMM?
ぐらっ
WHOOO
HUH?
ドサ
THUUD
KYAH.
KE...
...KEITARO?
HUH?
SHISH
URRGH
!?
WHAT ARE YOU DOING?
ドサッ
BAM

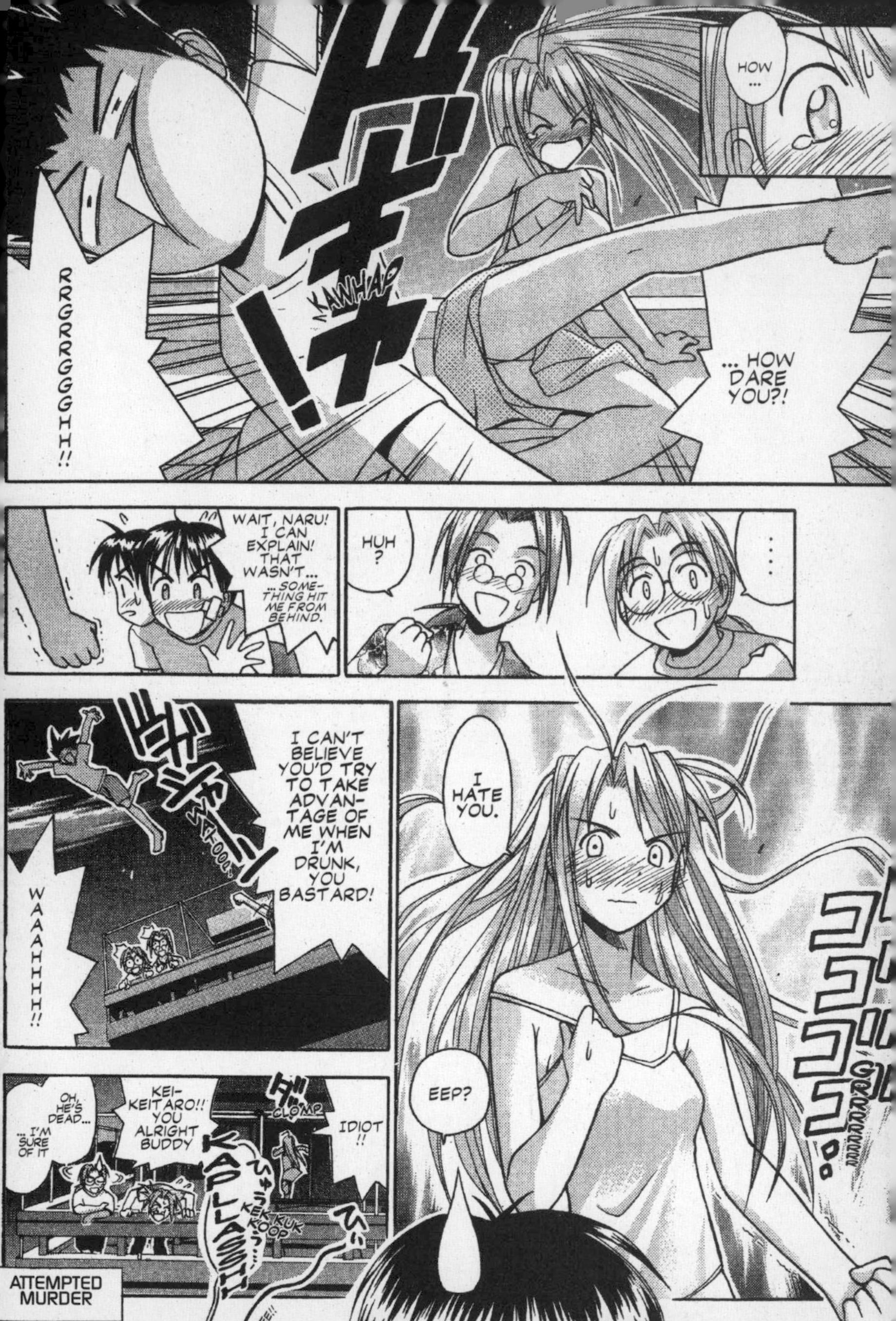
HOW ...
... HOW DARE YOU?!
KAWHAP
RRGRRGGHH!!
HUH ?
. . . .
WAIT, NARU! I CAN EXPLAIN! THAT WASN'T...
... SOMETHING HIT ME FROM BEHIND.
I HATE YOU.
EEP?
GRRRRRRR
I CAN'T BELIEVE YOU'D TRY TO TAKE ADVANTAGE OF ME WHEN I'M DRUNK, YOU BASTARD!
WAAAAHHHH!!
IDIOT !!
CLOMP
KEI-KEITARO!! YOU ALRIGHT BUDDY
OH, HE'S DEAD...
... I'M SURE OF IT
KEK KUK KOOP
KAPLLASSHH
HEEEE!!
ATTEMPTED MURDER

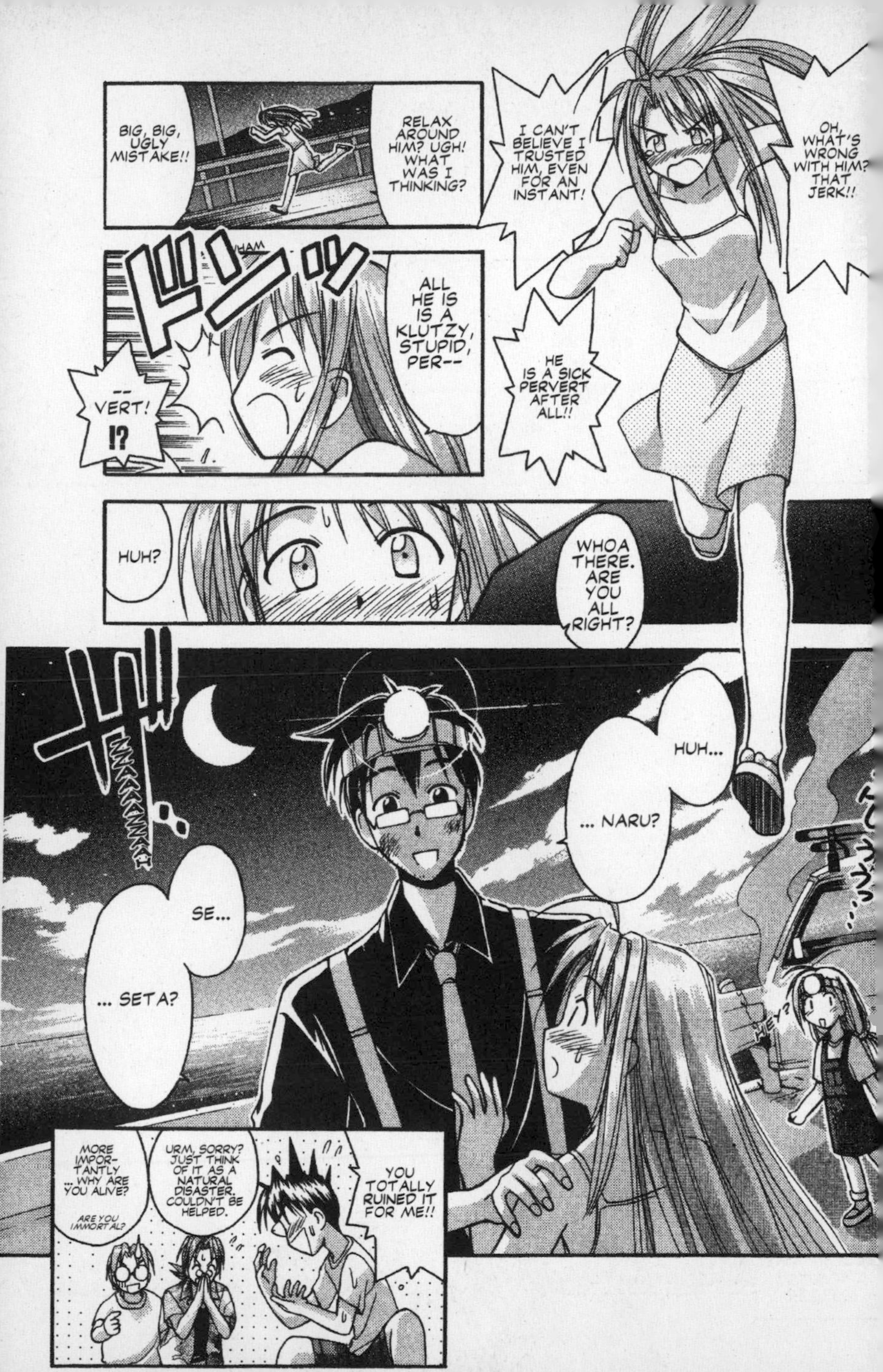
OH, WHAT'S WRONG WITH HIM? THAT JERK!!
I CAN'T BELIEVE I TRUSTED HIM, EVEN FOR AN INSTANT!
HE IS A SICK PERVERT AFTER ALL!!
RELAX AROUND HIM? UGH! WHAT WAS I THINKING?
BIG, BIG, UGLY MISTAKE!!
ALL HE IS IS A KLUTZY, STUPID, PER--
WHAM
--VERT!
!?
WHOA THERE. ARE YOU ALL RIGHT?
HUH?
HUH...
... NARU?
SE...
... SETA?
HEY?
YOU TOTALLY RUINED IT FOR ME!!
URM, SORRY? JUST THINK OF IT AS A NATURAL DISASTER. COULDN'T BE HELPED.
MORE IMPOR-TANTLY ... WHY ARE YOU ALIVE?
ARE YOU IMMORTAL?

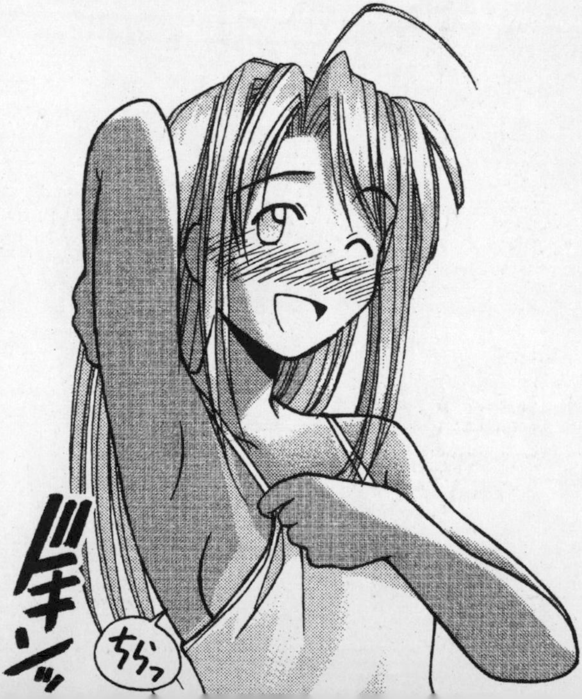
ドキンッ
ちらっ

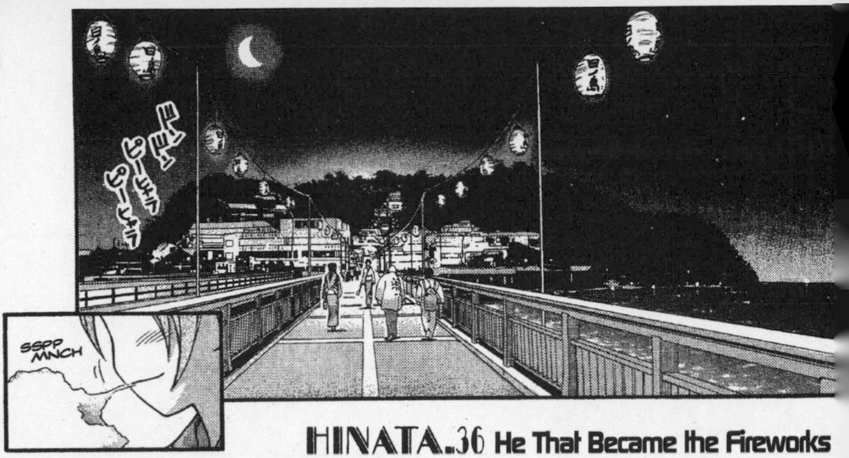
SSPP MNCH

HINATA.36 He That Became the Fireworks

Love Hina

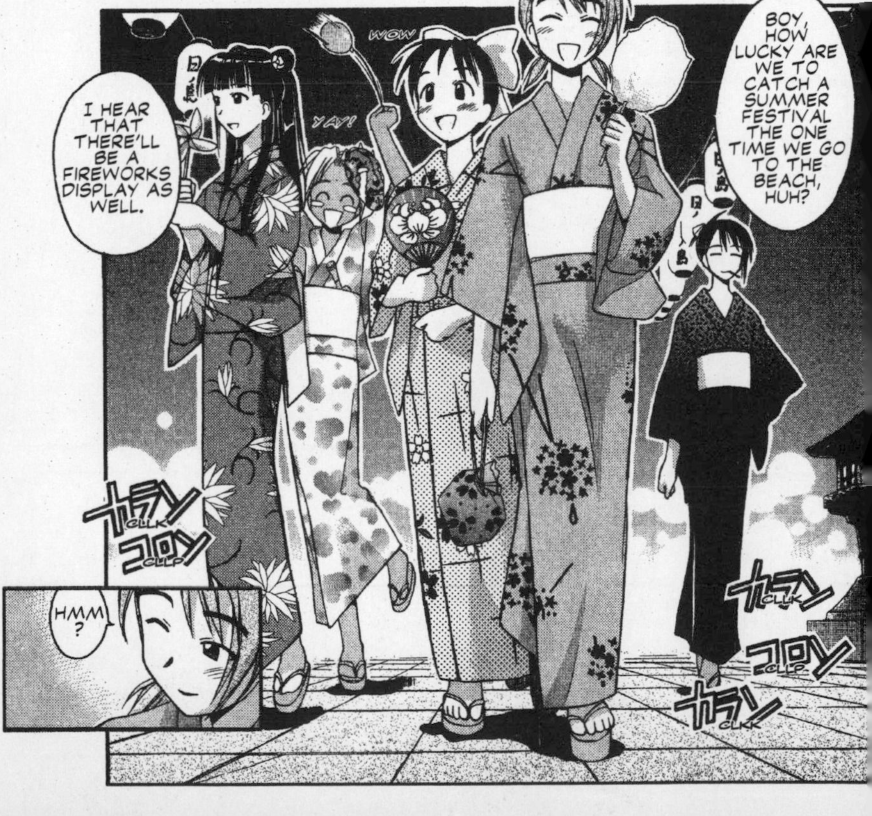
BOY, HOW LUCKY ARE WE TO CATCH A SUMMER FESTIVAL THE ONE TIME WE GO TO THE BEACH, HUH?
WOW
YAY!
I HEAR THAT THERE'LL BE A FIREWORKS DISPLAY AS WELL.
CLLK
CLLP
CLLK
CLLP
CLKK
HMM?

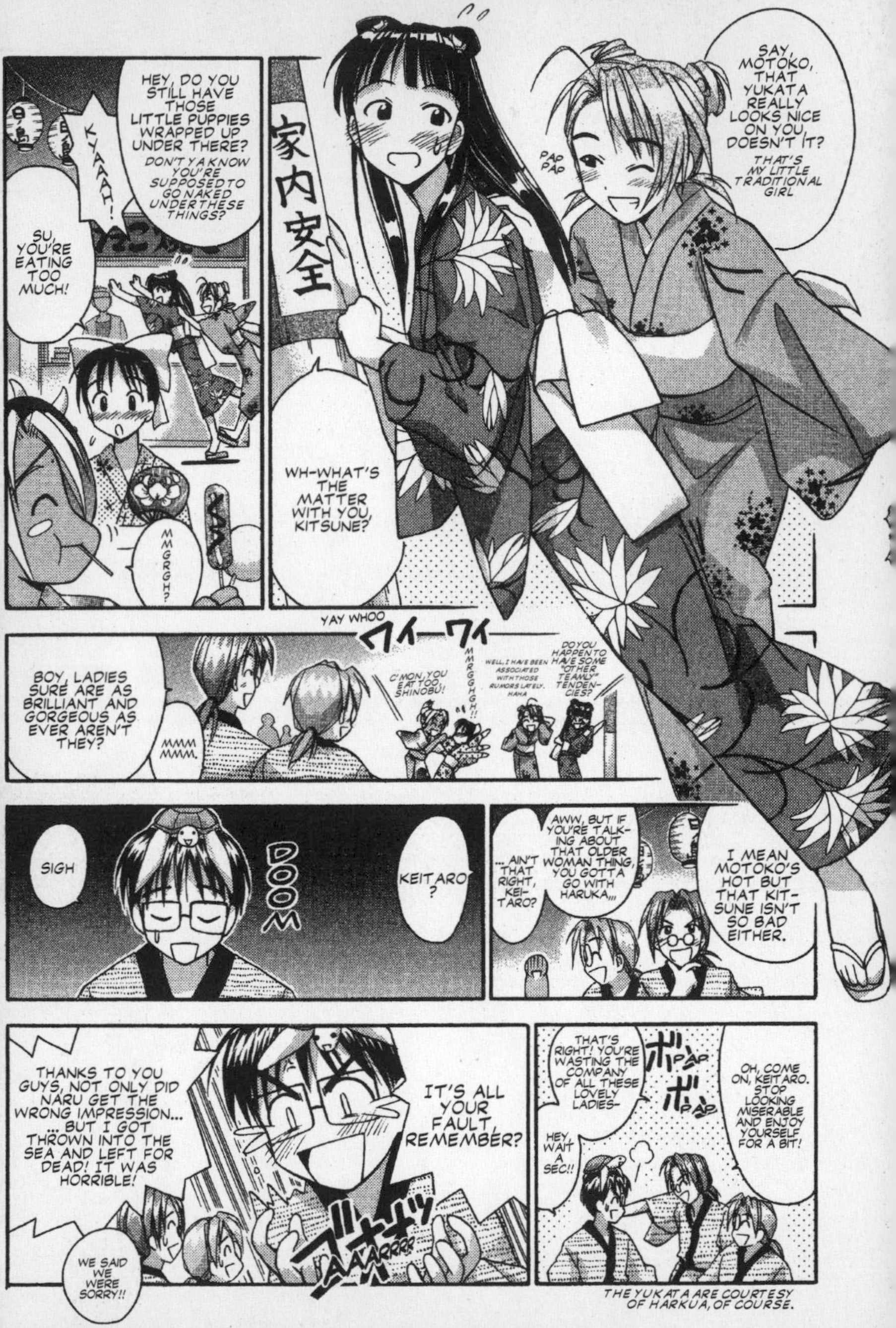
SAY, MOTOKO, THAT YUKATA REALLY LOOKS NICE ON YOU, DOESN'T IT?
THAT'S MY LITTLE TRADITIONAL GIRL
PAP PAP
家内安全
WH-WHAT'S THE MATTER WITH YOU, KITSUNE?
HEY, DO YOU STILL HAVE THOSE LITTLE PUPPIES WRAPPED UP UNDER THERE?
DON'T YA KNOW YOU'RE SUPPOSED TO GO NAKED UNDER THESE THINGS?
KYAAAH!
SU, YOU'RE EATING TOO MUCH!
MMGRGH?
YAY WHOO
ワイーワイ
DO YOU HAPPEN TO HAVE SOME "OTHER TEAMLY" TENDENCIES?
WELL, I HAVE BEEN ASSOCIATED WITH THOSE RUMORS LATELY. HAHA
MMRGGHGH!!
C'MON, YOU EAT TOO, SHINOBU!
BOY, LADIES SURE ARE AS BRILLIANT AND GORGEOUS AS EVER AREN'T THEY?
MMM MMM.
I MEAN MOTOKO'S HOT BUT THAT KIT-SUNE ISN'T SO BAD EITHER.
AWW, BUT IF YOU'RE TALK-ING ABOUT THAT OLDER WOMAN THING, YOU GOTTA GO WITH HARUKA...
...AIN'T THAT RIGHT, KEI-TARO?
KEITARO?
DOOM
SIGH
OH, COME ON, KEITARO. STOP LOOKING MISERABLE AND ENJOY YOURSELF FOR A BIT!
THAT'S RIGHT! YOU'RE WASTING THE COMPANY OF ALL THESE LOVELY LADIES-
PAP PAP
HEY, WAIT A SEC!!
IT'S ALL YOUR FAULT, REMEMBER?
THANKS TO YOU GUYS, NOT ONLY DID NARU GET THE WRONG IMPRESSION... ...BUT I GOT THROWN INTO THE SEA AND LEFT FOR DEAD! IT WAS HORRIBLE!
AAARRRR
WE SAID WE WERE SORRY!!

THE YUKATA ARE COURTESY OF HARKUA, OF COURSE.

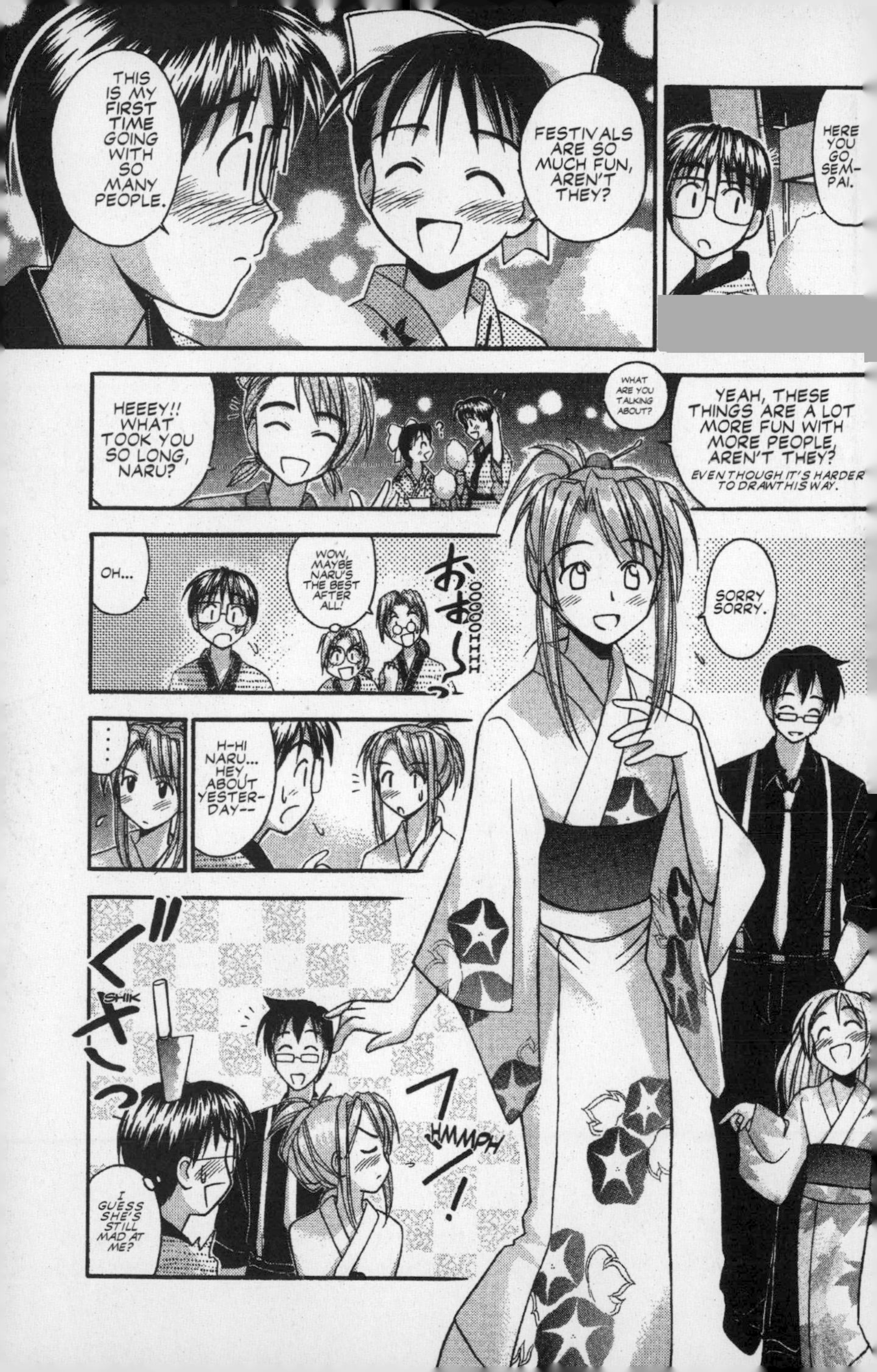
HERE YOU GO, SEMPAI.
FESTIVALS ARE SO MUCH FUN, AREN'T THEY?
THIS IS MY FIRST TIME GOING WITH SO MANY PEOPLE.
YEAH, THESE THINGS ARE A LOT MORE FUN WITH MORE PEOPLE, AREN'T THEY?
EVEN THOUGH IT'S HARDER TO DRAW THIS WAY.
WHAT ARE YOU TALKING ABOUT?
HEEEY!! WHAT TOOK YOU SO LONG, NARU?
SORRY SORRY.
OOOOOOHHHH
WOW, MAYBE NARU'S THE BEST AFTER ALL!
OH...
H-HI NARU... HEY, ABOUT YESTERDAY--
....
HMMPH
SHIK
I GUESS SHE'S STILL MAD AT ME?

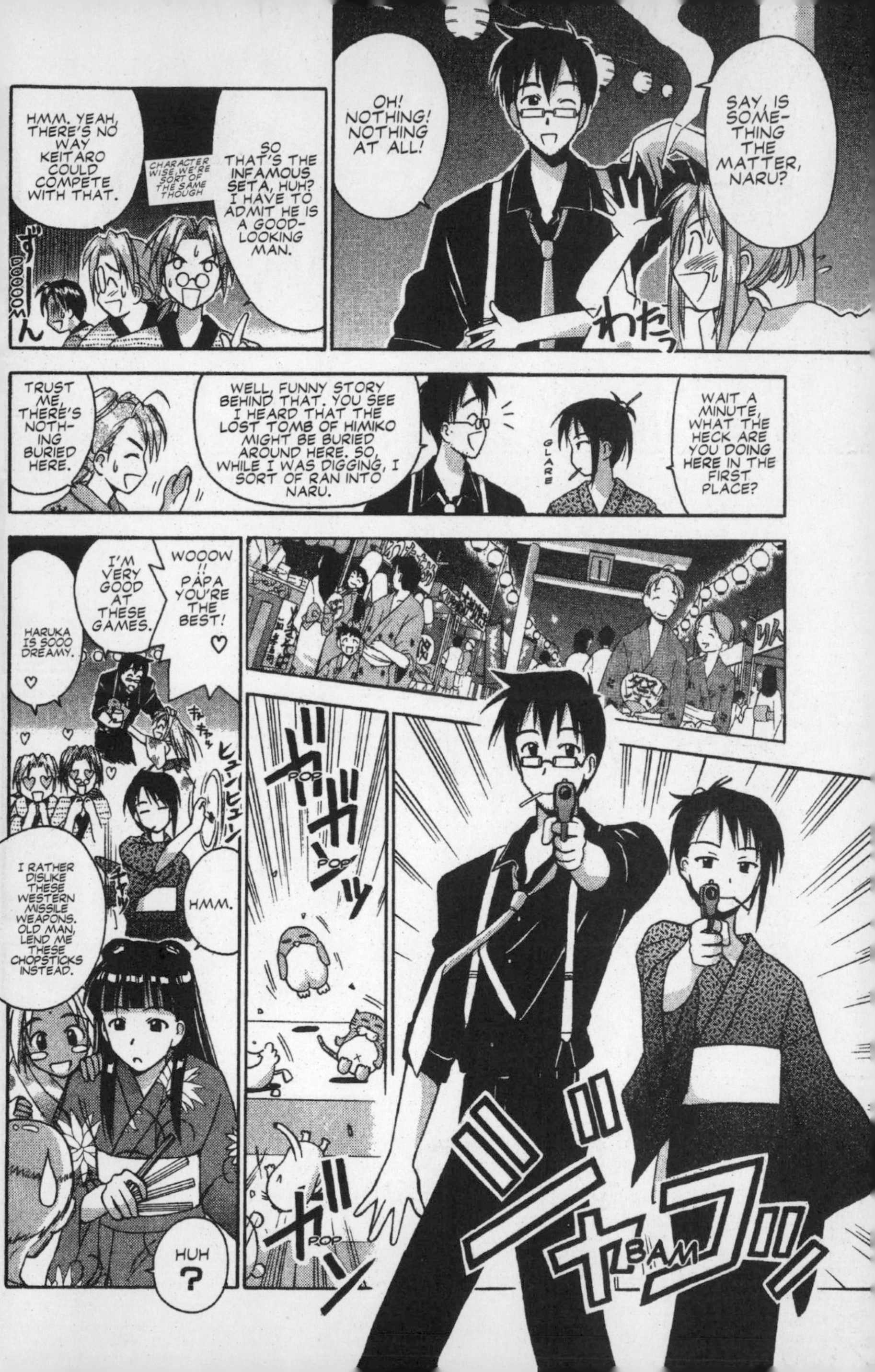
SAY, IS SOMETHING THE MATTER, NARU?
OH! NOTHING! NOTHING AT ALL!
わたっ
SO THAT'S THE INFAMOUS SETA, HUH? I HAVE TO ADMIT HE IS A GOOD-LOOKING MAN.
CHARACTER WISE WE'RE SORT OF THE SAME THOUGH
HMM. YEAH, THERE'S NO WAY KEITARO COULD COMPETE WITH THAT.
DOOOOOM
WAIT A MINUTE, WHAT THE HECK ARE YOU DOING HERE IN THE FIRST PLACE?
GLARE
WELL, FUNNY STORY BEHIND THAT. YOU SEE I HEARD THAT THE LOST TOMB OF HIMIKO MIGHT BE BURIED AROUND HERE. SO, WHILE I WAS DIGGING, I SORT OF RAN INTO NARU.
TRUST ME, THERE'S NOTHING BURIED HERE.
BAM
POP
POP
POP
WOOOW!! PAPA YOU'RE THE BEST!
I'M VERY GOOD AT THESE GAMES.
HARUKA IS SOOO DREAMY.
HMM.
I RATHER DISLIKE THESE WESTERN MISSILE WEAPONS. OLD MAN, LEND ME THESE CHOPSTICKS INSTEAD.
HUH?

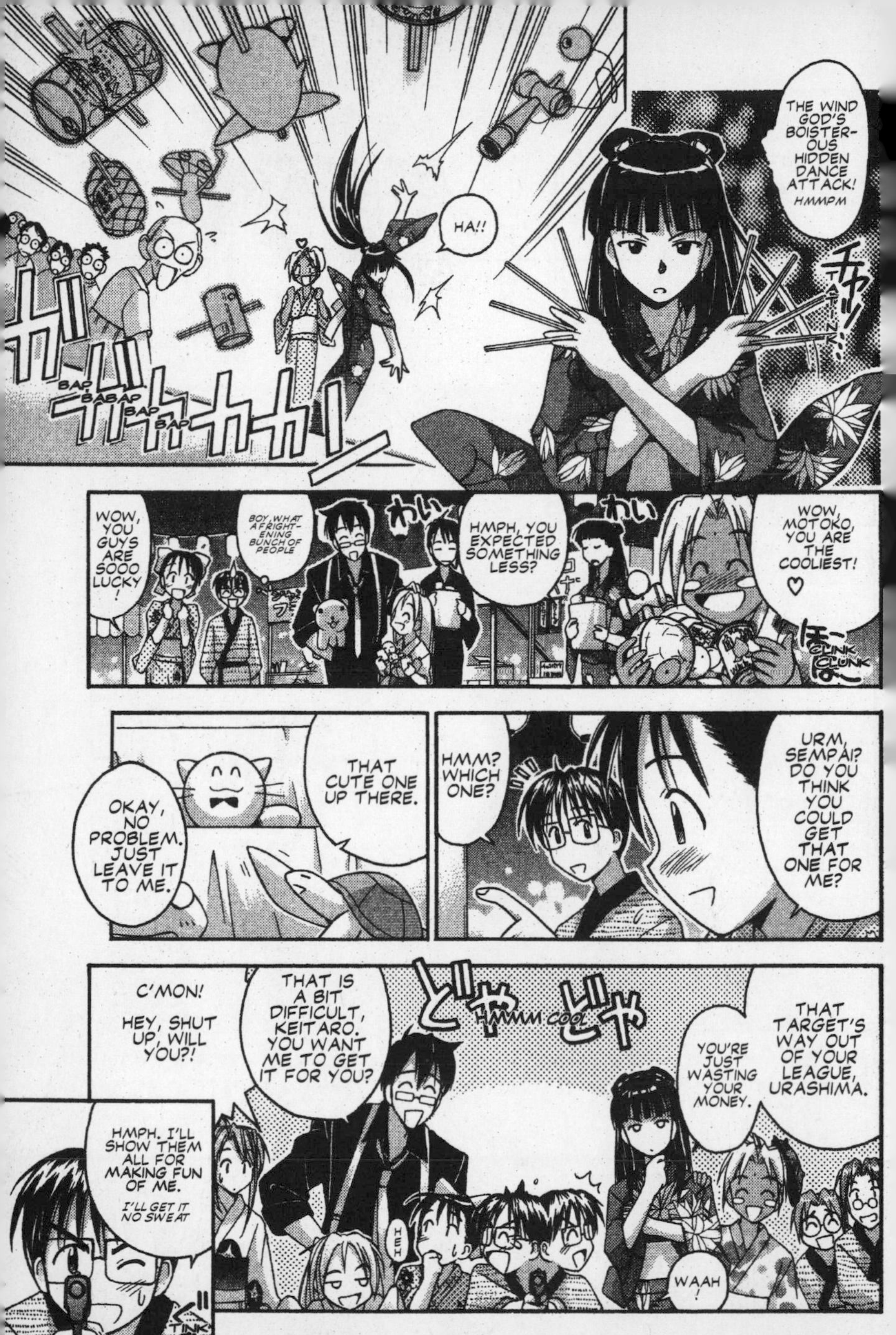
THE WIND GOD'S BOISTEROUS HIDDEN DANCE ATTACK!
HMMPM
TINK!!
HA!!
BAP BABAP BAP BAP
WOW, MOTOKO, YOU ARE THE COOLIEST! ♡
CLUNK CLUNK
わい
HMPH, YOU EXPECTED SOMETHING LESS?
わい
BOY, WHAT A FRIGHTENING BUNCH OF PEOPLE
WOW, YOU GUYS ARE SOOO LUCKY!
URM, SEMPAI? DO YOU THINK YOU COULD GET THAT ONE FOR ME?
HMM? WHICH ONE?
THAT CUTE ONE UP THERE.
OKAY, NO PROBLEM. JUST LEAVE IT TO ME.
THAT TARGET'S WAY OUT OF YOUR LEAGUE, URASHIMA.
YOU'RE JUST WASTING YOUR MONEY.
WAAH!
HMMM COOL
THAT IS A BIT DIFFICULT, KEITARO. YOU WANT ME TO GET IT FOR YOU?
HEH
C'MON!
HEY, SHUT UP, WILL YOU?!
HMPH. I'LL SHOW THEM ALL FOR MAKING FUN OF ME.
I'LL GET IT NO SWEAT
TINK

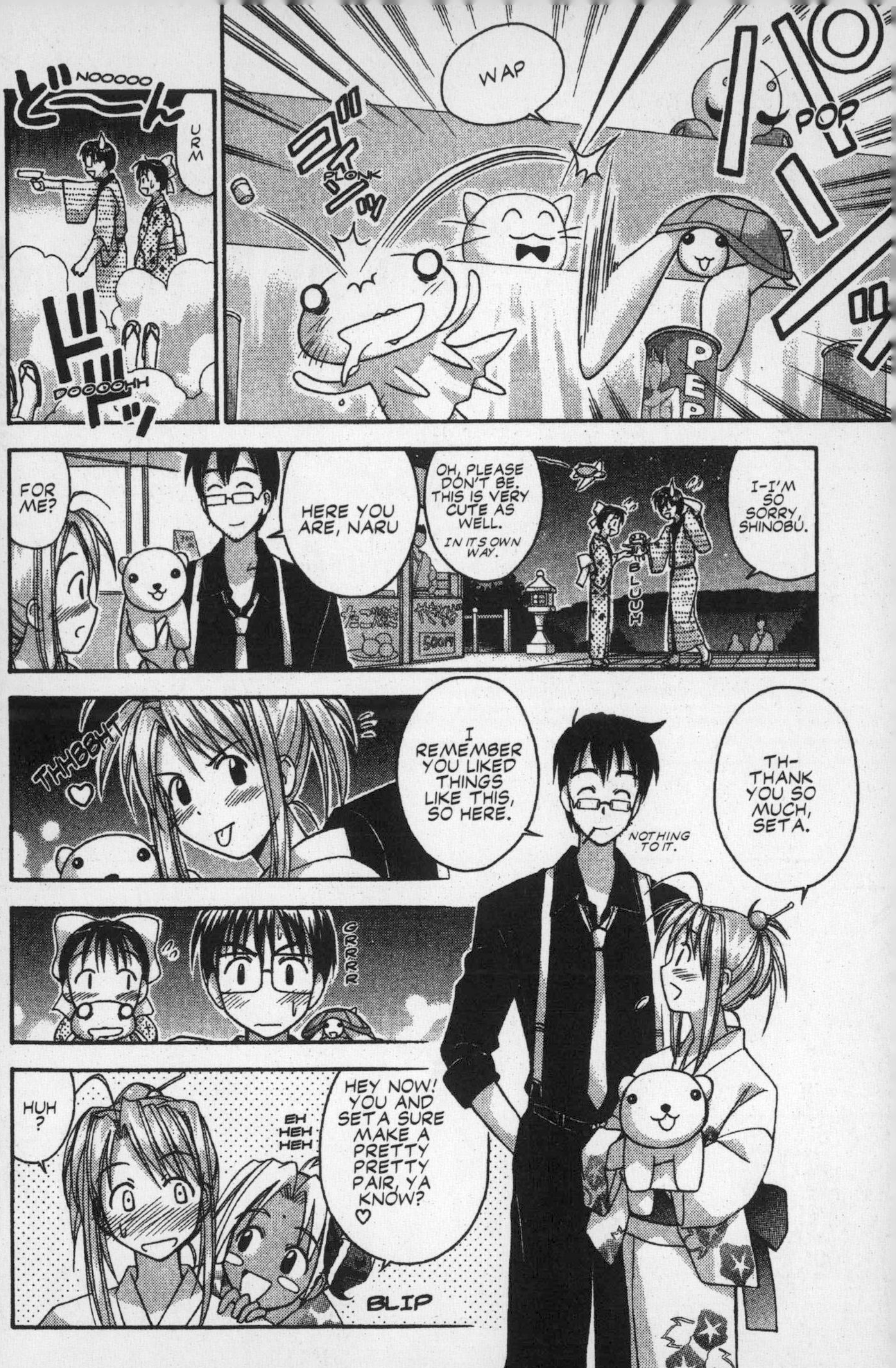
POP
WAP
PLONK
NOOOOO
URM
DOOOOHH
I-I'M SO SORRY, SHINOBU.
OH, PLEASE DON'T BE. THIS IS VERY CUTE AS WELL.
IN ITS OWN WAY.
BLUUH
HERE YOU ARE, NARU
FOR ME?
TH-THANK YOU SO MUCH, SETA.
I REMEMBER YOU LIKED THINGS LIKE THIS, SO HERE.
NOTHING TO IT.
THHBBHT
GRRRR
HEY NOW! YOU AND SETA SURE MAKE A PRETTY PRETTY PAIR, YA KNOW? ♡
EH HEH HEH
HUH?
BLIP

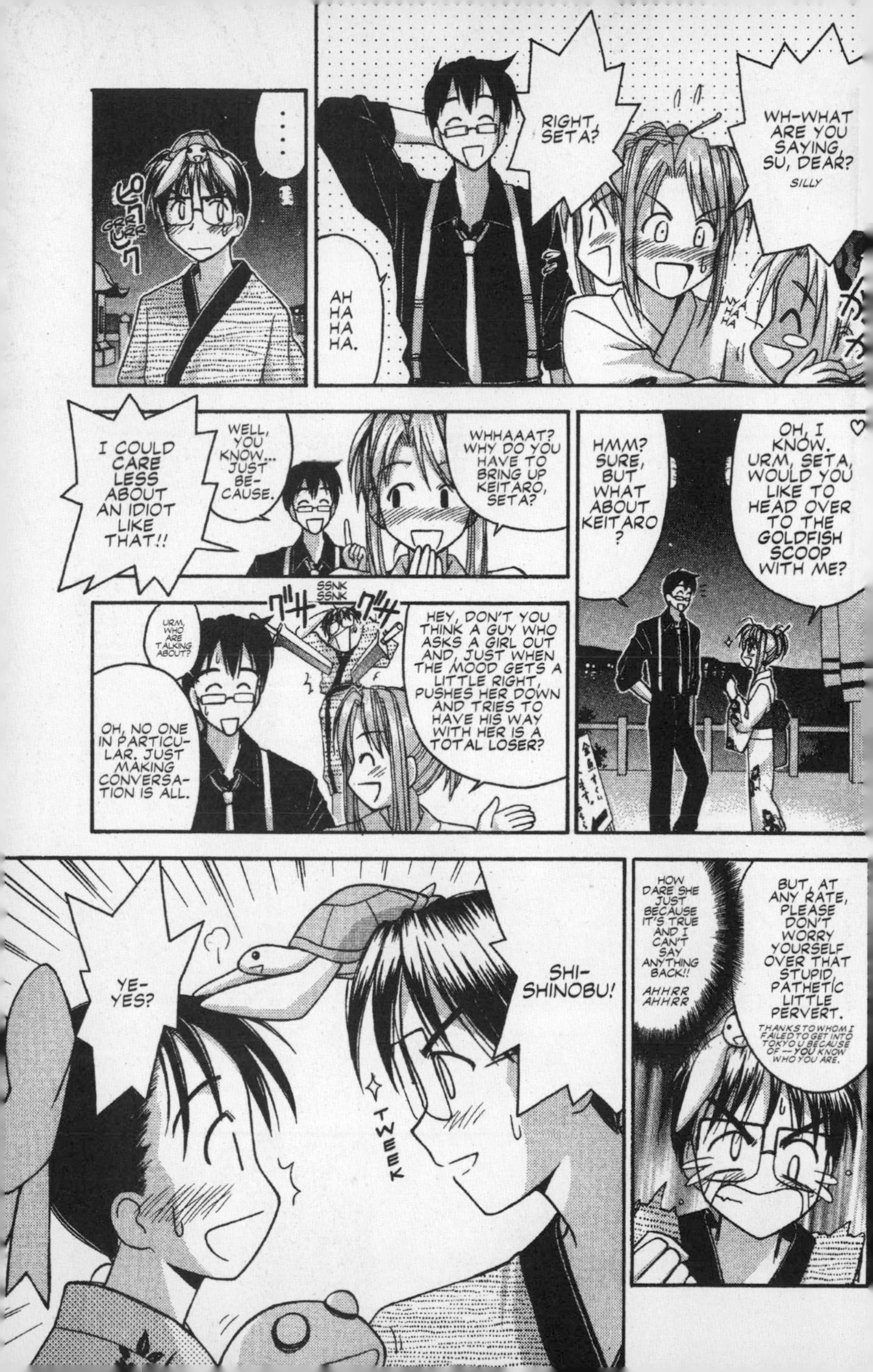
WH-WHAT ARE YOU SAYING, SU, DEAR?
SILLY
NYA HA HA HA
RIGHT, SETA?
AH HA HA HA.
. . . .
GRR URR
OH, I KNOW. URM, SETA, WOULD YOU LIKE TO HEAD OVER TO THE GOLDFISH SCOOP WITH ME?
HMM? SURE, BUT WHAT ABOUT KEITARO?
WHHAAAT? WHY DO YOU HAVE TO BRING UP KEITARO, SETA?
WELL, YOU KNOW... JUST BE-CAUSE.
I COULD CARE LESS ABOUT AN IDIOT LIKE THAT!!
HEY, DON'T YOU THINK A GUY WHO ASKS A GIRL OUT AND, JUST WHEN THE MOOD GETS A LITTLE RIGHT, PUSHES HER DOWN AND TRIES TO HAVE HIS WAY WITH HER IS A TOTAL LOSER?
SSNK SSNK
URM, WHO ARE TALKING ABOUT?
OH, NO ONE IN PARTICU-LAR. JUST MAKING CONVERSA-TION IS ALL.
BUT, AT ANY RATE, PLEASE DON'T WORRY YOURSELF OVER THAT STUPID, PATHETIC LITTLE PERVERT.
THANKS TO WHOM I FAILED TO GET INTO TOKYO U BECAUSE OF -- YOU KNOW WHO YOU ARE.
HOW DARE SHE JUST BECAUSE IT'S TRUE AND I CAN'T SAY ANYTHING BACK!!
AHHRR AHHRR
SHI-SHINOBU!
TWEEK
YE-YES?

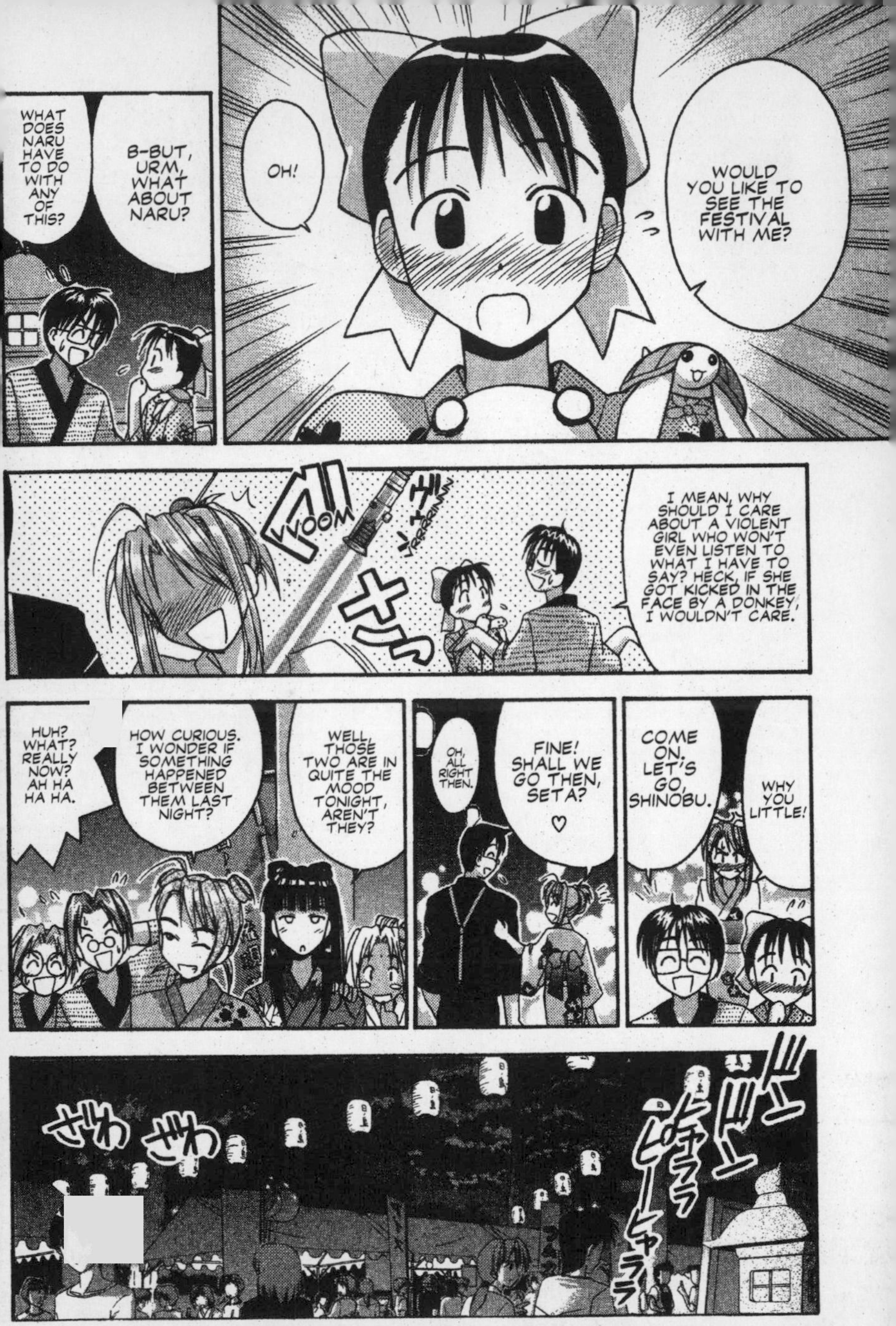
WOULD YOU LIKE TO SEE THE FESTIVAL WITH ME?
OH!
B-BUT, URM, WHAT ABOUT NARU?
WHAT DOES NARU HAVE TO DO WITH ANY OF THIS?
I MEAN, WHY SHOULD I CARE ABOUT A VIOLENT GIRL WHO WON'T EVEN LISTEN TO WHAT I HAVE TO SAY? HECK, IF SHE GOT KICKED IN THE FACE BY A DONKEY, I WOULDN'T CARE.
VRRRRINN
VOOM
WHY YOU LITTLE!
COME ON. LET'S GO, SHINOBU.
FINE! SHALL WE GO THEN, SETA? ♡
OH, ALL RIGHT THEN.
WELL, THOSE TWO ARE IN QUITE THE MOOD TONIGHT, AREN'T THEY?
HOW CURIOUS. I WONDER IF SOMETHING HAPPENED BETWEEN THEM LAST NIGHT?
HUH? WHAT? REALLY NOW? AH HA HA HA.
ざわ ざわ

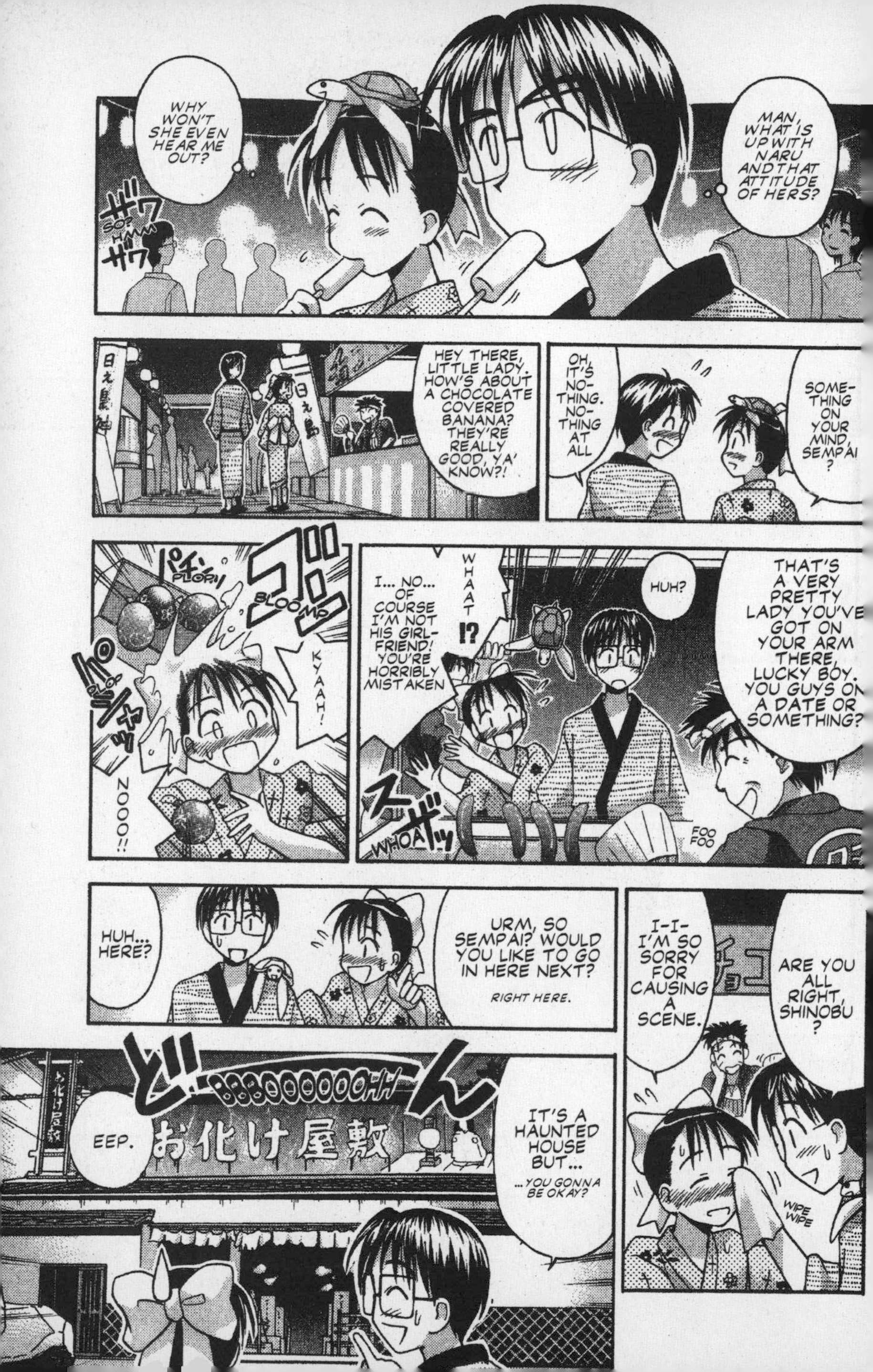
MAN, WHAT IS UP WITH NARU AND THAT ATTITUDE OF HERS?
WHY WON'T SHE EVEN HEAR ME OUT?
SOMETHING ON YOUR MIND, SEMPAI?
OH, IT'S NOTHING. NOTHING AT ALL
HEY THERE, LITTLE LADY. HOW'S ABOUT A CHOCOLATE COVERED BANANA? THEY'RE REALLY GOOD, YA' KNOW?!
THAT'S A VERY PRETTY LADY YOU'VE GOT ON YOUR ARM THERE, LUCKY BOY. YOU GUYS ON A DATE OR SOMETHING?
HUH?
FOO FOO
WHAAT!?
I... NO... OF COURSE I'M NOT HIS GIRLFRIEND! YOU'RE HORRIBLY MISTAKEN
WHOA
BLOOMP
PLOP
KYAAH!
NOOOO!!
ARE YOU ALL RIGHT, SHINOBU?
I-I-I'M SO SORRY FOR CAUSING A SCENE.
WIPE WIPE
URM, SO SEMPAI? WOULD YOU LIKE TO GO IN HERE NEXT?
RIGHT HERE.
HUH... HERE?
BBBOOOOOOOHH
お化け屋敷
IT'S A HAUNTED HOUSE BUT...
...YOU GONNA BE OKAY?
EEP.

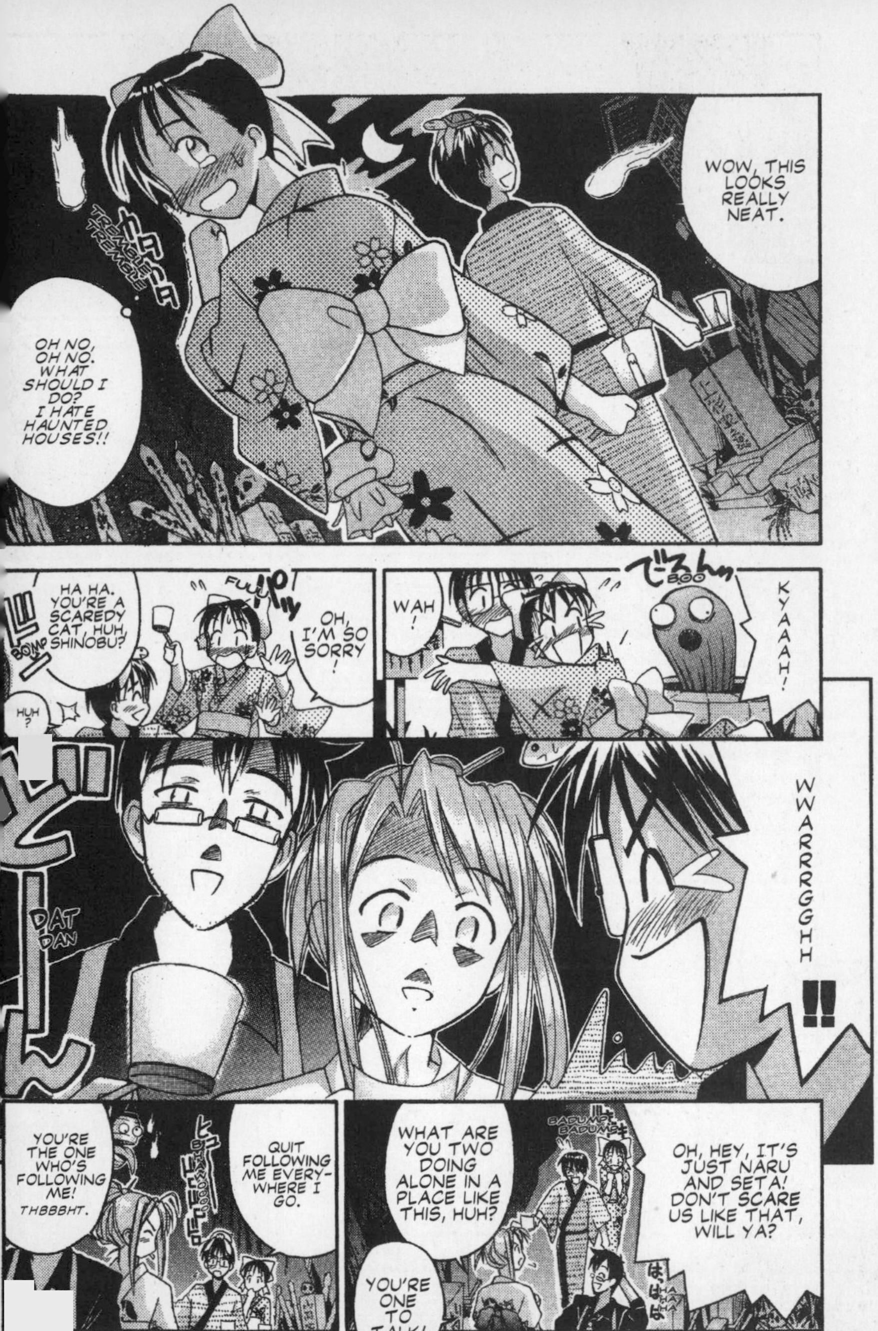
WOW, THIS LOOKS REALLY NEAT.
TREMBLE TREMBLE
OH NO, OH NO. WHAT SHOULD I DO? I HATE HAUNTED HOUSES!!
BOO
KYAAAH!
WAH!
OH, I'M SO SORRY!
HA HA. YOU'RE A SCAREDY CAT, HUH, SHINOBU?
BOMP
HUH?
WWARRRGGHH!!
DAT DAN
OH, HEY, IT'S JUST NARU AND SETA! DON'T SCARE US LIKE THAT, WILL YA?
BADUMP BADUMP
WHAT ARE YOU TWO DOING ALONE IN A PLACE LIKE THIS, HUH?
HA HA HA
YOU'RE ONE TO TALK!
QUIT FOLLOWING ME EVERY-WHERE I GO.
YOU'RE THE ONE WHO'S FOLLOWING ME!
THBBBHT.

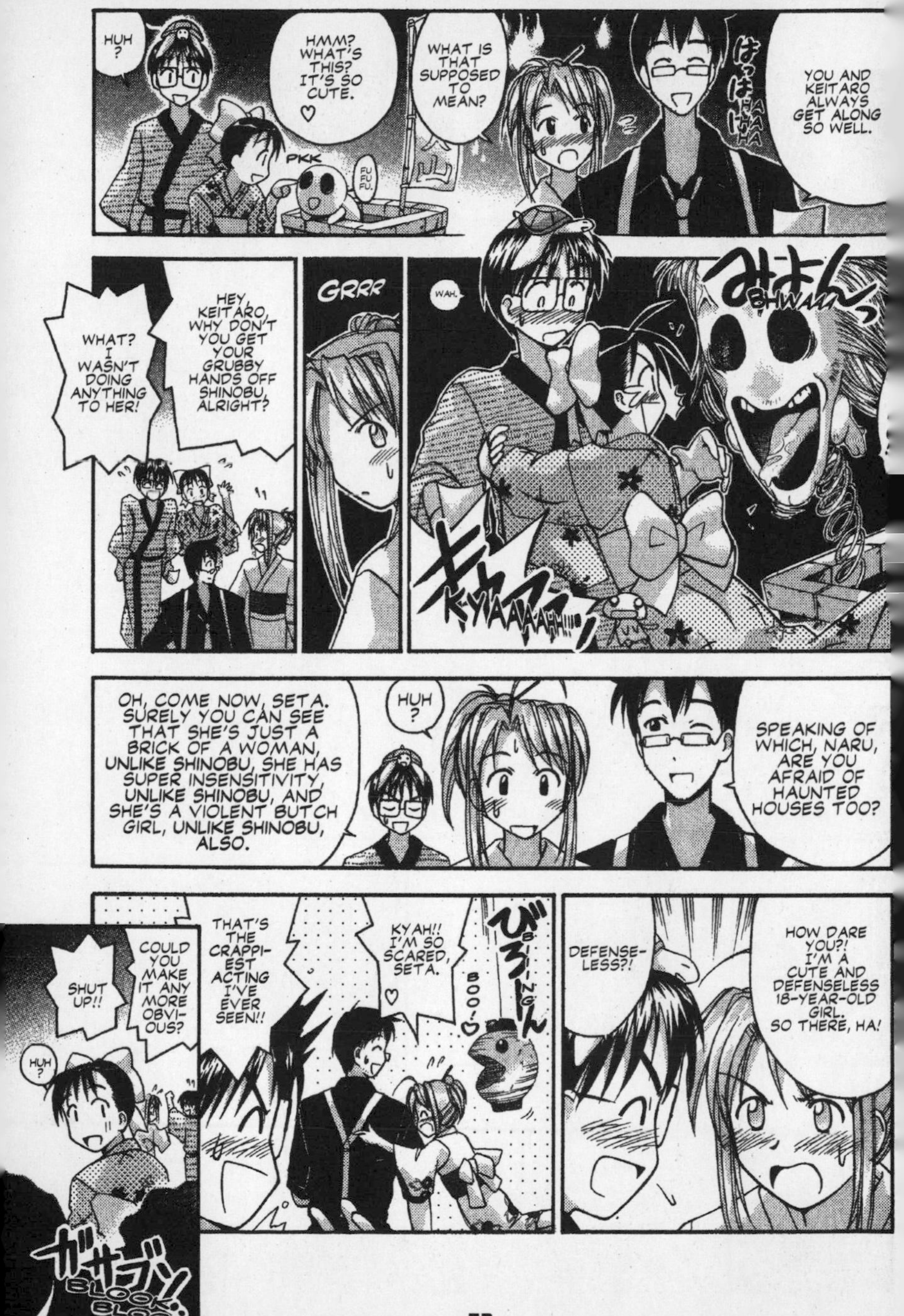
YOU AND KEITARO ALWAYS GET ALONG SO WELL.
HA HA HA
WHAT IS THAT SUPPOSED TO MEAN?
HMM? WHAT'S THIS? IT'S SO CUTE. ♡
FU FU FU.
PKK
HUH?
BHWAAAA
WAH.
KYAAAAAAHH!!!
GRRR
HEY, KEITARO, WHY DON'T YOU GET YOUR GRUBBY HANDS OFF SHINOBU, ALRIGHT?
WHAT? I WASN'T DOING ANYTHING TO HER!
SPEAKING OF WHICH, NARU, ARE YOU AFRAID OF HAUNTED HOUSES TOO?
HUH?
OH, COME NOW, SETA. SURELY YOU CAN SEE THAT SHE'S JUST A BRICK OF A WOMAN, UNLIKE SHINOBU, SHE HAS SUPER INSENSITIVITY, UNLIKE SHINOBU, AND SHE'S A VIOLENT BUTCH GIRL, UNLIKE SHINOBU, ALSO.
HOW DARE YOU?! I'M A CUTE AND DEFENSELESS 18-YEAR-OLD GIRL. SO THERE, HA!
DEFENSE-LESS?!
BIIING
BOO! ♡
KYAH!! I'M SO SCARED, SETA. ♡
THAT'S THE CRAPPIEST ACTING I'VE EVER SEEN!!
COULD YOU MAKE IT ANY MORE OBVIOUS?
SHUT UP!!
HUH?
BLOOK BLOOK

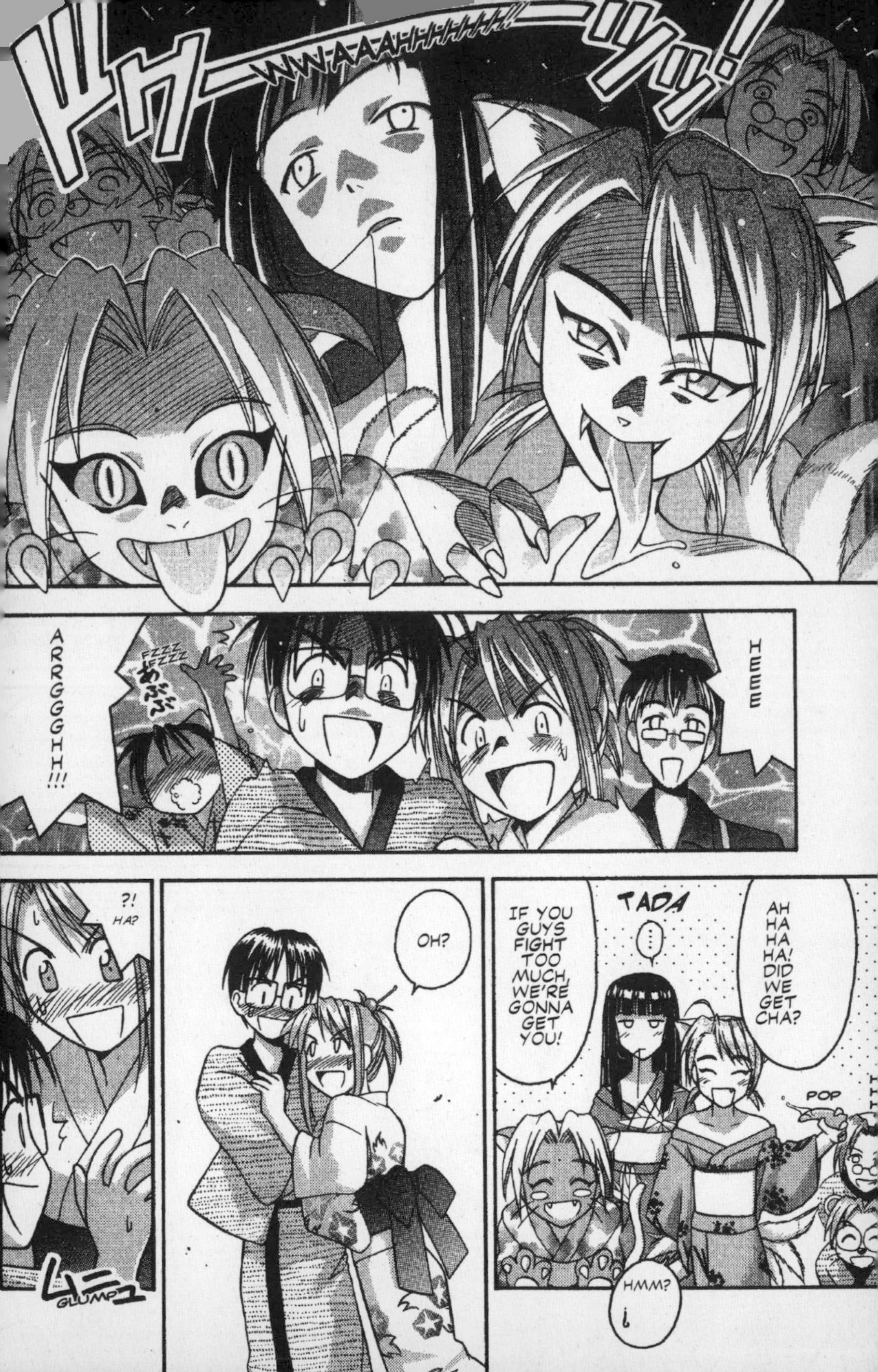

WWAAAHHHHHH!!
HEEE
ARRGGGH!!!
FZZZZ FZZZZ
あぶぶ
AH HA HA HA! DID WE GET CHA?
TADA
...
IF YOU GUYS FIGHT TOO MUCH, WE'RE GONNA GET YOU!
POP
HMM?
OH?
?!
HA?
GLUMP

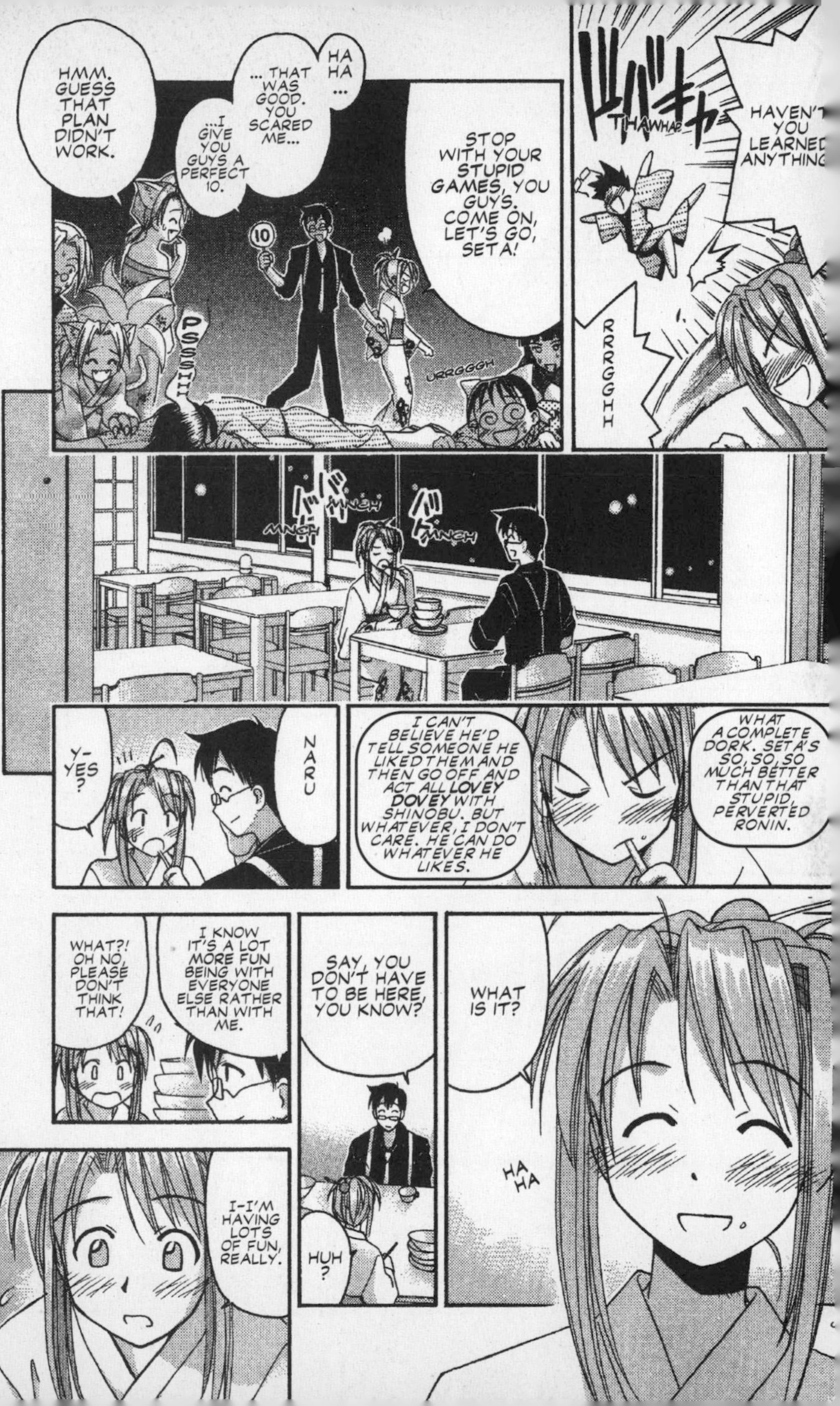
THAWHAP
HAVEN'T YOU LEARNED ANYTHING
RRRGGHH
STOP WITH YOUR STUPID GAMES, YOU GUYS. COME ON, LET'S GO, SETA!
HA HA ...
... THAT WAS GOOD. YOU SCARED ME...
...I GIVE YOU GUYS A PERFECT 10.
10
HMM. GUESS THAT PLAN DIDN'T WORK.
PSSSHH
URRGGGH
MNGH
MNGH
MNGH
WHAT A COMPLETE DORK. SETA'S SO, SO, SO MUCH BETTER THAN THAT STUPID, PERVERTED RONIN.
I CAN'T BELIEVE HE'D TELL SOMEONE HE LIKED THEM AND THEN GO OFF AND ACT ALL LOVEY DOVEY WITH SHINOBU. BUT WHATEVER, I DON'T CARE. HE CAN DO WHATEVER HE LIKES.
NARU
Y-YES?
WHAT IS IT?
HA HA
SAY, YOU DON'T HAVE TO BE HERE, YOU KNOW?
I KNOW IT'S A LOT MORE FUN BEING WITH EVERYONE ELSE RATHER THAN WITH ME.
WHAT?! OH NO, PLEASE DON'T THINK THAT!
HUH?
I-I'M HAVING LOTS OF FUN, REALLY.

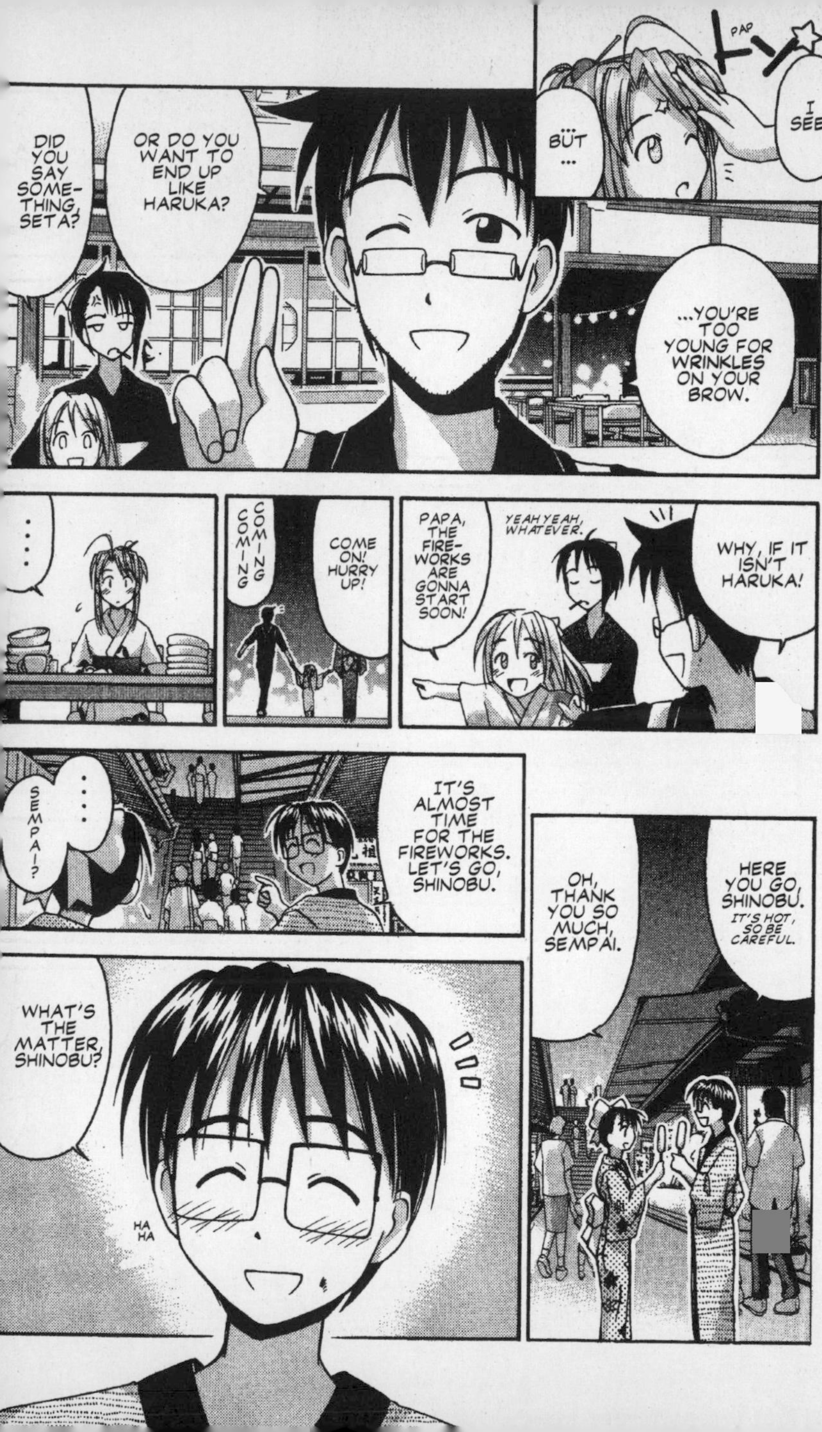
PAP
I SEE.
...BUT...
...YOU'RE TOO YOUNG FOR WRINKLES ON YOUR BROW.
OR DO YOU WANT TO END UP LIKE HARUKA?
DID YOU SAY SOMETHING, SETA?
WHY, IF IT ISN'T HARUKA!
YEAH YEAH, WHATEVER.
PAPA, THE FIRE-WORKS ARE GONNA START SOON!
COME ON! HURRY UP!
COMING COMING
....
HERE YOU GO, SHINOBU.
IT'S HOT, SO BE CAREFUL.
OH, THANK YOU SO MUCH, SEMPAI.
IT'S ALMOST TIME FOR THE FIREWORKS. LET'S GO, SHINOBU.
....SEMPAI?
WHAT'S THE MATTER, SHINOBU?
HA HA

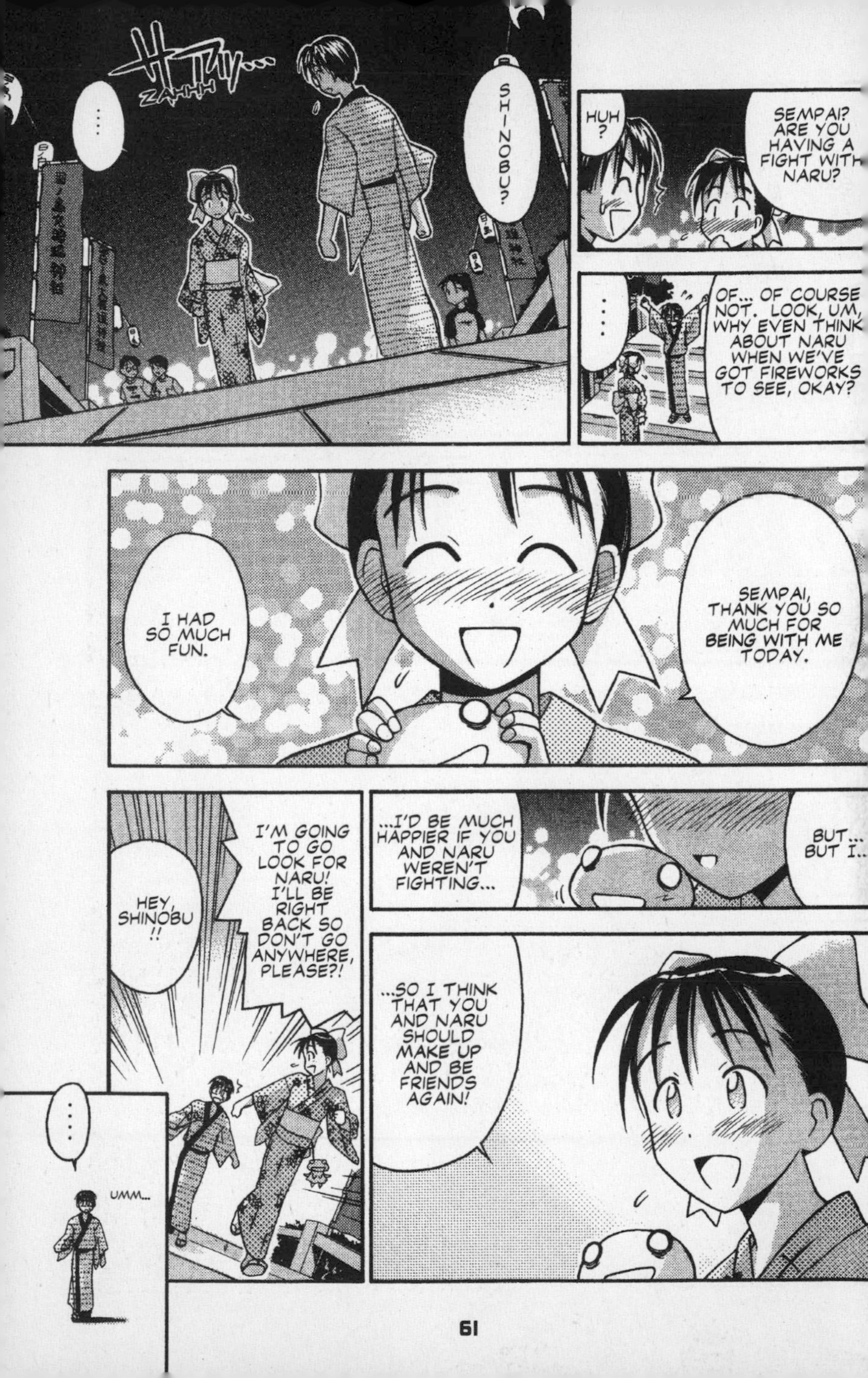
SEMPAI? ARE YOU HAVING A FIGHT WITH NARU?
HUH?
OF... OF COURSE NOT. LOOK, UM, WHY EVEN THINK ABOUT NARU WHEN WE'VE GOT FIREWORKS TO SEE, OKAY?
....
SHINOBU?
ZAHHH
....
SEMPAI, THANK YOU SO MUCH FOR BEING WITH ME TODAY.
I HAD SO MUCH FUN.
BUT... BUT I...
...I'D BE MUCH HAPPIER IF YOU AND NARU WEREN'T FIGHTING...
...SO I THINK THAT YOU AND NARU SHOULD MAKE UP AND BE FRIENDS AGAIN!
I'M GOING TO GO LOOK FOR NARU! I'LL BE RIGHT BACK SO DON'T GO ANYWHERE, PLEASE?!
HEY, SHINOBU!!
....
UMM...

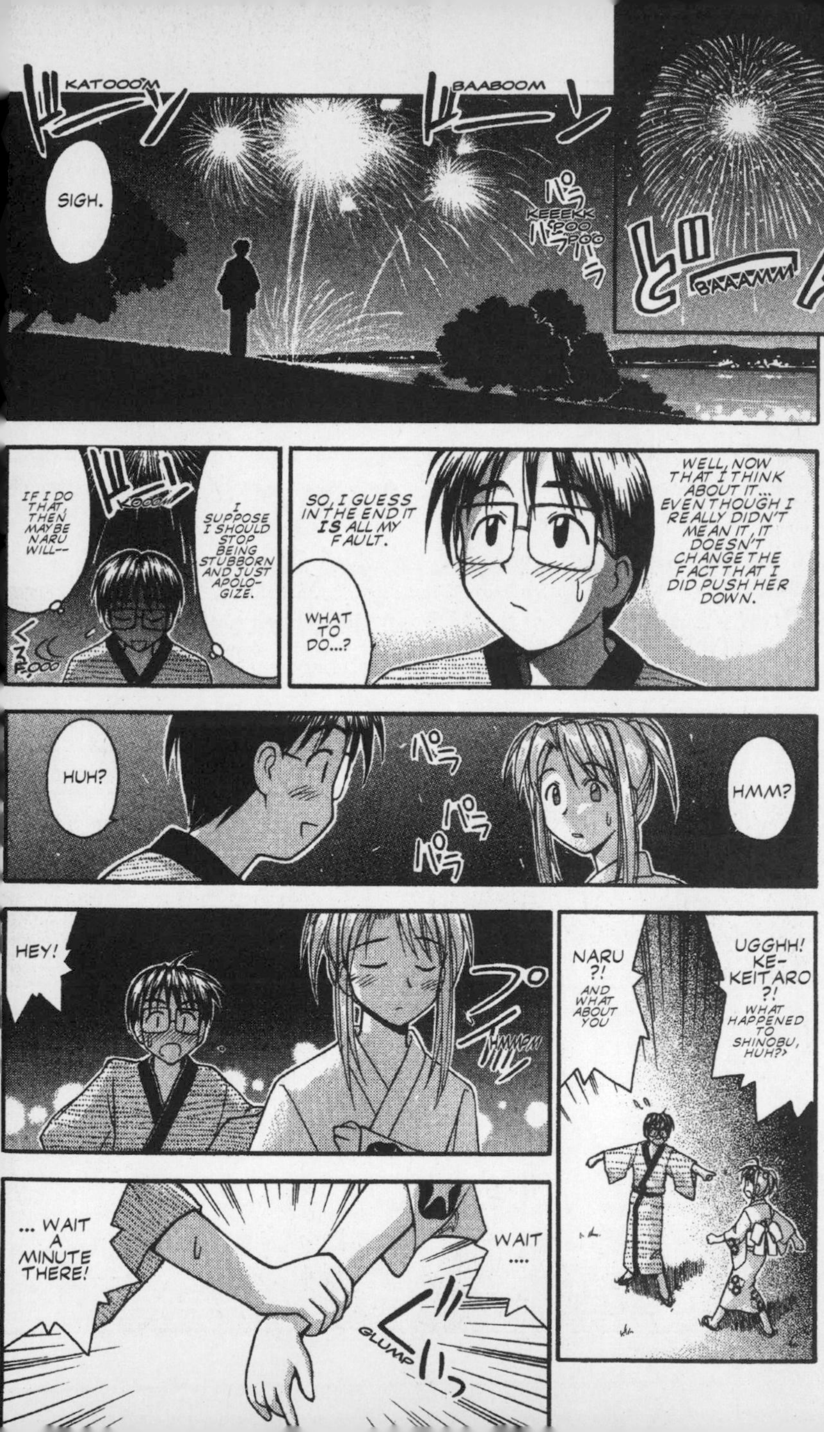
BAAAMM
BAABOOM
KEEEKK POO POO
KATOOOM
SIGH.
WELL, NOW THAT I THINK ABOUT IT... EVEN THOUGH I REALLY DIDN'T MEAN IT, IT DOESN'T CHANGE THE FACT THAT I DID PUSH HER DOWN.
SO, I GUESS IN THE END IT IS ALL MY FAULT.
WHAT TO DO...?
I SUPPOSE I SHOULD STOP BEING STUBBORN AND JUST APOLOGIZE.
IF I DO THAT, THEN MAYBE NARU WILL--
HMM?
HUH?
UGGHH! KE-KEITARO?! WHAT HAPPENED TO SHINOBU, HUH?>
NARU?! AND WHAT ABOUT YOU
HMMPH
HEY!
WAIT ....
... WAIT A MINUTE THERE!
GLUMP

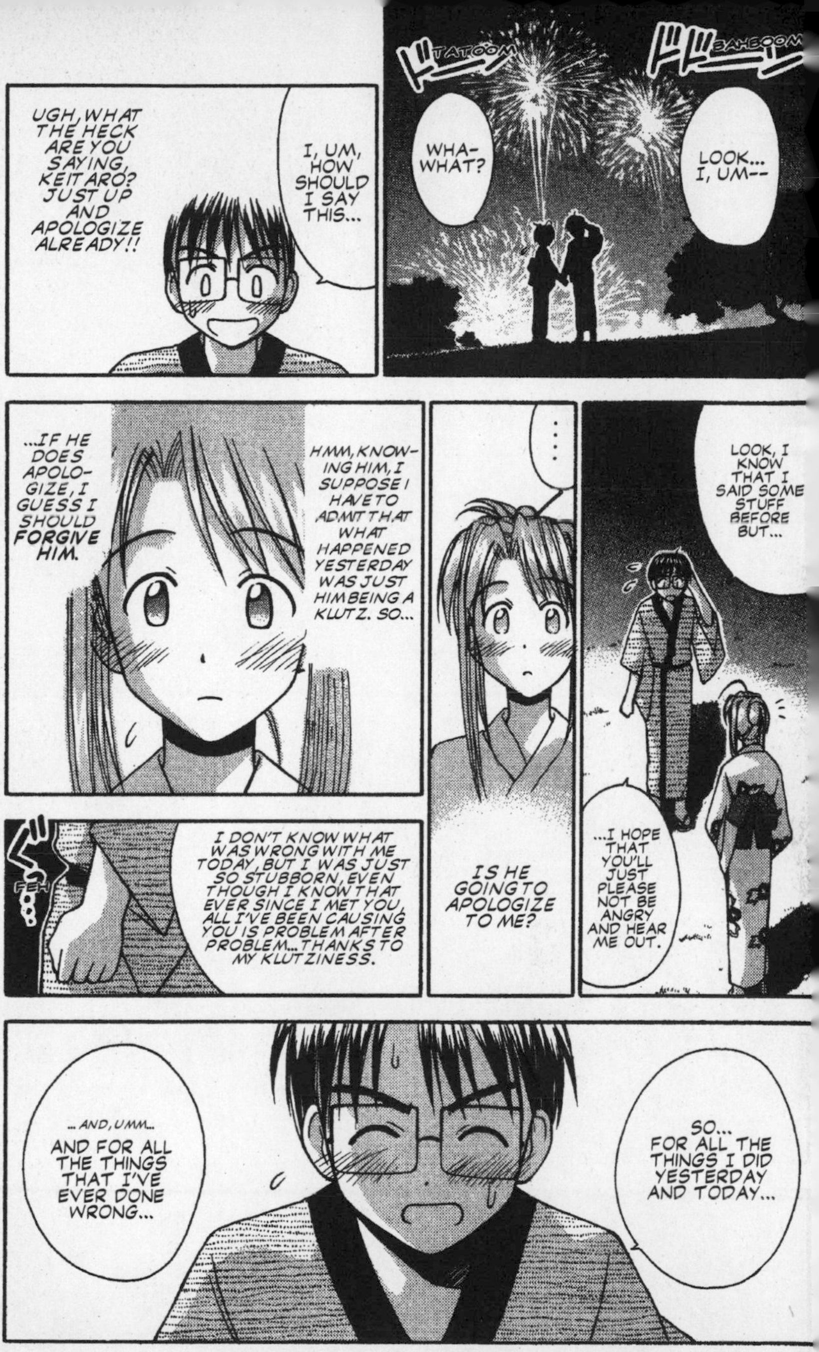
BAHOOM
TATOOM
LOOK... I, UM--
WHA-WHAT?
I, UM, HOW SHOULD I SAY THIS...
UGH, WHAT THE HECK ARE YOU SAYING, KEITARO? JUST UP AND APOLOGIZE ALREADY!!
LOOK, I KNOW THAT I SAID SOME STUFF BEFORE BUT...
...I HOPE THAT YOU'LL JUST PLEASE NOT BE ANGRY AND HEAR ME OUT.
....
IS HE GOING TO APOLOGIZE TO ME?
HMM, KNOWING HIM, I SUPPOSE I HAVE TO ADMIT THAT WHAT HAPPENED YESTERDAY WAS JUST HIM BEING A KLUTZ. SO...
...IF HE DOES APOLOGIZE, I GUESS I SHOULD FORGIVE HIM.
I DON'T KNOW WHAT WAS WRONG WITH ME TODAY, BUT I WAS JUST SO STUBBORN, EVEN THOUGH I KNOW THAT EVER SINCE I MET YOU, ALL I'VE BEEN CAUSING YOU IS PROBLEM AFTER PROBLEM...THANKS TO MY KLUTZINESS.
FEH
SO... FOR ALL THE THINGS I DID YESTERDAY AND TODAY...
...AND, UMM... AND FOR ALL THE THINGS THAT I'VE EVER DONE WRONG...

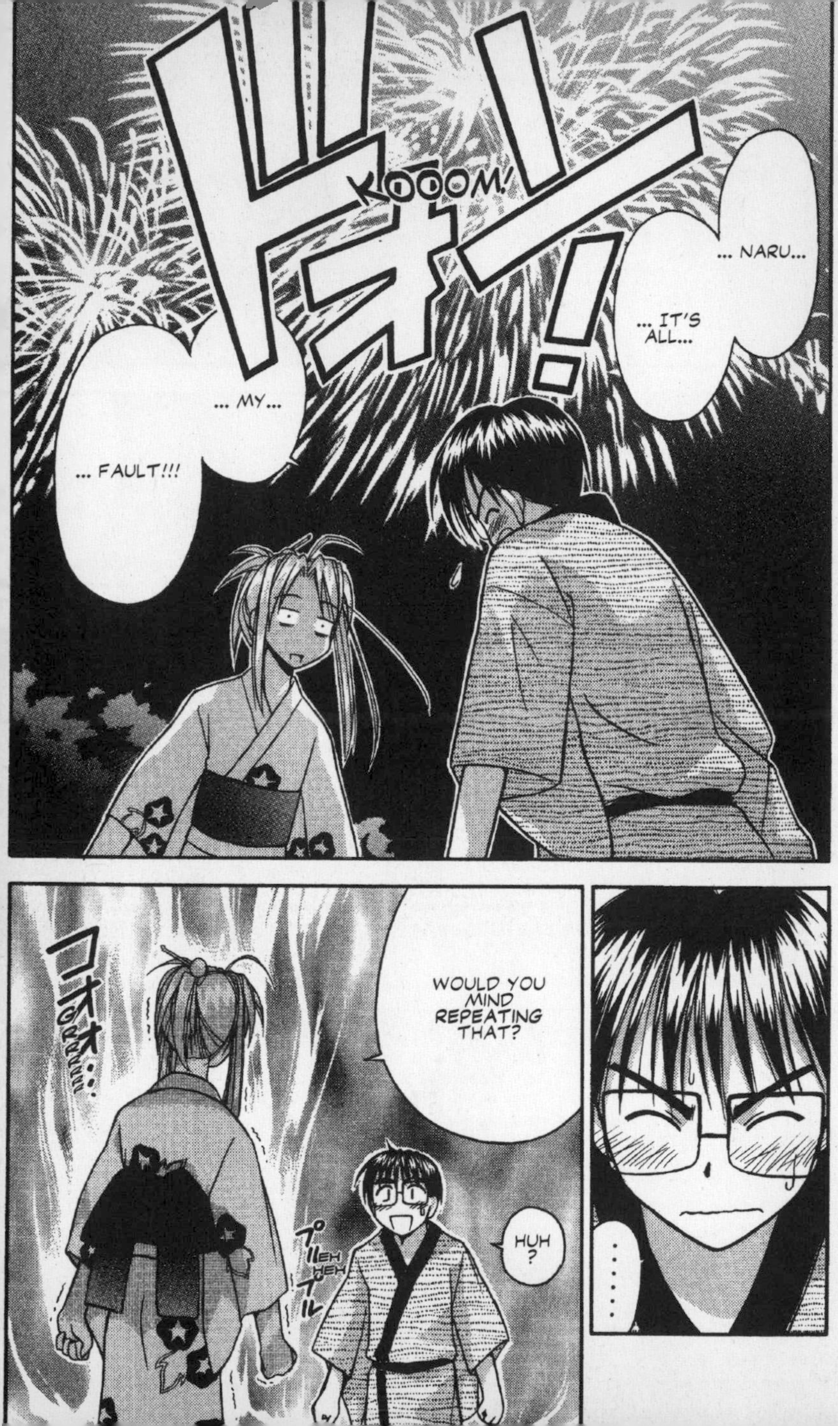
ドォン!
KOOOM!
... NARU...
... IT'S ALL...
... MY...
... FAULT!!!
......
WOULD YOU MIND REPEATING THAT?
HUH?
プルプル
EH HEH
コオオ...
GRRRRRRR...

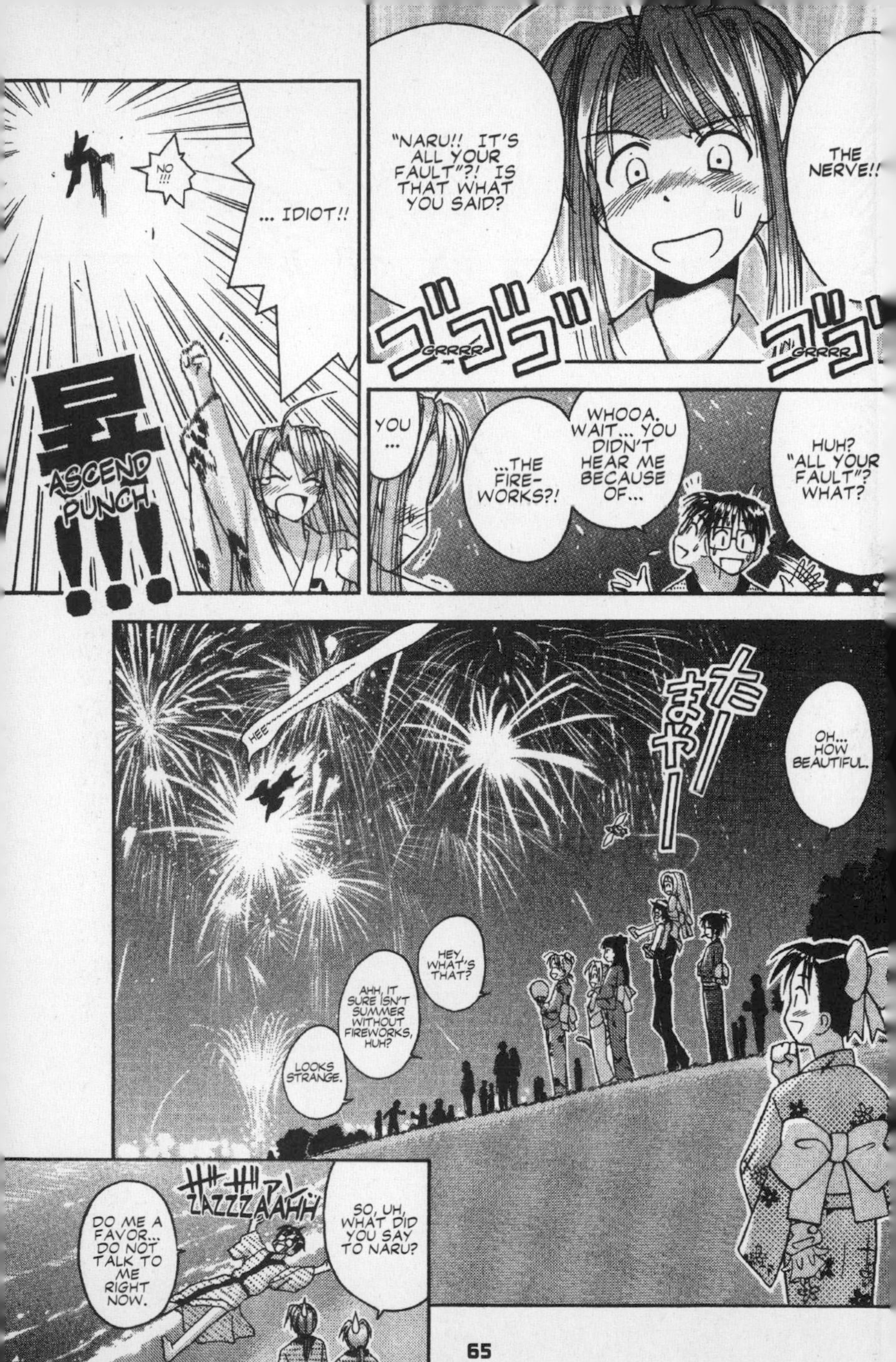
THE NERVE!!
"NARU!! IT'S ALL YOUR FAULT"?! IS THAT WHAT YOU SAID?
GRRRR
GRRRR
HUH? "ALL YOUR FAULT"? WHAT?
WHOOA. WAIT... YOU DIDN'T HEAR ME BECAUSE OF...
...THE FIRE-WORKS?!
YOU ...
... IDIOT!!
NO !!!
ASCEND PUNCH !!!
OH... HOW BEAUTIFUL.
HEE~
HEY, WHAT'S THAT?
AHH, IT SURE ISN'T SUMMER WITHOUT FIREWORKS, HUH?
LOOKS STRANGE.
SO, UH, WHAT DID YOU SAY TO NARU?
ZAZZZZAAHH
DO ME A FAVOR... DO NOT TALK TO ME RIGHT NOW.

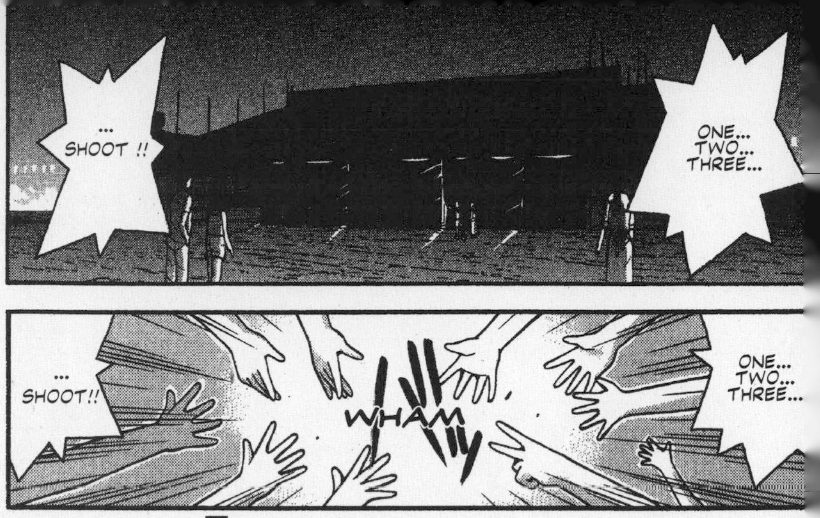
ONE... TWO... THREE...
... SHOOT !!
ONE... TWO... THREE...
... SHOOT!!
WHAM

Love Hina

HINATA.37 Lovely Goku and Her Funtastic Friends. ♡

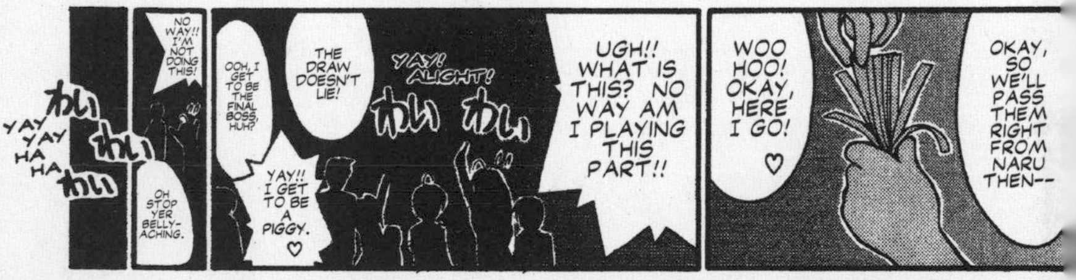
OKAY, SO WE'LL PASS THEM RIGHT FROM NARU THEN--
WOO HOO! OKAY, HERE I GO! ♡
UGH!! WHAT IS THIS? NO WAY AM I PLAYING THIS PART!!
YAY! ALIGHT!
わい わい
THE DRAW DOESN'T LIE!
YAY!! I GET TO BE A PIGGY. ♡
OOH, I GET TO BE THE FINAL BOSS, HUH?
NO WAY!! I'M NOT DOING THIS!
OH STOP YER BELLY-ACHING.
わい わい わい
YAY YAY HA HA

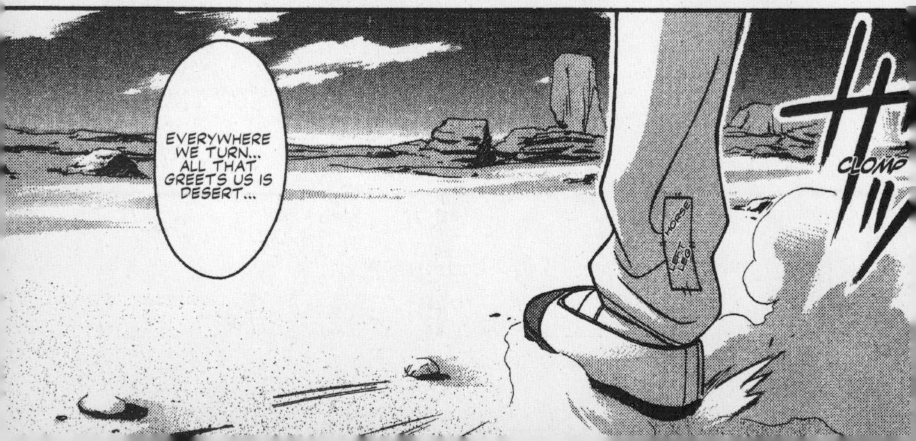
CLOMP
EVERYWHERE WE TURN... ALL THAT GREETS US IS DESERT...

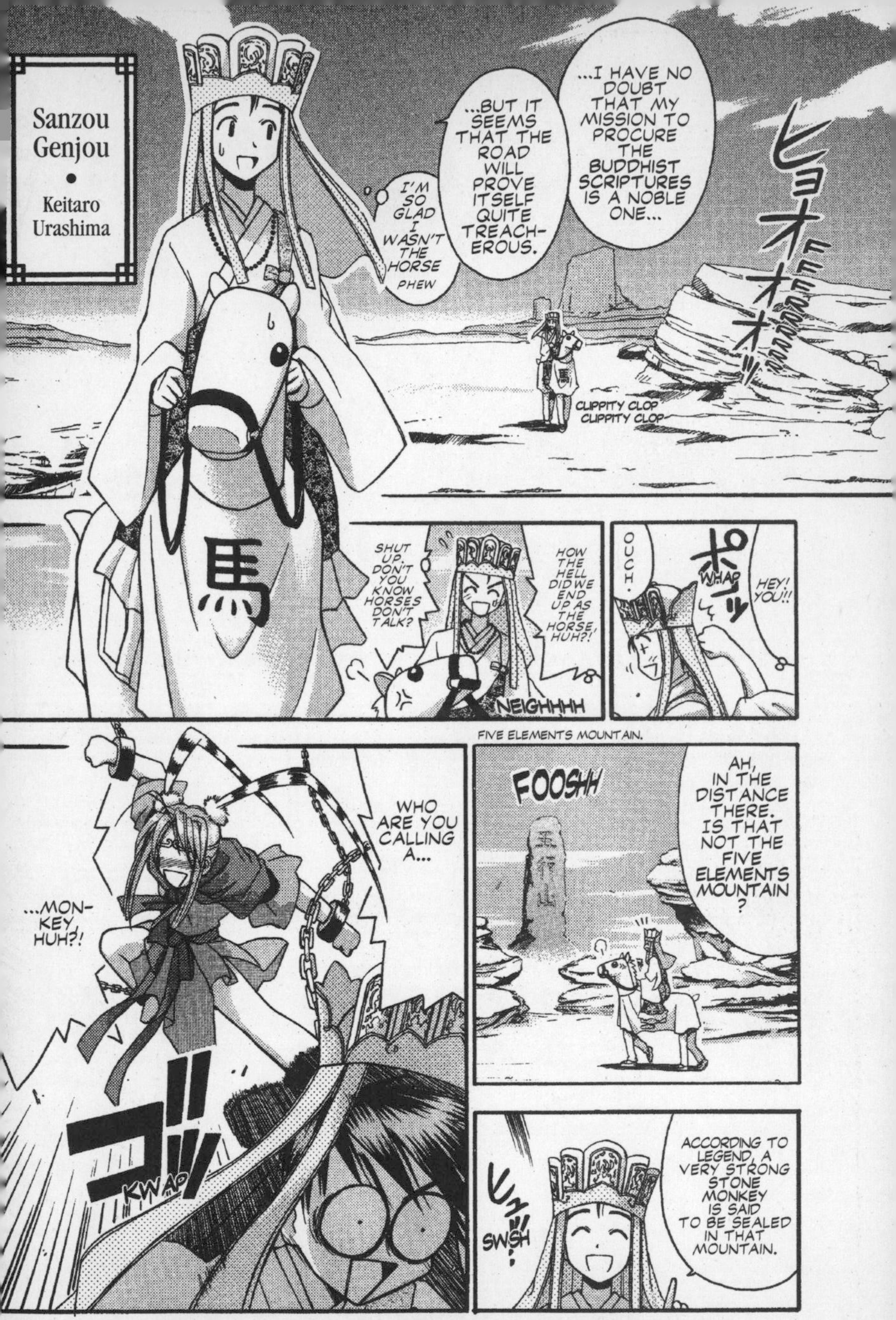
...I HAVE NO DOUBT THAT MY MISSION TO PROCURE THE BUDDHIST SCRIPTURES IS A NOBLE ONE...
...BUT IT SEEMS THAT THE ROAD WILL PROVE ITSELF QUITE TREACH-EROUS.
I'M SO GLAD I WASN'T THE HORSE
PHEW
Sanzou Genjou • Keitaro Urashima
CLIPPITY CLOP CLIPPITY CLOP
HEY! YOU!!
WHAP
OUCH.
HOW THE HELL DID WE END UP AS THE HORSE, HUH?!
SHUT UP. DON'T YOU KNOW HORSES DON'T TALK?
NEIGHHHH
FIVE ELEMENTS MOUNTAIN.
AH, IN THE DISTANCE THERE. IS THAT NOT THE FIVE ELEMENTS MOUNTAIN?
FOOSHH
ACCORDING TO LEGEND, A VERY STRONG STONE MONKEY IS SAID TO BE SEALED IN THAT MOUNTAIN.
SWSH
WHO ARE YOU CALLING A...
...MON-KEY, HUH?!
KWAP

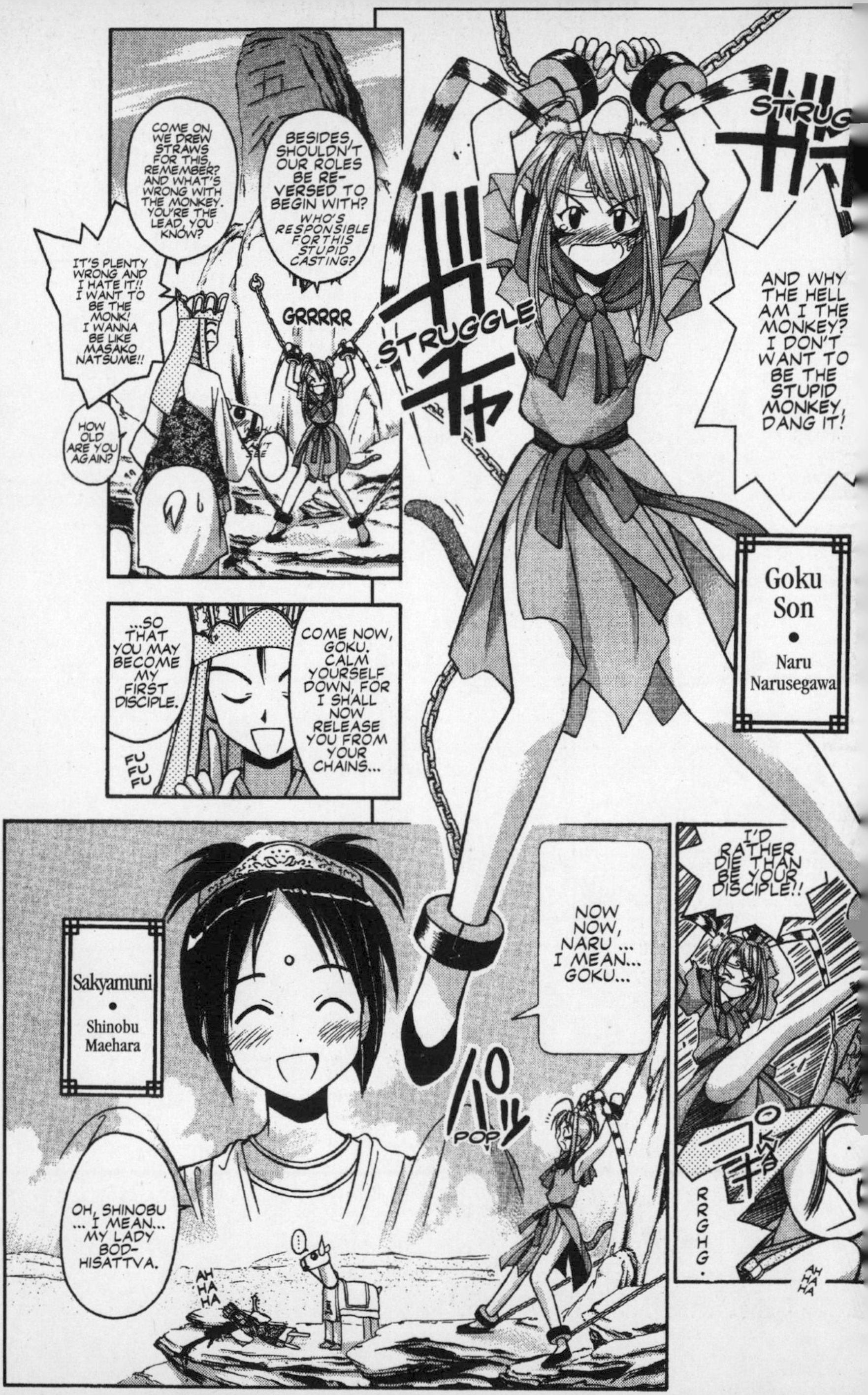
STRUG
AND WHY THE HELL AM I THE MONKEY? I DON'T WANT TO BE THE STUPID MONKEY, DANG IT!
STRUGGLE
Goku Son • Naru Narusegawa
BESIDES, SHOULDN'T OUR ROLES BE RE-VERSED TO BEGIN WITH? WHO'S RESPONSIBLE FOR THIS STUPID CASTING?
COME ON, WE DREW STRAWS FOR THIS, REMEMBER? AND WHAT'S WRONG WITH THE MONKEY. YOU'RE THE LEAD, YOU KNOW?
IT'S PLENTY WRONG AND I HATE IT!! I WANT TO BE THE MONK! I WANNA BE LIKE MASAKO NATSUME!!
GRRRRR
HOW OLD ARE YOU AGAIN?
COME NOW, GOKU. CALM YOURSELF DOWN, FOR I SHALL NOW RELEASE YOU FROM YOUR CHAINS...
...SO THAT YOU MAY BECOME MY FIRST DISCIPLE.
FU FU FU
I'D RATHER DIE THAN BE YOUR DISCIPLE!!
RRGHG.
AH HA HA HA
NOW NOW, NARU ... I MEAN... GOKU...
POP
Sakyamuni • Shinobu Maehara
OH, SHINOBU ... I MEAN... MY LADY BOD-HISATTVA.
...
AH HA HA

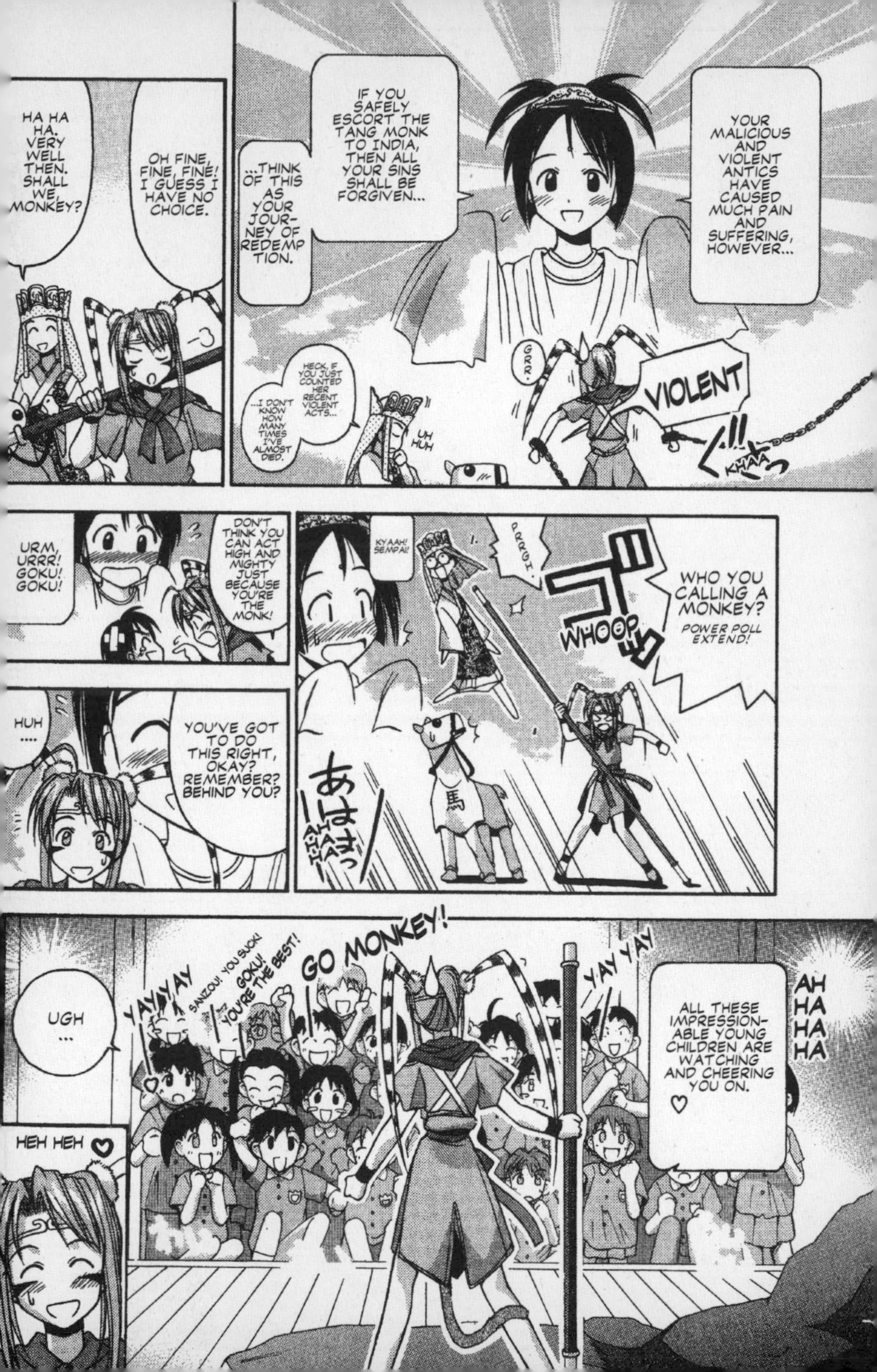
YOUR MALICIOUS AND VIOLENT ANTICS HAVE CAUSED MUCH PAIN AND SUFFERING, HOWEVER...
IF YOU SAFELY ESCORT THE TANG MONK TO INDIA, THEN ALL YOUR SINS SHALL BE FORGIVEN...
...THINK OF THIS AS YOUR JOURNEY OF REDEMPTION.
GRR.
VIOLENT
KHAA
HECK, IF YOU JUST COUNTED HER RECENT VIOLENT ACTS...
...I DON'T KNOW HOW MANY TIMES I'VE ALMOST DIED.
UH HUH
OH FINE, FINE, FINE! I GUESS I HAVE NO CHOICE.
HA HA HA. VERY WELL THEN. SHALL WE, MONKEY?
WHO YOU CALLING A MONKEY?
POWER POLL EXTEND!
PRRGH!
WHOOP
KYAAH! SEMPAI!
あはは
AH HA HA
DON'T THINK YOU CAN ACT HIGH AND MIGHTY JUST BECAUSE YOU'RE THE MONK!
URM, URRR! GOKU! GOKU!
YOU'VE GOT TO DO THIS RIGHT, OKAY? REMEMBER? BEHIND YOU?
HUH ....
AH HA HA HA
ALL THESE IMPRESSIONABLE YOUNG CHILDREN ARE WATCHING AND CHEERING YOU ON.
YAY YAY
GO MONKEY!
GOKU! YOU'RE THE BEST!
SANZOU! YOU SUCK!
YAY YAY
UGH ...
HEH HEH

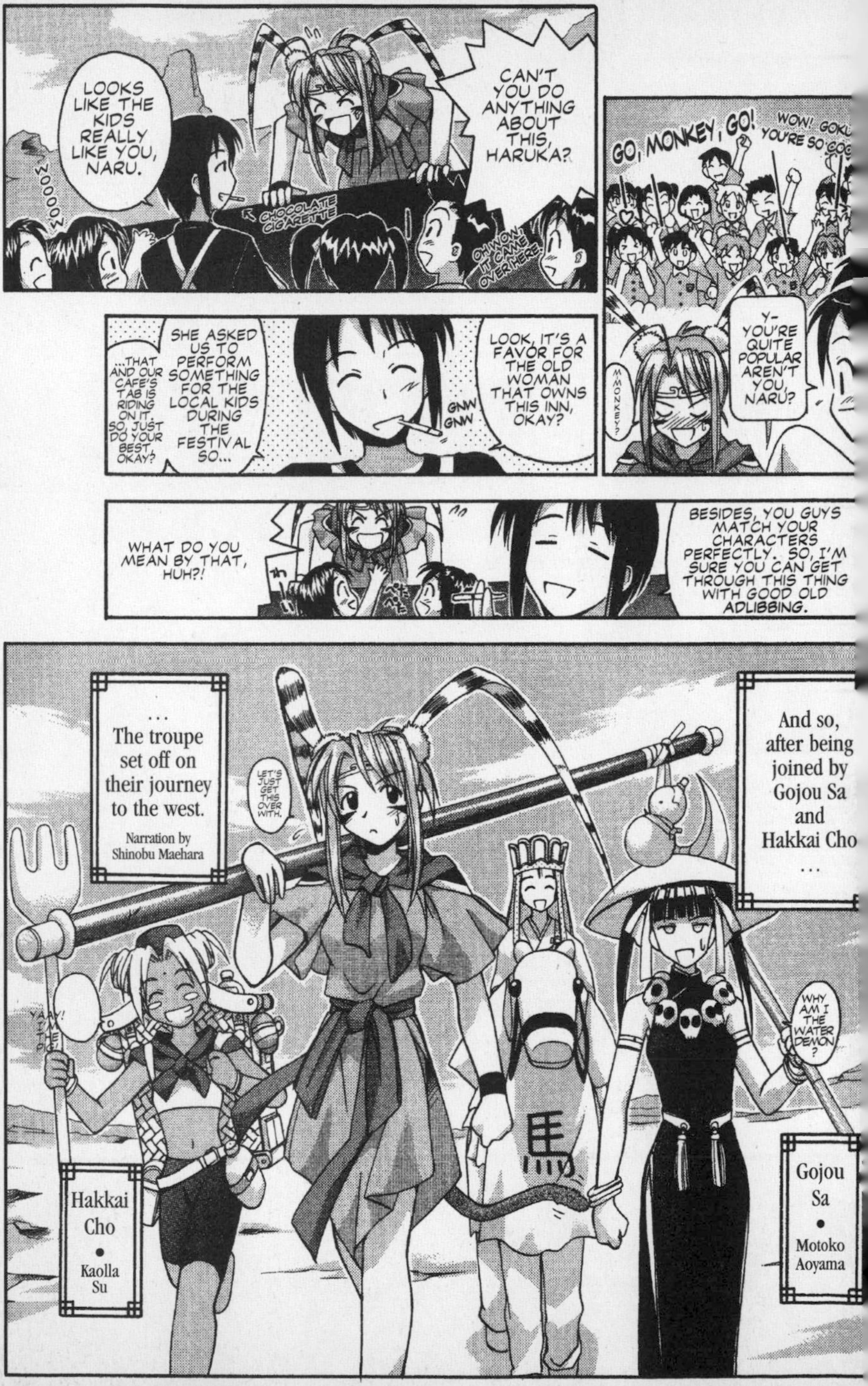

CAN'T YOU DO ANYTHING ABOUT THIS, HARUKA?
OH WOW! IT CAME OVER HERE.
LOOKS LIKE THE KIDS REALLY LIKE YOU, NARU.
CHOCOLATE CIGARETTE
WOOOOW
WOW! GOKU YOU'RE SO COO
GO, MONKEY, GO!
Y-YOU'RE QUITE POPULAR AREN'T YOU, NARU?
M-MONKEY?
LOOK, IT'S A FAVOR FOR THE OLD WOMAN THAT OWNS THIS INN, OKAY?
GNW GNW
SHE ASKED US TO PERFORM SOMETHING FOR THE LOCAL KIDS DURING THE FESTIVAL SO...
...THAT AND OUR CAFE'S TAB IS RIDING ON IT. SO, JUST DO YOUR BEST, OKAY?
BESIDES, YOU GUYS MATCH YOUR CHARACTERS PERFECTLY. SO, I'M SURE YOU CAN GET THROUGH THIS THING WITH GOOD OLD ADLIBBING.
WHAT DO YOU MEAN BY THAT, HUH?!
And so, after being joined by Gojou Sa and Hakkai Cho ...
WHY AM I THE WATER DEMON?
LET'S JUST GET THIS OVER WITH.
... The troupe set off on their journey to the west.
Narration by Shinobu Maehara
YAAY! I'M THE PIG!
Gojou Sa • Motoko Aoyama
Hakkai Cho • Kaolla Su

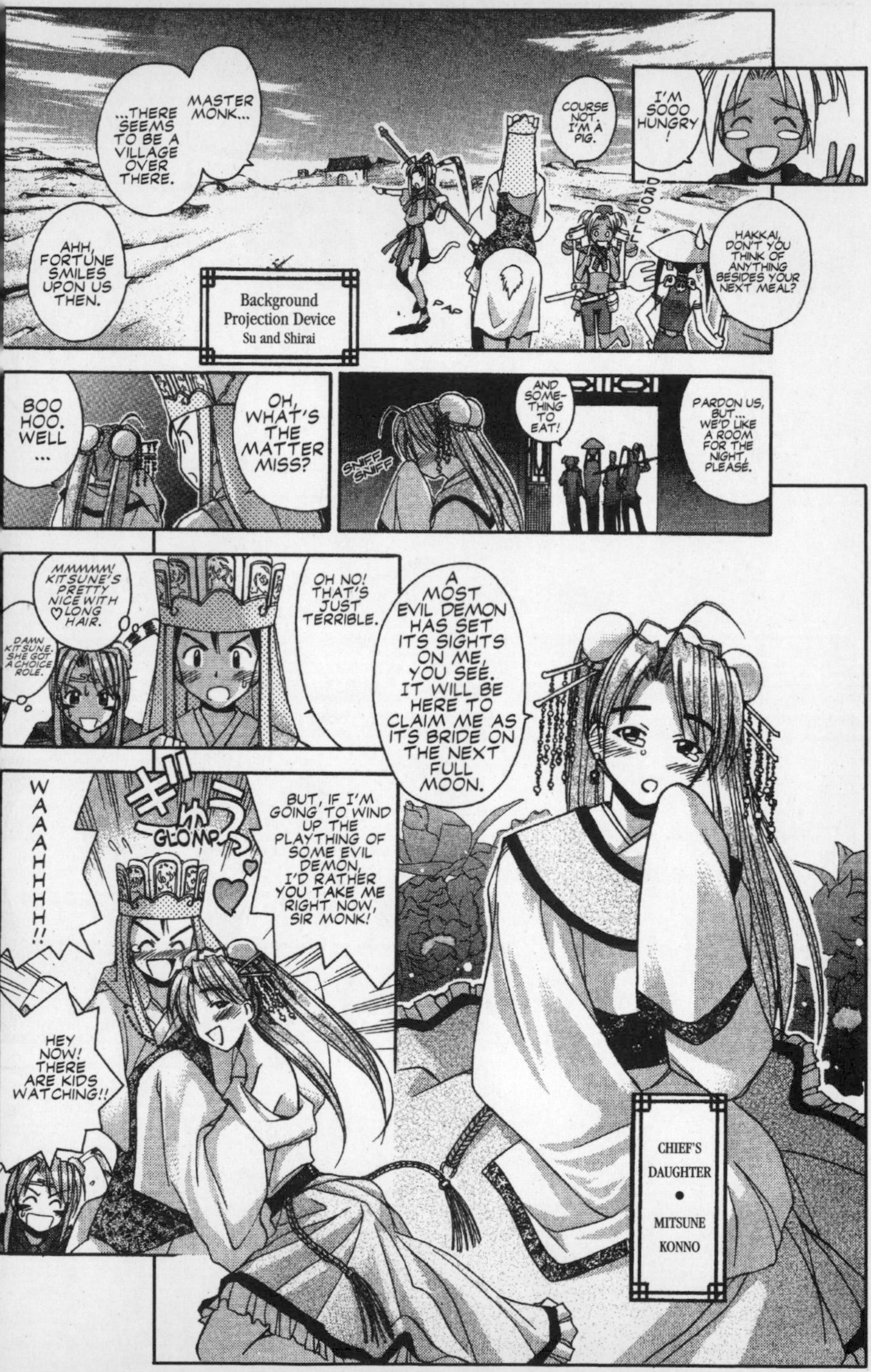
I'M SOOO HUNGRY!
HAKKAI, DON'T YOU THINK OF ANYTHING BESIDES YOUR NEXT MEAL?
DROOLL
COURSE NOT. I'M A PIG.
MASTER MONK...
...THERE SEEMS TO BE A VILLAGE OVER THERE.
AHH, FORTUNE SMILES UPON US THEN.
PAD
Background Projection Device Su and Shirai
PARDON US, BUT... WE'D LIKE A ROOM FOR THE NIGHT, PLEASE.
AND SOMETHING TO EAT!
SNIFF SNIFF
OH, WHAT'S THE MATTER MISS?
BOO HOO. WELL ...
A MOST EVIL DEMON HAS SET ITS SIGHTS ON ME, YOU SEE. IT WILL BE HERE TO CLAIM ME AS ITS BRIDE ON THE NEXT FULL MOON.
CHIEF'S DAUGHTER • MITSUNE KONNO
OH NO! THAT'S JUST TERRIBLE.
MMMMM! KITSUNE'S PRETTY NICE WITH ♡ LONG HAIR.
DAMN KITSUNE. SHE GOT A CHOICE ROLE.
BUT, IF I'M GOING TO WIND UP THE PLAYTHING OF SOME EVIL DEMON, I'D RATHER YOU TAKE ME RIGHT NOW, SIR MONK!
GLOMP
WAAAAHHHH!!
HEY NOW! THERE ARE KIDS WATCHING!!

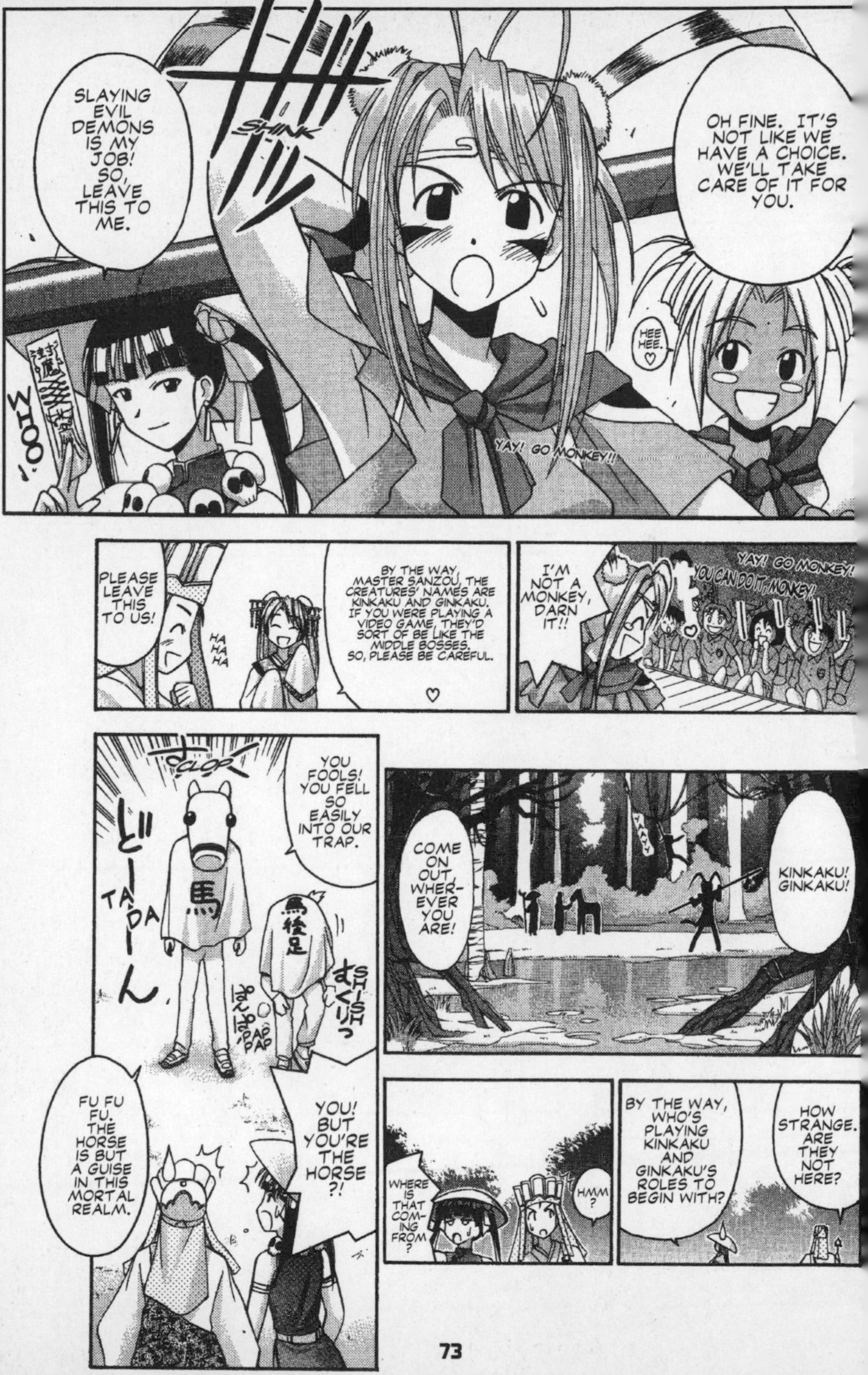

OH FINE. IT'S NOT LIKE WE HAVE A CHOICE. WE'LL TAKE CARE OF IT FOR YOU.
HEE HEE. ♡
YAY! GO MONKEY!!
SHINK
SLAYING EVIL DEMONS IS MY JOB! SO, LEAVE THIS TO ME.
WHOO!
YAY! GO MONKEY!
YOU CAN DO IT, MONKEY!
I'M NOT A MONKEY, DARN IT!!
BY THE WAY, MASTER SANZOU, THE CREATURES' NAMES ARE KINKAKU AND GINKAKU. IF YOU WERE PLAYING A VIDEO GAME, THEY'D SORT OF BE LIKE THE MIDDLE BOSSES. SO, PLEASE BE CAREFUL. ♡
HA HA HA
PLEASE LEAVE THIS TO US!
KINKAKU! GINKAKU!
COME ON OUT, WHEREVER YOU ARE!
HOW STRANGE. ARE THEY NOT HERE?
BY THE WAY, WHO'S PLAYING KINKAKU AND GINKAKU'S ROLES TO BEGIN WITH?
HMM?
WHERE IS THAT COMING FROM?
CLOP
YOU FOOLS! YOU FELL SO EASILY INTO OUR TRAP.
TA-DA
SHISH
PAP PAP
YOU! BUT YOU'RE THE HORSE?!
FU FU FU. THE HORSE IS BUT A GUISE IN THIS MORTAL REALM.

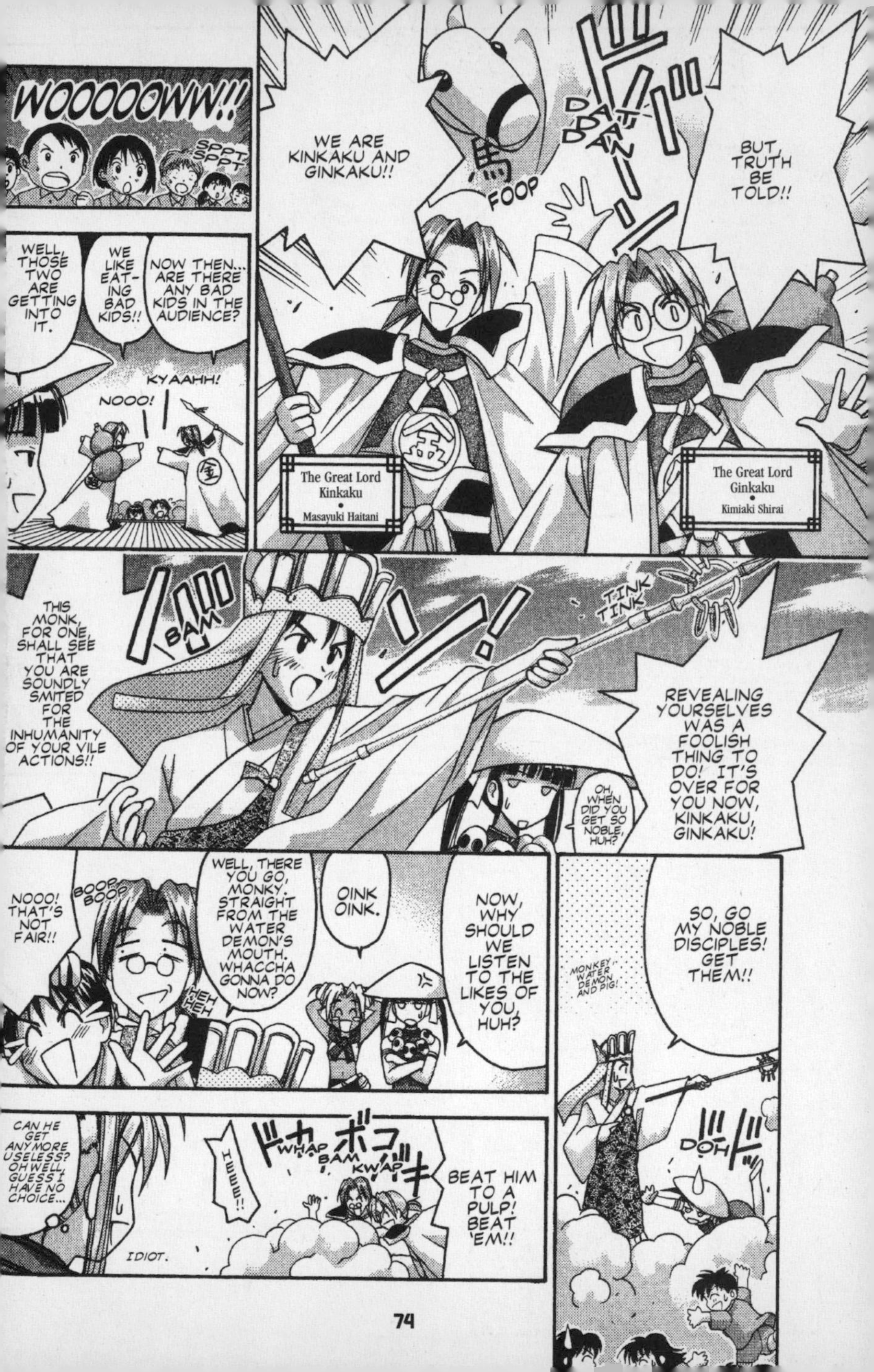
BUT, TRUTH BE TOLD!!
DA DA DAN
WE ARE KINKAKU AND GINKAKU!!
FOOP
The Great Lord Ginkaku • Kimiaki Shirai
The Great Lord Kinkaku • Masayuki Haitani
WOOOOOWW!!
SPPT, SPPT
NOW THEN... ARE THERE ANY BAD KIDS IN THE AUDIENCE?
WE LIKE EATING BAD KIDS!!
WELL, THOSE TWO ARE GETTING INTO IT.
KYAAHH!
NOOO!
REVEALING YOURSELVES WAS A FOOLISH THING TO DO! IT'S OVER FOR YOU NOW, KINKAKU, GINKAKU!
TINK TINK
OH, WHEN DID YOU GET SO NOBLE, HUH?
BAM
THIS MONK, FOR ONE, SHALL SEE THAT YOU ARE SOUNDLY SMITED FOR THE INHUMANITY OF YOUR VILE ACTIONS!!
SO, GO MY NOBLE DISCIPLES! GET THEM!!
MONKEY, WATER DEMON AND PIG!
DOH
NOW, WHY SHOULD WE LISTEN TO THE LIKES OF YOU, HUH?
OINK OINK.
WELL, THERE YOU GO, MONKY. STRAIGHT FROM THE WATER DEMON'S MOUTH. WHACCHA GONNA DO NOW?
HEH HEH
BOOP BOOP
NOOO! THAT'S NOT FAIR!!
BEAT HIM TO A PULP! BEAT 'EM!!
WHAP BAM KWAP
HEEEE!!
CAN HE GET ANYMORE USELESS? OH WELL, GUESS I HAVE NO CHOICE...
IDIOT.

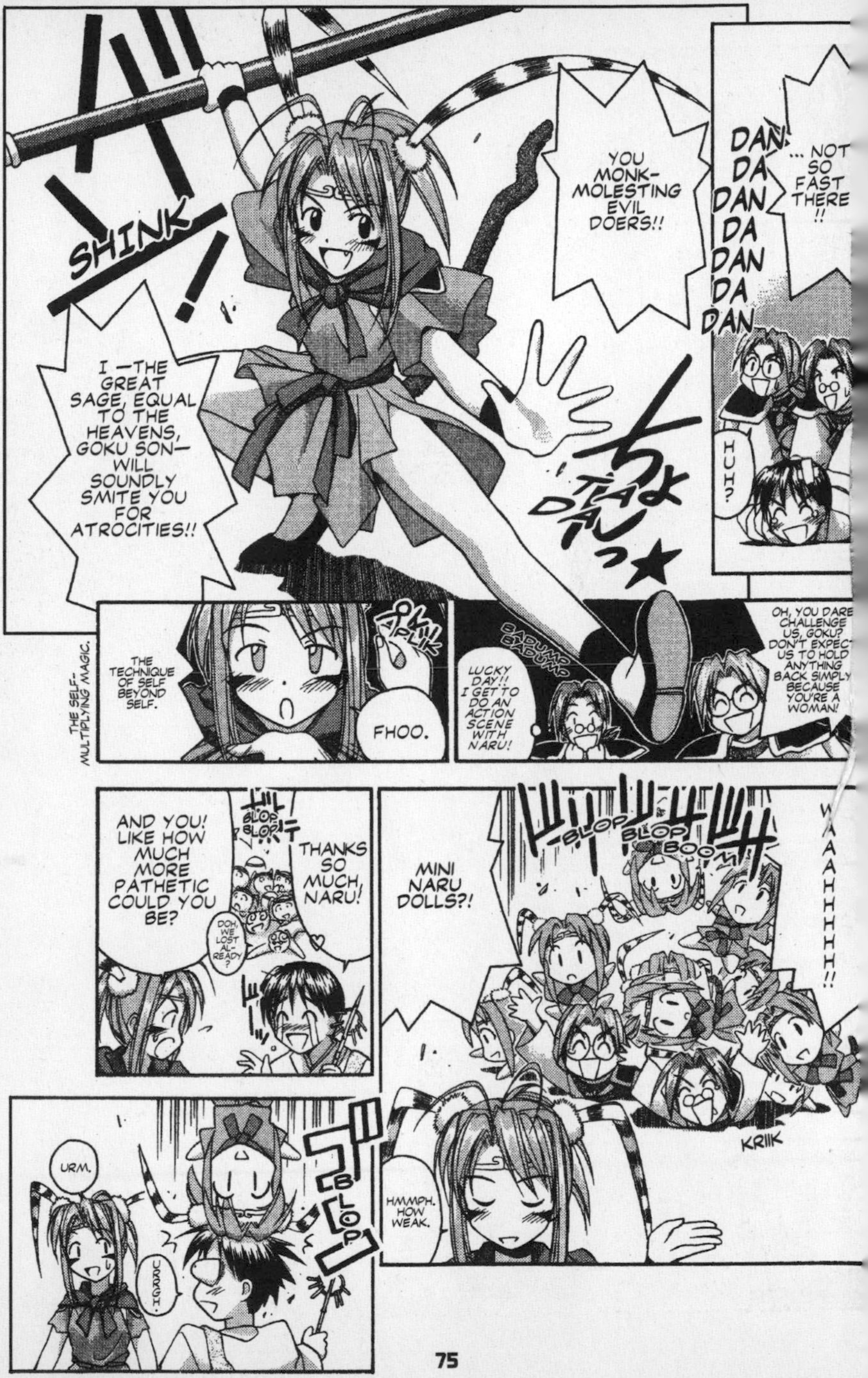

... NOT SO FAST THERE!!
DAN DA DAN DA DAN DA DAN DA DAN
HUH?
YOU MONK-MOLESTING EVIL DOERS!!
SHINK
I—THE GREAT SAGE, EQUAL TO THE HEAVENS, GOKU SON—WILL SOUNDLY SMITE YOU FOR ATROCITIES!!
TIA DAN
OH, YOU DARE CHALLENGE US, GOKU? DON'T EXPECT US TO HOLD ANYTHING BACK SIMPLY BECAUSE YOU'RE A WOMAN!
BADUMP BADUMP
LUCKY DAY!! I GET TO DO AN ACTION SCENE WITH NARU!
PLIK
THE TECHNIQUE OF SELF BEYOND SELF.
FHOO.
THE SELF-MULTIPLYING MAGIC.
WAAAHHHHH!!
BLOP BLOP BOOM
MINI NARU DOLLS?!
KRIIK
HMMPH. HOW WEAK.
THANKS SO MUCH, NARU!
BLOP BLOP
AND YOU! LIKE HOW MUCH MORE PATHETIC COULD YOU BE?
DOH, WE LOST AL-READY?
CBLOP
URM.
URRGH.

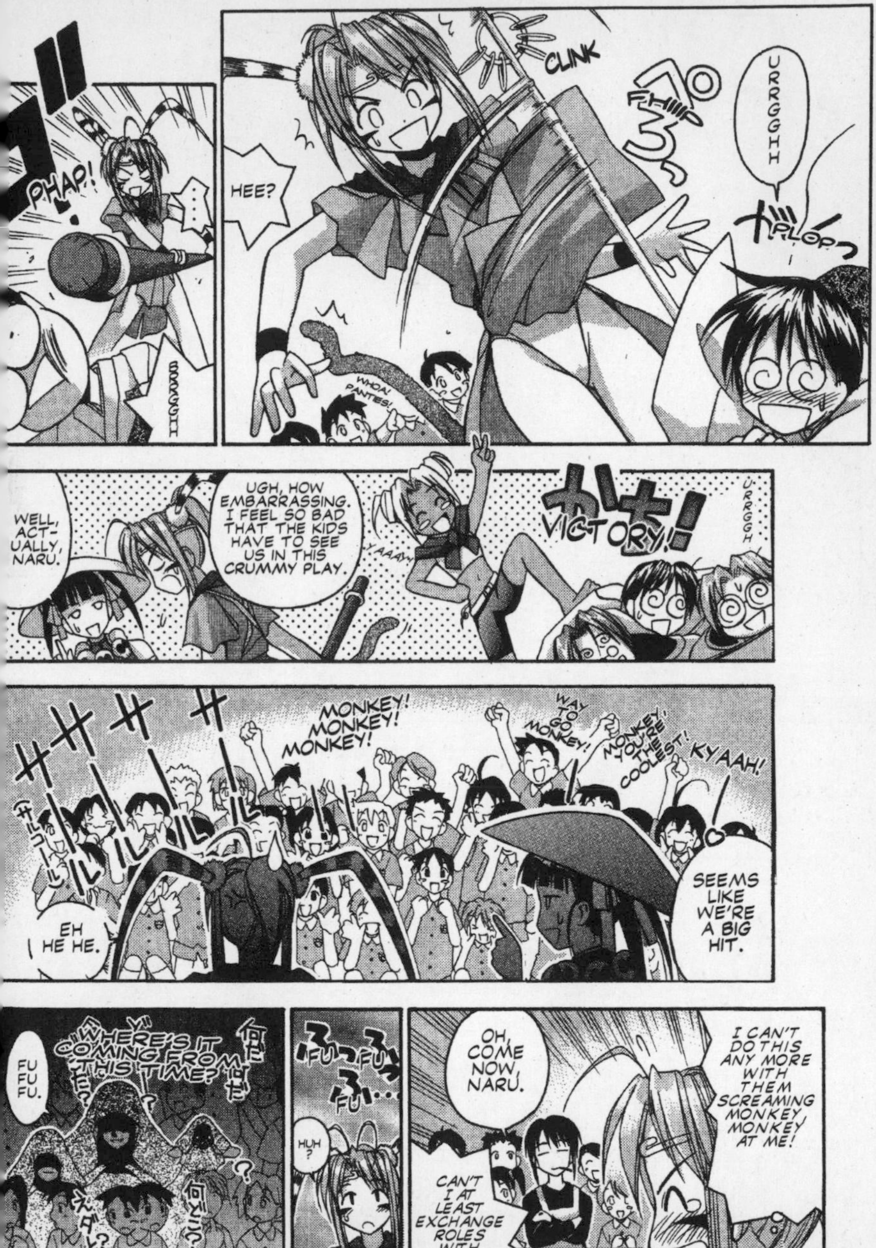
URRGGH
CLINK
FHIP
PLOP
HEE?
WHOA! PANTES!
PHAP!
BRRGGH
URRGGH
VICTORY!
UGH, HOW EMBARRASSING. I FEEL SO BAD THAT THE KIDS HAVE TO SEE US IN THIS CRUMMY PLAY.
WELL, ACTUALLY, NARU.
KYAAH!
MONKEY, YOU'RE THE COOLEST!
WAY TO GO MONKEY!
MONKEY! MONKEY! MONKEY!
SEEMS LIKE WE'RE A BIG HIT.
EH HE HE.
I CAN'T DO THIS ANY MORE WITH THEM SCREAMING MONKEY, MONKEY AT ME!
OH, COME NOW, NARU.
CAN'T I AT LEAST EXCHANGE ROLES WITH SOMEONE ELSE!?!?
FU FU FU...
HUH?
WHERE'S IT COMING FROM THIS TIME?
FU FU FU.

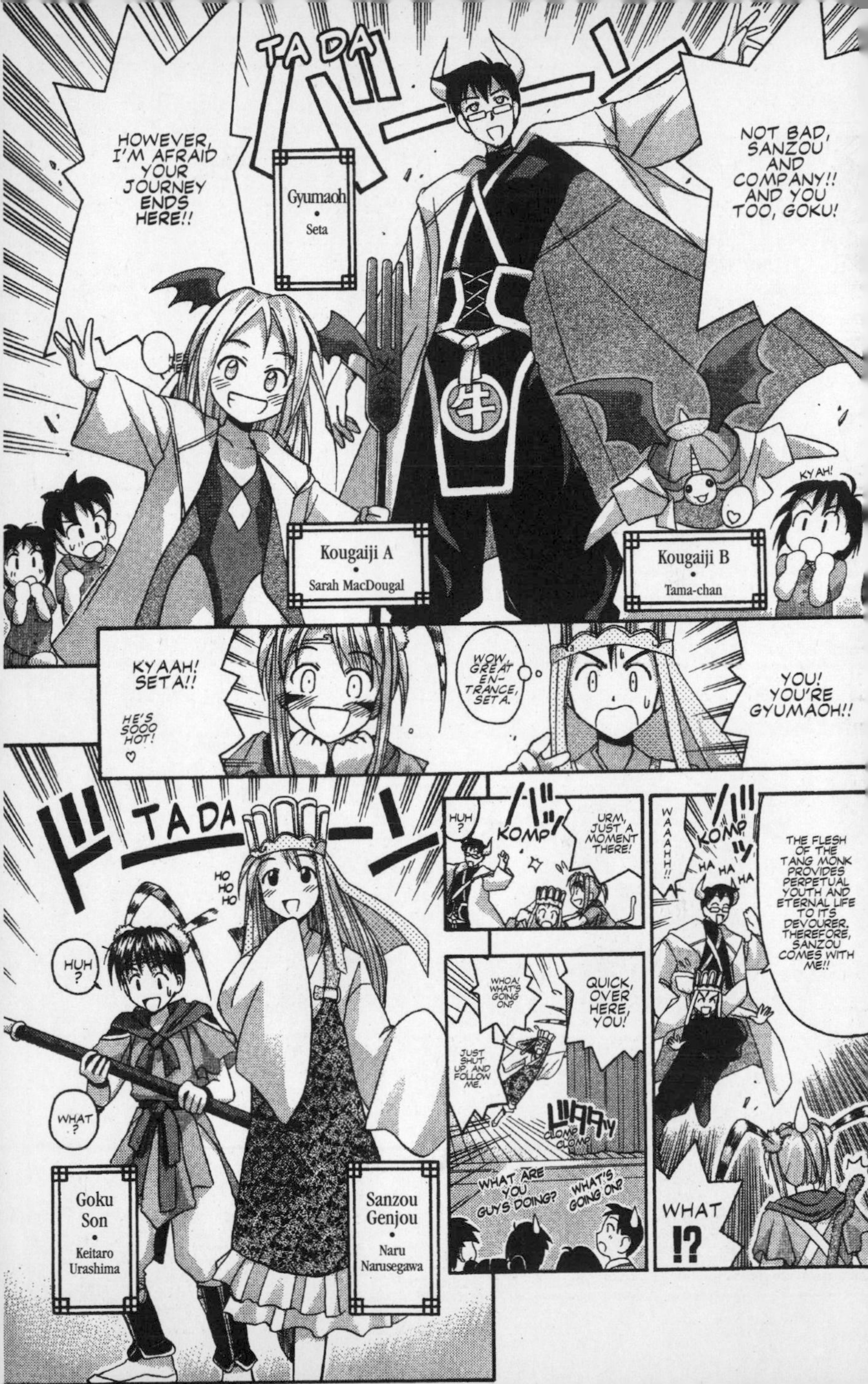
TA DA
NOT BAD, SANZOU AND COMPANY!! AND YOU TOO, GOKU!
HOWEVER, I'M AFRAID YOUR JOURNEY ENDS HERE!!
Gyumaoh • Seta
KYAH!
Kougaiji B • Tama-chan
Kougaiji A • Sarah MacDougal
YOU! YOU'RE GYUMAOH!!
WOW, GREAT EN-TRANCE, SETA.
KYAAH! SETA!!
HE'S SOOO HOT! ♡
KOMP
WAAAAHH!!
HA HA HA
THE FLESH OF THE TANG MONK PROVIDES PERPETUAL YOUTH AND ETERNAL LIFE TO ITS DEVOURER. THEREFORE, SANZOU COMES WITH ME!!
WHAT !?
URM, JUST A MOMENT THERE!
KOMP
HUH ?
QUICK, OVER HERE, YOU!
WHOA! WHAT'S GOING ON?
JUST SHUT UP, AND FOLLOW ME.
CLOMP CLOMP
WHAT'S GOING ON?
WHAT ARE YOU GUYS DOING?
TA DA
HO HO HO
HUH ?
WHAT ?
Sanzou Genjou • Naru Narusegawa
Goku Son • Keitaro Urashima

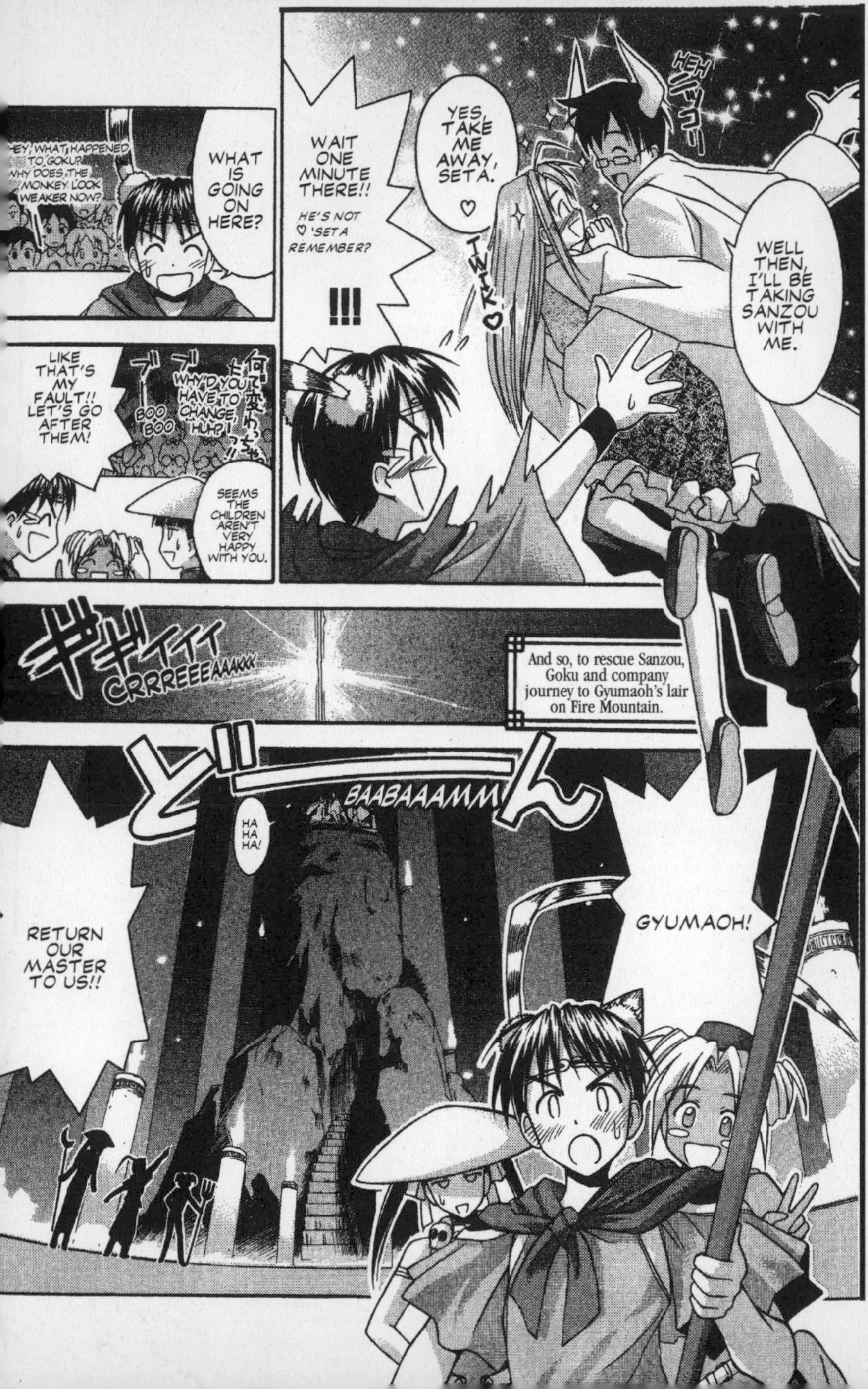
HEH
WELL THEN, I'LL BE TAKING SANZOU WITH ME.
YES, TAKE ME AWAY, SETA. ♡
TWIK♡
WAIT ONE MINUTE THERE!!
HE'S NOT ♡'SETA REMEMBER?
!!!
WHAT IS GOING ON HERE?
HEY, WHAT HAPPENED TO GOKU? WHY DOES THE MONKEY LOOK WEAKER NOW?
WHY'D YOU HAVE TO CHANGE HUH?
BOO BOO
SEEMS THE CHILDREN AREN'T VERY HAPPY WITH YOU.
LIKE THAT'S MY FAULT!! LET'S GO AFTER THEM!
And so, to rescue Sanzou, Goku and company journey to Gyumaoh's lair on Fire Mountain.
CRRREEEAAAKKK
BAABAAAMM
GYUMAOH!
HA HA HA!
RETURN OUR MASTER TO US!!

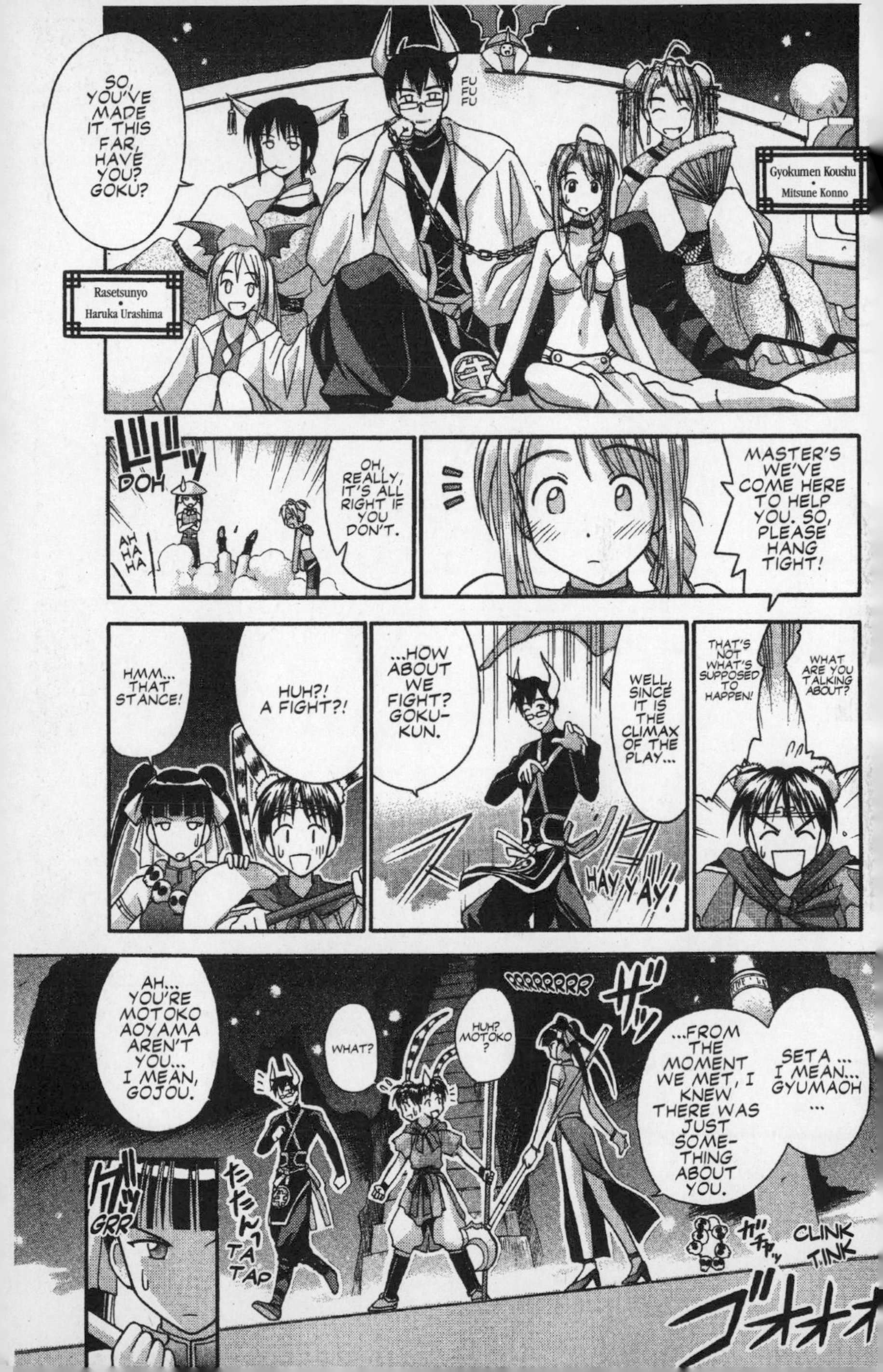
Gyokumen Koushu • Mitsune Konno
FU FU FU
SO, YOU'VE MADE IT THIS FAR, HAVE YOU? GOKU?
Rasetsunyo • Haruka Urashima
MASTER'S WE'VE COME HERE TO HELP YOU. SO, PLEASE HANG TIGHT!
OH, REALLY, IT'S ALL RIGHT IF YOU DON'T.
DOH
AH HA HA
WHAT ARE YOU TALKING ABOUT?
THAT'S NOT WHAT'S SUPPOSED TO HAPPEN!
WELL, SINCE IT IS THE CLIMAX OF THE PLAY...
...HOW ABOUT WE FIGHT? GOKU-KUN.
HAY YAY!
HUH?! A FIGHT?!
HMM... THAT STANCE!
SETA ... I MEAN... GYUMAOH ...
...FROM THE MOMENT WE MET, I KNEW THERE WAS JUST SOME-THING ABOUT YOU.
HUH? MOTOKO ?
WHAT?
AH... YOU'RE MOTOKO AOYAMA AREN'T YOU... I MEAN, GOJOU.
RRRRRRRR
CLINK T.INK
TA TAP
GRR

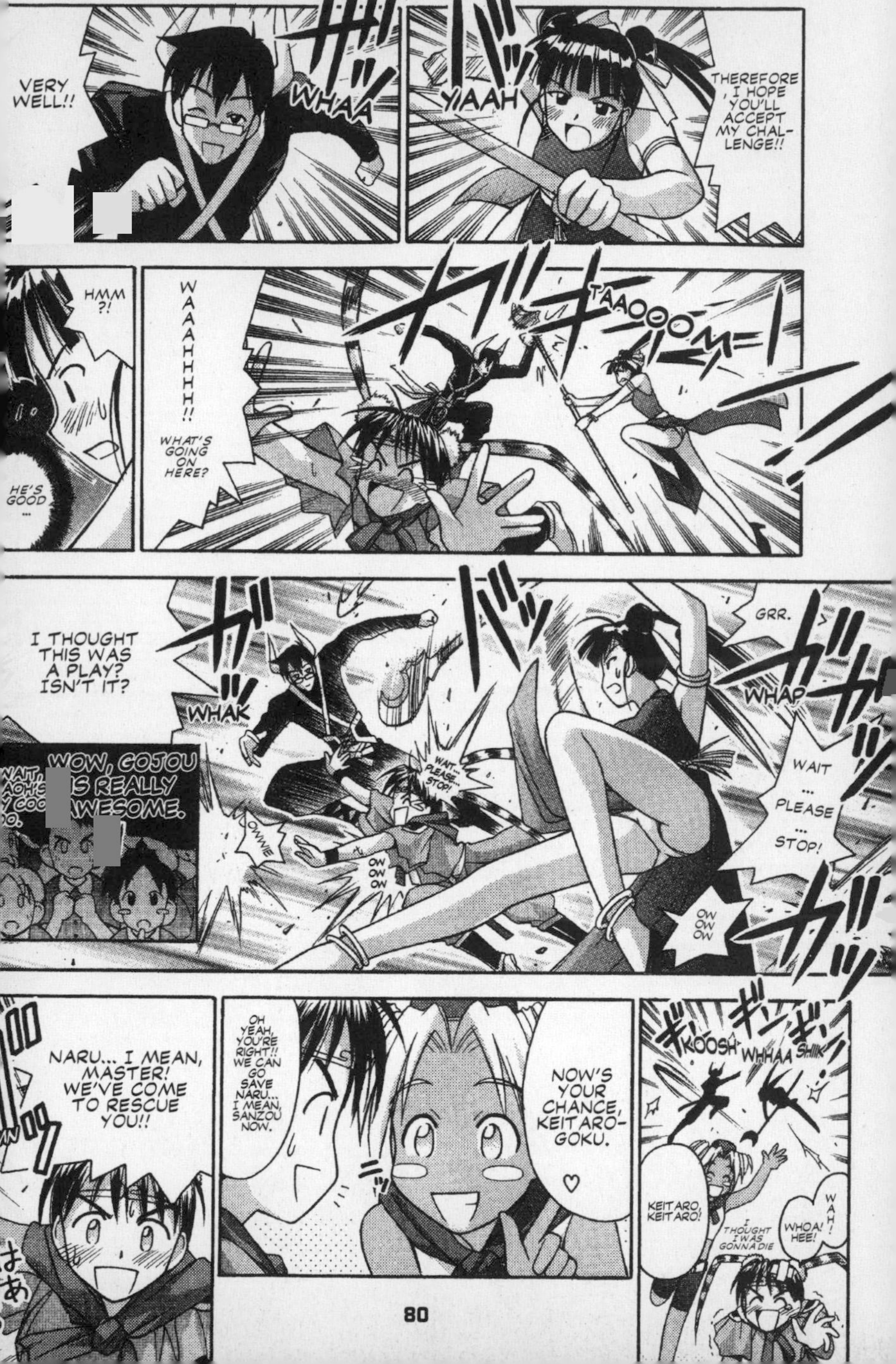

YIAAH
THEREFORE, I HOPE YOU'LL ACCEPT MY CHAL-LENGE!!
WHAA
VERY WELL!!
TAAOOOOM
WAAAAHHHH!!
WHAT'S GOING ON HERE?
HMM ?!
HE'S GOOD ...
GRR.
WHAP
WAIT ... PLEASE ... STOP!
OW OW OW
WHAK
I THOUGHT THIS WAS A PLAY? ISN'T IT?
WAIT... PLEASE... STOP!
OWWW
OW OW OW
WOW, GOJOU IS REALLY AWESOME.
KOOSH
WHHAA
SHIIK
KEITARO, KEITARO!
WAH!
WHOA! HEE!
I THOUGHT I WAS GONNA DIE
NOW'S YOUR CHANCE, KEITARO-GOKU.
OH YEAH, YOU'RE RIGHT!! WE CAN GO SAVE NARU... I MEAN, SANZOU NOW.
NARU... I MEAN, MASTER! WE'VE COME TO RESCUE YOU!!
はあ

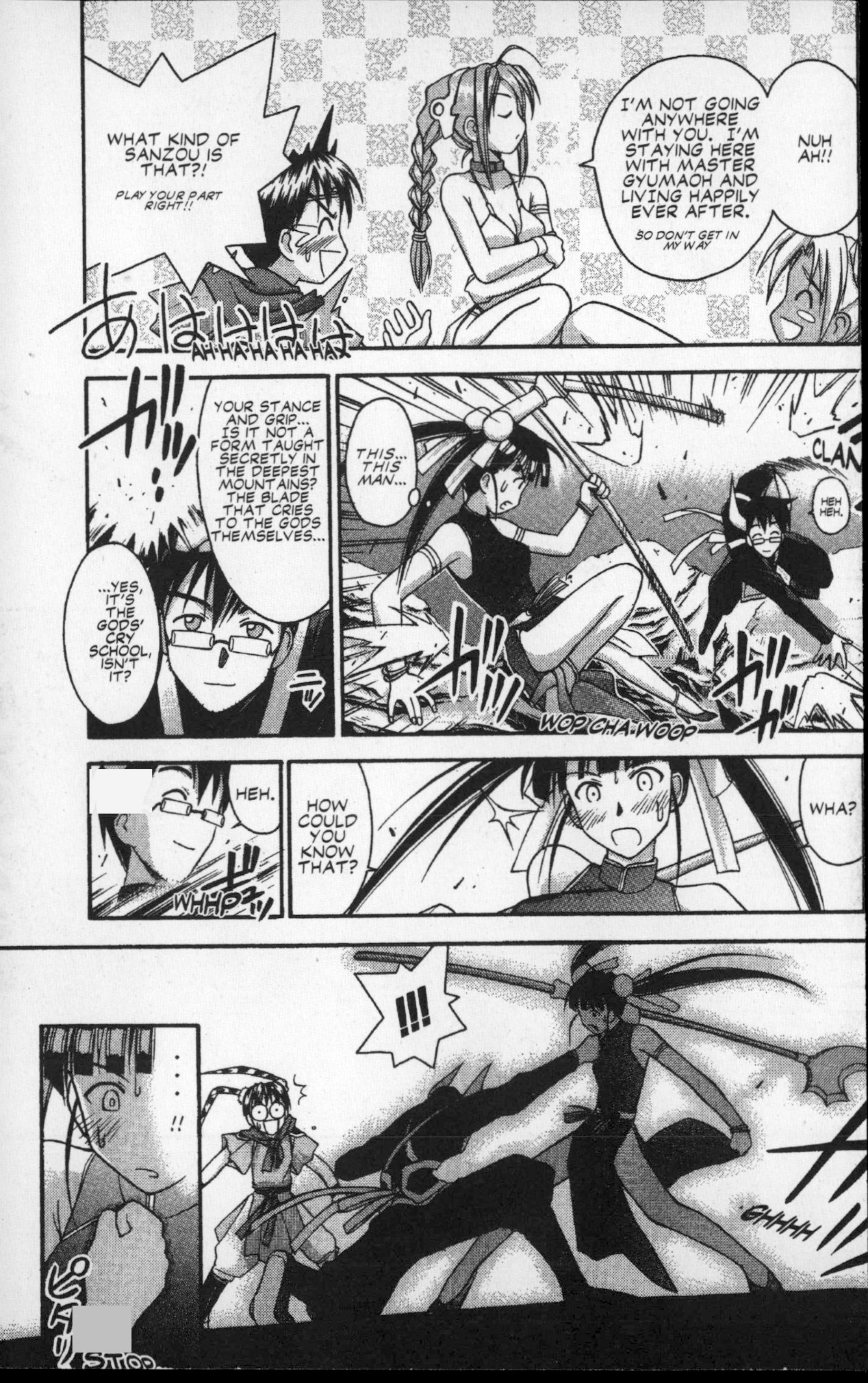

NUH AH!!
I'M NOT GOING ANYWHERE WITH YOU. I'M STAYING HERE WITH MASTER GYUMAOH AND LIVING HAPPILY EVER AFTER.
SO DON'T GET IN MY WAY
WHAT KIND OF SANZOU IS THAT?!
PLAY YOUR PART RIGHT!!
あははははは
AH HA HA HA HA
CLAN
THIS... THIS MAN...
HEH HEH.
WOP CHA WOOP
YOUR STANCE AND GRIP... IS IT NOT A FORM TAUGHT SECRETLY IN THE DEEPEST MOUNTAINS? THE BLADE THAT CRIES TO THE GODS THEMSELVES...
...YES, IT'S THE GODS' CRY SCHOOL, ISN'T IT?
WHA?
HOW COULD YOU KNOW THAT?
HEH.
WHHP
!!!
GHHHH
....
!!
STOP

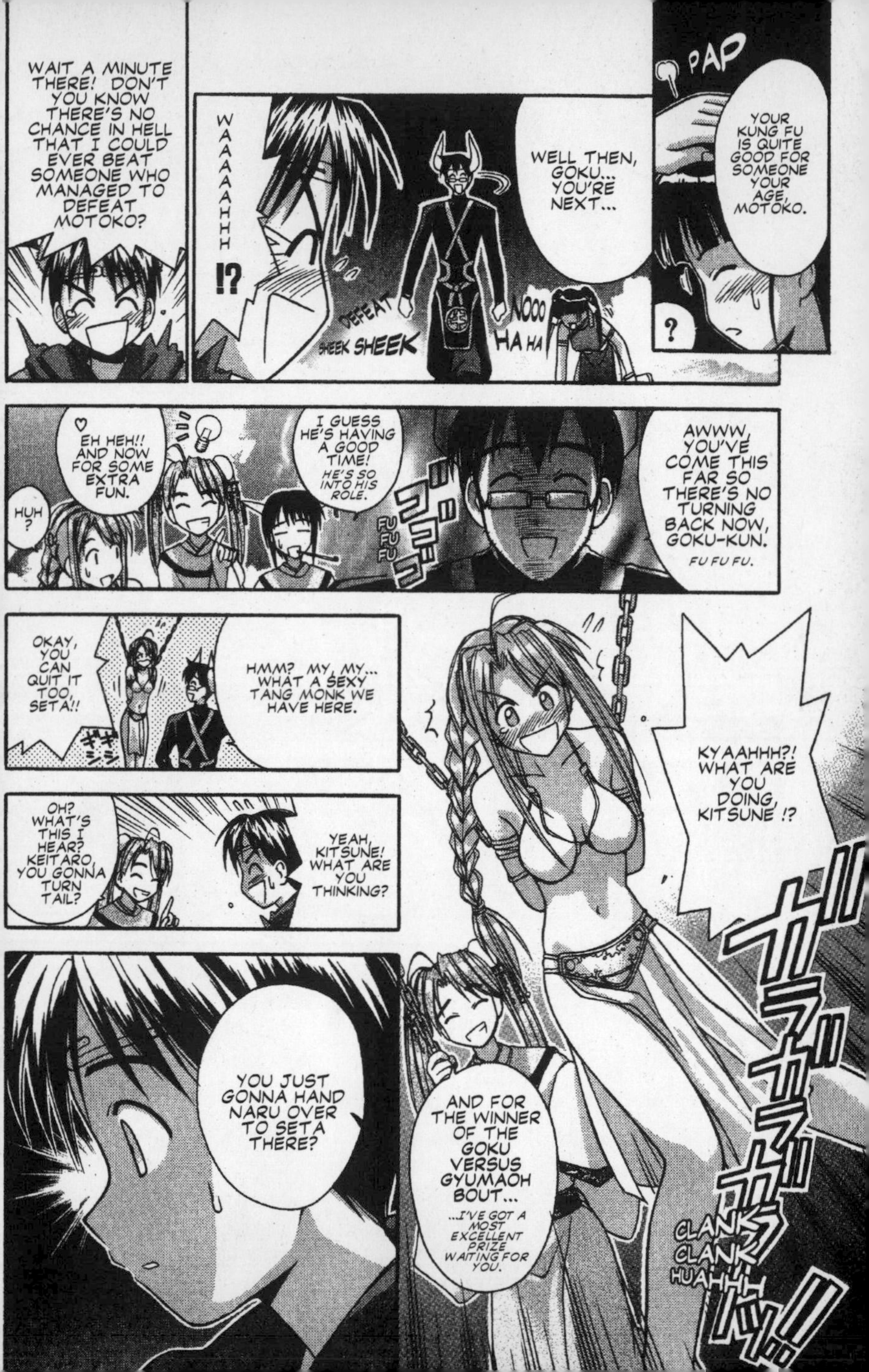
PAP
YOUR KUNG FU IS QUITE GOOD FOR SOMEONE YOUR AGE, MOTOKO.
?
WELL THEN, GOKU... YOU'RE NEXT...
NOOO HA HA
DEFEAT
SHEEK SHEEK
WAAAAAAHHH !?
WAIT A MINUTE THERE! DON'T YOU KNOW THERE'S NO CHANCE IN HELL THAT I COULD EVER BEAT SOMEONE WHO MANAGED TO DEFEAT MOTOKO?
AWWW, YOU'VE COME THIS FAR SO THERE'S NO TURNING BACK NOW, GOKU-KUN.
FU FU FU.
FU FU FU
I GUESS HE'S HAVING A GOOD TIME! HE'S SO INTO HIS ROLE.
♡ EH HEH!! AND NOW FOR SOME EXTRA FUN.
HUH ?
KYAAHHH?! WHAT ARE YOU DOING, KITSUNE !?
CLANKS CLANK HUAHHH
AND FOR THE WINNER OF THE GOKU VERSUS GYUMAOH BOUT...
...I'VE GOT A MOST EXCELLENT PRIZE WAITING FOR YOU.
HMM? MY, MY... WHAT A SEXY TANG MONK WE HAVE HERE.
OKAY, YOU CAN QUIT IT TOO, SETA!!
YEAH, KITSUNE! WHAT ARE YOU THINKING?
OH? WHAT'S THIS I HEAR? KEITARO, YOU GONNA TURN TAIL?
YOU JUST GONNA HAND NARU OVER TO SETA THERE?

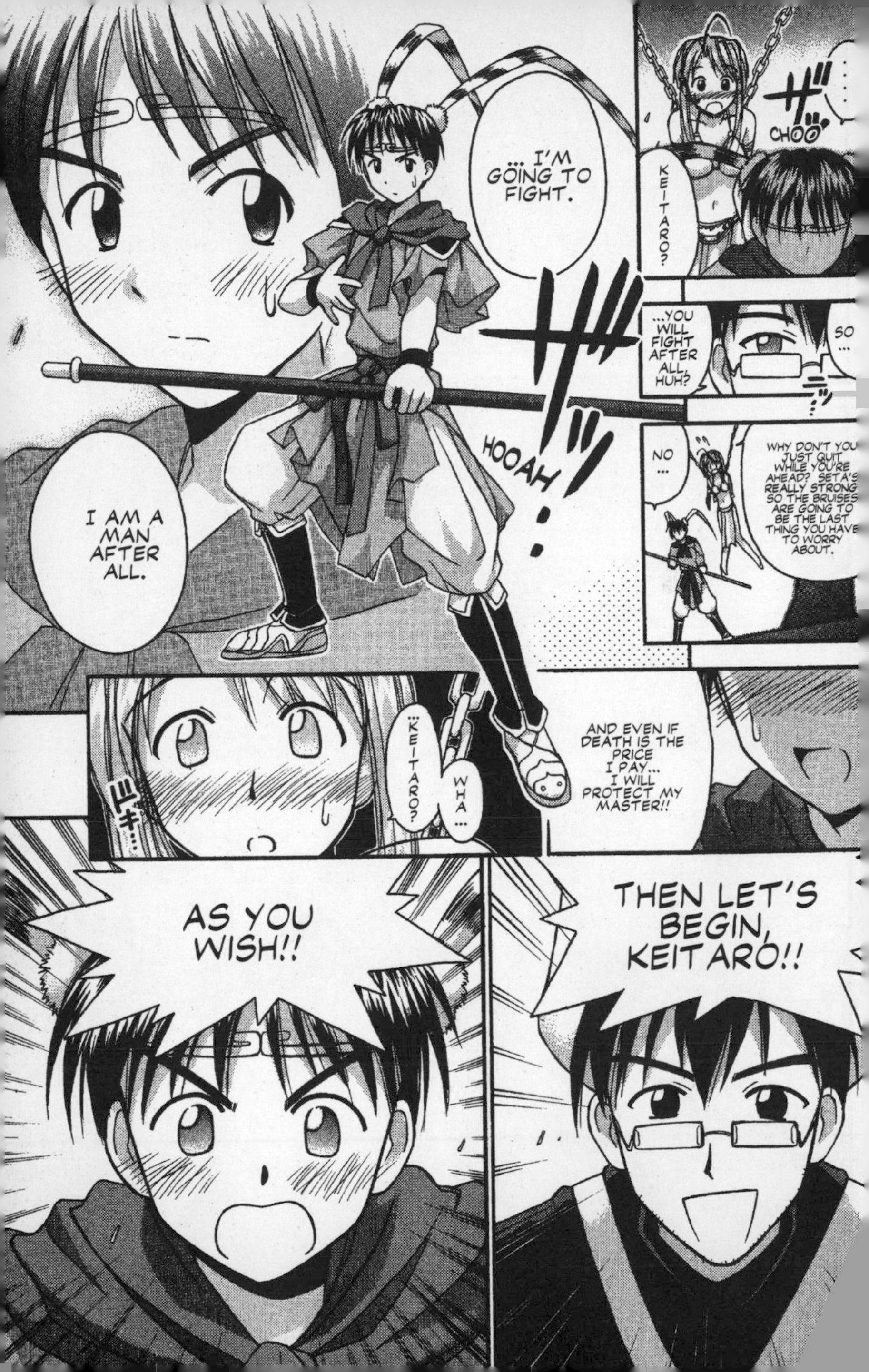
...
CHOO
KEITARO?
SO ...
...YOU WILL FIGHT AFTER ALL, HUH?
WHY DON'T YOU JUST QUIT WHILE YOU'RE AHEAD? SETA'S REALLY STRONG SO THE BRUISES ARE GOING TO BE THE LAST THING YOU HAVE TO WORRY ABOUT.
NO ...
... I'M GOING TO FIGHT.
HOOAH!!
I AM A MAN AFTER ALL.
AND EVEN IF DEATH IS THE PRICE I PAY... I WILL PROTECT MY MASTER!!
WHA ...
...KEITARO?
THEN LET'S BEGIN, KEITARO!!
AS YOU WISH!!

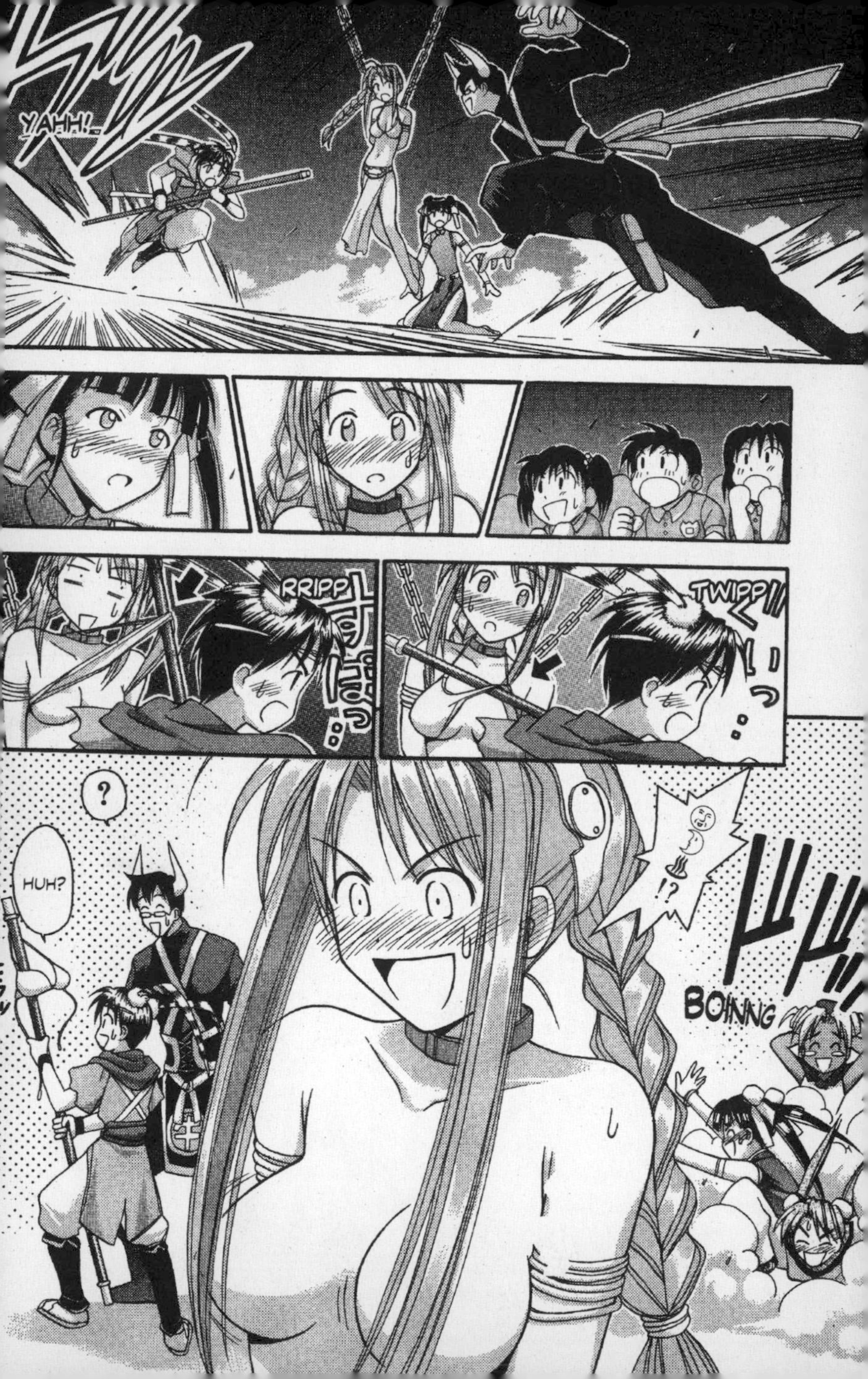
YAHH!
TWIPP
RRIPP
!?
BOINNG
?
HUH?

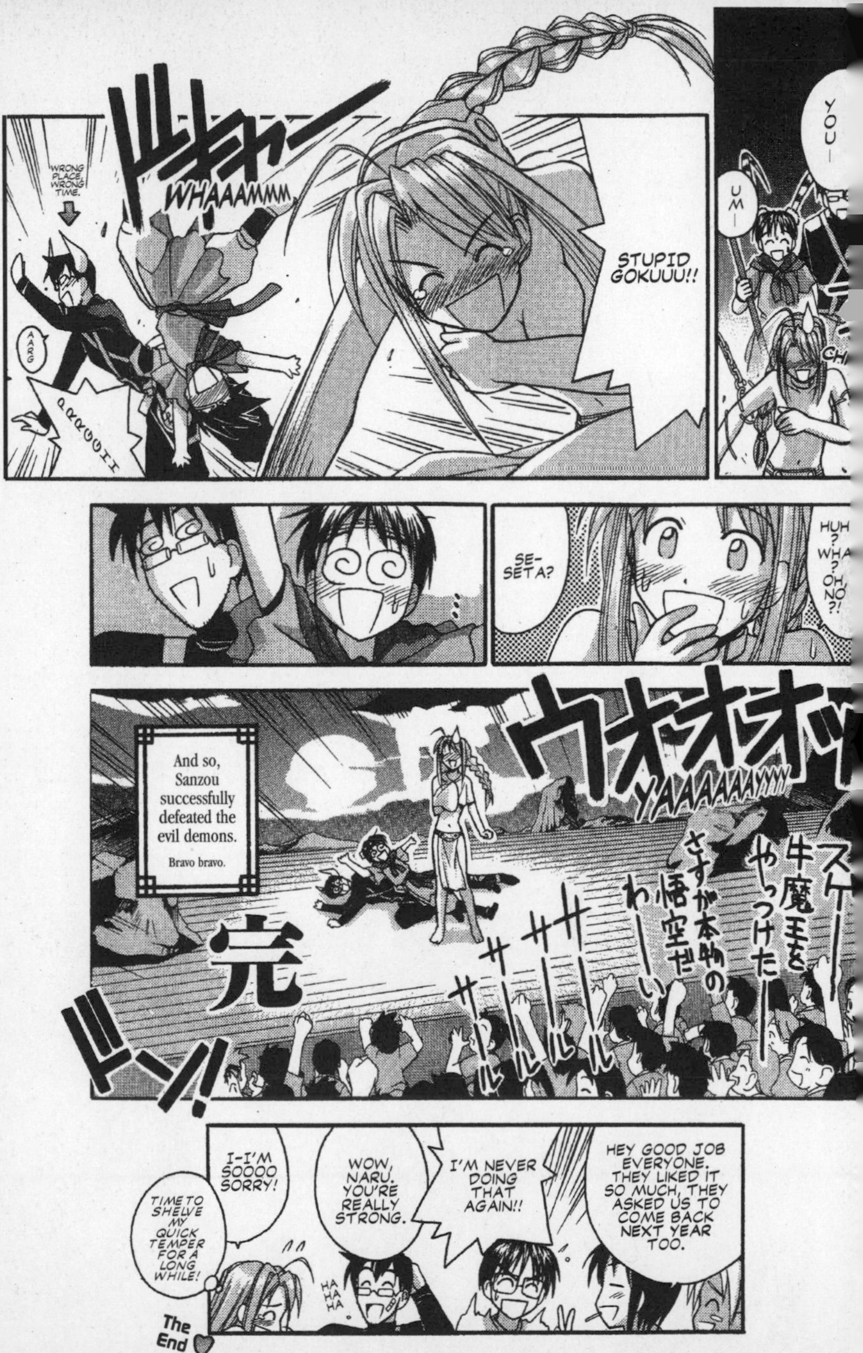
YOU—
UM—
WHAAAMMM
STUPID GOKUUU!!
WRONG PLACE, WRONG TIME.
AARG
HUH? WHA? OH, NO?!
SE-SETA?
YAAAAAAYYYY
スゲー
牛魔王をやっつけた—
さすが本物の悟空だわ——い
And so, Sanzou successfully defeated the evil demons.
Bravo bravo.
完
HEY GOOD JOB EVERYONE. THEY LIKED IT SO MUCH, THEY ASKED US TO COME BACK NEXT YEAR TOO.
I'M NEVER DOING THAT AGAIN!!
WOW, NARU. YOU'RE REALLY STRONG.
I-I'M SOOOO SORRY!
TIME TO SHELVE MY QUICK TEMPER FOR A LONG WHILE!
HA HA HA
The End

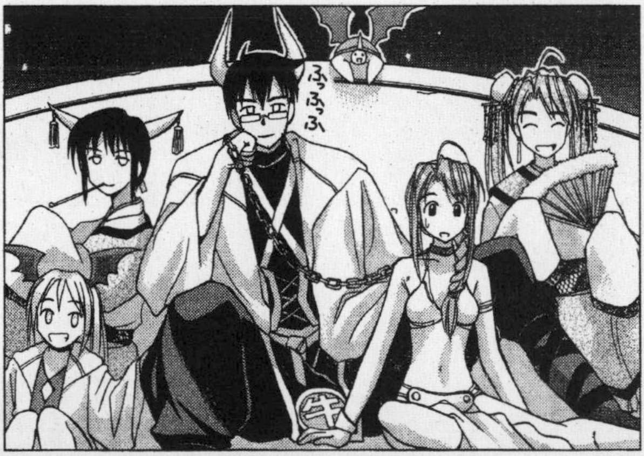
ふっふっふ

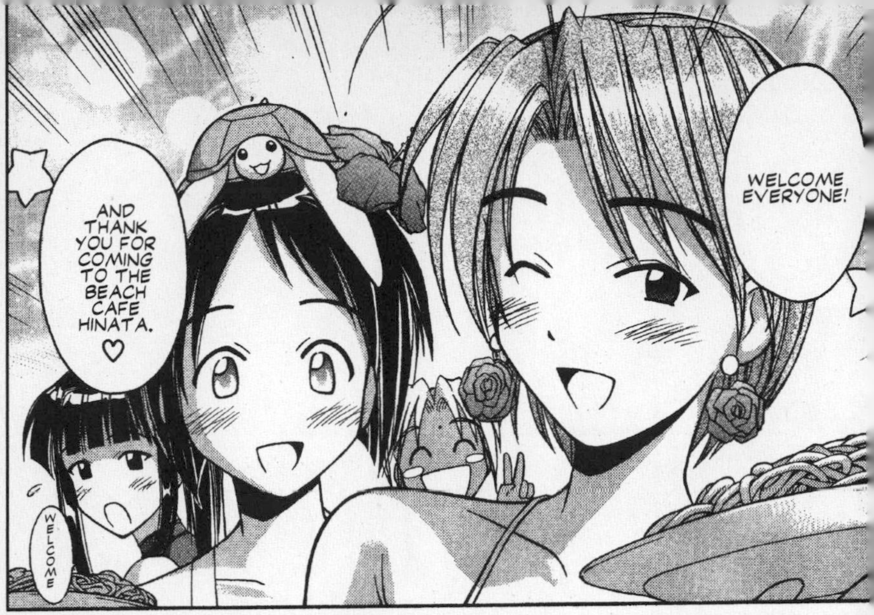
WELCOME EVERYONE!
AND THANK YOU FOR COMING TO THE BEACH CAFE HINATA. ♡
WELCOME

Love Hina

HINATA.38 A Happening and a Kiss ♡

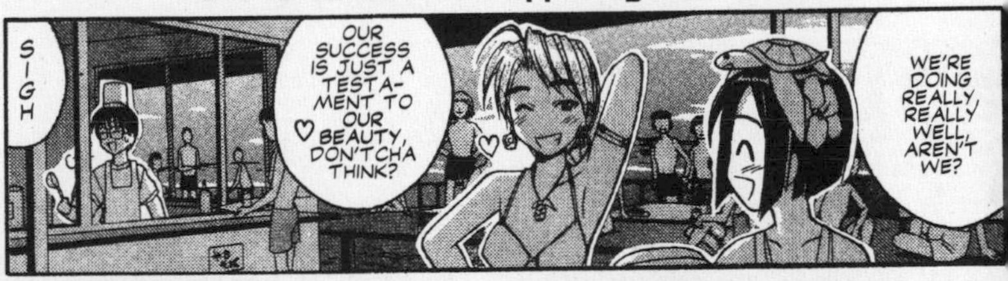
WE'RE DOING REALLY, REALLY WELL, AREN'T WE?
OUR SUCCESS IS JUST A TESTAMENT TO OUR BEAUTY, DON'TCHA THINK? ♡
SIGH

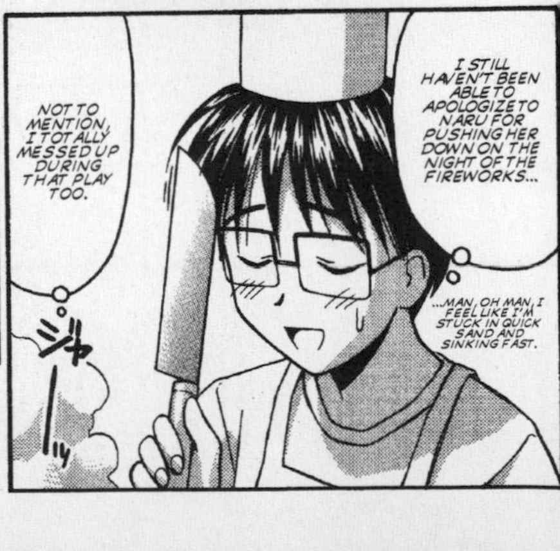
I STILL HAVEN'T BEEN ABLE TO APOLOGIZE TO NARU FOR PUSHING HER DOWN ON THE NIGHT OF THE FIREWORKS...
NOT TO MENTION, I TOTALLY MESSED UP DURING THAT PLAY TOO.
...MAN, OH MAN, I FEEL LIKE I'M STUCK IN QUICK SAND AND SINKING FAST.

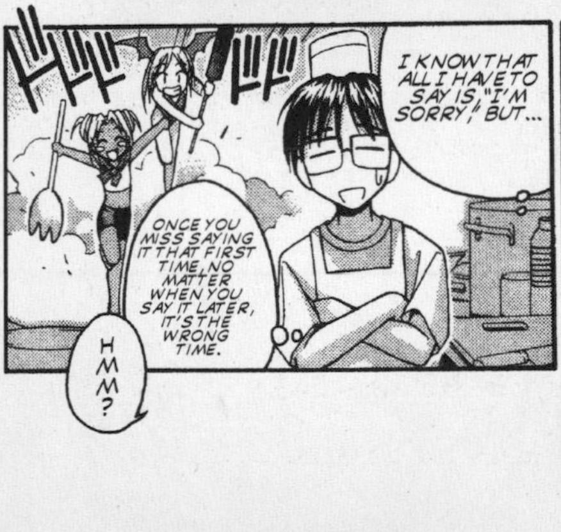
I KNOW THAT ALL I HAVE TO SAY IS, "I'M SORRY," BUT...
ONCE YOU MISS SAYING IT THAT FIRST TIME, NO MATTER WHEN YOU SAY IT LATER, IT'S THE WRONG TIME.
HMM?

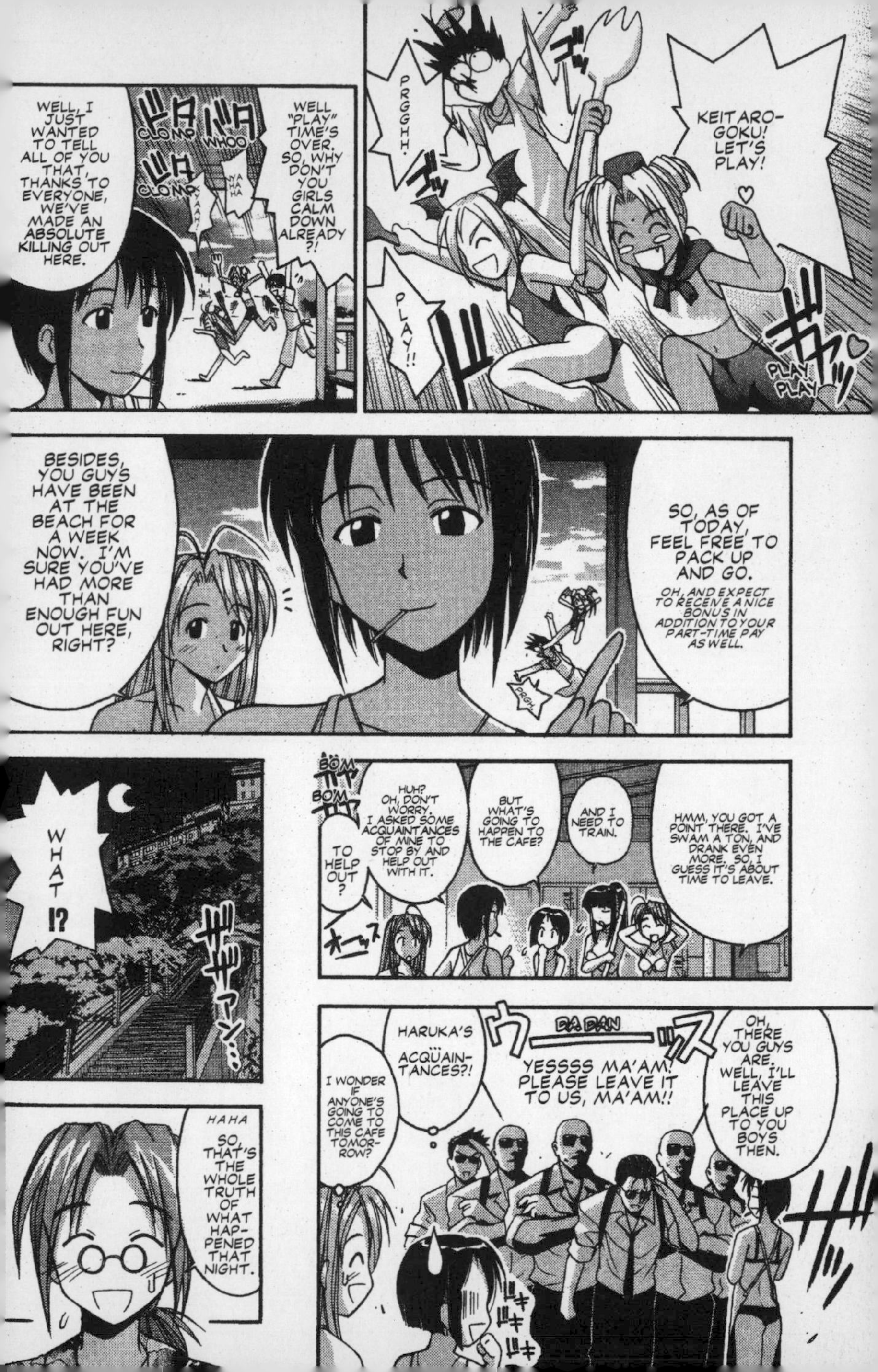
KEITARO-GOKU! LET'S PLAY!
PRGGH.
PLAY!!
PLAY PLAY
WELL "PLAY" TIME'S OVER. SO, WHY DON'T YOU GIRLS CALM DOWN ALREADY?!
CLOMP WHOO
CLOMP
NYA HA HA
YAAH!
WELL, I JUST WANTED TO TELL ALL OF YOU THAT, THANKS TO EVERYONE, WE'VE MADE AN ABSOLUTE KILLING OUT HERE.
SO, AS OF TODAY, FEEL FREE TO PACK UP AND GO.
OH, AND EXPECT TO RECEIVE A NICE BONUS IN ADDITION TO YOUR PART-TIME PAY AS WELL.
PRGGH
BESIDES, YOU GUYS HAVE BEEN AT THE BEACH FOR A WEEK NOW. I'M SURE YOU'VE HAD MORE THAN ENOUGH FUN OUT HERE, RIGHT?
HMM, YOU GOT A POINT THERE. I'VE SWAM A TON, AND DRANK EVEN MORE. SO, I GUESS IT'S ABOUT TIME TO LEAVE.
AND I NEED TO TRAIN.
BUT WHAT'S GOING TO HAPPEN TO THE CAFE?
HUH? OH, DON'T WORRY. I ASKED SOME ACQUAINTANCES OF MINE TO STOP BY AND HELP OUT WITH IT.
BOM BOM
TO HELP OUT?
OH, THERE YOU GUYS ARE. WELL, I'LL LEAVE THIS PLACE UP TO YOU BOYS THEN.
DA DAN
YESSSS MA'AM! PLEASE LEAVE IT TO US, MA'AM!!
HARUKA'S ACQUAINTANCES?!
I WONDER IF ANYONE'S GOING TO COME TO THIS CAFE TOMORROW?
WHAT !?
HAHA
SO, THAT'S THE WHOLE TRUTH OF WHAT HAPPENED THAT NIGHT.

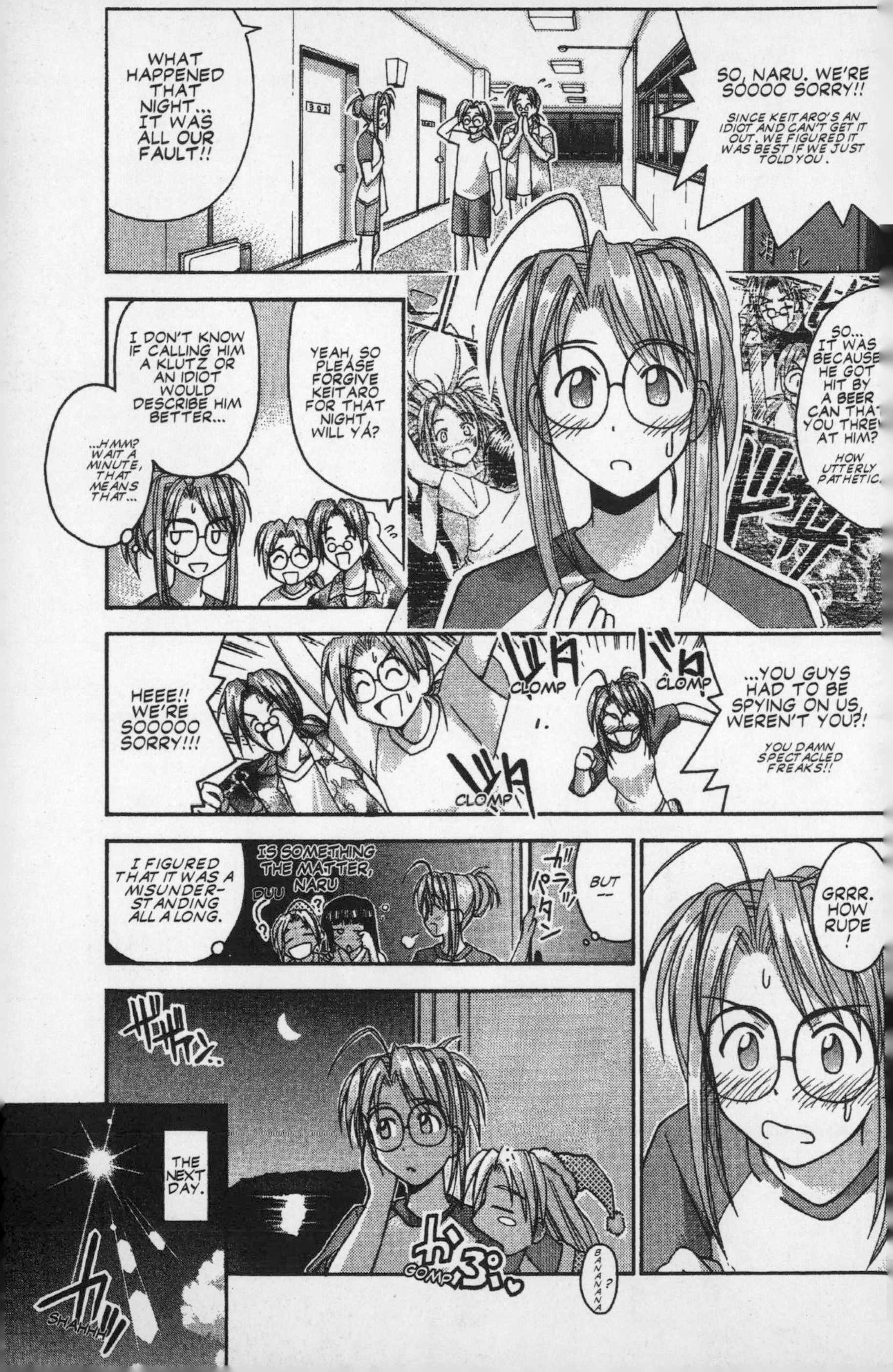
SO, NARU. WE'RE SOOOO SORRY!!
SINCE KEITARO'S AN IDIOT AND CAN'T GET IT OUT, WE FIGURED IT WAS BEST IF WE JUST TOLD YOU.
WHAT HAPPENED THAT NIGHT... IT WAS ALL OUR FAULT!!
SO... IT WAS BECAUSE HE GOT HIT BY A BEER CAN THAT YOU THREW AT HIM?
HOW UTTERLY PATHETIC.
YEAH, SO PLEASE FORGIVE KEITARO FOR THAT NIGHT, WILL YA?
I DON'T KNOW IF CALLING HIM A KLUTZ OR AN IDIOT WOULD DESCRIBE HIM BETTER...
...HMM? WAIT A MINUTE, THAT MEANS THAT...
...YOU GUYS HAD TO BE SPYING ON US, WEREN'T YOU?!
YOU DAMN SPECTACLED FREAKS!!
CLOMP
CLOMP
CLOMP
HEEE!! WE'RE SOOOOO SORRY!!!
GRRR. HOW RUDE!
BUT --
IS SOMETHING THE MATTER, NARU
DUU
I FIGURED THAT IT WAS A MISUNDER-STANDING ALL ALONG.
GOMP
BANANANA?
THE NEXT DAY.
SHAHHH

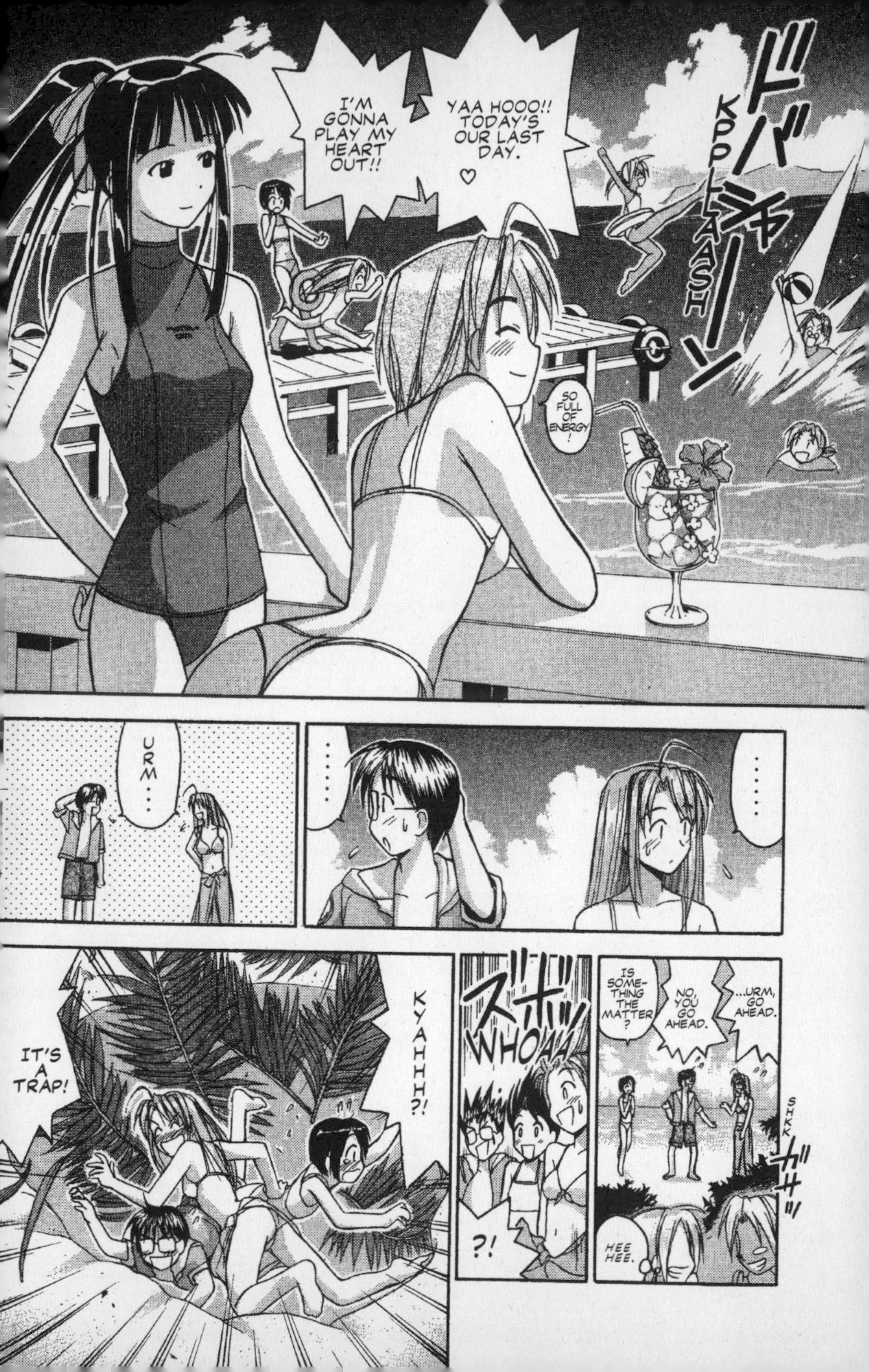
ドバシャーン
KPPLAASH
YAA HOOO!! TODAY'S OUR LAST DAY. ♡
I'M GONNA PLAY MY HEART OUT!!
SO FULL OF ENERGY!
......
......
URM...
...URM, GO AHEAD.
NO, YOU GO AHEAD.
IS SOMETHING THE MATTER?
SHKK
ガザッ
HEE HEE.
ズボッ
WHOAA
?!
KYAHHH?!
IT'S A TRAP!

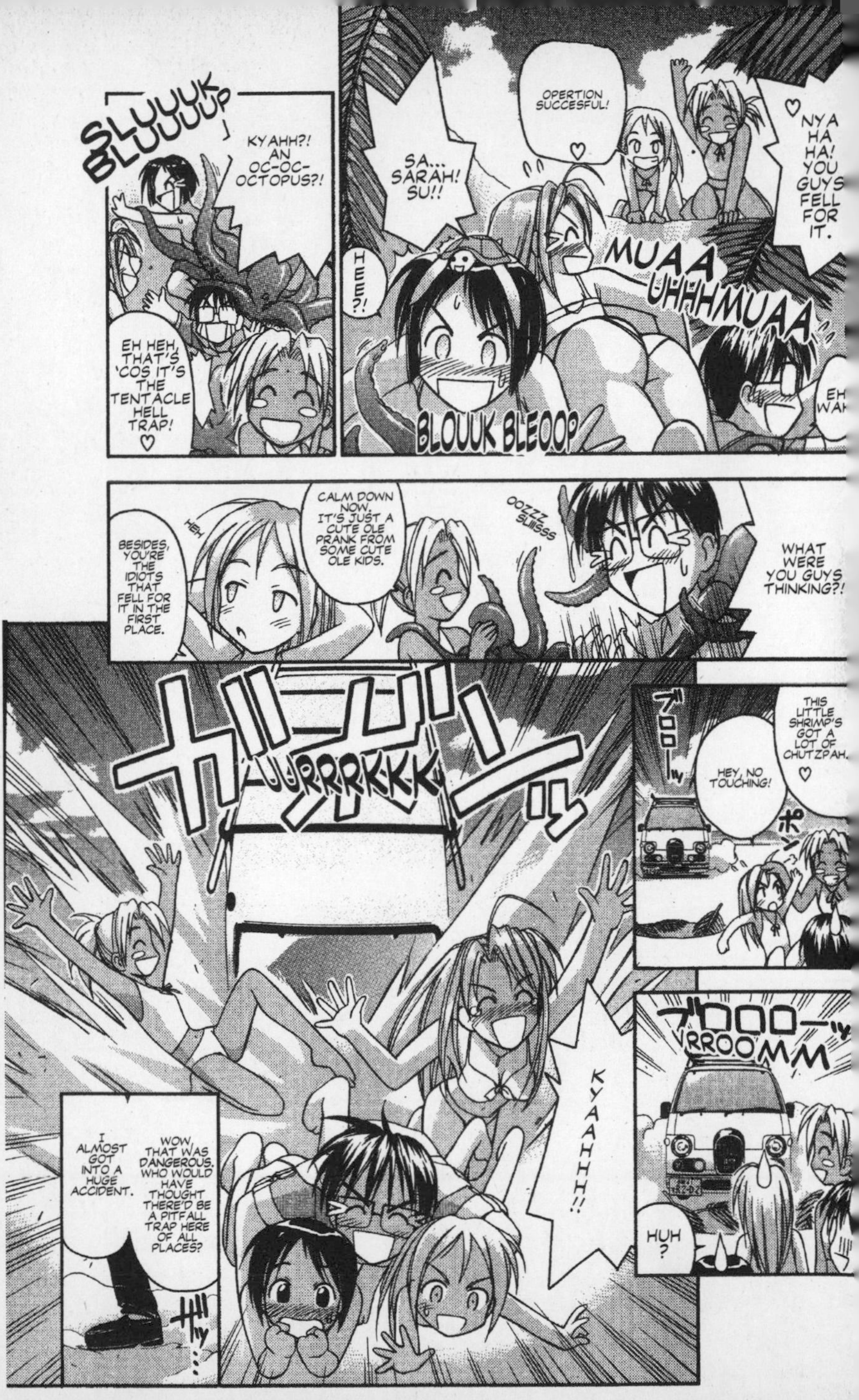

NYA HA HA! YOU GUYS FELL FOR IT. ♡
OPERTION SUCCESFUL! ♡
SA... SARAH! SU!!
MUAA UHHHMUAA
EH WAK
HEE?!
BLOUUK BLEOOP
SLUUUK BLUUUUP
KYAHH?! AN OC-OC-OCTOPUS?!
EH HEH, THAT'S 'COS IT'S THE TENTACLE HELL TRAP! ♡
WHAT WERE YOU GUYS THINKING?!
OOZZZ SLIIISSS
CALM DOWN NOW. IT'S JUST A CUTE OLE PRANK FROM SOME CUTE OLE KIDS.
HEH
BESIDES, YOU'RE THE IDIOTS THAT FELL FOR IT IN THE FIRST PLACE.
ブロロー
THIS LITTLE SHRIMP'S GOT A LOT OF CHUTZPAH. ♡
HEY, NO TOUCHING!
ポン
ブロロロー
VRROOMM
HUH?
UURRRKKK
KYAAHHH!!
WOW, THAT WAS DANGEROUS. WHO WOULD HAVE THOUGHT THERE'D BE A PITFALL TRAP HERE OF ALL PLACES?
I ALMOST GOT INTO A HUGE ACCIDENT.

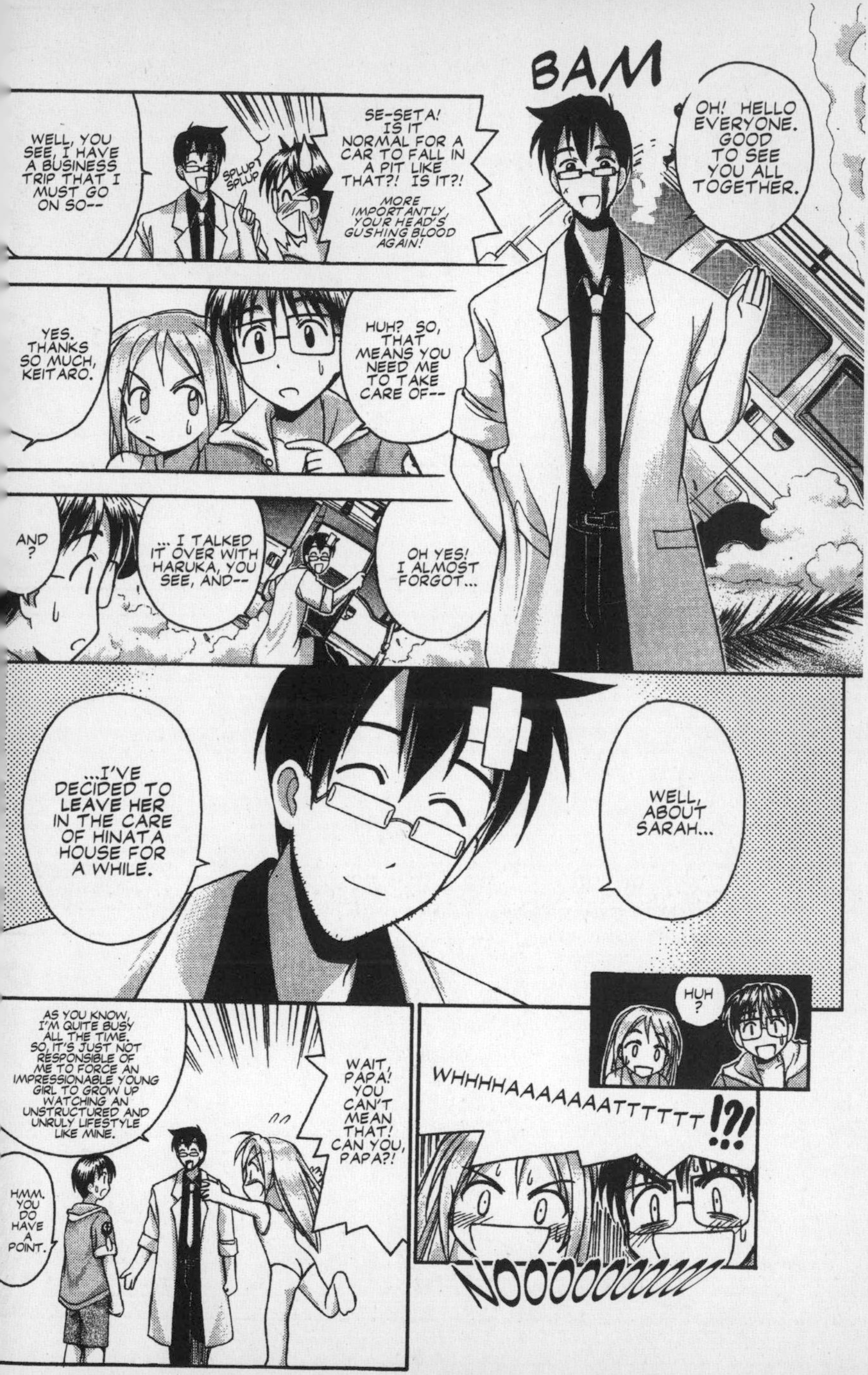
BAM
OH! HELLO EVERYONE. GOOD TO SEE YOU ALL TOGETHER.
SE-SETA! IS IT NORMAL FOR A CAR TO FALL IN A PIT LIKE THAT?! IS IT?!
MORE IMPORTANTLY, YOUR HEAD'S GUSHING BLOOD AGAIN!
SPLUP SPLUP
WELL, YOU SEE, I HAVE A BUSINESS TRIP THAT I MUST GO ON SO--
HUH? SO, THAT MEANS YOU NEED ME TO TAKE CARE OF--
YES. THANKS SO MUCH, KEITARO.
OH YES! I ALMOST FORGOT...
... I TALKED IT OVER WITH HARUKA, YOU SEE, AND--
AND ?
WELL, ABOUT SARAH...
...I'VE DECIDED TO LEAVE HER IN THE CARE OF HINATA HOUSE FOR A WHILE.
HUH ?
WHHHHAAAAAAAATTTTTT !?!
NOOOOOOOOO
WAIT, PAPA! YOU CAN'T MEAN THAT! CAN YOU, PAPA?!
AS YOU KNOW, I'M QUITE BUSY ALL THE TIME. SO, IT'S JUST NOT RESPONSIBLE OF ME TO FORCE AN IMPRESSIONABLE YOUNG GIRL TO GROW UP WATCHING AN UNSTRUCTURED AND UNRULY LIFESTYLE LIKE MINE.
HMM. YOU DO HAVE A POINT.

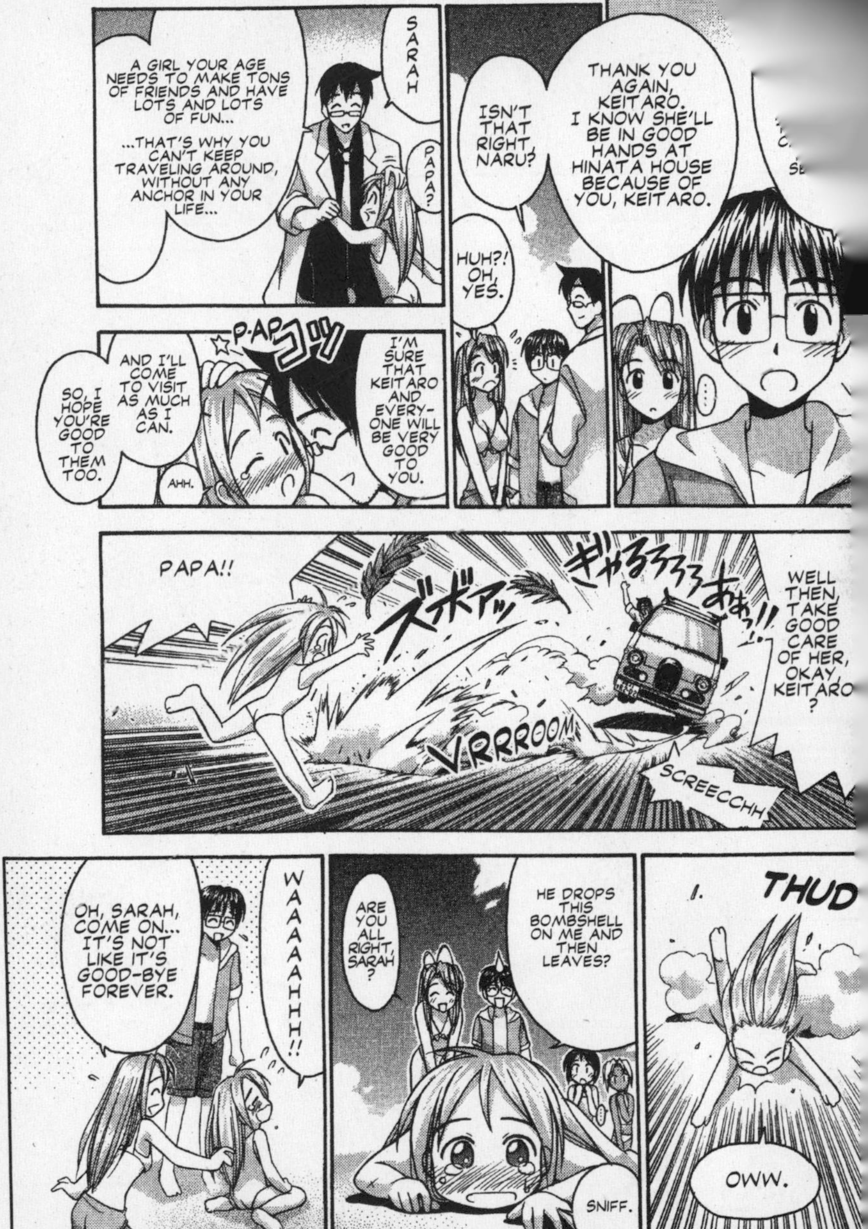
THANK YOU AGAIN, KEITARO. I KNOW SHE'LL BE IN GOOD HANDS AT HINATA HOUSE BECAUSE OF YOU, KEITARO.
...
ISN'T THAT RIGHT, NARU?
HUH?! OH, YES.
SARAH
PAPA?
A GIRL YOUR AGE NEEDS TO MAKE TONS OF FRIENDS AND HAVE LOTS AND LOTS OF FUN...
...THAT'S WHY YOU CAN'T KEEP TRAVELING AROUND, WITHOUT ANY ANCHOR IN YOUR LIFE...
I'M SURE THAT KEITARO AND EVERYONE WILL BE VERY GOOD TO YOU.
P-AP
AND I'LL COME TO VISIT AS MUCH AS I CAN.
SO, I HOPE YOU'RE GOOD TO THEM TOO.
AHH.
WELL THEN, TAKE GOOD CARE OF HER, OKAY, KEITARO?
SCREECCHH
VRRROOM
PAPA!!
THUD
OWW.
HE DROPS THIS BOMBSHELL ON ME AND THEN LEAVES?
ARE YOU ALL RIGHT, SARAH?
SNIFF.
WAAAAAAHHH!!
OH, SARAH, COME ON... IT'S NOT LIKE IT'S GOOD-BYE FOREVER.

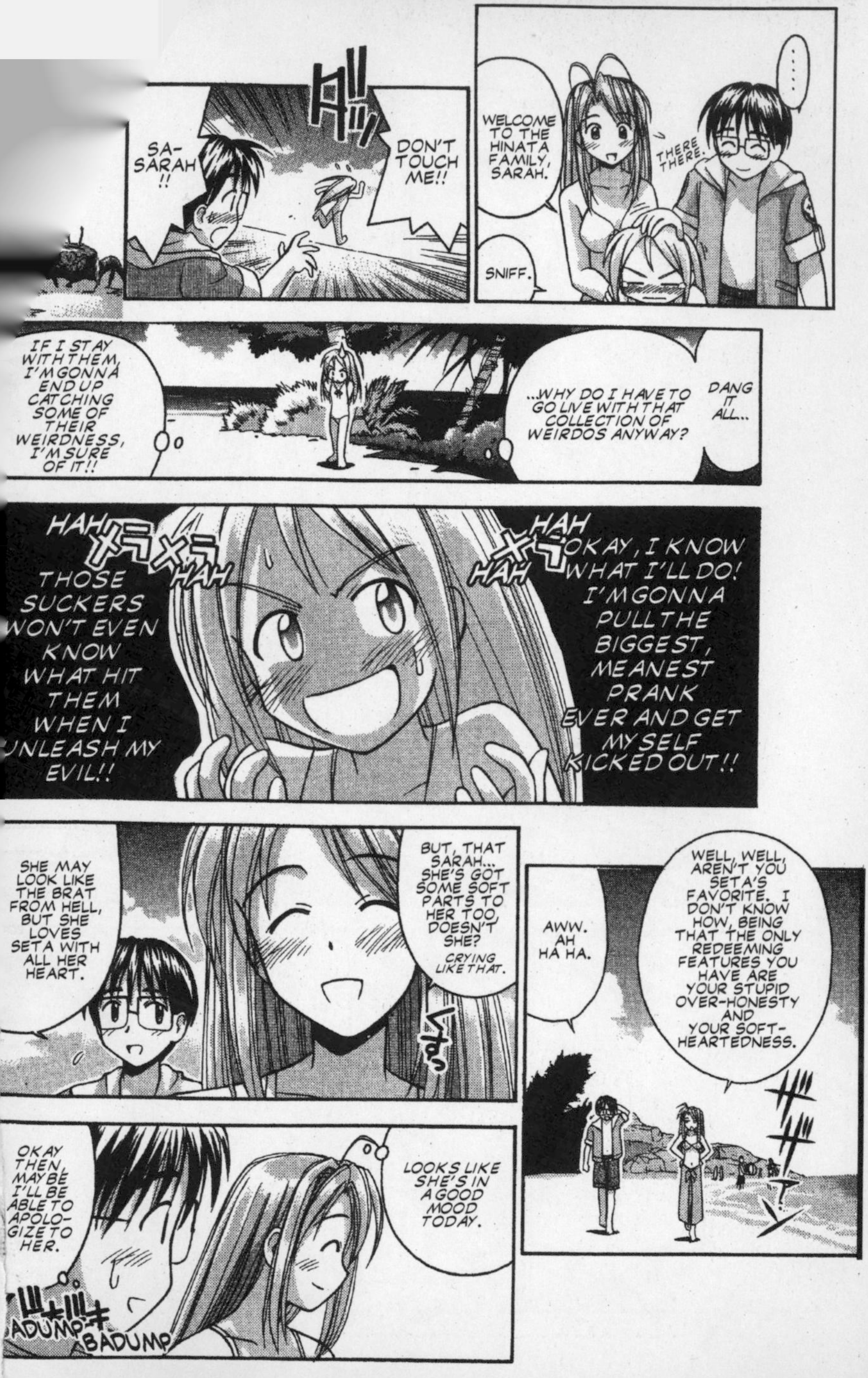
......
WELCOME TO THE HINATA FAMILY, SARAH.
THERE THERE.
SNIFF.
DON'T TOUCH ME!!
SA-SARAH!!
DANG IT ALL...
...WHY DO I HAVE TO GO LIVE WITH THAT COLLECTION OF WEIRDOS ANYWAY?
IF I STAY WITH THEM, I'M GONNA END UP CATCHING SOME OF THEIR WEIRDNESS, I'M SURE OF IT!!
HAH HAH
OKAY, I KNOW WHAT I'LL DO! I'M GONNA PULL THE BIGGEST, MEANEST PRANK EVER AND GET MYSELF KICKED OUT!!
HAH HAH
THOSE SUCKERS WON'T EVEN KNOW WHAT HIT THEM WHEN I UNLEASH MY EVIL!!
WELL, WELL, AREN'T YOU SETA'S FAVORITE. I DON'T KNOW HOW, BEING THAT THE ONLY REDEEMING FEATURES YOU HAVE ARE YOUR STUPID OVER-HONESTY AND YOUR SOFT-HEARTEDNESS.
AWW. AH HA HA.
BUT, THAT SARAH... SHE'S GOT SOME SOFT PARTS TO HER TOO, DOESN'T SHE?
CRYING LIKE THAT.
SHE MAY LOOK LIKE THE BRAT FROM HELL, BUT SHE LOVES SETA WITH ALL HER HEART.
LOOKS LIKE SHE'S IN A GOOD MOOD TODAY.
OKAY THEN, MAYBE I'LL BE ABLE TO APOLOGIZE TO HER.
BADUMP BADUMP

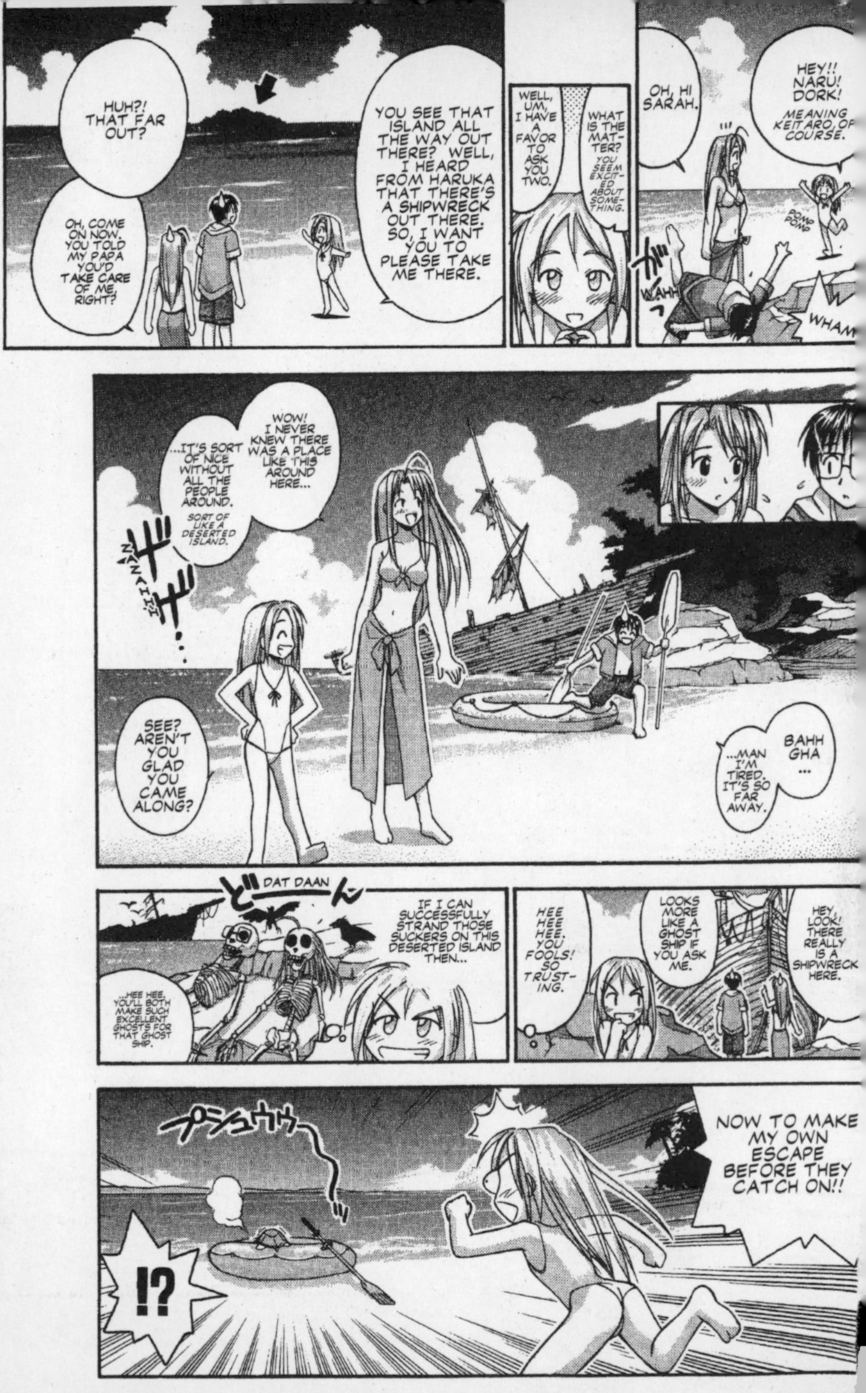
HEY!! NARU! DORK!
MEANING KEITARO, OF COURSE.
POMP POMP
WAHH
WHAM
OH, HI SARAH.
WHAT IS THE MATTER? YOU SEEM EXCITED ABOUT SOMETHING.
WELL, UM, I HAVE A FAVOR TO ASK YOU TWO.
YOU SEE THAT ISLAND ALL THE WAY OUT THERE? WELL, I HEARD FROM HARUKA THAT THERE'S A SHIPWRECK OUT THERE. SO, I WANT YOU TO PLEASE TAKE ME THERE.
HUH?! THAT FAR OUT?
OH, COME ON NOW. YOU TOLD MY PAPA YOU'D TAKE CARE OF ME, RIGHT?
BAHH GHA...
...MAN I'M TIRED. IT'S SO FAR AWAY.
WOW! I NEVER KNEW THERE WAS A PLACE LIKE THIS AROUND HERE...
...IT'S SORT OF NICE WITHOUT ALL THE PEOPLE AROUND.
SORT OF LIKE A DESERTED ISLAND.
ZAZAHHH
SEE? AREN'T YOU GLAD YOU CAME ALONG?
HEY, LOOK! THERE REALLY IS A SHIPWRECK HERE.
LOOKS MORE LIKE A GHOST SHIP IF YOU ASK ME.
HEE HEE HEE. YOU FOOLS! SO TRUSTING.
IF I CAN SUCCESSFULLY STRAND THOSE SUCKERS ON THIS DESERTED ISLAND THEN...
DAT DAAN
...HEE HEE. YOU'LL BOTH MAKE SUCH EXCELLENT GHOSTS FOR THAT GHOST SHIP.
NOW TO MAKE MY OWN ESCAPE BEFORE THEY CATCH ON!!
!?

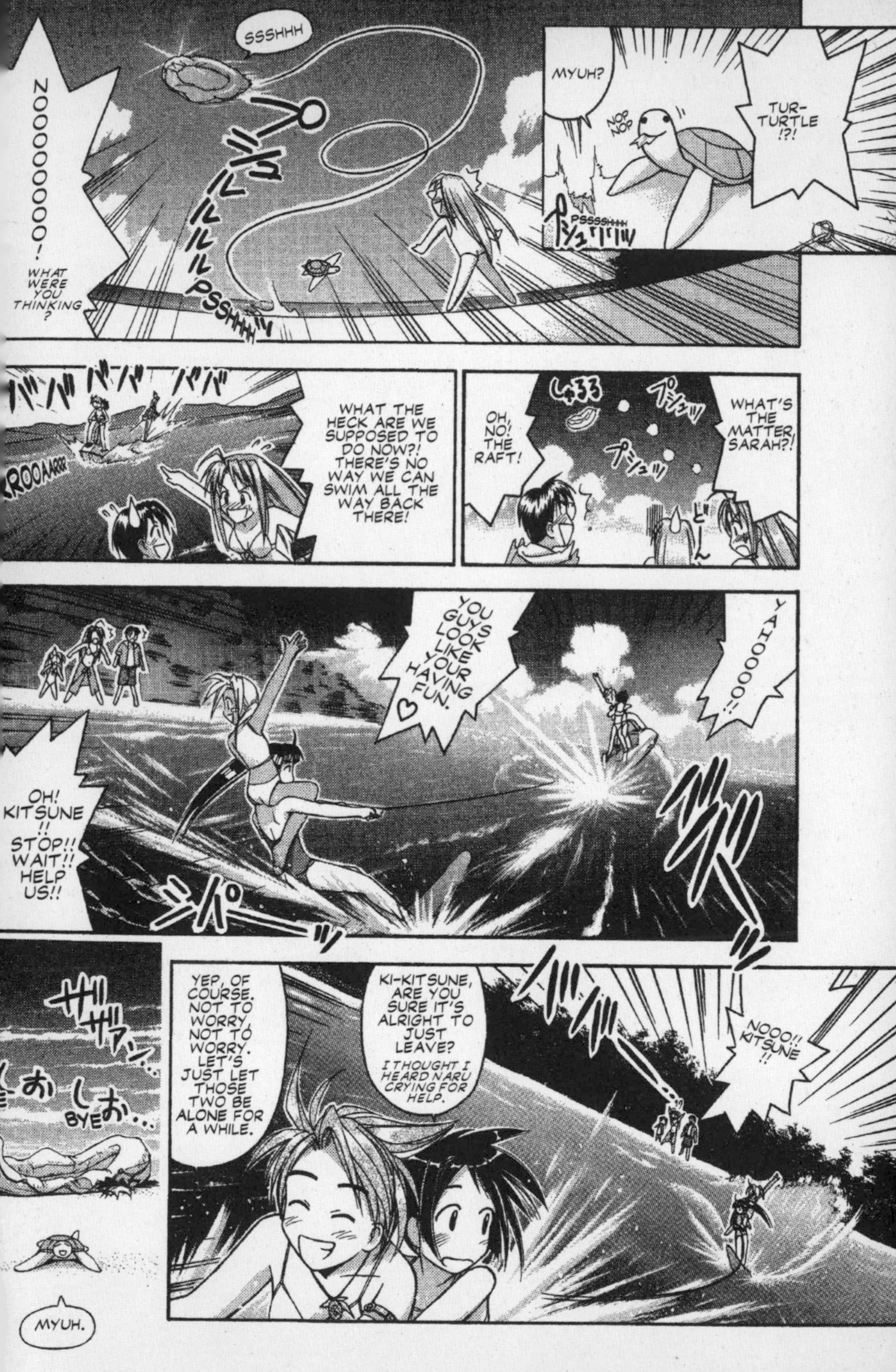

MYUH?
TUR-TURTLE !?!
NOP NOP
PSSSHHHH
SSSHHH
NOOOOOOOOOO! WHAT WERE YOU THINKING?
PSSHHHH
WHAT'S THE MATTER SARAH?!
OH, NO! THE RAFT!
WHAT THE HECK ARE WE SUPPOSED TO DO NOW?! THERE'S NO WAY WE CAN SWIM ALL THE WAY BACK THERE!
KROOAARRR
YAHOOOOO!!
YOU GUYS LOOK LIKE YOUR HAVING FUN. ♥
OH! KITSUNE!! STOP!! WAIT!! HELP US!!
NOOO!! KITSUNE!!
KI-KITSUNE, ARE YOU SURE IT'S ALRIGHT TO JUST LEAVE? I THOUGHT I HEARD NARU CRYING FOR HELP.
YEP, OF COURSE. NOT TO WORRY, NOT TO WORRY. LET'S JUST LET THOSE TWO BE ALONE FOR A WHILE.
BYE
MYUH.

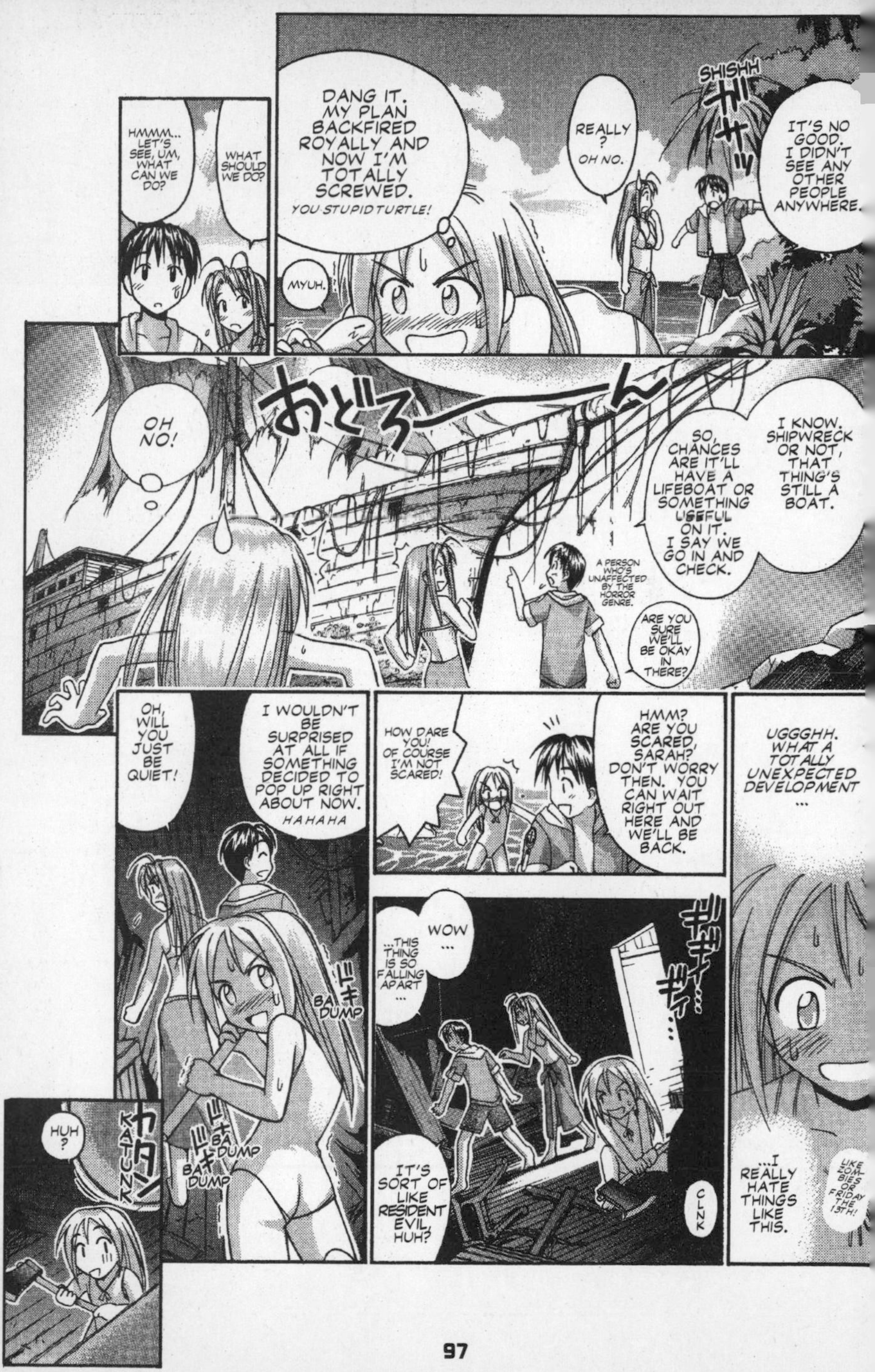
SHISHH
IT'S NO GOOD. I DIDN'T SEE ANY OTHER PEOPLE ANYWHERE.
REALLY? OH NO.
DANG IT. MY PLAN BACKFIRED ROYALLY AND NOW I'M TOTALLY SCREWED.
YOU STUPID TURTLE!
MYUH.
WHAT SHOULD WE DO?
HMMM... LET'S SEE, UM, WHAT CAN WE DO?
I KNOW. SHIPWRECK OR NOT, THAT THING'S STILL A BOAT.
SO, CHANCES ARE IT'LL HAVE A LIFEBOAT OR SOMETHING USEFUL ON IT. I SAY WE GO IN AND CHECK.
A PERSON WHO'S UNAFFECTED BY THE HORROR GENRE.
ARE YOU SURE WE'LL BE OKAY IN THERE?
おどろ───ん
OH NO!
UGGGHH. WHAT A TOTALLY UNEXPECTED DEVELOPMENT ...
...I REALLY HATE THINGS LIKE THIS.
LIKE ZOMBIES OR FRIDAY THE 13TH!
HMM? ARE YOU SCARED, SARAH? DON'T WORRY THEN. YOU CAN WAIT RIGHT OUT HERE AND WE'LL BE BACK.
HOW DARE YOU! OF COURSE I'M NOT SCARED!
WOW ...
...THIS THING IS SO FALLING APART ...
CLNK
IT'S SORT OF LIKE RESIDENT EVIL, HUH?
I WOULDN'T BE SURPRISED AT ALL IF SOMETHING DECIDED TO POP UP RIGHT ABOUT NOW.
HAHAHA
OH, WILL YOU JUST BE QUIET!
BA DUMP
BA DUMP
BA DUMP
KATUNK
HUH?

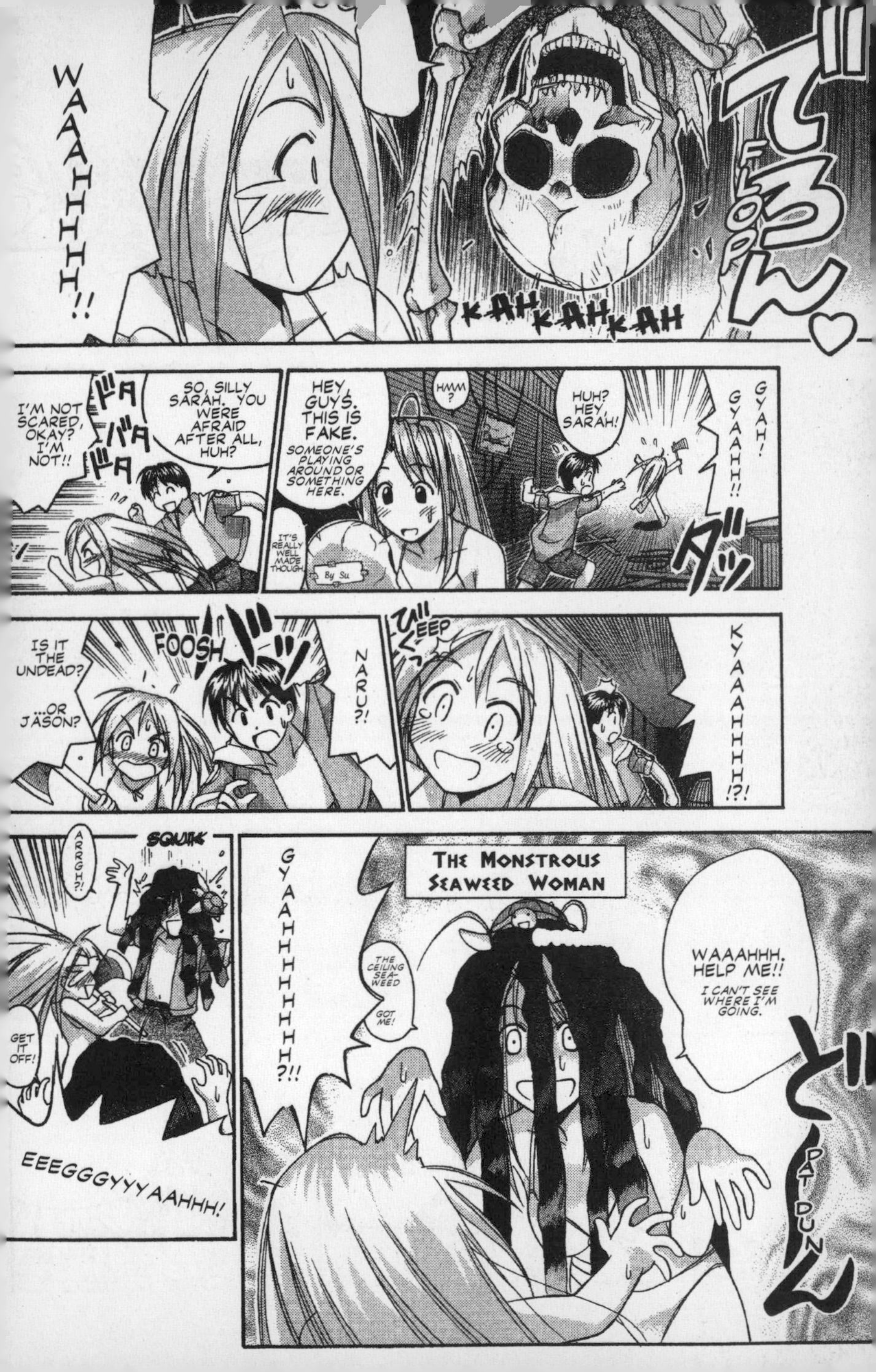
でろん♥
FLOP
KAH KAH KAH
WAAAHHHHH!!
GYAH! GYAAAHH!!
HUH? HEY, SARAH!
ダッ
HMM?
HEY, GUYS. THIS IS FAKE. SOMEONE'S PLAYING AROUND OR SOMETHING HERE.
IT'S REALLY WELL MADE THOUGH
By Su
SO, SILLY SARAH. YOU WERE AFRAID AFTER ALL, HUH?
ドタバタドタ
I'M NOT SCARED, OKAY? I'M NOT!!
KYAAAAHHHH!?!
EEP
NARU?!
FOOSH
IS IT THE UNDEAD? ...OR JASON?
PAT DUN
WAAAHHH. HELP ME!! I CAN'T SEE WHERE I'M GOING.
THE MONSTROUS SEAWEED WOMAN
GYAAHHHHHHHH?!!
THE CEILING SEAWEED GOT ME!
SQUIK
ARRGH?!
GET IT OFF!
EEEGGGYYYAAHHH!

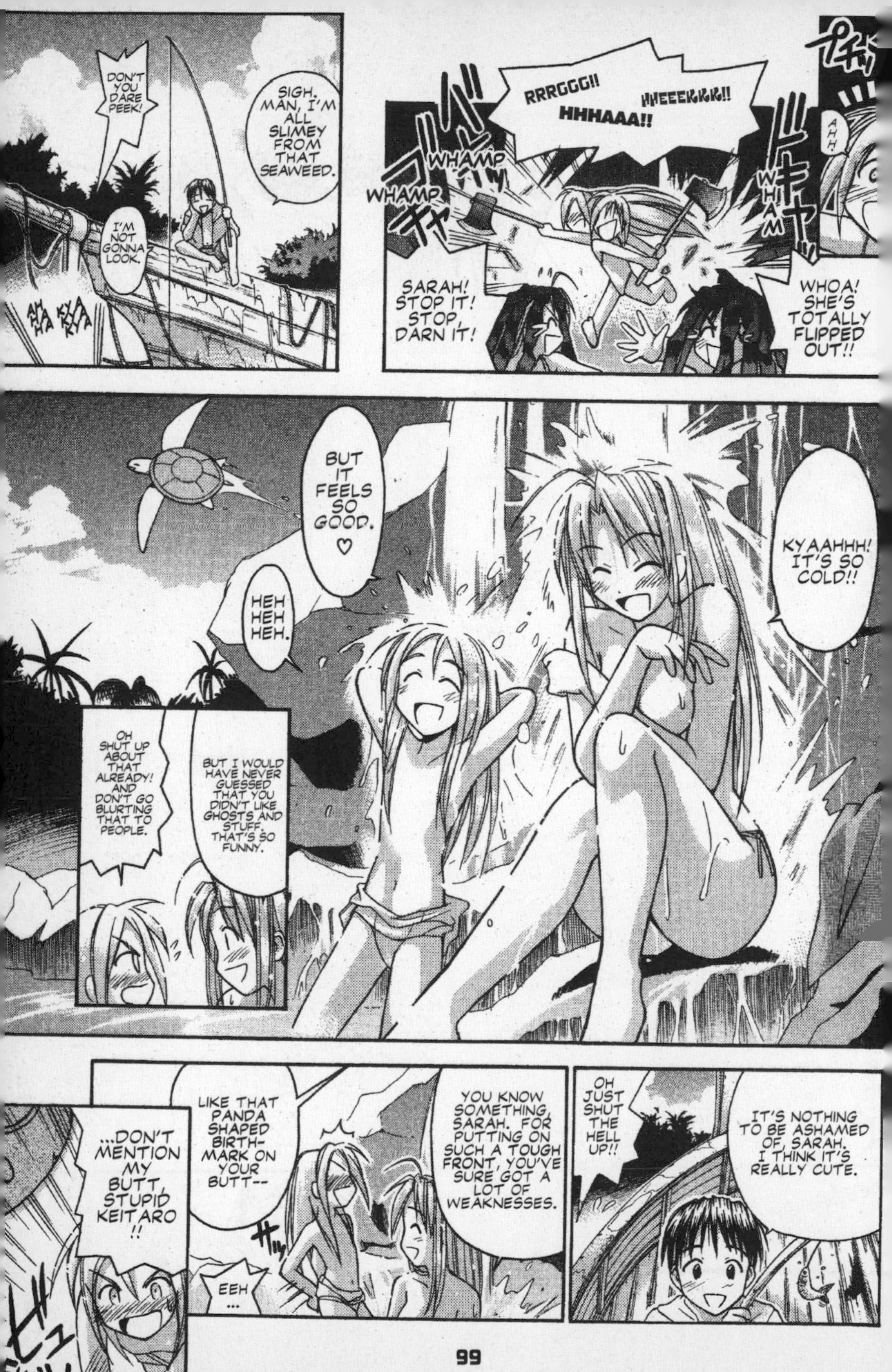
AHH!
RRRGGG!!
HHEEEKKKK!!
HHHAAA!!
WHAM
WHAMP
WHAMP
WHOA! SHE'S TOTALLY FLIPPED OUT!!
SARAH! STOP IT! STOP, DARN IT!
SIGH. MAN, I'M ALL SLIMEY FROM THAT SEAWEED.
DON'T YOU DARE PEEK!
I'M NOT GONNA LOOK.
AH HA KYA HA KYA
KYAAHHH! IT'S SO COLD!!
BUT IT FEELS SO GOOD. ♡
HEH HEH HEH.
BUT I WOULD HAVE NEVER GUESSED THAT YOU DIDN'T LIKE GHOSTS AND STUFF. THAT'S SO FUNNY.
OH SHUT UP ABOUT THAT ALREADY! AND DON'T GO BLURTING THAT TO PEOPLE.
IT'S NOTHING TO BE ASHAMED OF, SARAH. I THINK IT'S REALLY CUTE.
OH JUST SHUT THE HELL UP!!
YOU KNOW SOMETHING, SARAH. FOR PUTTING ON SUCH A TOUGH FRONT, YOU'VE SURE GOT A LOT OF WEAKNESSES.
LIKE THAT PANDA SHAPED BIRTH-MARK ON YOUR BUTT--
EEH ...
...DON'T MENTION MY BUTT, STUPID KEITARO!!

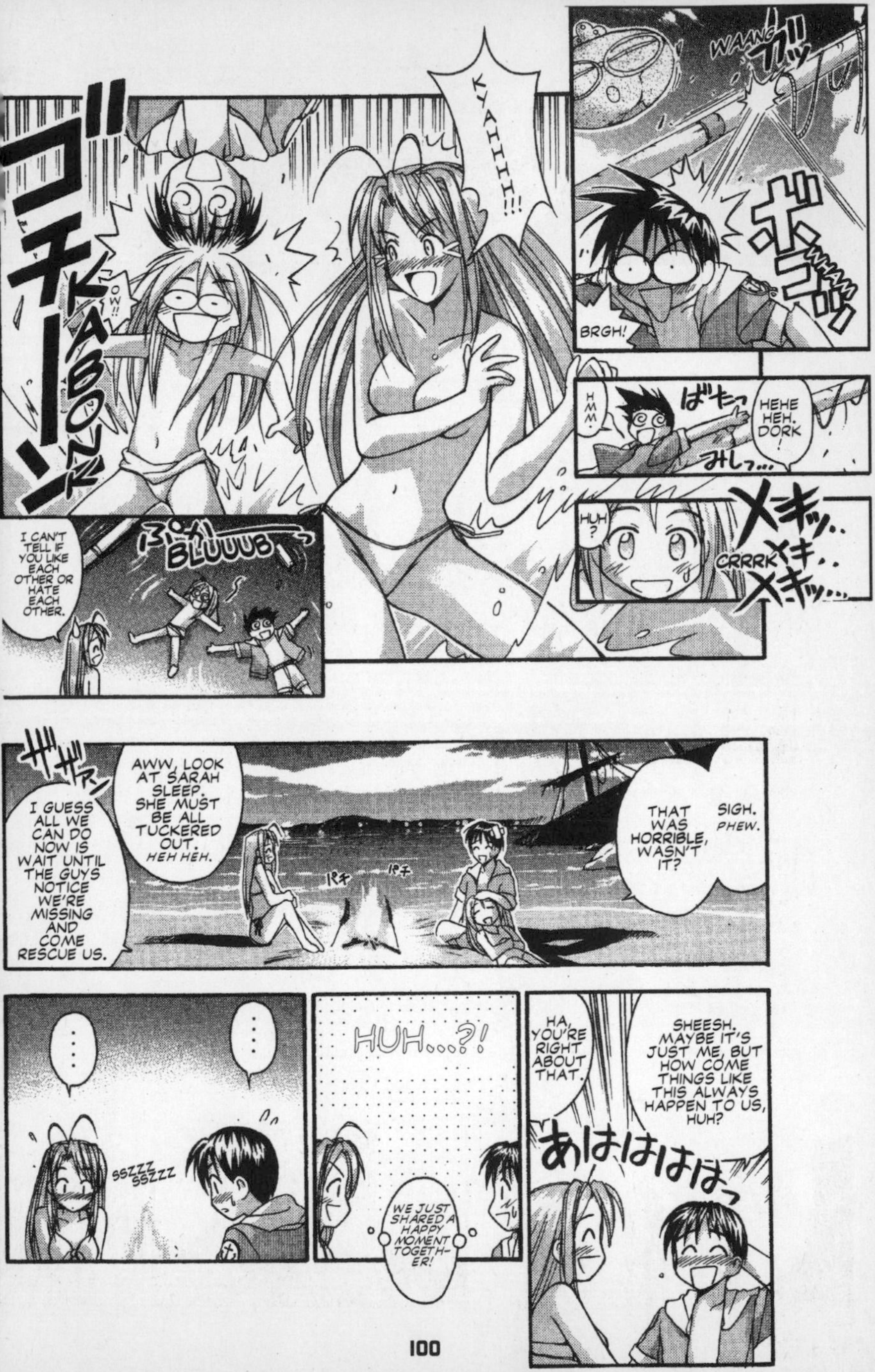
WAANG
ブッ
WHAM
ボコッ
BRGH!
HMM.
HEHE HEH. DORK!
ばキっ
みしっ...
HUH?
メキッ..
CRRRK
メキ..
メキッ...
KYAHHHH!!!
ゴチーン
KABONK
OW!!
BLUUUB
I CAN'T TELL IF YOU LIKE EACH OTHER OR HATE EACH OTHER.
ザザァン
SIGH. PHEW.
THAT WAS HORRIBLE, WASN'T IT?
AWW, LOOK AT SARAH SLEEP. SHE MUST BE ALL TUCKERED OUT. HEH HEH.
I GUESS ALL WE CAN DO NOW IS WAIT UNTIL THE GUYS NOTICE WE'RE MISSING AND COME RESCUE US.
パチ
パチ
SHEESH. MAYBE IT'S JUST ME, BUT HOW COME THINGS LIKE THIS ALWAYS HAPPEN TO US, HUH?
HA, YOU'RE RIGHT ABOUT THAT.
あははははっ
HUH...?!
WE JUST SHARED A HAPPY MOMENT TOGETH-ER!
...
...
SSZZZ SSZZZ

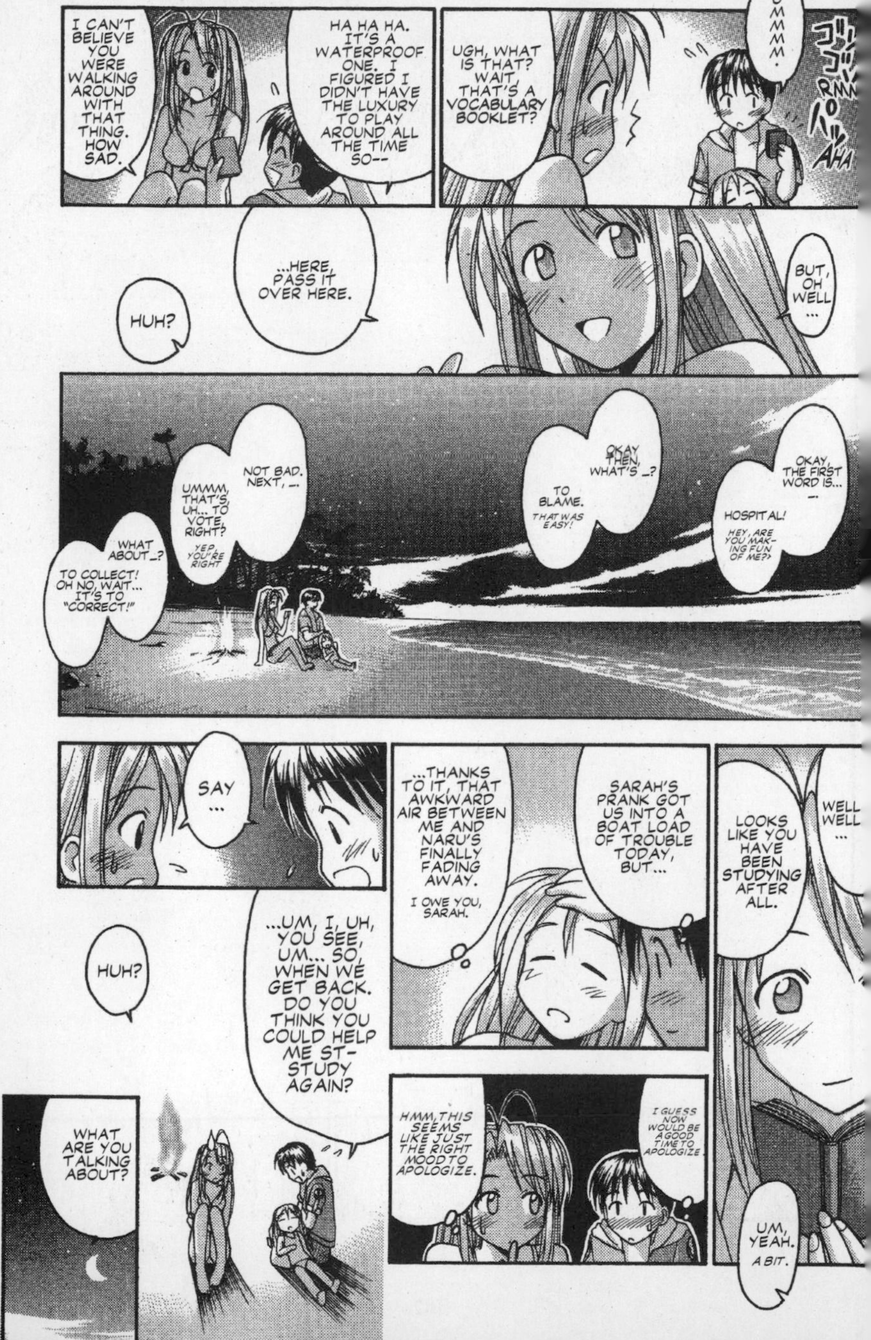
UMMMM.
RMM
AHA
UGH, WHAT IS THAT? WAIT, THAT'S A VOCABULARY BOOKLET?
HA HA HA. IT'S A WATERPROOF ONE. I FIGURED I DIDN'T HAVE THE LUXURY TO PLAY AROUND ALL THE TIME SO--
I CAN'T BELIEVE YOU WERE WALKING AROUND WITH THAT THING. HOW SAD.
BUT, OH WELL...
...HERE, PASS IT OVER HERE.
HUH?
OKAY, THE FIRST WORD IS... _
HOSPITAL!
HEY, ARE YOU MAKING FUN OF ME?>
OKAY THEN, WHAT'S _?
TO BLAME.
THAT WAS EASY!
NOT BAD. NEXT, _.
UMMM, THAT'S, UH... TO VOTE, RIGHT?
YEP, YOU'RE RIGHT
WHAT ABOUT _?
TO COLLECT! OH NO, WAIT... IT'S TO "CORRECT!"
WELL WELL...
LOOKS LIKE YOU HAVE BEEN STUDYING AFTER ALL.
UM, YEAH.
A BIT.
SARAH'S PRANK GOT US INTO A BOAT LOAD OF TROUBLE TODAY, BUT...
...THANKS TO IT, THAT AWKWARD AIR BETWEEN ME AND NARU'S FINALLY FADING AWAY.
I OWE YOU, SARAH.
I GUESS NOW WOULD BE A GOOD TIME TO APOLOGIZE
HMM, THIS SEEMS LIKE JUST THE RIGHT MOOD TO APOLOGIZE.
SAY...
...UM, I, UH, YOU SEE, UM... SO, WHEN WE GET BACK. DO YOU THINK YOU COULD HELP ME ST-STUDY AGAIN?
HUH?
WHAT ARE YOU TALKING ABOUT?

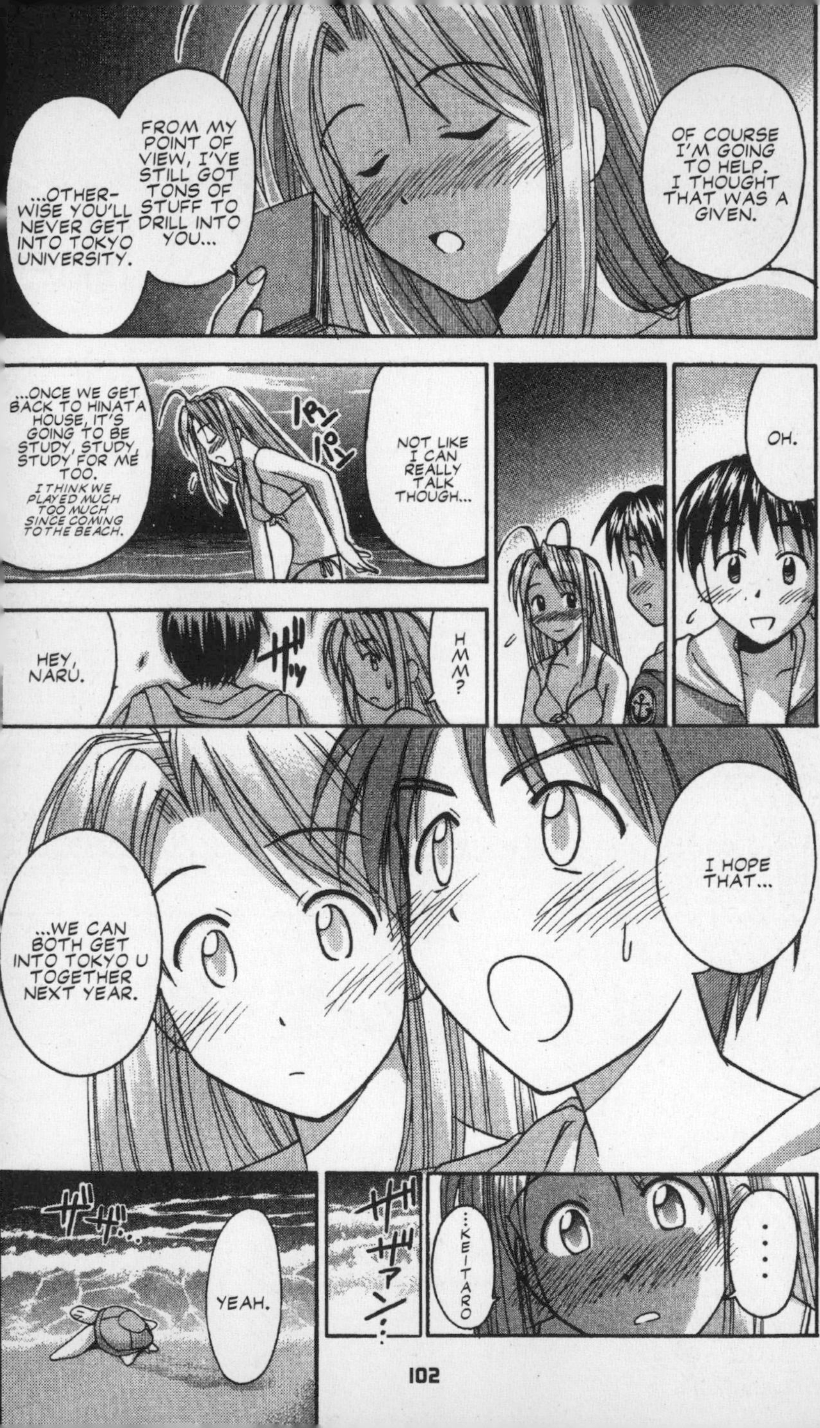
OF COURSE I'M GOING TO HELP. I THOUGHT THAT WAS A GIVEN.
FROM MY POINT OF VIEW, I'VE STILL GOT TONS OF STUFF TO DRILL INTO YOU...
...OTHER-WISE YOU'LL NEVER GET INTO TOKYO UNIVERSITY.
OH.
NOT LIKE I CAN REALLY TALK THOUGH...
...ONCE WE GET BACK TO HINATA HOUSE, IT'S GOING TO BE STUDY, STUDY, STUDY FOR ME TOO.
I THINK WE PLAYED MUCH TOO MUCH SINCE COMING TO THE BEACH.
HMM?
HEY, NARU.
I HOPE THAT...
...WE CAN BOTH GET INTO TOKYO U TOGETHER NEXT YEAR.
....
...KEITARO
ザザァン…
YEAH.
ザザ…

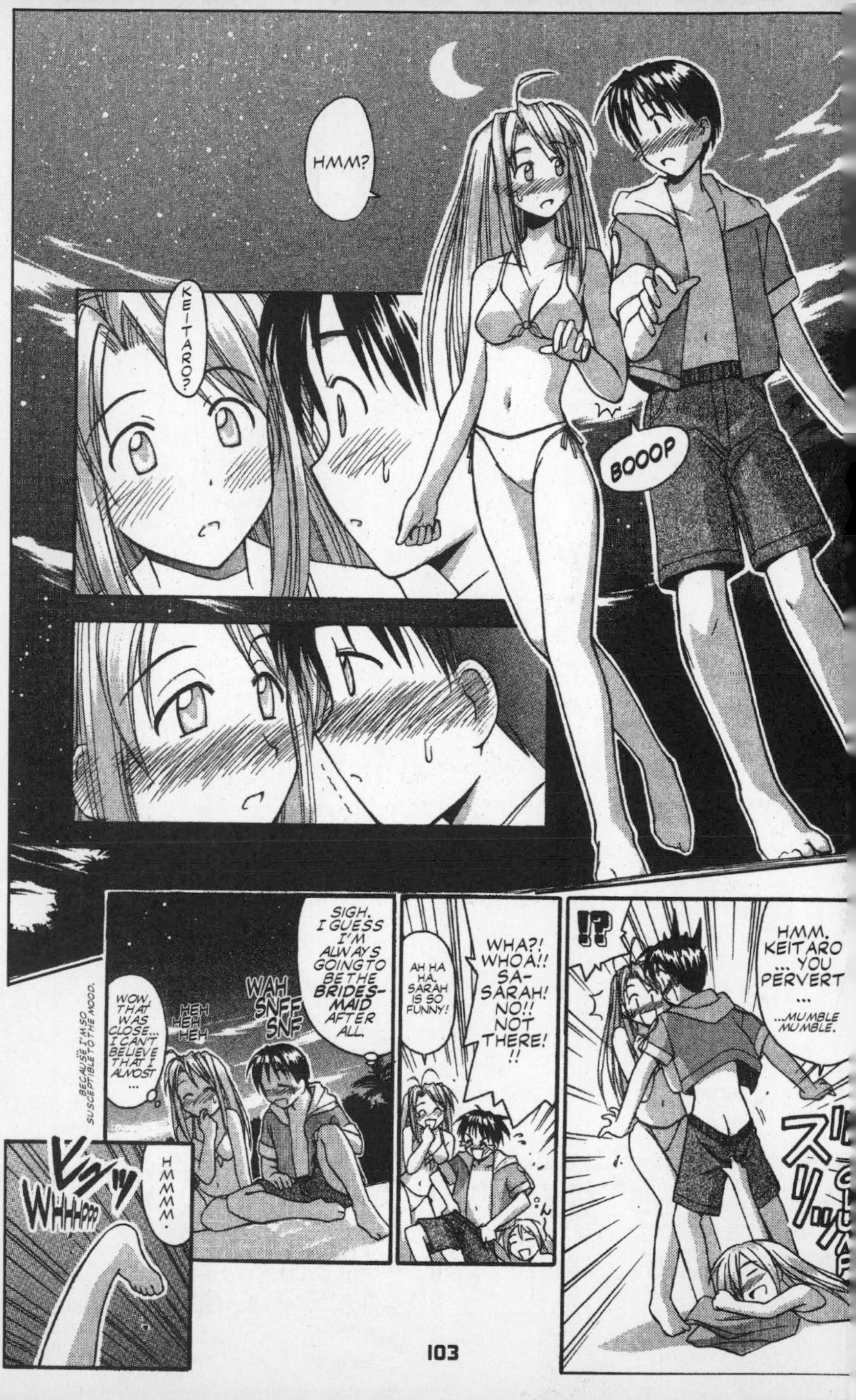
HMM?
KEI-TARO?
BOOOP
!?
HMM. KEITARO ... YOU PERVERT ...
...MUMBLE MUMBLE.
スルッ
WHA?! WHOA!! SA-SARAH! NO!! NOT THERE! !!
AH HA HA. SARAH IS SO FUNNY!
SIGH. I GUESS I'M ALWAYS GOING TO BE THE BRIDES-MAID AFTER ALL.
WAH SNFF SNF
HEH HEH HEH
WOW, THAT WAS CLOSE... I CAN'T BELIEVE THAT I ALMOST ...
...BECAUSE I'M SO SUSCEPTIBLE TO THE MOOD.
HMMMM.
ビシッ
WHHHPPP

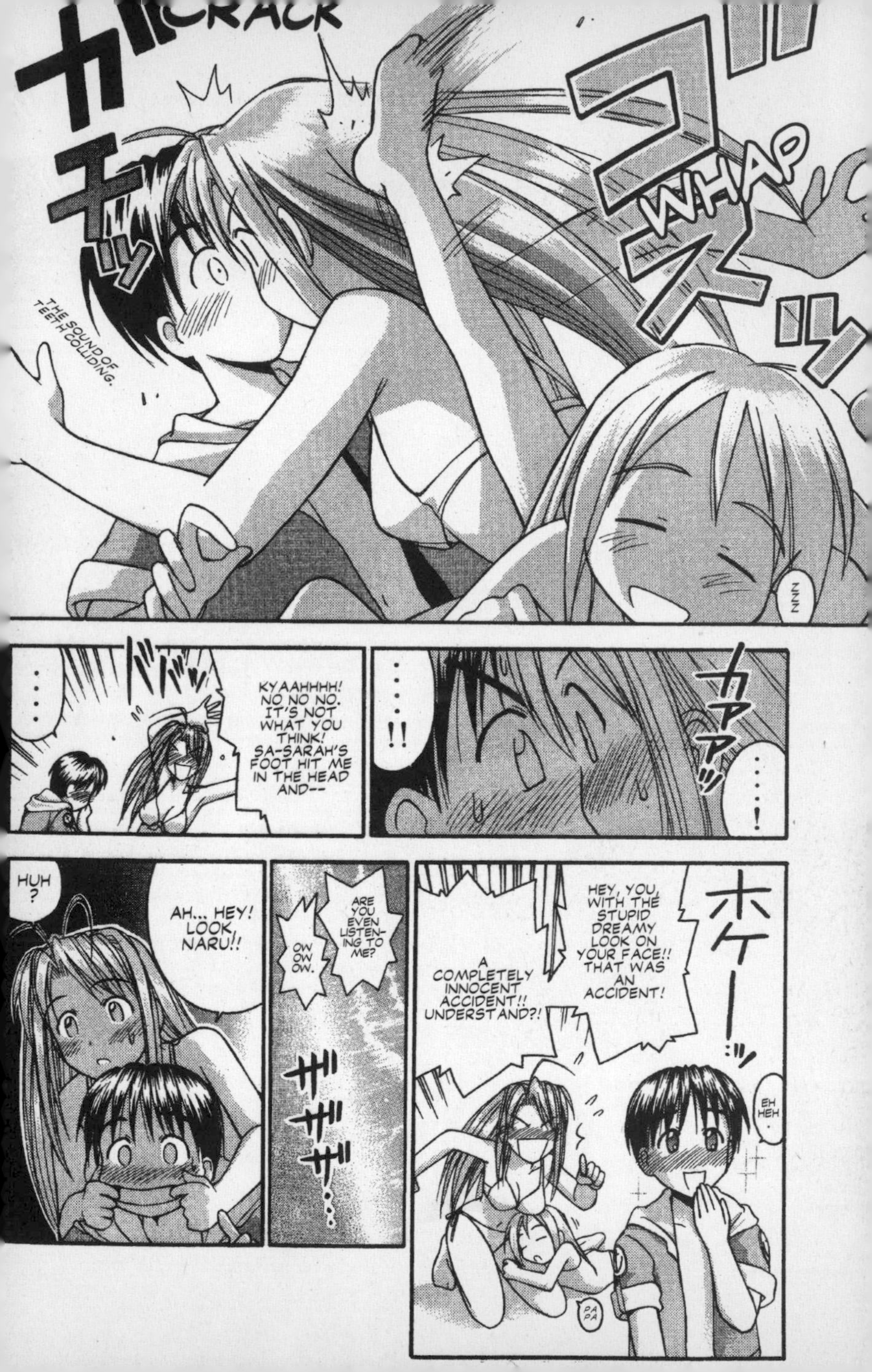
WHAP
CRACK
THE SOUND OF TEETH COLLIDING.
ZZZ
....!
....!!
KYAAHHHH! NO NO NO. IT'S NOT WHAT YOU THINK! SA-SARAH'S FOOT HIT ME IN THE HEAD AND--
....
HEY, YOU, WITH THE STUPID DREAMY LOOK ON YOUR FACE!! THAT WAS AN ACCIDENT!
A COMPLETELY INNOCENT ACCIDENT!! UNDERSTAND?!
EH HEH.
PA PA
ARE YOU EVEN LISTENING TO ME?
OW OW OW.
AH... HEY! LOOK, NARU!!
HUH?

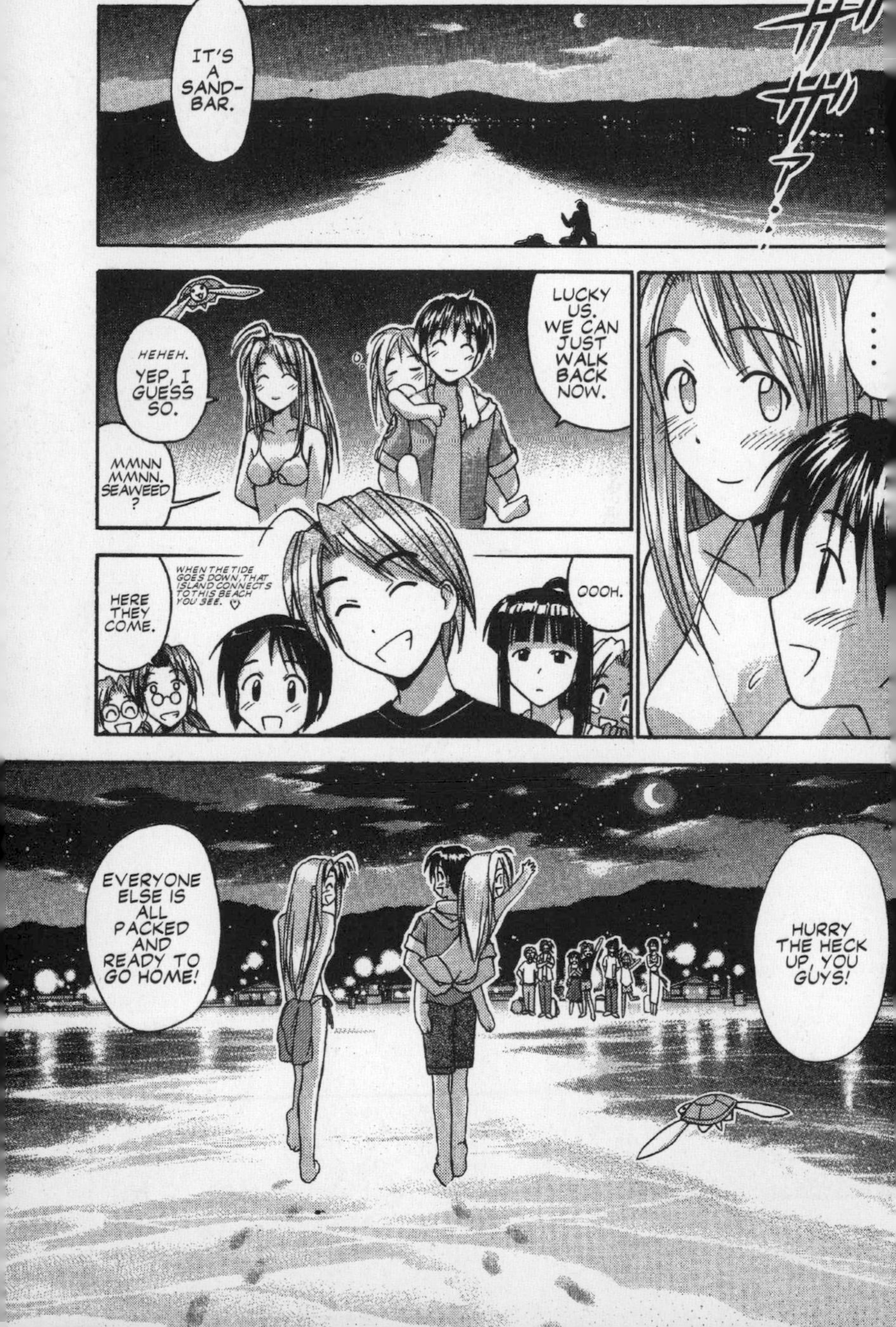
IT'S A SANDBAR.
....
LUCKY US. WE CAN JUST WALK BACK NOW.
HEHEH. YEP, I GUESS SO.
MMNN MMNN. SEAWEED?
OOOH.
WHEN THE TIDE GOES DOWN, THAT ISLAND CONNECTS TO THIS BEACH YOU SEE. ♡
HERE THEY COME.
HURRY THE HECK UP, YOU GUYS!
EVERYONE ELSE IS ALL PACKED AND READY TO GO HOME!

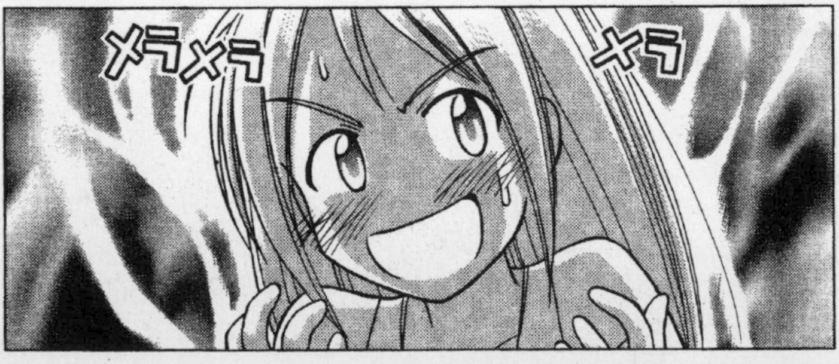
メラメラ
メラ

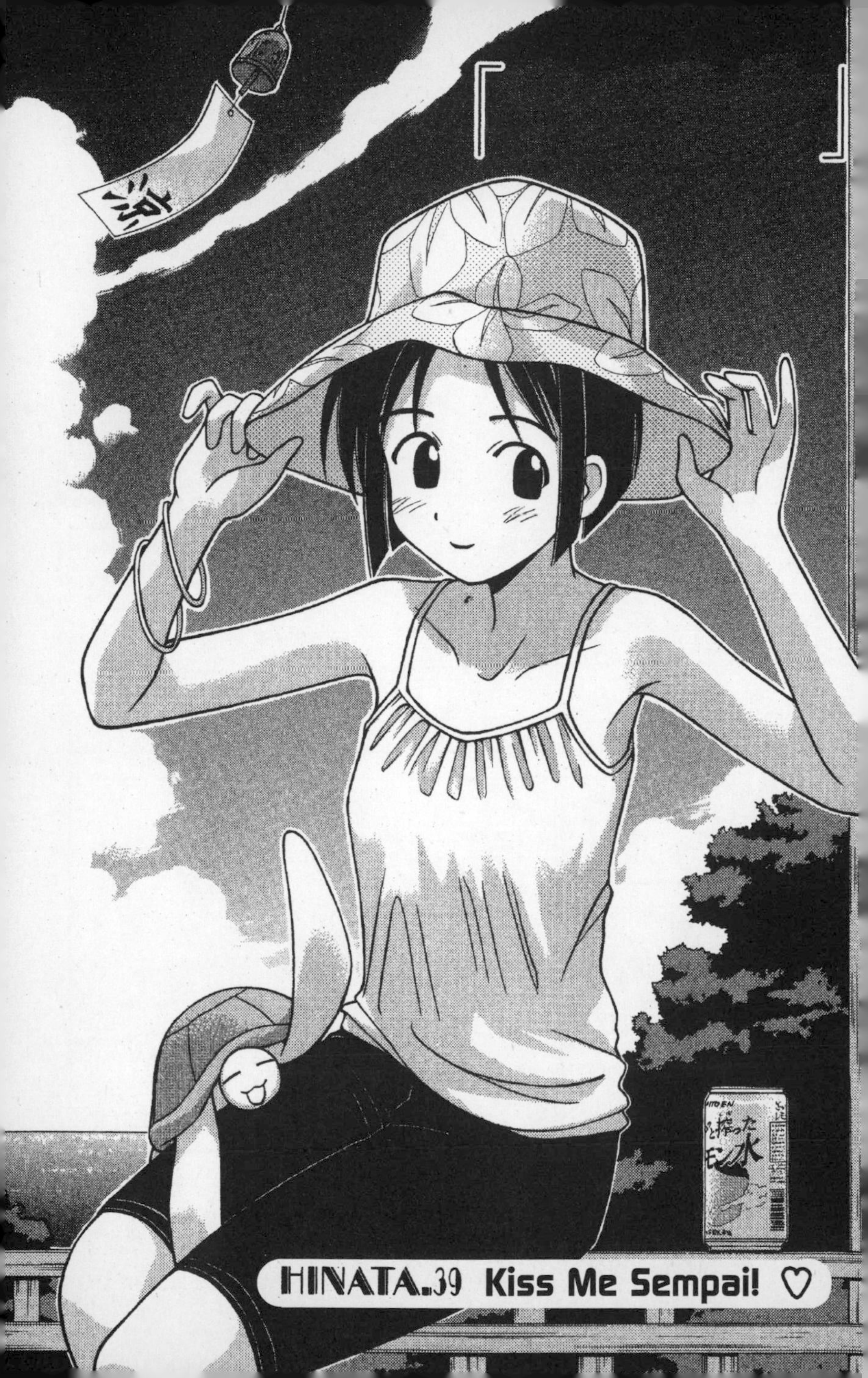
涼
HINATA.39 Kiss Me Sempai! ♡

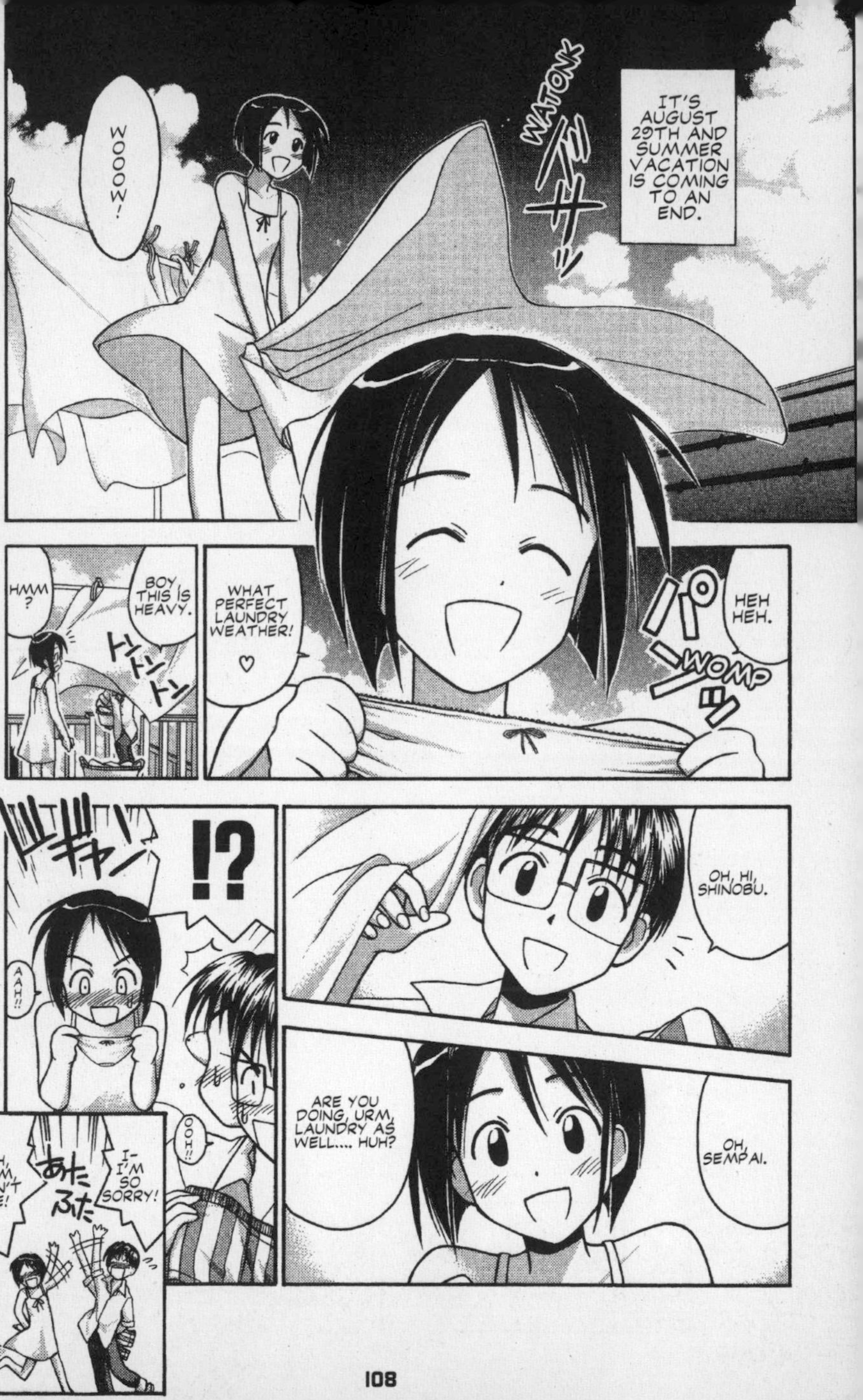
IT'S AUGUST 29TH AND SUMMER VACATION IS COMING TO AN END.
WATONK
WOOOW!
HEH HEH.
パーンッ
WOMP
WHAT PERFECT LAUNDRY WEATHER! ♡
BOY THIS IS HEAVY.
HMM?
トントントン
OH, HI, SHINOBU.
OH, SEMPAI.
ARE YOU DOING, URM, LAUNDRY AS WELL.... HUH?
ドギャーン!
!?
AAH!!
OOH!!
I-I'M SO SORRY!
あたふた
OH, URM, DON'T BE!

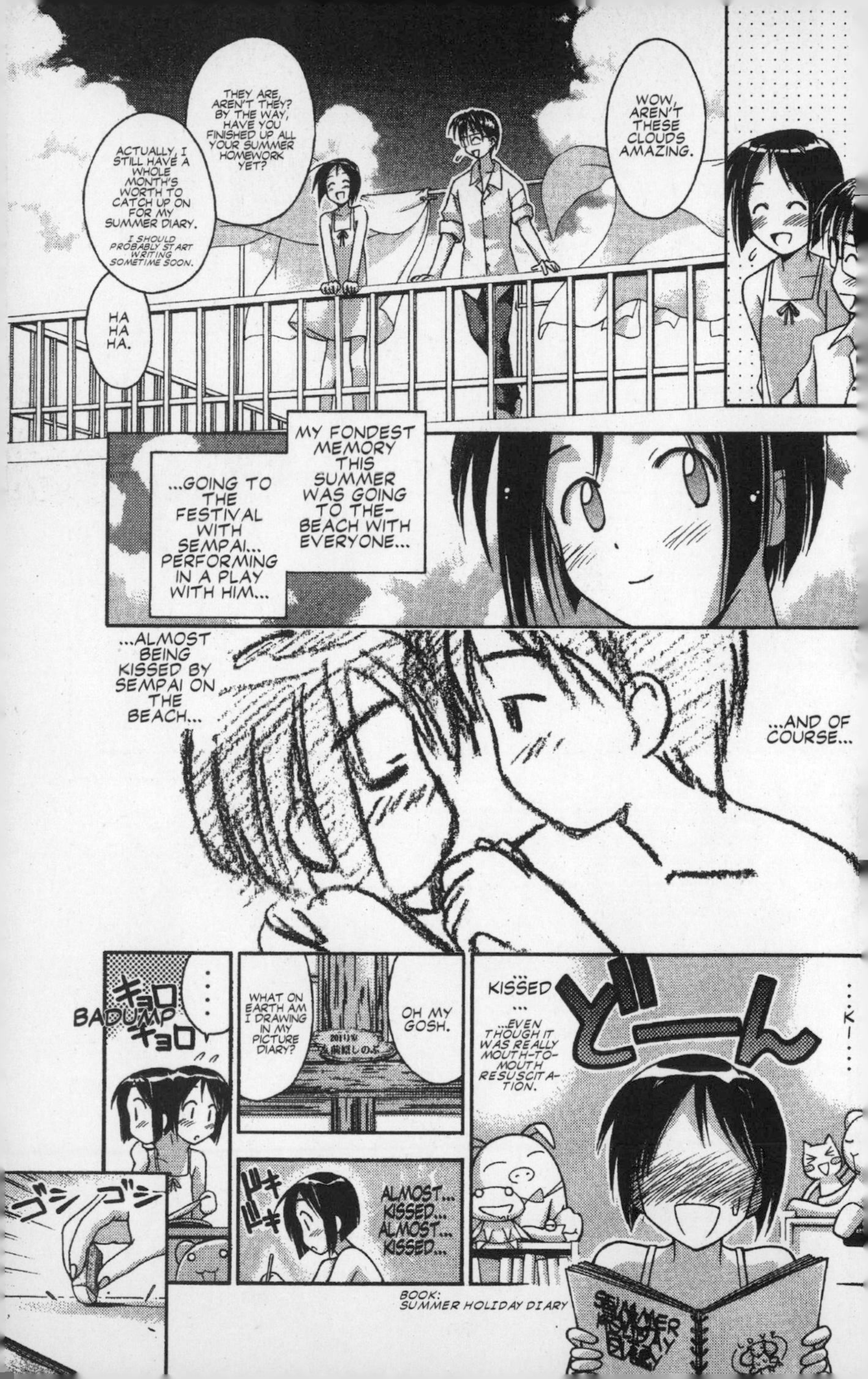
WOW, AREN'T THESE CLOUDS AMAZING.
THEY ARE, AREN'T THEY? BY THE WAY, HAVE YOU FINISHED UP ALL YOUR SUMMER HOMEWORK YET?
ACTUALLY, I STILL HAVE A WHOLE MONTH'S WORTH TO CATCH UP ON FOR MY SUMMER DIARY.
I SHOULD PROBABLY START WRITING SOMETIME SOON.
HA HA HA.
MY FONDEST MEMORY THIS SUMMER WAS GOING TO THE BEACH WITH EVERYONE...
...GOING TO THE FESTIVAL WITH SEMPAI... PERFORMING IN A PLAY WITH HIM...
...ALMOST BEING KISSED BY SEMPAI ON THE BEACH...
...AND OF COURSE...
...KI...
...KISSED...
...EVEN THOUGH IT WAS REALLY MOUTH-TO-MOUTH RESUSCITATION.
どーん
BOOK: SUMMER HOLIDAY DIARY
OH MY GOSH.
WHAT ON EARTH AM I DRAWING IN MY PICTURE DIARY?
....
キョロ キョロ
BADUMP
ドキ ドキ
ALMOST... KISSED... ALMOST... KISSED...
ゴシ ゴシ

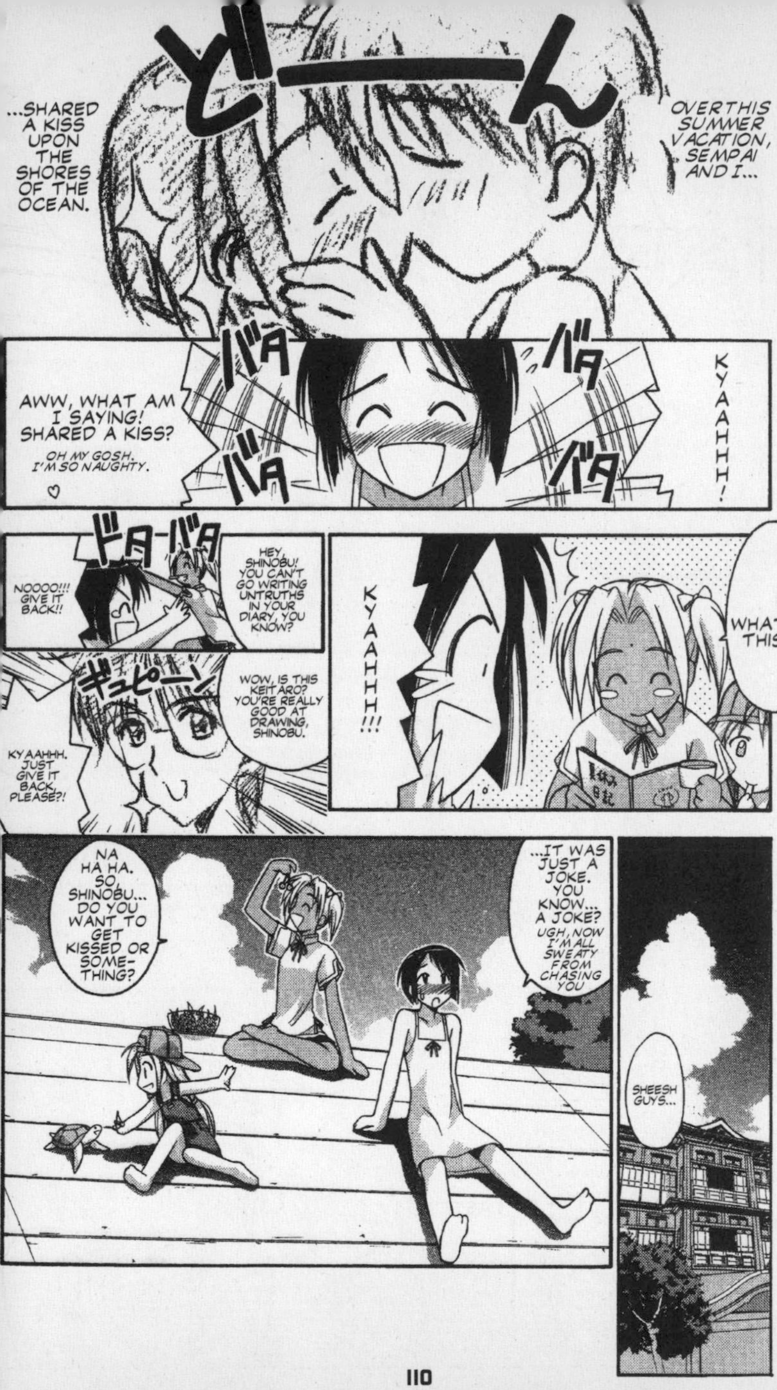
どーん
OVER THIS SUMMER VACATION, SEMPAI AND I...
...SHARED A KISS UPON THE SHORES OF THE OCEAN.
KYAAHHH!
バタ
バタ
バタ
バタ
AWW, WHAT AM I SAYING! SHARED A KISS?
OH MY GOSH. I'M SO NAUGHTY. ♡
WHAT'S THIS?
KYAAHHH!!!
HEY, SHINOBU! YOU CAN'T GO WRITING UNTRUTHS IN YOUR DIARY, YOU KNOW?
ドタバタ
NOOOO!!! GIVE IT BACK!!
WOW, IS THIS KEITARO? YOU'RE REALLY GOOD AT DRAWING, SHINOBU.
ギュピーン
KYAAHHH. JUST GIVE IT BACK, PLEASE?!
SHEESH GUYS...
...IT WAS JUST A JOKE. YOU KNOW... A JOKE?
UGH, NOW I'M ALL SWEATY FROM CHASING YOU
NA HA HA. SO, SHINOBU... DO YOU WANT TO GET KISSED OR SOMETHING?

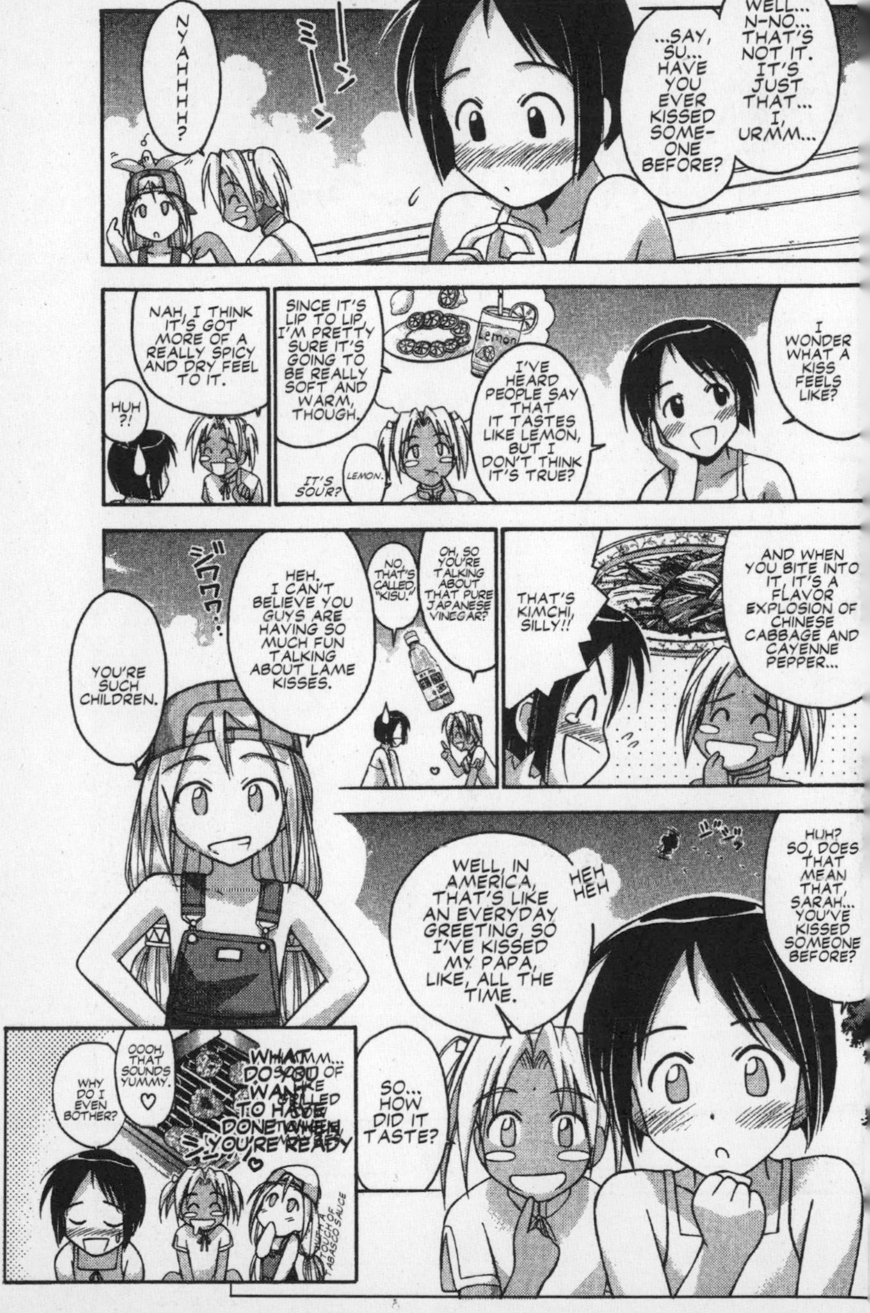
WELL... N-NO... THAT'S NOT IT. IT'S JUST THAT... I, URMM...
...SAY, SU... HAVE YOU EVER KISSED SOMEONE BEFORE?
NYAHHHH?
I WONDER WHAT A KISS FEELS LIKE?
I'VE HEARD PEOPLE SAY THAT IT TASTES LIKE LEMON, BUT I DON'T THINK IT'S TRUE?
SINCE IT'S LIP TO LIP, I'M PRETTY SURE IT'S GOING TO BE REALLY SOFT AND WARM, THOUGH.
Lemon
LEMON.
IT'S SOUR?
NAH, I THINK IT'S GOT MORE OF A REALLY SPICY AND DRY FEEL TO IT.
HUH?!
AND WHEN YOU BITE INTO IT, IT'S A FLAVOR EXPLOSION OF CHINESE CABBAGE AND CAYENNE PEPPER...
THAT'S KIMCHI, SILLY!!
OH, SO YOU'RE TALKING ABOUT THAT PURE JAPANESE VINEGAR?
NO, THAT'S CALLED "KISU."
HEH. I CAN'T BELIEVE YOU GUYS ARE HAVING SO MUCH FUN TALKING ABOUT LAME KISSES.
YOU'RE SUCH CHILDREN.
HUH? SO, DOES THAT MEAN THAT, SARAH... YOU'VE KISSED SOMEONE BEFORE?
HEH HEH
WELL, IN AMERICA, THAT'S LIKE AN EVERYDAY GREETING, SO I'VE KISSED MY PAPA, LIKE, ALL THE TIME.
SO... HOW DID IT TASTE?
WHAT DO YOU WANT TO HAVE DONE WHEN YOU'RE READY
UMM... SORT OF LIKE GRILLED
WITH A TOUCH OF TABASCO SAUCE
OOOH, THAT SOUNDS YUMMY. ♡
WHY DO I EVEN BOTHER?

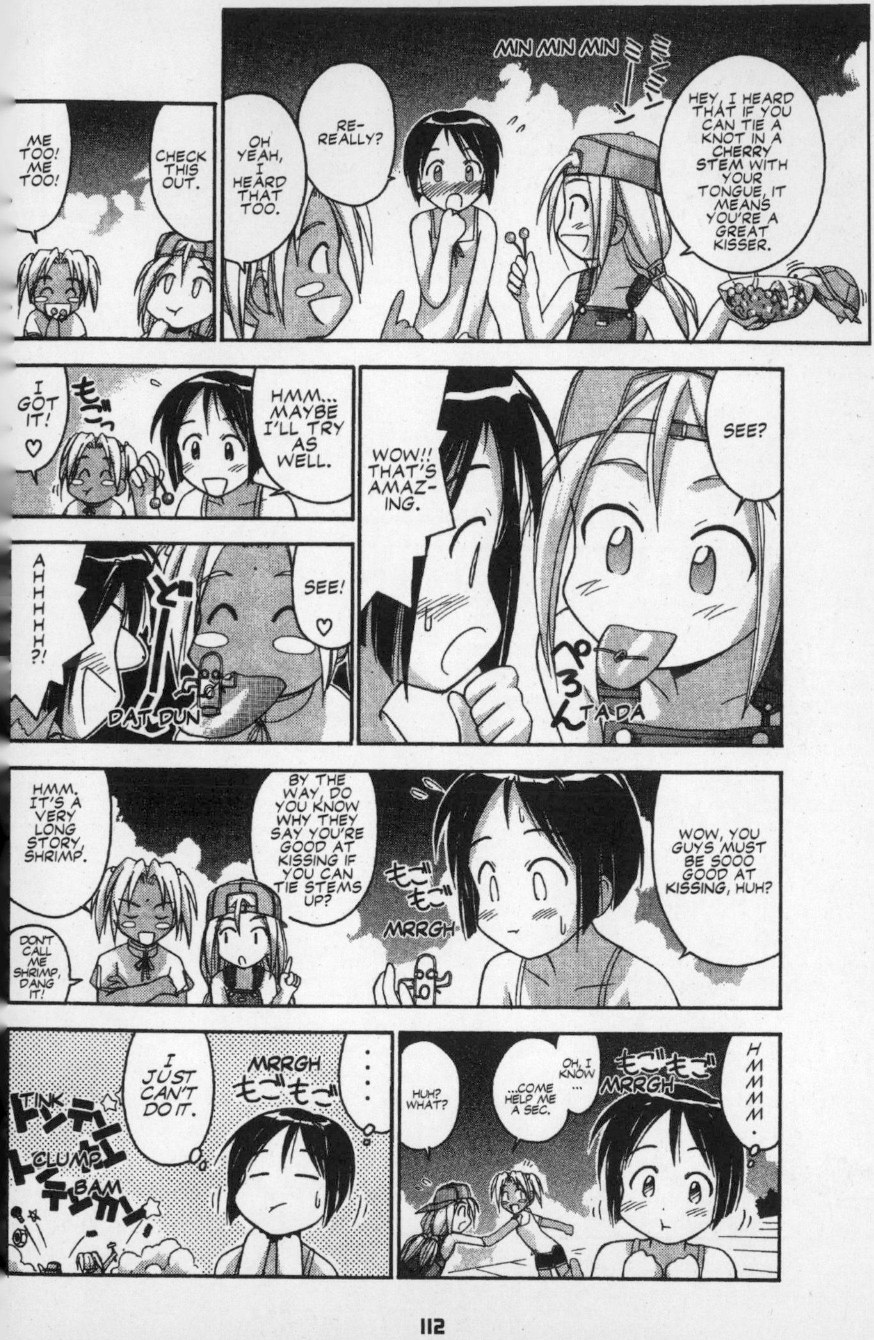
MIN MIN MIN
HEY, I HEARD THAT IF YOU CAN TIE A KNOT IN A CHERRY STEM WITH YOUR TONGUE, IT MEANS YOU'RE A GREAT KISSER.
RE-REALLY?
OH YEAH, I HEARD THAT TOO.
CHECK THIS OUT.
ME TOO! ME TOO!
SEE?
WOW!! THAT'S AMAZ-ING.
ぺろん
TA DA
HMM... MAYBE I'LL TRY AS WELL.
もごっ
I GOT IT! ♡
SEE! ♡
DAT DUN
AHHHHH?!
WOW, YOU GUYS MUST BE SOOO GOOD AT KISSING, HUH?
もごもご
MRRGH
BY THE WAY, DO YOU KNOW WHY THEY SAY YOU'RE GOOD AT KISSING IF YOU CAN TIE STEMS UP?
HMM. IT'S A VERY LONG STORY, SHRIMP.
DON'T CALL ME SHRIMP, DANG IT!
HMMMM.
もごもご
MRRGH
OH, I KNOW...
...COME HELP ME A SEC.
HUH? WHAT?
....
MRRGH
もごもご
I JUST CAN'T DO IT.
TINK
CLUMP
BAM

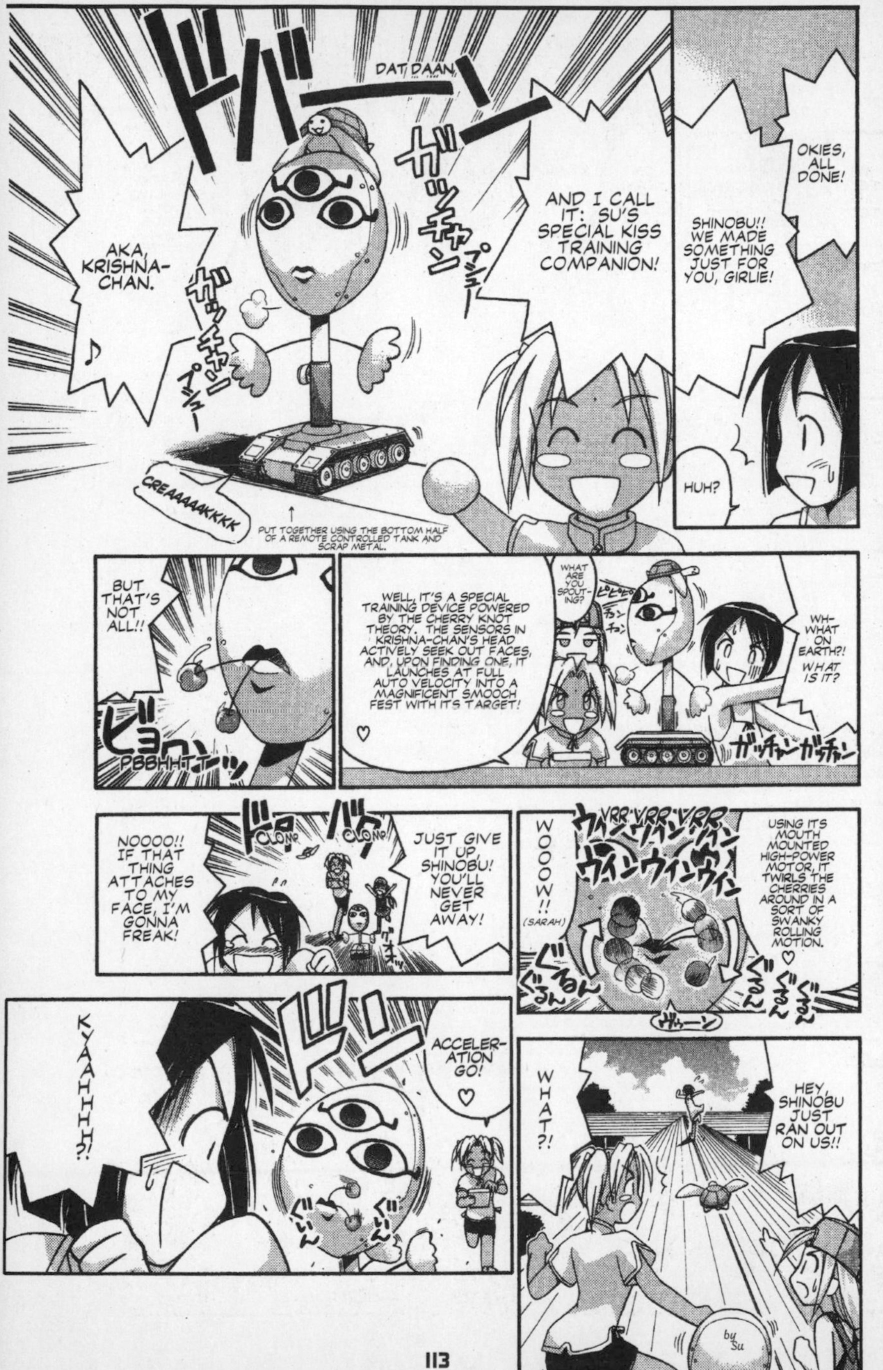
OKIES, ALL DONE!
SHINOBU!! WE MADE SOMETHING JUST FOR YOU, GIRLIE!
HUH?
AND I CALL IT: SU'S SPECIAL KISS TRAINING COMPANION!
DAT DAAN
AKA, KRISHNA-CHAN. ♪
CREAAAAAKKKK
PUT TOGETHER USING THE BOTTOM HALF OF A REMOTE CONTROLLED TANK AND SCRAP METAL.
WH-WHAT ON EARTH?! WHAT IS IT?
WHAT ARE YOU SPOUTING?
WELL, IT'S A SPECIAL TRAINING DEVICE POWERED BY THE CHERRY KNOT THEORY. THE SENSORS IN KRISHNA-CHAN'S HEAD ACTIVELY SEEK OUT FACES, AND, UPON FINDING ONE, IT LAUNCHES AT FULL AUTO VELOCITY INTO A MAGNIFICENT SMOOCH FEST WITH ITS TARGET! ♡
BUT THAT'S NOT ALL!!
PBBHHT
USING ITS MOUTH MOUNTED HIGH-POWER MOTOR, IT TWIRLS THE CHERRIES AROUND IN A SORT OF SWANKY ROLLING MOTION.
VRR VRR VRR
WOOOOW!! (SARAH)
JUST GIVE IT UP, SHINOBU! YOU'LL NEVER GET AWAY!
CLOMP CLOMP
NOOOO!! IF THAT THING ATTACHES TO MY FACE, I'M GONNA FREAK!
HEY, SHINOBU JUST RAN OUT ON US!!
WHAT?!
by Su
ACCELER-ATION GO! ♡
KYAAHHH?!

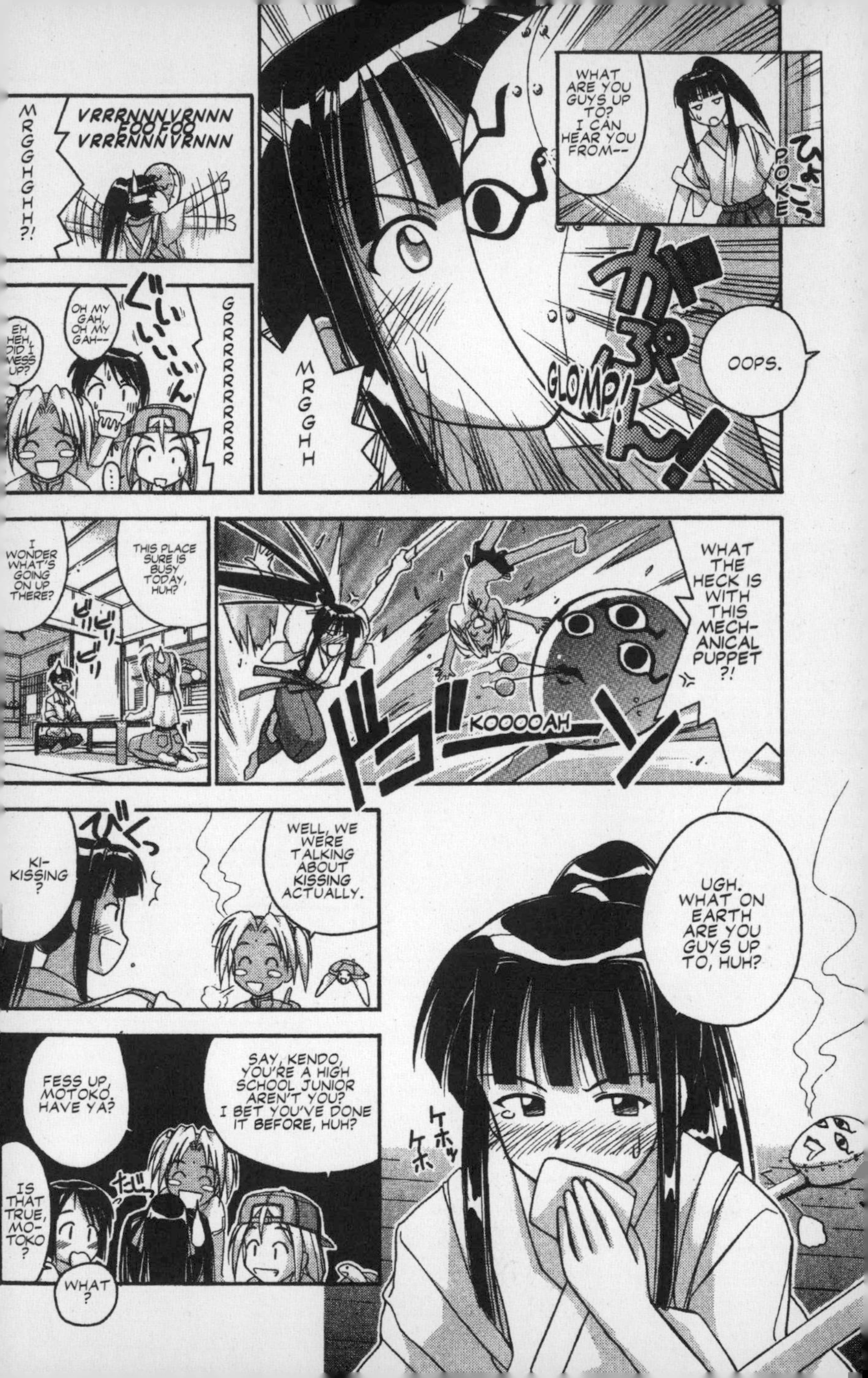
WHAT ARE YOU GUYS UP TO? I CAN HEAR YOU FROM--
ひょこっ
POKE
MRGGHH
かぷん!
GLOMP!
OOPS.
VRRRNNNVRNNN FOOFOO VRRRNNNVRNNN
MRGGHGHH?!
GRRRRRRRRRR
ぐいいいいん
OH MY GAH, OH MY GAH--
EH HEH, DID I MESS UP?
...
WHAT THE HECK IS WITH THIS MECHANICAL PUPPET?!
ドゴーン
KOOOOAH
THIS PLACE SURE IS BUSY TODAY, HUH?
I WONDER WHAT'S GOING ON UP THERE?
ビリビリ
UGH. WHAT ON EARTH ARE YOU GUYS UP TO, HUH?
ケホッ ケホ
WELL, WE WERE TALKING ABOUT KISSING ACTUALLY.
びくっ
KI-KISSING?
SAY, KENDO, YOU'RE A HIGH SCHOOL JUNIOR AREN'T YOU? I BET YOU'VE DONE IT BEFORE, HUH?
FESS UP, MOTOKO, HAVE YA?
IS THAT TRUE, MOTOKO?
WHAT?

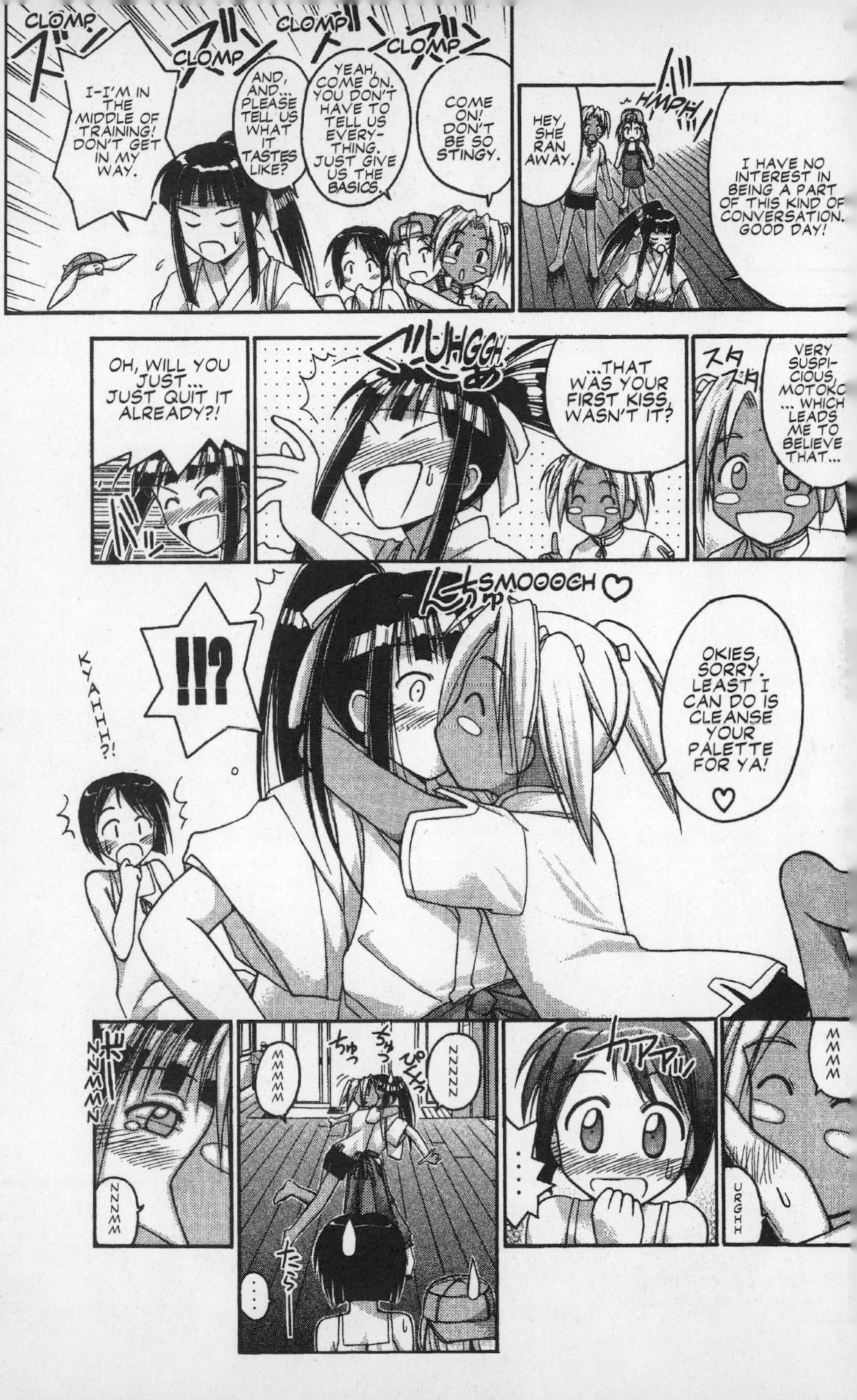
HMPH
I HAVE NO INTEREST IN BEING A PART OF THIS KIND OF CONVERSATION. GOOD DAY!
HEY, SHE RAN AWAY.
CLOMP
CLOMP
CLOMP
CLOMP
COME ON! DON'T BE SO STINGY.
YEAH, COME ON. YOU DON'T HAVE TO TELL US EVERY-THING. JUST GIVE US THE BASICS.
AND, AND... PLEASE TELL US WHAT IT TASTES LIKE?
I-I'M IN THE MIDDLE OF TRAINING! DON'T GET IN MY WAY.
VERY SUSPI-CIOUS, MOTOKO ... WHICH LEADS ME TO BELIEVE THAT...
...THAT WAS YOUR FIRST KISS, WASN'T IT?
UHGGH
OH, WILL YOU JUST... JUST QUIT IT ALREADY?!
SMOOOCH ♡
OKIES, SORRY. LEAST I CAN DO IS CLEANSE YOUR PALETTE FOR YA! ♡
!!?
KYAHHH?!
MMMM
URGHH
...
NNNNN
MMMMM
....
NNMMMN
NNNMM

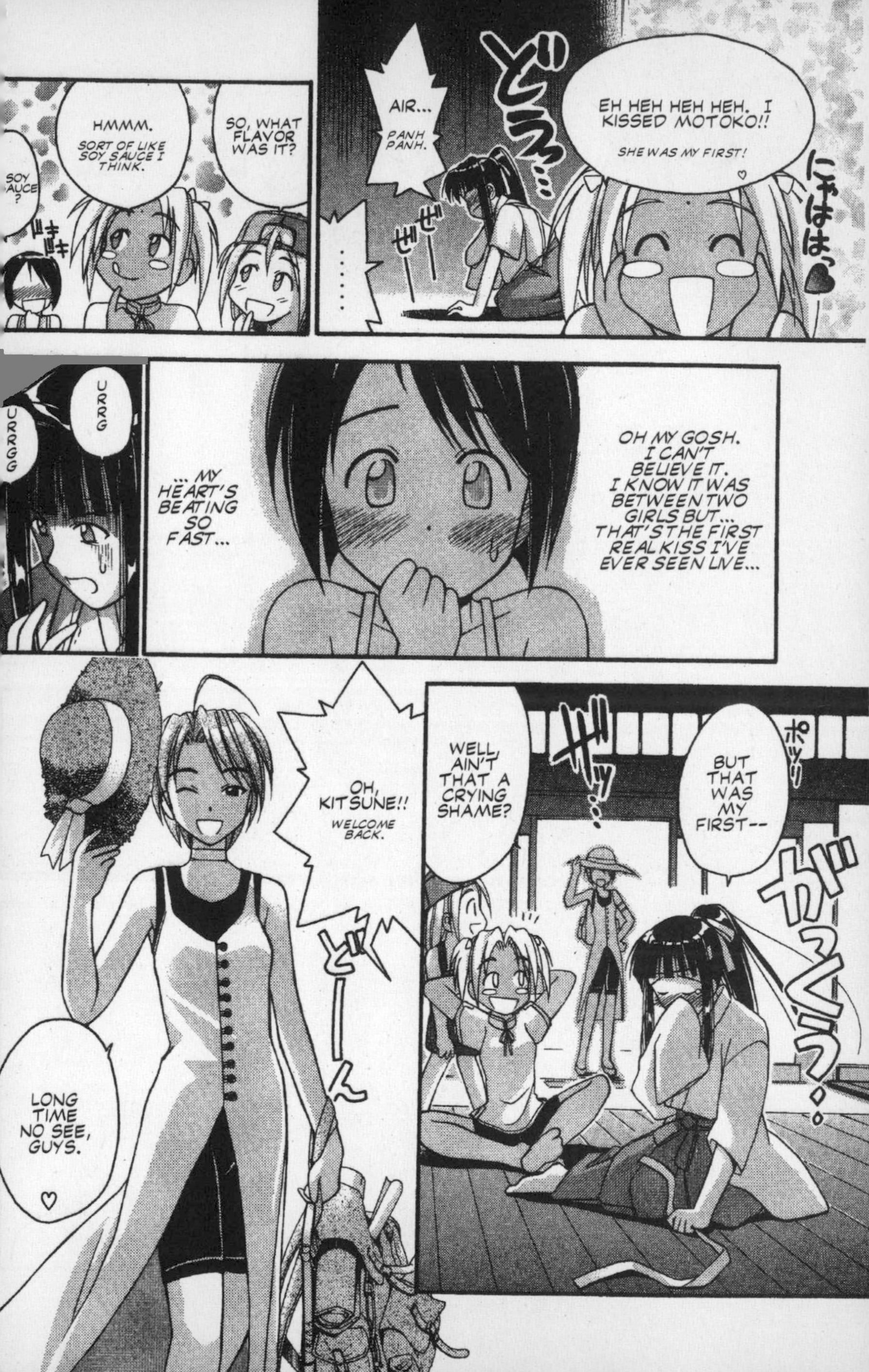

EH HEH HEH HEH. I KISSED MOTOKO!!
SHE WAS MY FIRST! ♡
にゃははっ♥
どうっ...
AIR... PANH PANH.
ぜ ぜ
......
SO, WHAT FLAVOR WAS IT?
HMMM. SORT OF LIKE SOY SAUCE I THINK.
SOY AUCE ?
ドキドキ
OH MY GOSH. I CAN'T BELIEVE IT. I KNOW IT WAS BETWEEN TWO GIRLS BUT... THAT'S THE FIRST REAL KISS I'VE EVER SEEN LIVE...
...MY HEART'S BEATING SO FAST...
URRG
URRGG
ポッ
BUT THAT WAS MY FIRST--
がっくぅっ。
ザッ...
WELL, AIN'T THAT A CRYING SHAME?
OH, KITSUNE!!
WELCOME BACK.
どーん
LONG TIME NO SEE, GUYS. ♡

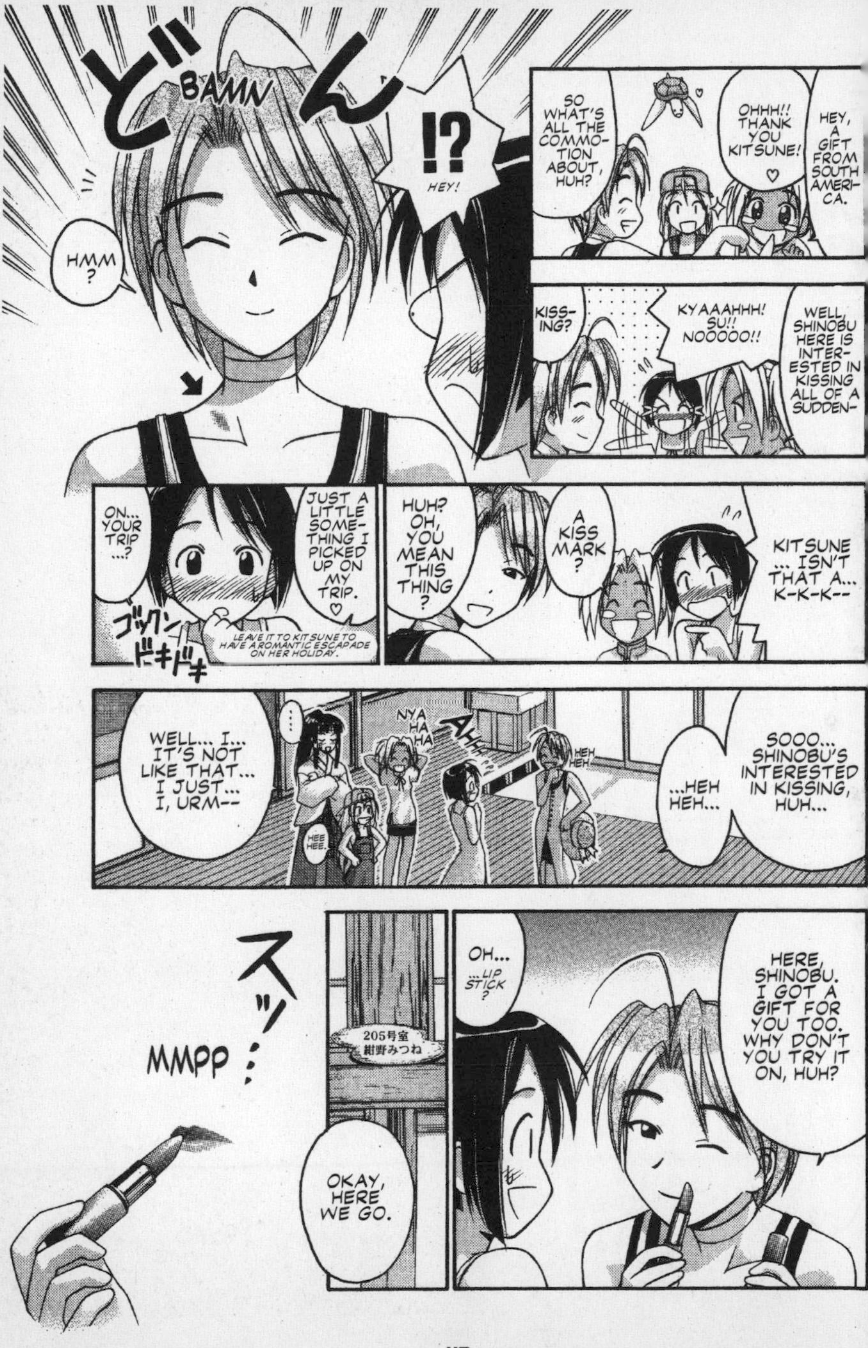
HEY, A GIFT FROM SOUTH AMERI-CA.
OHHH!! THANK YOU KITSUNE! ♡
SO WHAT'S ALL THE COMMO-TION ABOUT, HUH?
WELL, SHINOBU HERE IS INTER-ESTED IN KISSING ALL OF A SUDDEN-
KYAAAHHH! SU!! NOOOOO!!
KISS-ING?
どばん BAMN
!? HEY!
HMM ?
KITSUNE ... ISN'T THAT A... K-K-K--
A KISS MARK ?
HUH? OH, YOU MEAN THIS THING ?
JUST A LITTLE SOME-THING I PICKED UP ON MY TRIP. ♡
ON... YOUR TRIP ...?
LEAVE IT TO KITSUNE TO HAVE A ROMANTIC ESCAPADE ON HER HOLIDAY.
ゴックン ドキドキ
SOOO... SHINOBU'S INTERESTED IN KISSING, HUH...
...HEH HEH...
HEH HEH
AHH!?
NYA HA HA
....
HEE HEE.
WELL... I... IT'S NOT LIKE THAT... I JUST... I, URM--
HERE, SHINOBU. I GOT A GIFT FOR YOU TOO. WHY DON'T YOU TRY IT ON, HUH?
OH... ...LIP STICK ?
205号室 紺野みつね
OKAY, HERE WE GO.
スッ
MMPP

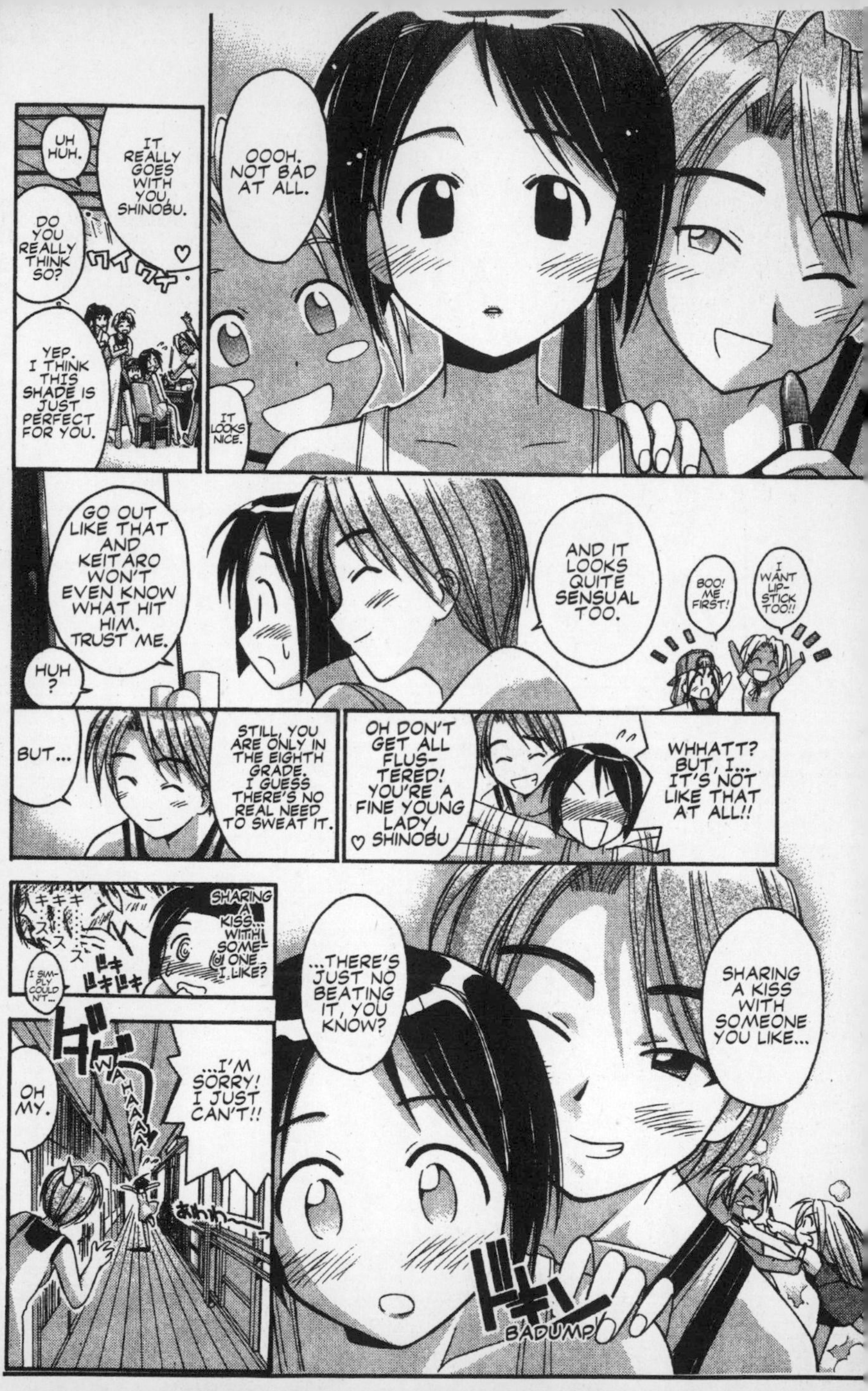
OOOH. NOT BAD AT ALL.
IT LOOKS NICE.
IT REALLY GOES WITH YOU, SHINOBU.
UH HUH.
DO YOU REALLY THINK SO? ♡
ワイワイ
YEP. I THINK THIS SHADE IS JUST PERFECT FOR YOU.
AND IT LOOKS QUITE SENSUAL TOO.
I WANT LIP-STICK TOO!!
BOO! ME FIRST!
GO OUT LIKE THAT AND KEITARO WON'T EVEN KNOW WHAT HIT HIM. TRUST ME.
HUH?
OH DON'T GET ALL FLUS-TERED! YOU'RE A FINE YOUNG LADY, ♡ SHINOBU
WHHATT? BUT, I... IT'S NOT LIKE THAT AT ALL!!
STILL, YOU ARE ONLY IN THE EIGHTH GRADE. I GUESS THERE'S NO REAL NEED TO SWEAT IT.
BUT...
SHARING A KISS WITH SOMEONE YOU LIKE...
...THERE'S JUST NO BEATING IT, YOU KNOW?
ドキン
BADUMP!
SHARING A KISS... WITH SOME-ONE I LIKE?
ドキドキ
I SIM-PLY COULD N'T...
...I'M SORRY! I JUST CAN'T!!
WAHAHAA!
OH MY.

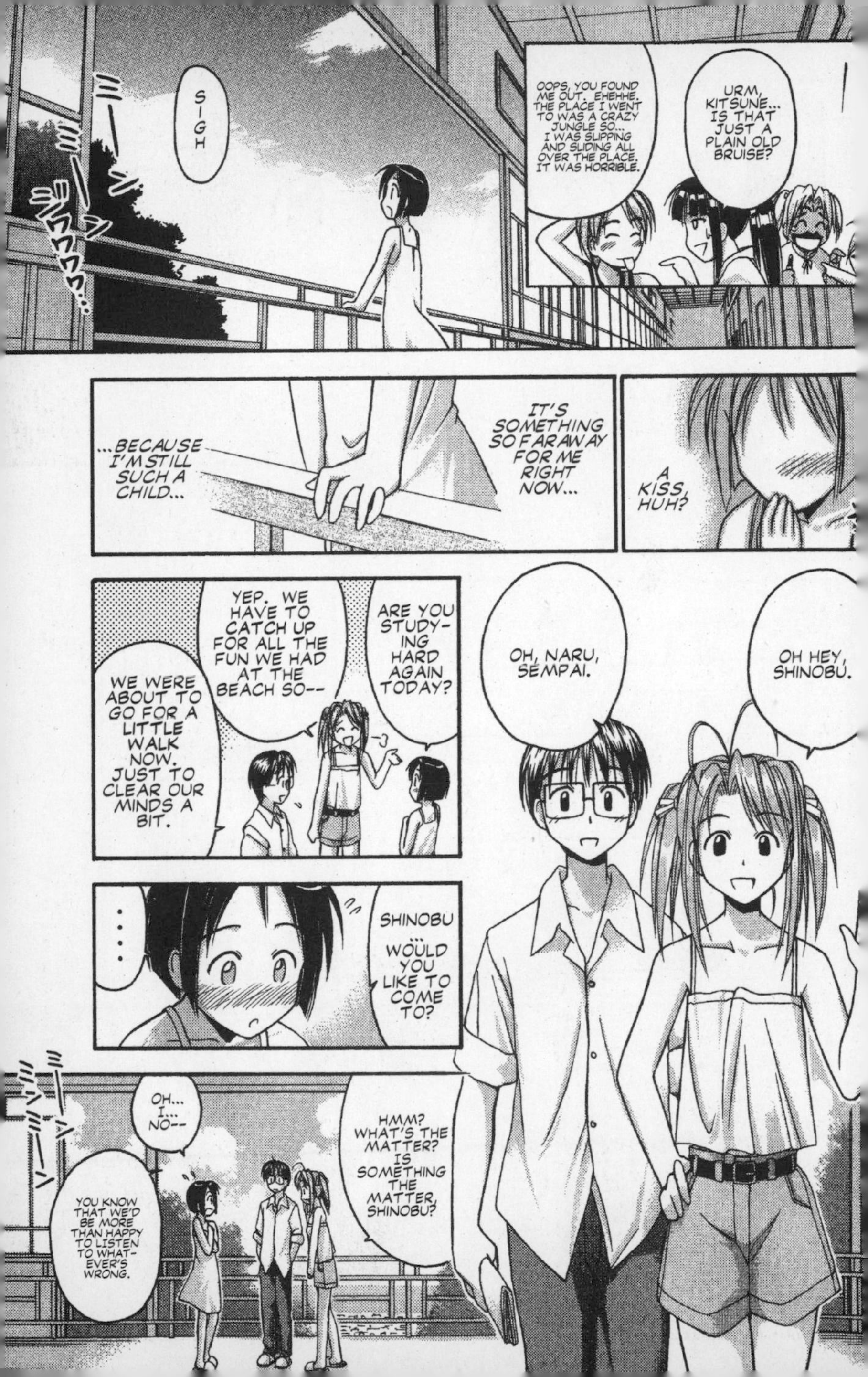
URM, KITSUNE... IS THAT JUST A PLAIN OLD BRUISE?
OOPS, YOU FOUND ME OUT. EHEHHE. THE PLACE I WENT TO WAS A CRAZY JUNGLE SO... I WAS SLIPPING AND SLIDING ALL OVER THE PLACE. IT WAS HORRIBLE.
ミーン ミーン
ジワワワワ…
SIGH
A KISS, HUH?
IT'S SOMETHING SO FARAWAY FOR ME RIGHT NOW...
...BECAUSE I'M STILL SUCH A CHILD...
OH HEY, SHINOBU.
OH, NARU, SEMPAI.
ARE YOU STUDYING HARD AGAIN TODAY?
YEP. WE HAVE TO CATCH UP FOR ALL THE FUN WE HAD AT THE BEACH SO--
WE WERE ABOUT TO GO FOR A LITTLE WALK NOW. JUST TO CLEAR OUR MINDS A BIT.
SHINOBU... WOULD YOU LIKE TO COME TO?
....
HMM? WHAT'S THE MATTER? IS SOMETHING THE MATTER, SHINOBU?
OH... I... NO--
YOU KNOW THAT WE'D BE MORE THAN HAPPY TO LISTEN TO WHATEVER'S WRONG.
ミーン ミーン

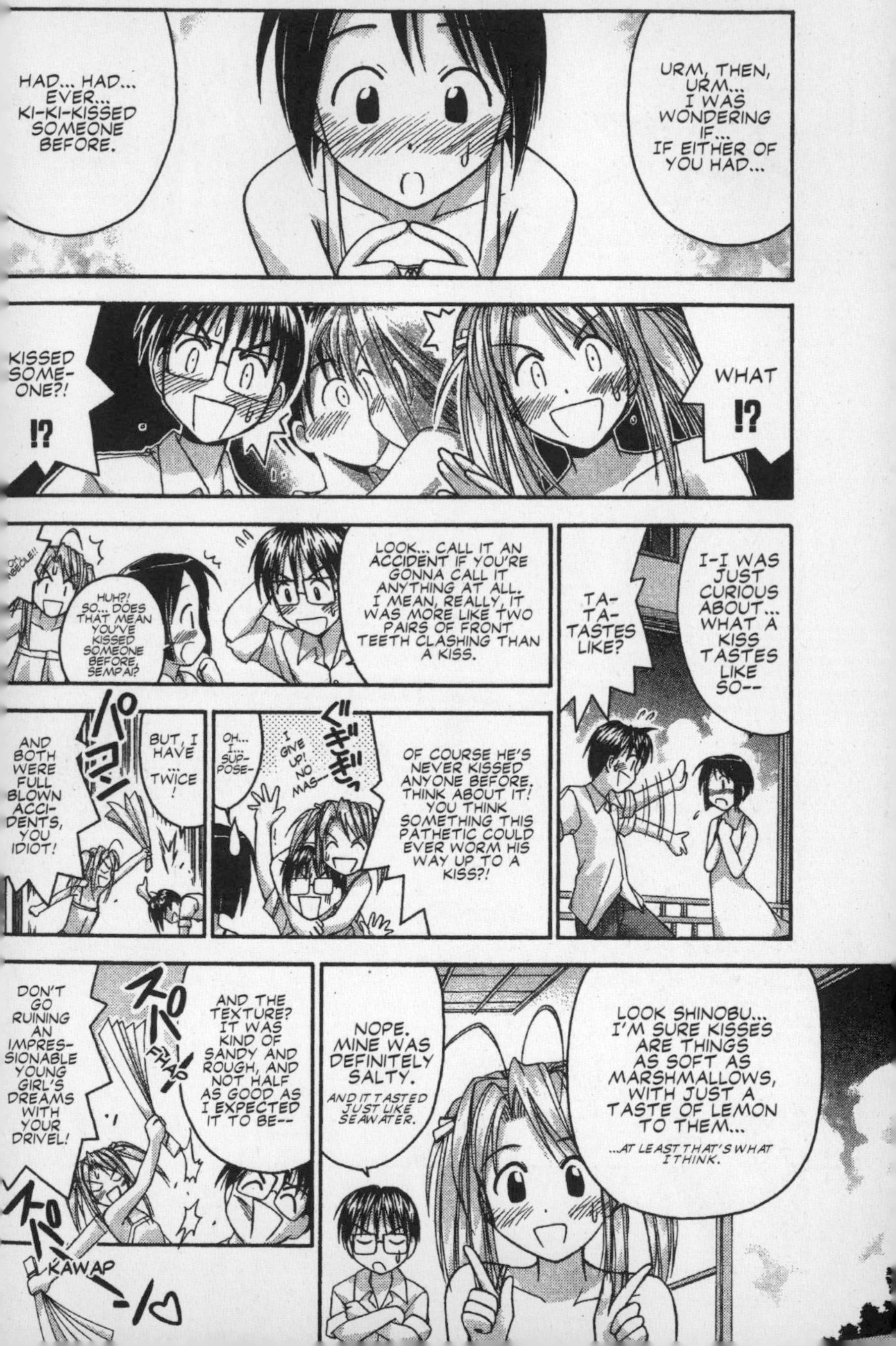
URM, THEN, URM... I WAS WONDERING IF... IF EITHER OF YOU HAD...
HAD... HAD... EVER... KI-KI-KISSED SOMEONE BEFORE.
WHAT !?
KISSED SOME-ONE?! !?
I-I WAS JUST CURIOUS ABOUT... WHAT A KISS TASTES LIKE SO--
TA-TA-TASTES LIKE?
LOOK... CALL IT AN ACCIDENT IF YOU'RE GONNA CALL IT ANYTHING AT ALL. I MEAN, REALLY, IT WAS MORE LIKE TWO PAIRS OF FRONT TEETH CLASHING THAN A KISS.
HUH?! SO... DOES THAT MEAN YOU'VE KISSED SOMEONE BEFORE, SEMPAI?
OF COURSE HE'S NEVER KISSED ANYONE BEFORE. THINK ABOUT IT! YOU THINK SOMETHING THIS PATHETIC COULD EVER WORM HIS WAY UP TO A KISS?!
I GIVE UP! NO MAS--
OH... I... SUP-POSE--
BUT, I HAVE... TWICE!
AND BOTH WERE FULL BLOWN ACCI-DENTS, YOU IDIOT!
LOOK SHINOBU... I'M SURE KISSES ARE THINGS AS SOFT AS MARSHMALLOWS, WITH JUST A TASTE OF LEMON TO THEM...
...AT LEAST THAT'S WHAT I THINK.
NOPE. MINE WAS DEFINITELY SALTY.
AND IT TASTED JUST LIKE SEAWATER.
AND THE TEXTURE? IT WAS KIND OF SANDY AND ROUGH, AND NOT HALF AS GOOD AS I EXPECTED IT TO BE--
FWAP
DON'T GO RUINING AN IMPRESSIONABLE YOUNG GIRL'S DREAMS WITH YOUR DRIVEL!
KAWAP

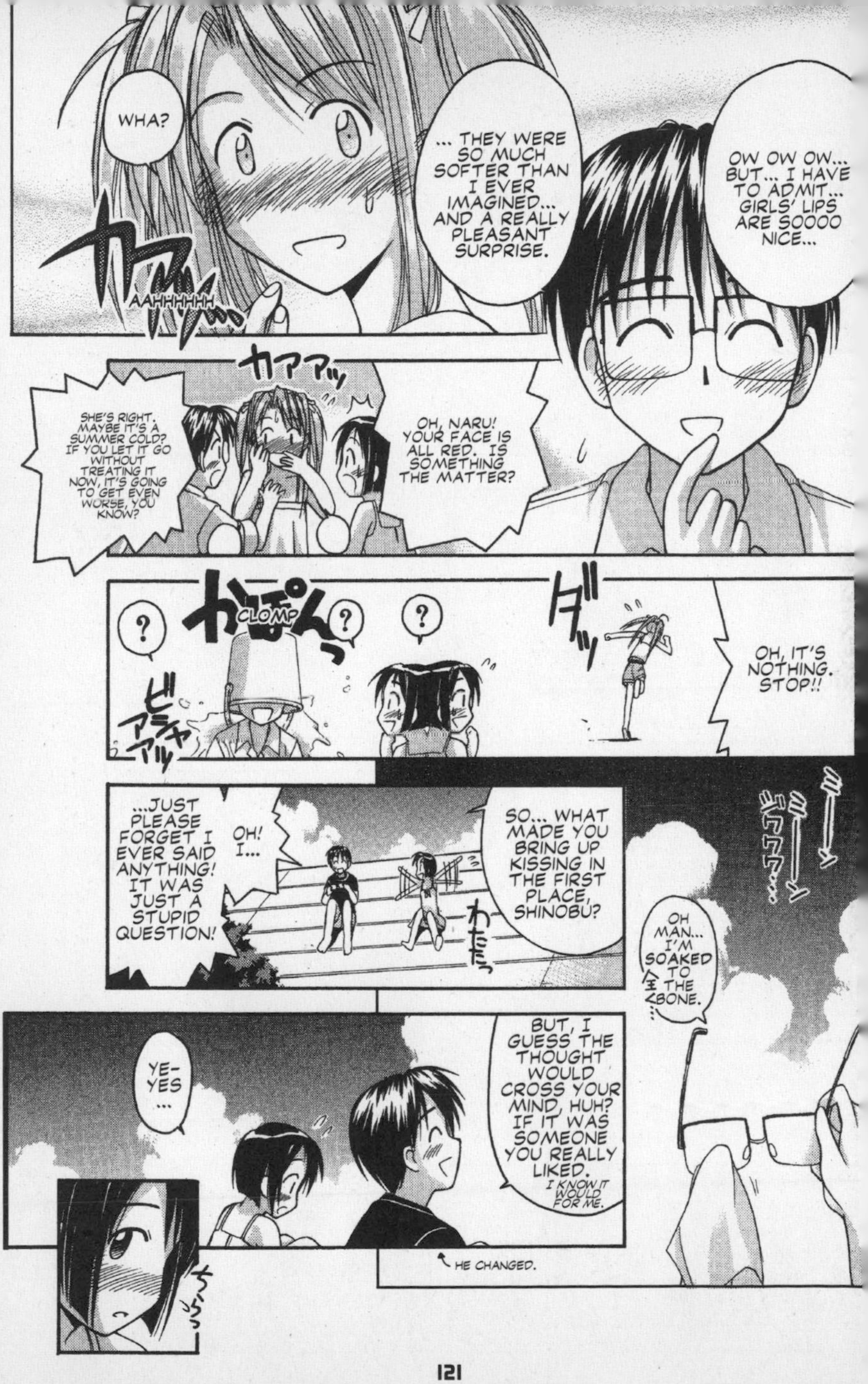
OW OW OW... BUT... I HAVE TO ADMIT... GIRLS' LIPS ARE SOOOO NICE...
... THEY WERE SO MUCH SOFTER THAN I EVER IMAGINED... AND A REALLY PLEASANT SURPRISE.
WHA?
AAHHHHHH
OH, NARU! YOUR FACE IS ALL RED. IS SOMETHING THE MATTER?
SHE'S RIGHT. MAYBE IT'S A SUMMER COLD? IF YOU LET IT GO WITHOUT TREATING IT NOW, IT'S GOING TO GET EVEN WORSE, YOU KNOW?
OH, IT'S NOTHING. STOP!!
?
?
CLOMP
?
OH MAN... I'M SOAKED TO THE BONE.
SO... WHAT MADE YOU BRING UP KISSING IN THE FIRST PLACE, SHINOBU?
OH! I...
...JUST PLEASE FORGET I EVER SAID ANYTHING! IT WAS JUST A STUPID QUESTION!
BUT, I GUESS THE THOUGHT WOULD CROSS YOUR MIND, HUH? IF IT WAS SOMEONE YOU REALLY LIKED.
I KNOW IT WOULD FOR ME.
HE CHANGED.
YE-YES ...

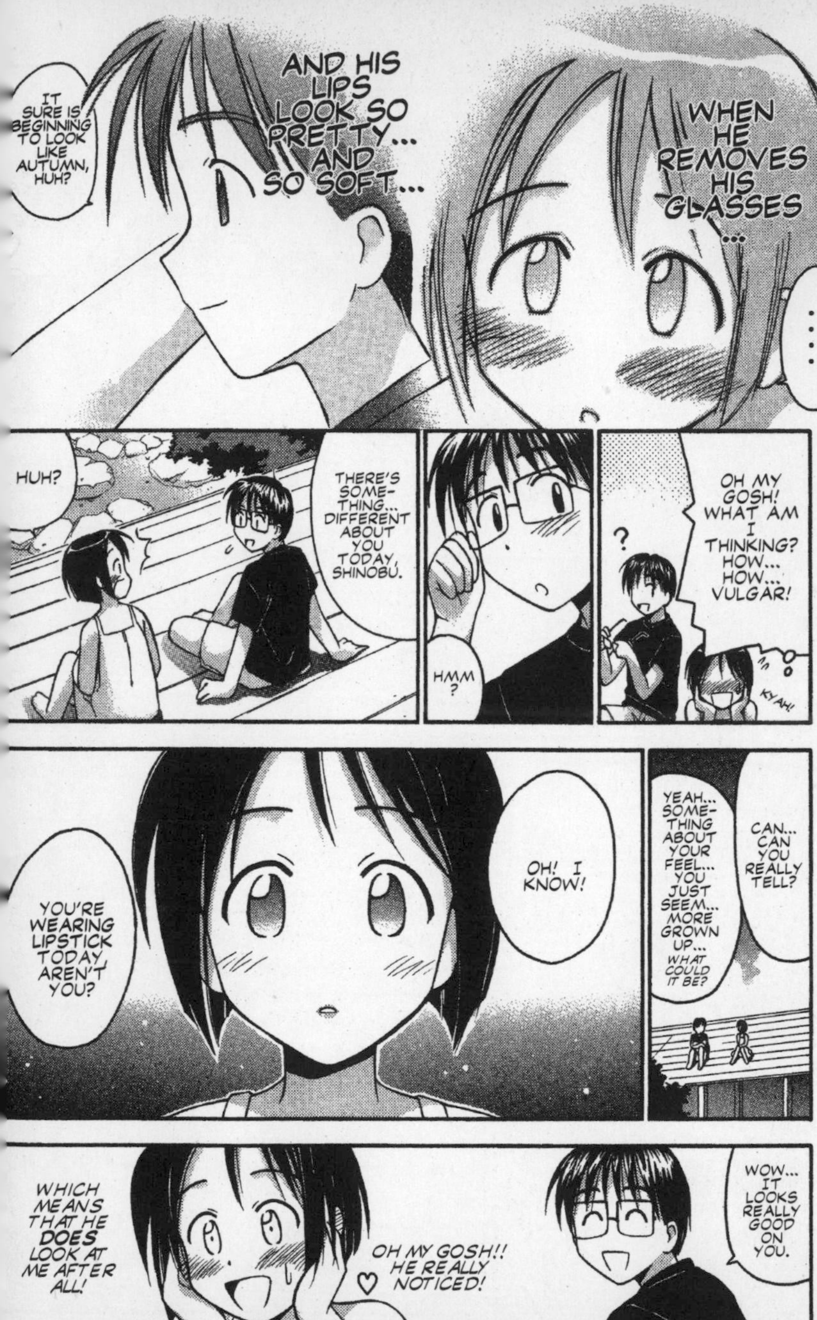
WHEN HE REMOVES HIS GLASSES...
....
AND HIS LIPS LOOK SO PRETTY... AND SO SOFT...
IT SURE IS BEGINNING TO LOOK LIKE AUTUMN, HUH?
OH MY GOSH! WHAT AM I THINKING? HOW... HOW... VULGAR!
?
KYAH!
HMM?
THERE'S SOME-THING... DIFFERENT ABOUT YOU TODAY, SHINOBU.
HUH?
CAN... CAN YOU REALLY TELL?
YEAH... SOME-THING ABOUT YOUR FEEL... YOU JUST SEEM... MORE GROWN UP... WHAT COULD IT BE?
OH! I KNOW!
YOU'RE WEARING LIPSTICK TODAY, AREN'T YOU?
WOW... IT LOOKS REALLY GOOD ON YOU.
OH MY GOSH!! HE REALLY NOTICED!
WHICH MEANS THAT HE DOES LOOK AT ME AFTER ALL!

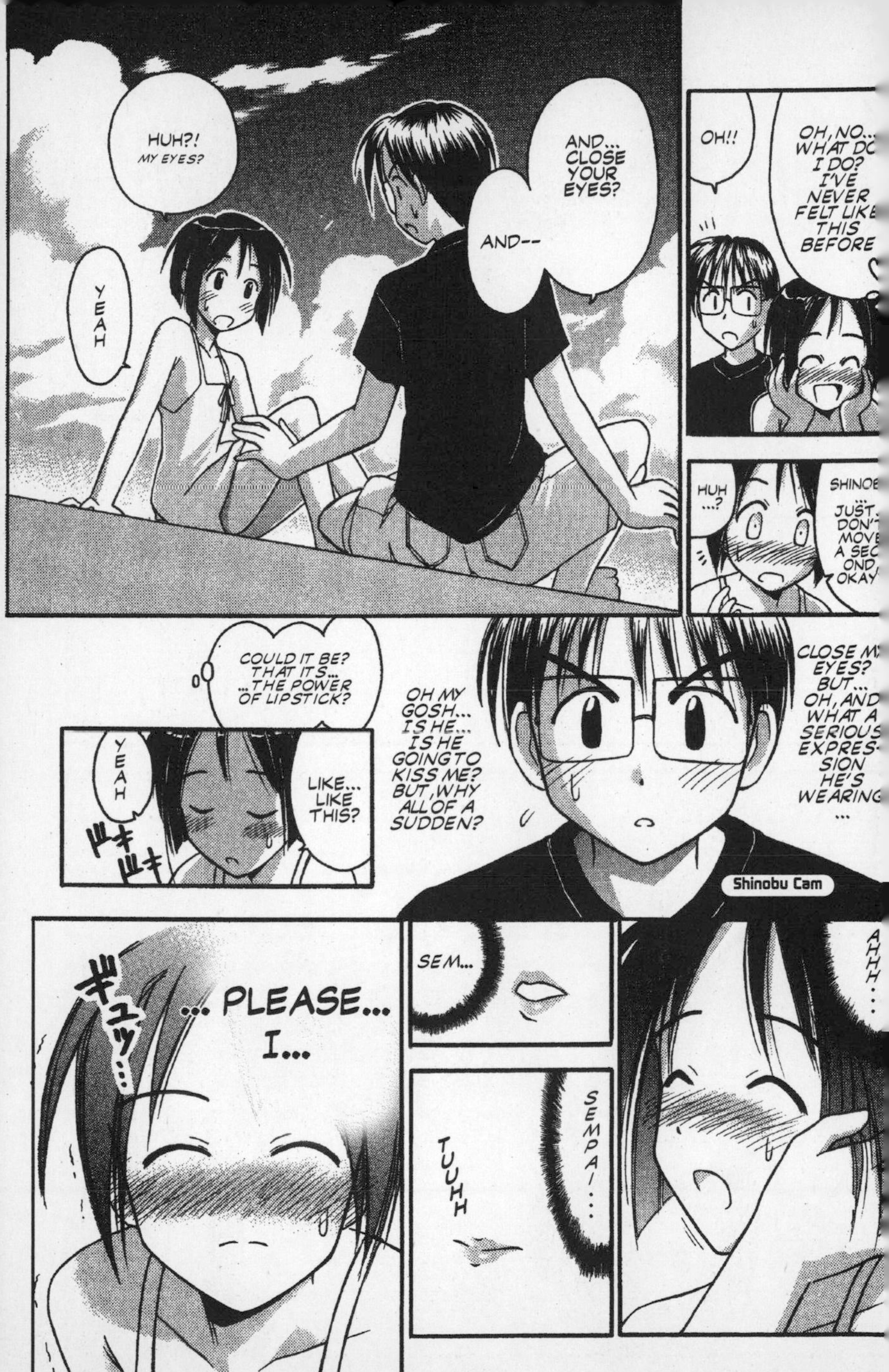
OH, NO... WHAT DO I DO? I'VE NEVER FELT LIKE THIS BEFORE
OH!!
SHINOB ... JUST... DON'T MOVE A SEC OND, OKAY
HUH ...?
AND... CLOSE YOUR EYES?
AND--
HUH?! MY EYES?
YEAH
CLOSE MY EYES? BUT... OH, AND WHAT A SERIOUS EXPRES-SION HE'S WEARING ...
OH MY GOSH... IS HE... IS HE GOING TO KISS ME? BUT, WHY ALL OF A SUDDEN?
Shinobu Cam
COULD IT BE? THAT ITS... ...THE POWER OF LIPSTICK?
LIKE... LIKE THIS?
YEAH
ドキ ドキ
AHHH...
SEM...
SEMPAI...
TUUHH
ギュッ...
... PLEASE... I...

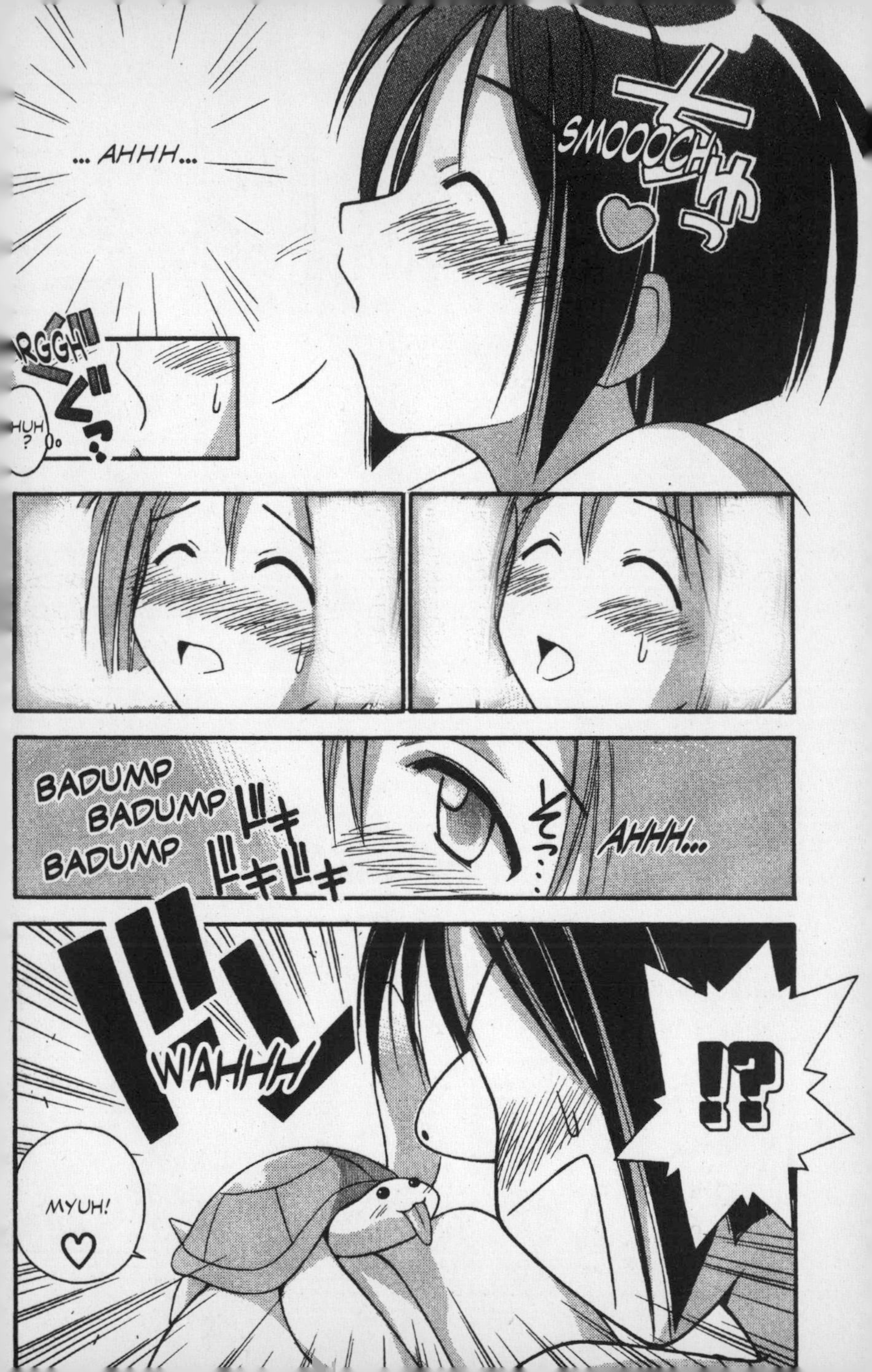
SMOOOCH
ちゅっ
... AHHH...
ARGGH
ぐっ
HUH?
AHHH...
BADUMP BADUMP BADUMP
ドキドキドキ
!?
WAHHH
MYUH! ♡

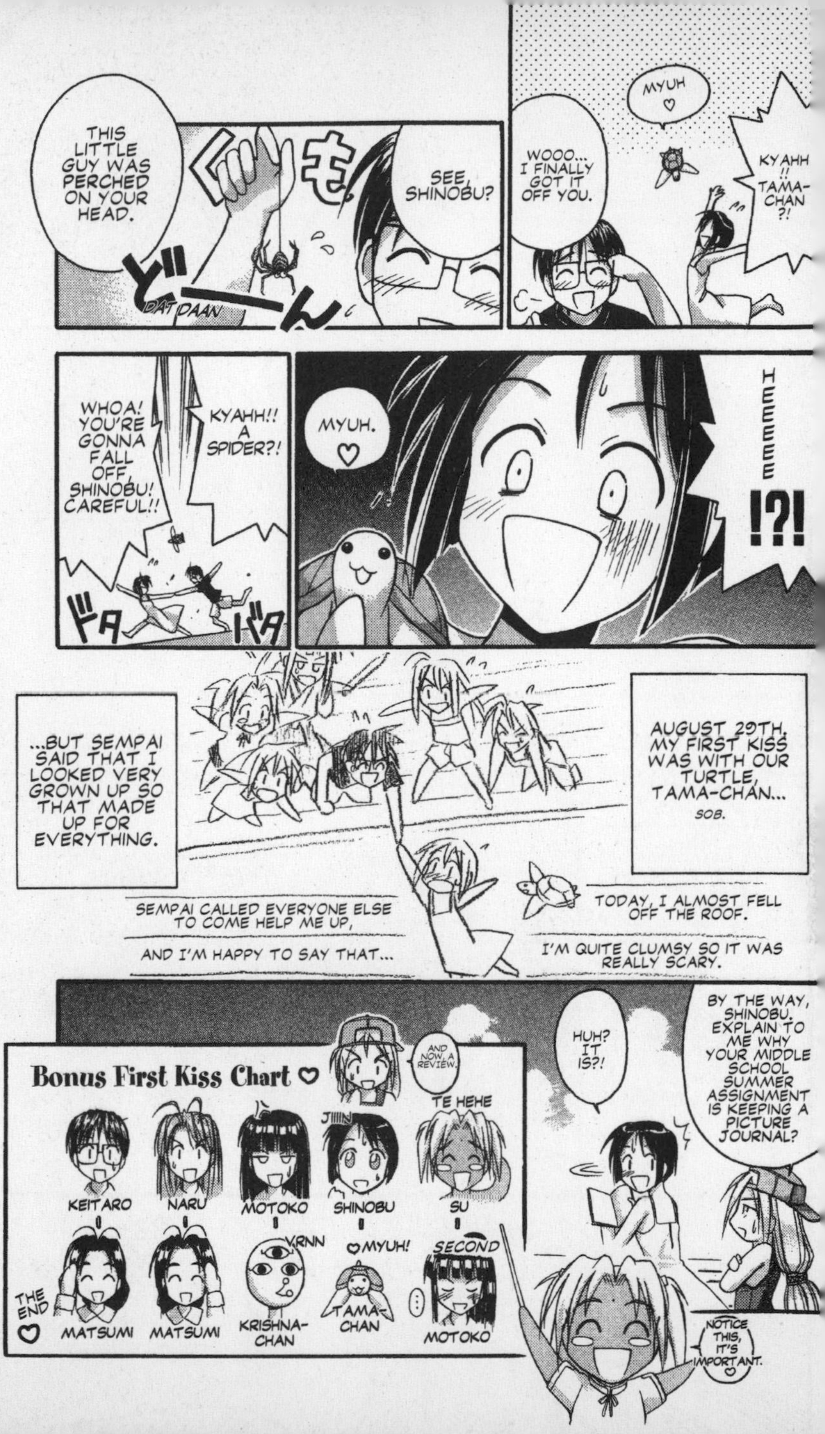
MYUH ♡
KYAHH!! TAMA-CHAN?!
WOOO... I FINALLY GOT IT OFF YOU.
SEE, SHINOBU?
THIS LITTLE GUY WAS PERCHED ON YOUR HEAD.
DAT DAAN
HEEEEE !?!
MYUH. ♡
KYAHH!! A SPIDER?!
WHOA! YOU'RE GONNA FALL OFF, SHINOBU! CAREFUL!!
TODAY, I ALMOST FELL OFF THE ROOF.
I'M QUITE CLUMSY SO IT WAS REALLY SCARY.
SEMPAI CALLED EVERYONE ELSE TO COME HELP ME UP,
AND I'M HAPPY TO SAY THAT...
AUGUST 29TH. MY FIRST KISS WAS WITH OUR TURTLE, TAMA-CHAN...
SOB.
...BUT SEMPAI SAID THAT I LOOKED VERY GROWN UP SO THAT MADE UP FOR EVERYTHING.
BY THE WAY, SHINOBU. EXPLAIN TO ME WHY YOUR MIDDLE SCHOOL SUMMER ASSIGNMENT IS KEEPING A PICTURE JOURNAL?
HUH? IT IS?!
AND NOW, A REVIEW.
NOTICE THIS, IT'S IMPORTANT. ♡
Bonus First Kiss Chart ♡
KEITARO
NARU
MOTOKO
JIIIN
SHINOBU
TE HEHE
SU
MATSUMI
MATSUMI
VRNN
KRISHNA-CHAN
♡MYUH!
TAMA-CHAN
SECOND
...
MOTOKO
THE END ♡

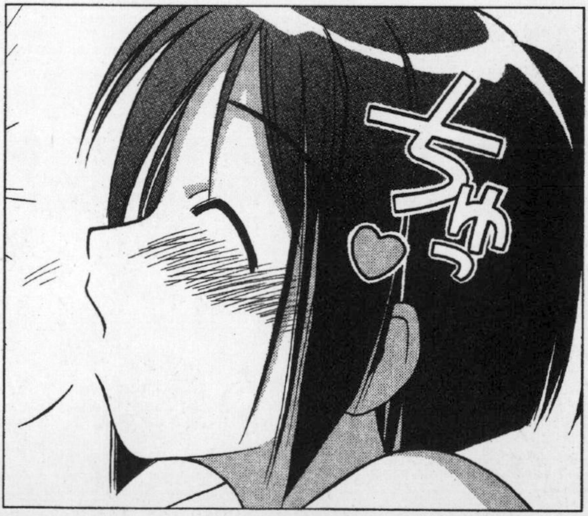
ちゅっ

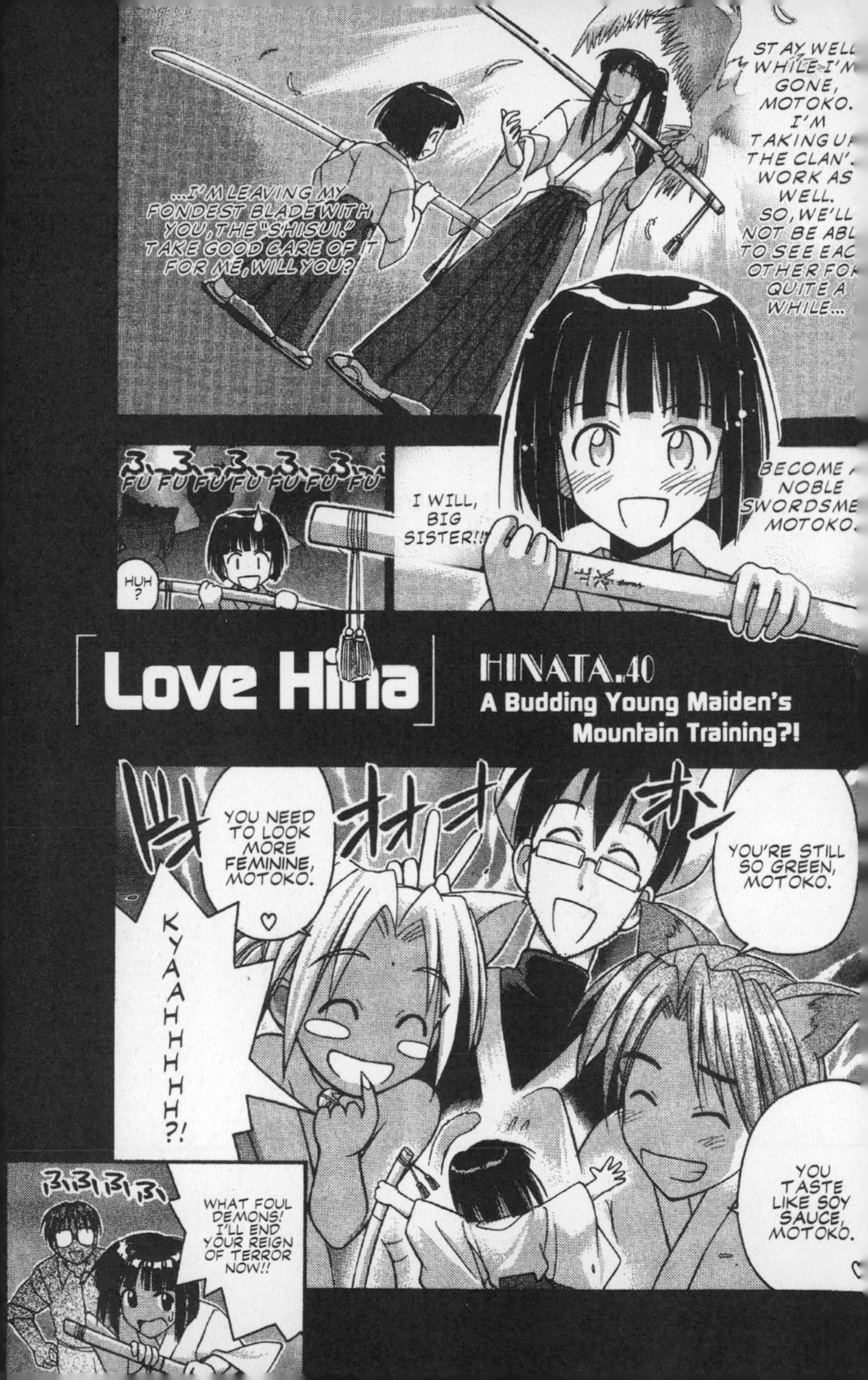
STAY WELL WHILE I'M GONE, MOTOKO. I'M TAKING U THE CLAN'. WORK AS WELL. SO, WE'LL NOT BE ABL TO SEE EAC OTHER FO QUITE A WHILE...
...I'M LEAVING MY FONDEST BLADE WITH YOU, THE "SHISUI." TAKE GOOD CARE OF IT FOR ME, WILL YOU?
BECOME NOBLE SWORDSME MOTOKO.
I WILL, BIG SISTER!!!
ふっふっふっふっふっ
FU FU FU FU FU FU FU
HUH?
Love Hina
HINATA.40
A Budding Young Maiden's Mountain Training?!
YOU'RE STILL SO GREEN, MOTOKO.
YOU NEED TO LOOK MORE FEMININE, MOTOKO. ♡
YOU TASTE LIKE SOY SAUCE, MOTOKO.
KYAAHHHHHH?!
ふふふふ
WHAT FOUL DEMONS! I'LL END YOUR REIGN OF TERROR NOW!!

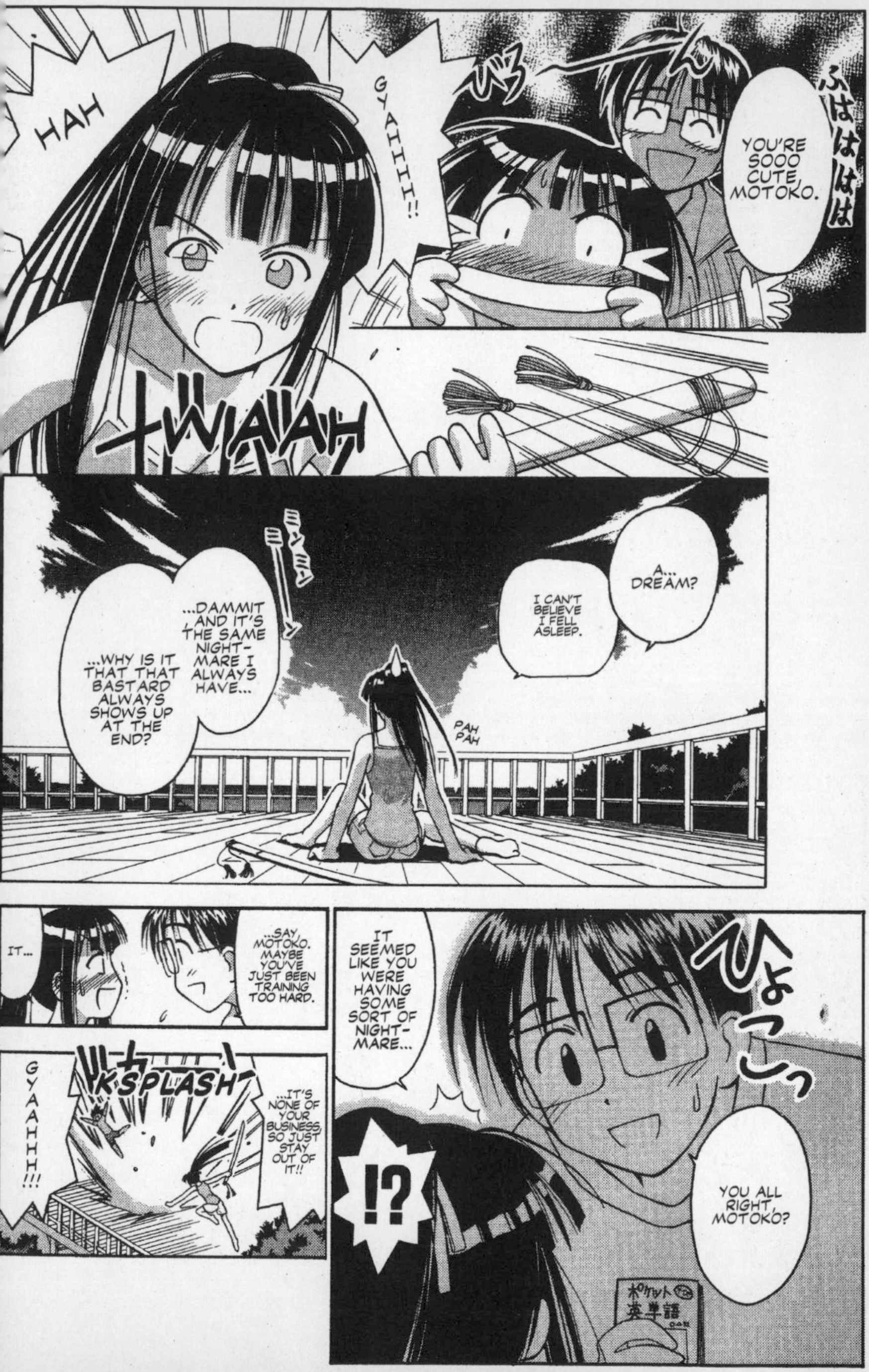
ふはははは
YOU'RE SOOO CUTE, MOTOKO.
GYAHHHH!!
HAH
WAAAH
A... DREAM?
I CAN'T BELIEVE I FELL ASLEEP.
...DAMMIT AND IT'S THE SAME NIGHTMARE I ALWAYS HAVE...
...WHY IS IT THAT THAT BASTARD ALWAYS SHOWS UP AT THE END?
PAH PAH
ひょこっ
IT SEEMED LIKE YOU WERE HAVING SOME SORT OF NIGHTMARE...
YOU ALL RIGHT, MOTOKO?
!?
ポケット英単語
...SAY MOTOKO. MAYBE YOU'VE JUST BEEN TRAINING TOO HARD.
IT...
...IT'S NONE OF YOUR BUSINESS, SO JUST STAY OUT OF IT!!
KSPLASH
GYAAHHH!!!

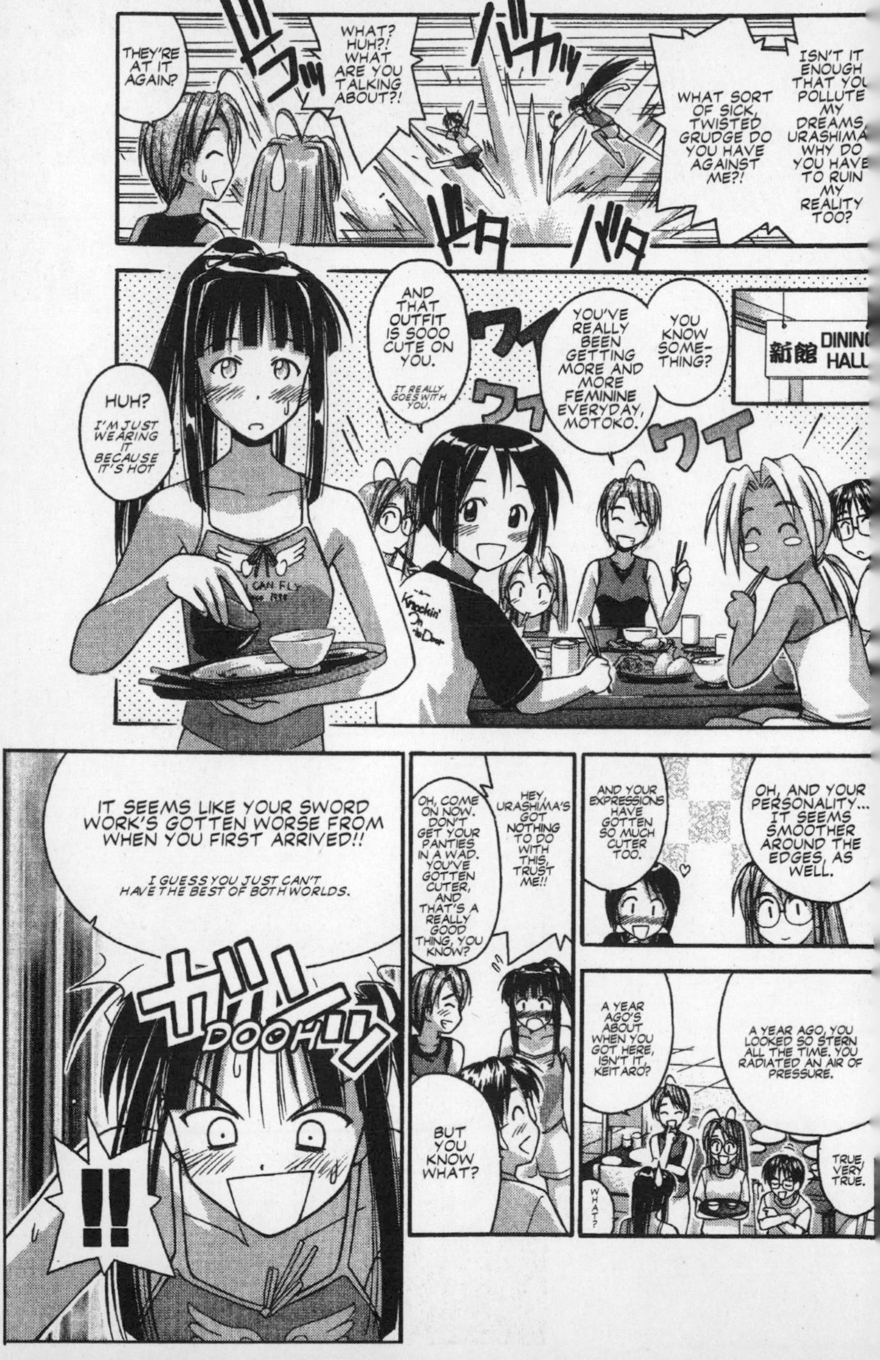
ISN'T IT ENOUGH THAT YOU POLLUTE MY DREAMS, URASHIMA? WHY DO YOU HAVE TO RUIN MY REALITY TOO?
WHAT SORT OF SICK, TWISTED GRUDGE DO YOU HAVE AGAINST ME?!
WHAT? HUH?! WHAT ARE YOU TALKING ABOUT?!
THEY'RE AT IT AGAIN?
ドタ バタ
新館 DINING HALL
YOU KNOW SOME-THING?
YOU'VE REALLY BEEN GETTING MORE AND MORE FEMININE EVERYDAY, MOTOKO.
ワイ ワイ ワイ
AND THAT OUTFIT IS SOOO CUTE ON YOU.
IT REALLY GOES WITH YOU.
HUH?
I'M JUST WEARING IT BECAUSE IT'S HOT
OH, AND YOUR PERSONALITY... IT SEEMS SMOOTHER AROUND THE EDGES, AS WELL.
AND YOUR EXPRESSIONS HAVE GOTTEN SO MUCH CUTER TOO.
A YEAR AGO, YOU LOOKED SO STERN ALL THE TIME. YOU RADIATED AN AIR OF PRESSURE.
TRUE, VERY TRUE.
A YEAR AGO'S ABOUT WHEN YOU GOT HERE, ISN'T IT, KEITARO?
WHAT?
HEY, URASHIMA'S GOT NOTHING TO DO WITH THIS, TRUST ME!!
OH, COME ON NOW. DON'T GET YOUR PANTIES IN A WAD. YOU'VE GOTTEN CUTER, AND THAT'S A REALLY GOOD THING, YOU KNOW?
BUT YOU KNOW WHAT?
IT SEEMS LIKE YOUR SWORD WORK'S GOTTEN WORSE FROM WHEN YOU FIRST ARRIVED!!
I GUESS YOU JUST CAN'T HAVE THE BEST OF BOTH WORLDS.
!!

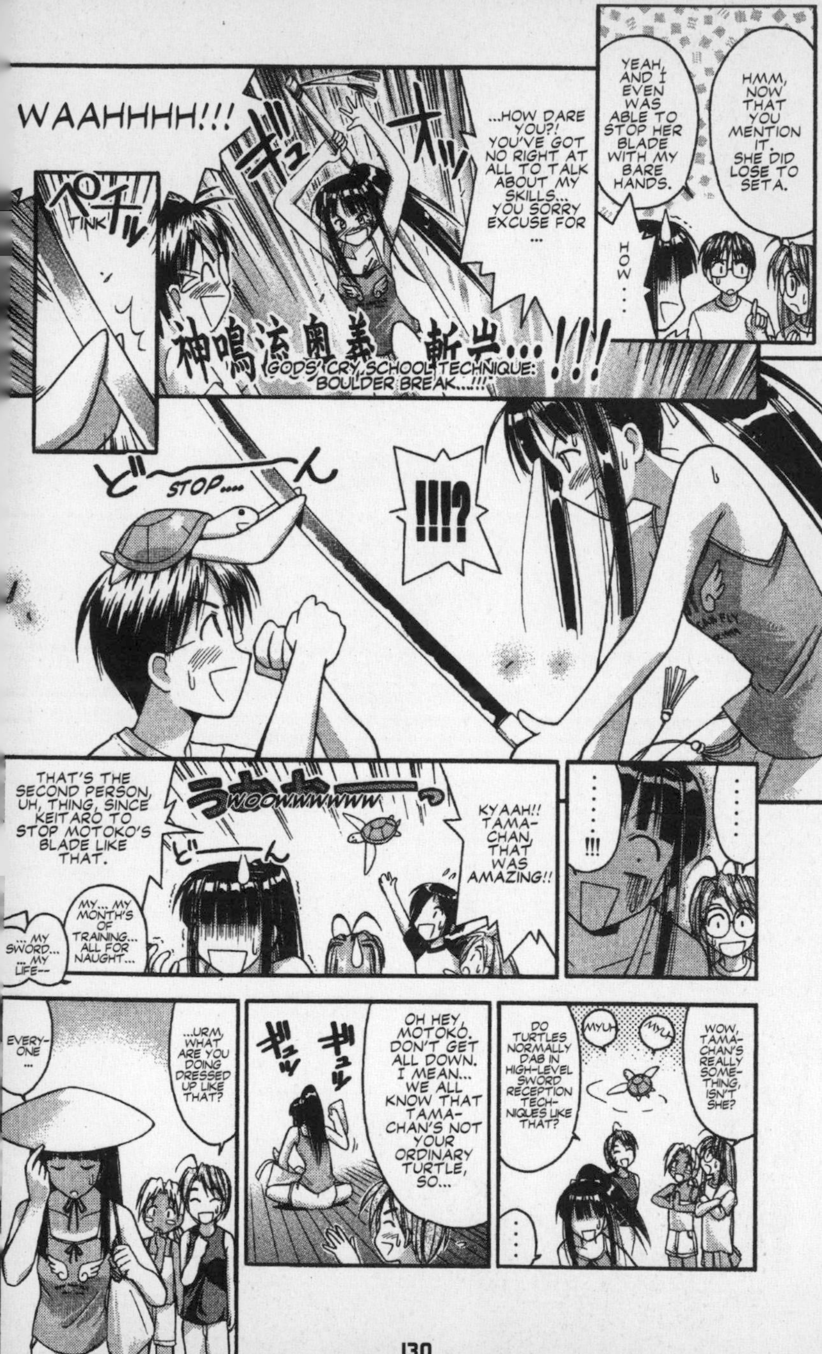
HMM, NOW THAT YOU MENTION IT. SHE DID LOSE TO SETA.
YEAH, AND I EVEN WAS ABLE TO STOP HER BLADE WITH MY BARE HANDS.
HOW...
...HOW DARE YOU?! YOU'VE GOT NO RIGHT AT ALL TO TALK ABOUT MY SKILLS... YOU SORRY EXCUSE FOR ...
WAAHHHH!!!
神鳴流奥義 斬岩…!!!
GODS' CRY SCHOOL TECHNIQUE: BOULDER BREAK...!!!
TINK
!!!?
STOP....
......
!!!
......
KYAAH!! TAMA-CHAN, THAT WAS AMAZING!!
WOOWWWWWW
THAT'S THE SECOND PERSON, UH, THING, SINCE KEITARO TO STOP MOTOKO'S BLADE LIKE THAT.
MY... MY MONTH'S OF TRAINING... ALL FOR NAUGHT...
... MY SWORD... ... MY LIFE--
WOW, TAMA-CHAN'S REALLY SOMETHING, ISN'T SHE?
MYU
MYU
DO TURTLES NORMALLY DAB IN HIGH-LEVEL SWORD RECEPTION TECHNIQUES LIKE THAT?
....
OH HEY, MOTOKO. DON'T GET ALL DOWN. I MEAN... WE ALL KNOW THAT TAMA-CHAN'S NOT YOUR ORDINARY TURTLE, SO...
...URM, WHAT ARE YOU DOING DRESSED UP LIKE THAT?
EVERY-ONE ...

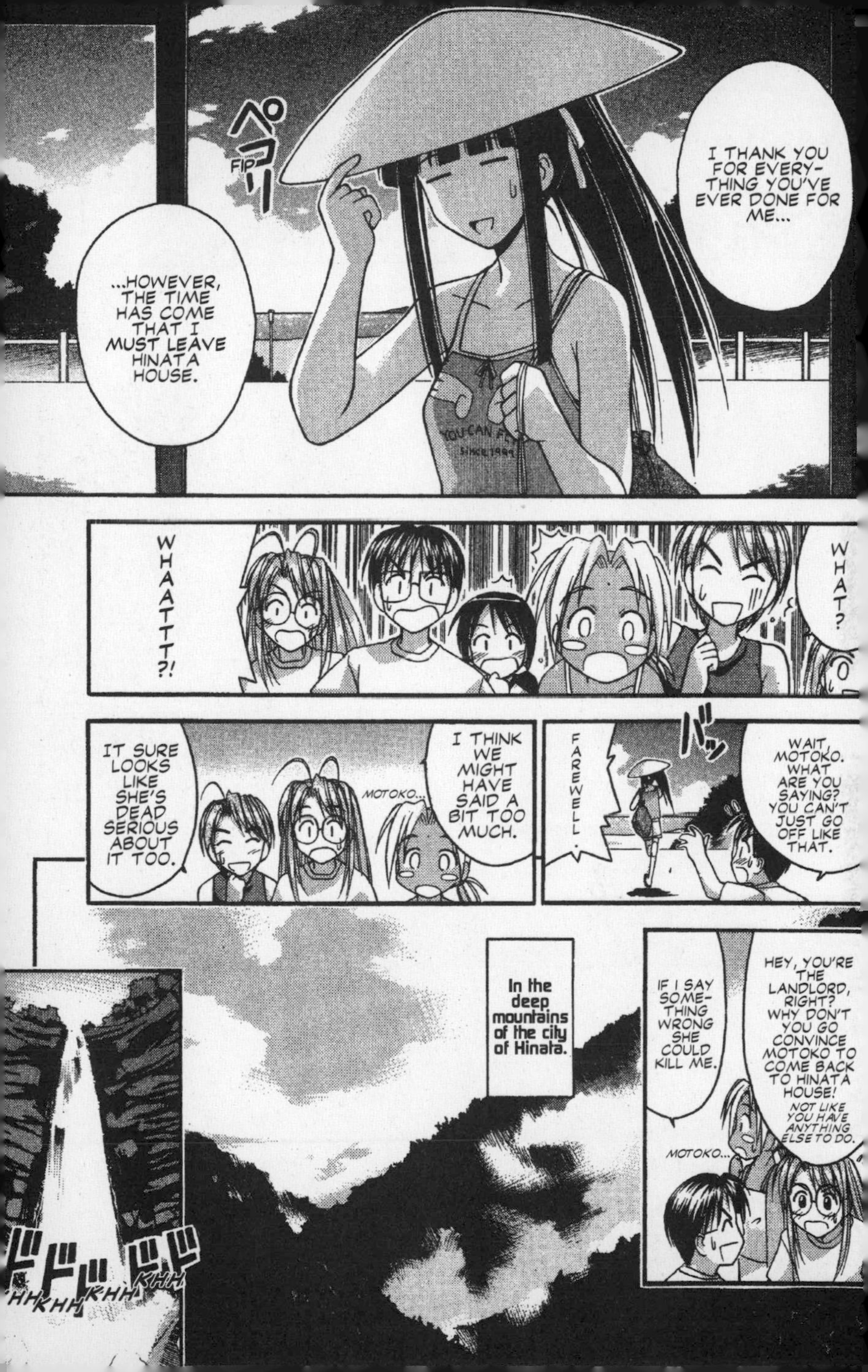
I THANK YOU FOR EVERY-THING YOU'VE EVER DONE FOR ME...
FIP
...HOWEVER, THE TIME HAS COME THAT I MUST LEAVE HINATA HOUSE.
WHAT?
WHAATTTT?!
WAIT, MOTOKO. WHAT ARE YOU SAYING? YOU CAN'T JUST GO OFF LIKE THAT.
FAREWELL.
I THINK WE MIGHT HAVE SAID A BIT TOO MUCH.
MOTOKO...
IT SURE LOOKS LIKE SHE'S DEAD SERIOUS ABOUT IT TOO.
HEY, YOU'RE THE LANDLORD, RIGHT? WHY DON'T YOU GO CONVINCE MOTOKO TO COME BACK TO HINATA HOUSE!
NOT LIKE YOU HAVE ANYTHING ELSE TO DO.
IF I SAY SOME-THING WRONG SHE COULD KILL ME.
MOTOKO...
In the deep mountains of the city of Hinata.
KHH KHH KHH

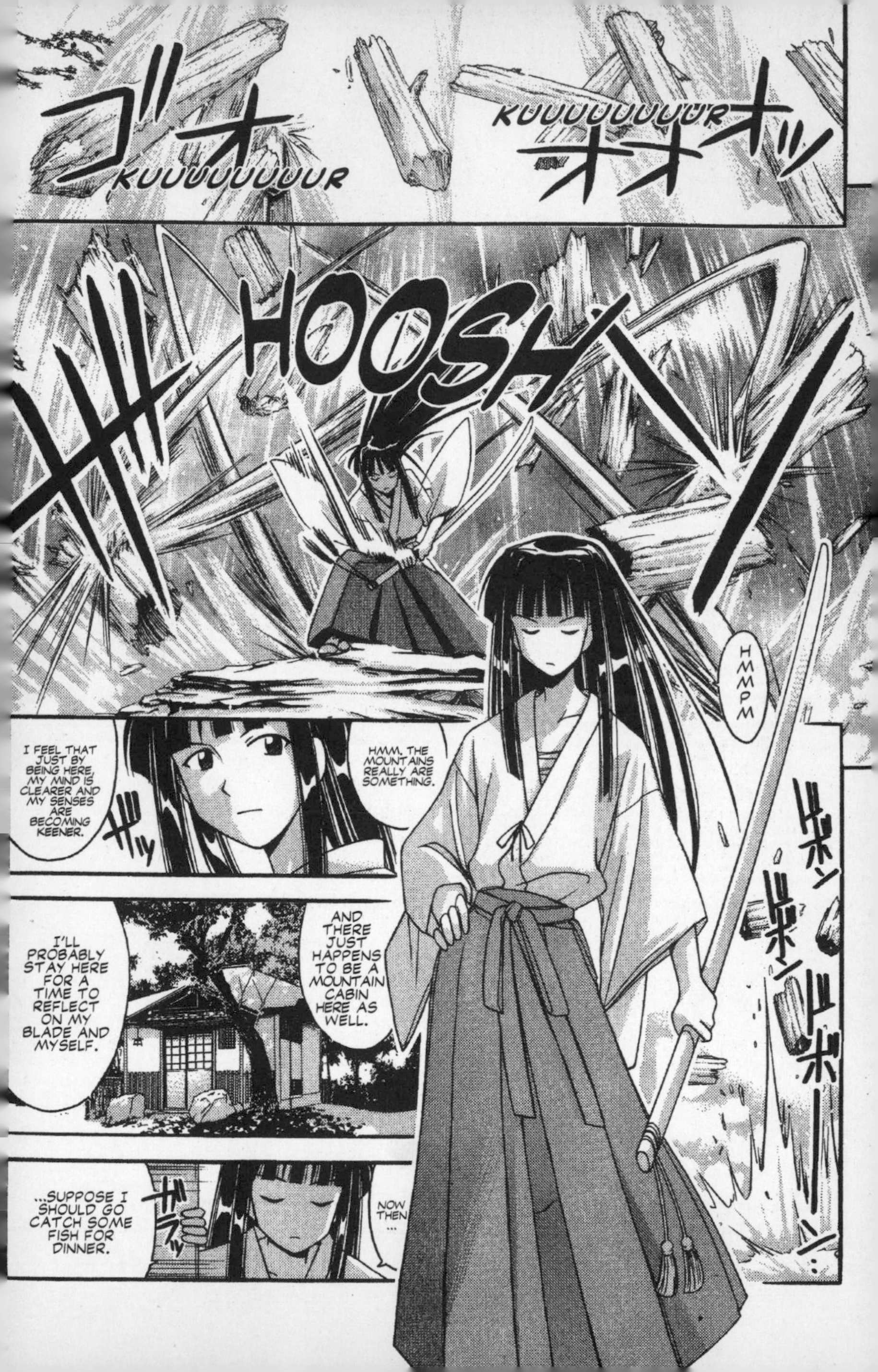
KUUUUUUUUUR
KUUUUUUUUUR
HOOSH
HMMPM
HMM. THE MOUNTAINS REALLY ARE SOMETHING.
I FEEL THAT JUST BY BEING HERE, MY MIND IS CLEARER AND MY SENSES ARE BECOMING KEENER.
AND THERE JUST HAPPENS TO BE A MOUNTAIN CABIN HERE AS WELL.
I'LL PROBABLY STAY HERE FOR A TIME TO REFLECT ON MY BLADE AND MYSELF.
NOW THEN...
...SUPPOSE I SHOULD GO CATCH SOME FISH FOR DINNER.

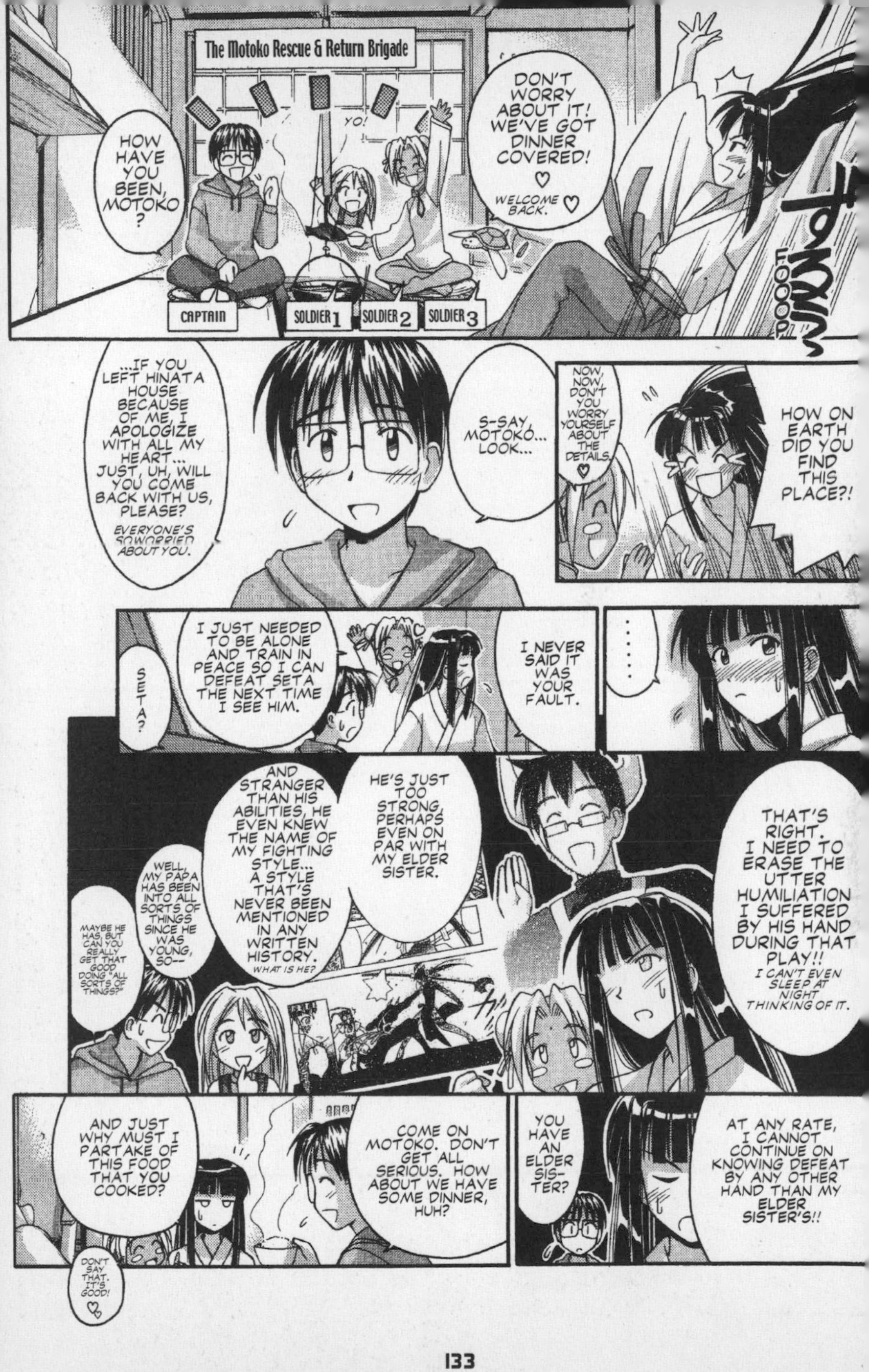

FOOOP
DON'T WORRY ABOUT IT! WE'VE GOT DINNER COVERED! ♡
WELCOME BACK. ♡
YO!
HOW HAVE YOU BEEN, MOTOKO?
The Motoko Rescue & Return Brigade
CAPTAIN
SOLDIER 1
SOLDIER 2
SOLDIER 3
HOW ON EARTH DID YOU FIND THIS PLACE?!
NOW, NOW, DON'T YOU WORRY YOURSELF ABOUT THE DETAILS. ♡
S-SAY, MOTOKO... LOOK...
...IF YOU LEFT HINATA HOUSE BECAUSE OF ME, I APOLOGIZE WITH ALL MY HEART... JUST, UH, WILL YOU COME BACK WITH US, PLEASE?
EVERYONE'S SO WORRIED ABOUT YOU.
......
I NEVER SAID IT WAS YOUR FAULT.
I JUST NEEDED TO BE ALONE AND TRAIN IN PEACE SO I CAN DEFEAT SETA THE NEXT TIME I SEE HIM.
SETA?
THAT'S RIGHT. I NEED TO ERASE THE UTTER HUMILIATION I SUFFERED BY HIS HAND DURING THAT PLAY!!
I CAN'T EVEN SLEEP AT NIGHT THINKING OF IT.
HE'S JUST TOO STRONG, PERHAPS EVEN ON PAR WITH MY ELDER SISTER.
AND STRANGER THAN HIS ABILITIES, HE EVEN KNEW THE NAME OF MY FIGHTING STYLE... A STYLE THAT'S NEVER BEEN MENTIONED IN ANY WRITTEN HISTORY.
WHAT IS HE?
WELL, MY PAPA HAS BEEN INTO ALL SORTS OF THINGS SINCE HE WAS YOUNG, SO--
MAYBE HE HAS, BUT CAN YOU REALLY GET THAT GOOD DOING "ALL SORTS OF THINGS?"
AT ANY RATE, I CANNOT CONTINUE ON KNOWING DEFEAT BY ANY OTHER HAND THAN MY ELDER SISTER'S!!
YOU HAVE AN ELDER SISTER?
COME ON MOTOKO. DON'T GET ALL SERIOUS. HOW ABOUT WE HAVE SOME DINNER, HUH?
AND JUST WHY MUST I PARTAKE OF THIS FOOD THAT YOU COOKED?
DON'T SAY THAT. IT'S GOOD! ♡

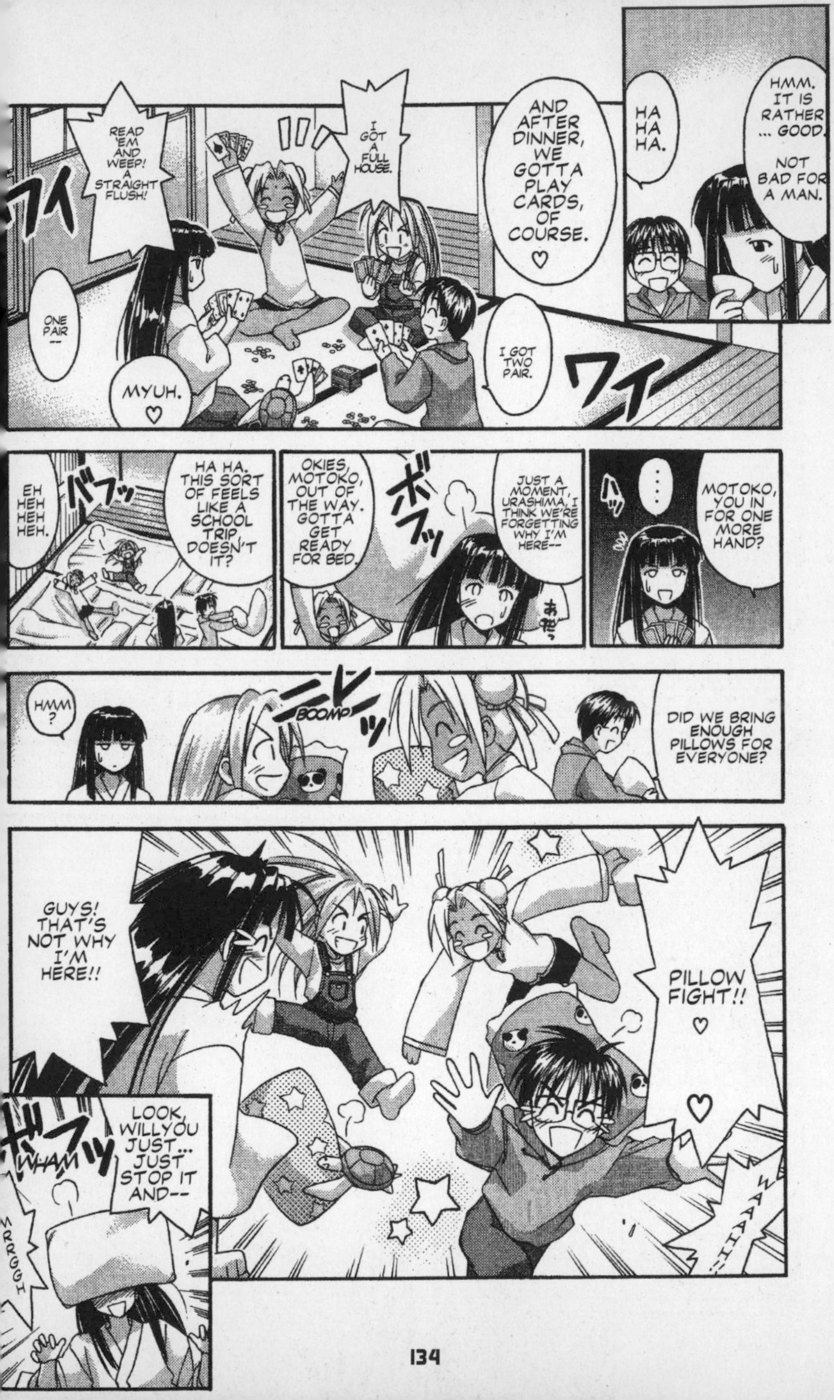
HMM. IT IS RATHER ... GOOD.
NOT BAD FOR A MAN.
HA HA HA.
AND AFTER DINNER, WE GOTTA PLAY CARDS, OF COURSE. ♡
I GOT A FULL HOUSE.
READ 'EM AND WEEP! A STRAIGHT FLUSH!
ワイ
ワイ
I GOT TWO PAIR.
ONE PAIR --
MYUH. ♡
MOTOKO, YOU IN FOR ONE MORE HAND?
. . . .
JUST A MOMENT, URASHIMA, I THINK WE'RE FORGETTING WHY I'M HERE--
ボフッ
OKIES, MOTOKO, OUT OF THE WAY. GOTTA GET READY FOR BED.
HA HA. THIS SORT OF FEELS LIKE A SCHOOL TRIP DOESN'T IT?
バフッ
EH HEH HEH HEH.
DID WE BRING ENOUGH PILLOWS FOR EVERYONE?
BOOMP
HMM ?
PILLOW FIGHT!! ♡
WAAAH!!
GUYS! THAT'S NOT WHY I'M HERE!!
LOOK, WILLYOU JUST... JUST STOP IT AND--
WHAM
MRRGGH

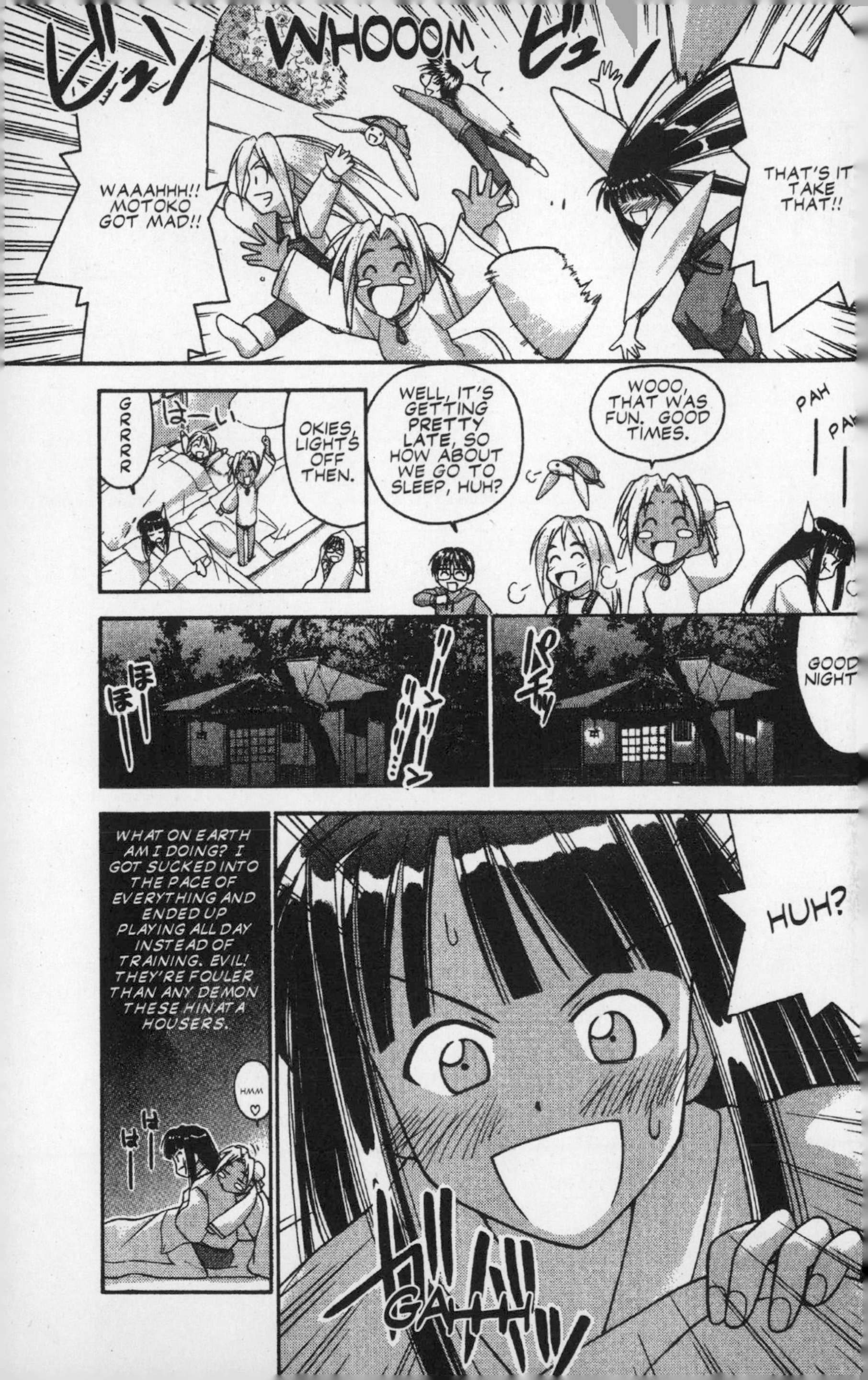

WHOOOM
THAT'S IT TAKE THAT!!
WAAAHHH!! MOTOKO GOT MAD!!
PAH PAH
WOOO, THAT WAS FUN. GOOD TIMES.
WELL, IT'S GETTING PRETTY LATE, SO HOW ABOUT WE GO TO SLEEP, HUH?
OKIES, LIGHTS OFF THEN.
はーい
GRRRR
GOOD NIGHT
HUH?
GAHH
WHAT ON EARTH AM I DOING? I GOT SUCKED INTO THE PACE OF EVERYTHING AND ENDED UP PLAYING ALL DAY INSTEAD OF TRAINING. EVIL! THEY'RE FOULER THAN ANY DEMON THESE HINATA HOUSERS.
HMM ♡

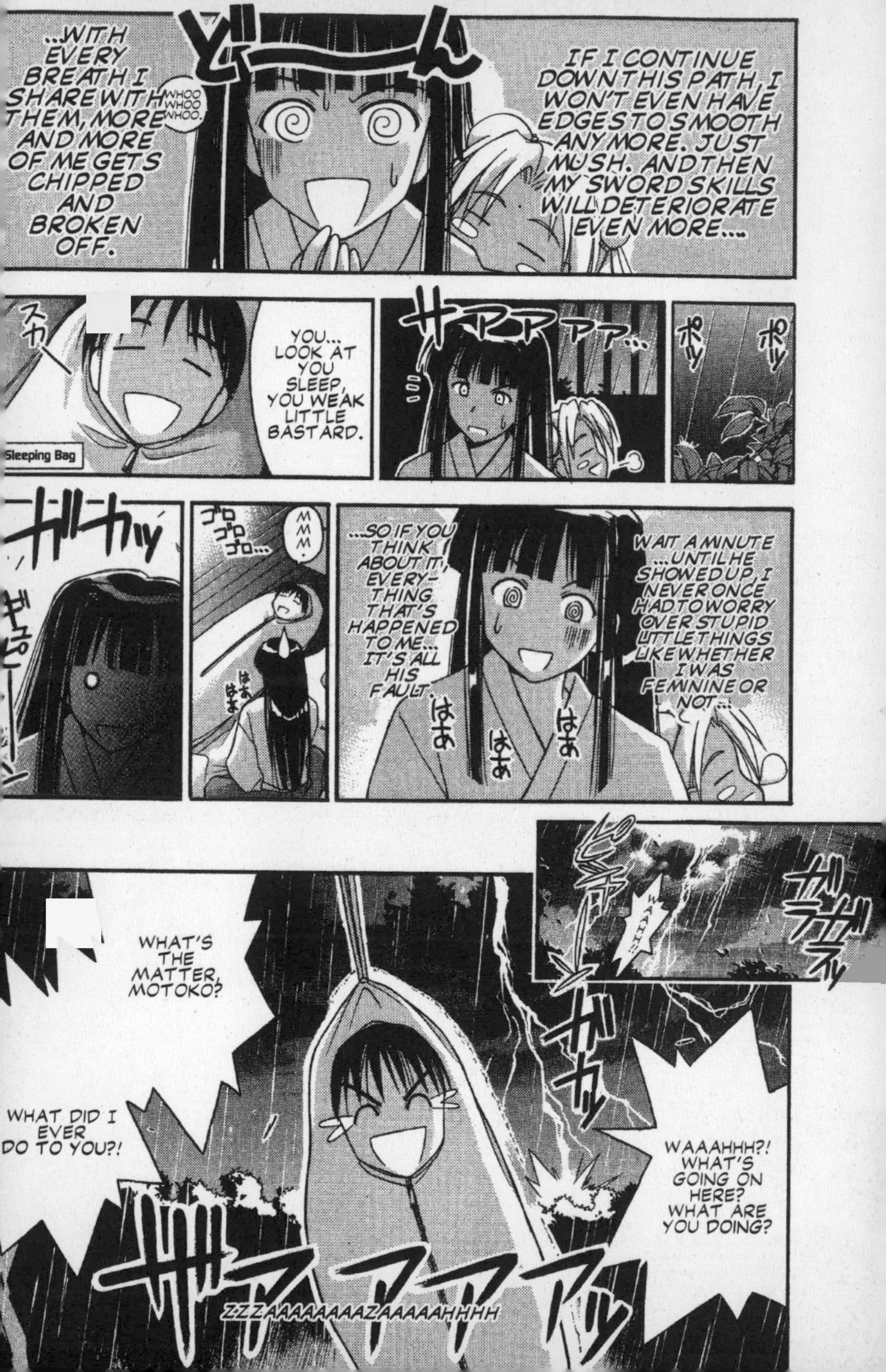
IF I CONTINUE DOWN THIS PATH, I WON'T EVEN HAVE EDGES TO SMOOTH ANYMORE. JUST MUSH. AND THEN MY SWORD SKILLS WILL DETERIORATE EVEN MORE...
WHOO WHOO WHOO.
...WITH EVERY BREATH I SHARE WITH THEM, MORE AND MORE OF ME GETS CHIPPED AND BROKEN OFF.
YOU... LOOK AT YOU SLEEP, YOU WEAK LITTLE BASTARD.
Sleeping Bag
WAIT A MINUTE ...UNTIL HE SHOWED UP, I NEVER ONCE HAD TO WORRY OVER STUPID LITTLE THINGS LIKE WHETHER I WAS FEMNINE OR NOT...
...SO IF YOU THINK ABOUT IT, EVERY-THING THAT'S HAPPENED TO ME... IT'S ALL HIS FAULT.
MMM...
WAAHH!!
WAAAHHH?! WHAT'S GOING ON HERE? WHAT ARE YOU DOING?
WHAT'S THE MATTER, MOTOKO?
WHAT DID I EVER DO TO YOU?!
ZZZAAAAAAAAZAAAAAHHHH

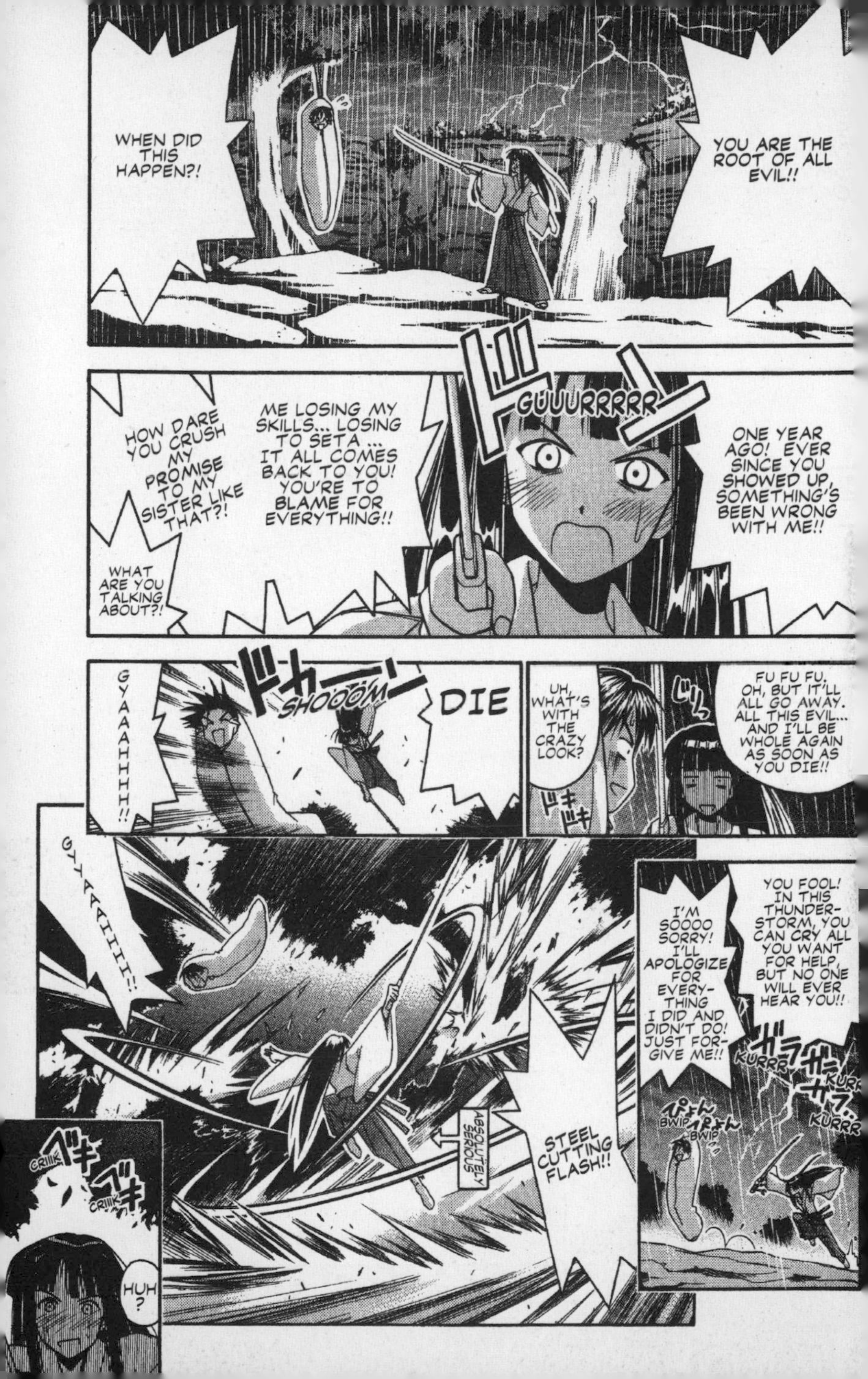
YOU ARE THE ROOT OF ALL EVIL!!
WHEN DID THIS HAPPEN?!
ONE YEAR AGO! EVER SINCE YOU SHOWED UP, SOMETHING'S BEEN WRONG WITH ME!!
GUUURRRRR
ME LOSING MY SKILLS... LOSING TO SETA ... IT ALL COMES BACK TO YOU! YOU'RE TO BLAME FOR EVERYTHING!!
HOW DARE YOU CRUSH MY PROMISE TO MY SISTER LIKE THAT?!
WHAT ARE YOU TALKING ABOUT?!
FU FU FU. OH, BUT IT'LL ALL GO AWAY. ALL THIS EVIL... AND I'LL BE WHOLE AGAIN AS SOON AS YOU DIE!!
UH, WHAT'S WITH THE CRAZY LOOK?
DIE
SHOOOM
GYAAAAHHHH!!
YOU FOOL! IN THIS THUNDER-STORM, YOU CAN CRY ALL YOU WANT FOR HELP, BUT NO ONE WILL EVER HEAR YOU!!
I'M SOOOO SORRY! I'LL APOLOGIZE FOR EVERY-THING I DID AND DIDN'T DO! JUST FOR-GIVE ME!!
KURRR
KURRR
KURRR
BWIP
BWIP
STEEL CUTTING FLASH!!
ABSOLUTELY SERIOUS
GYAAAAHHHH!!
CRIIIK
CRIIIK
HUH?

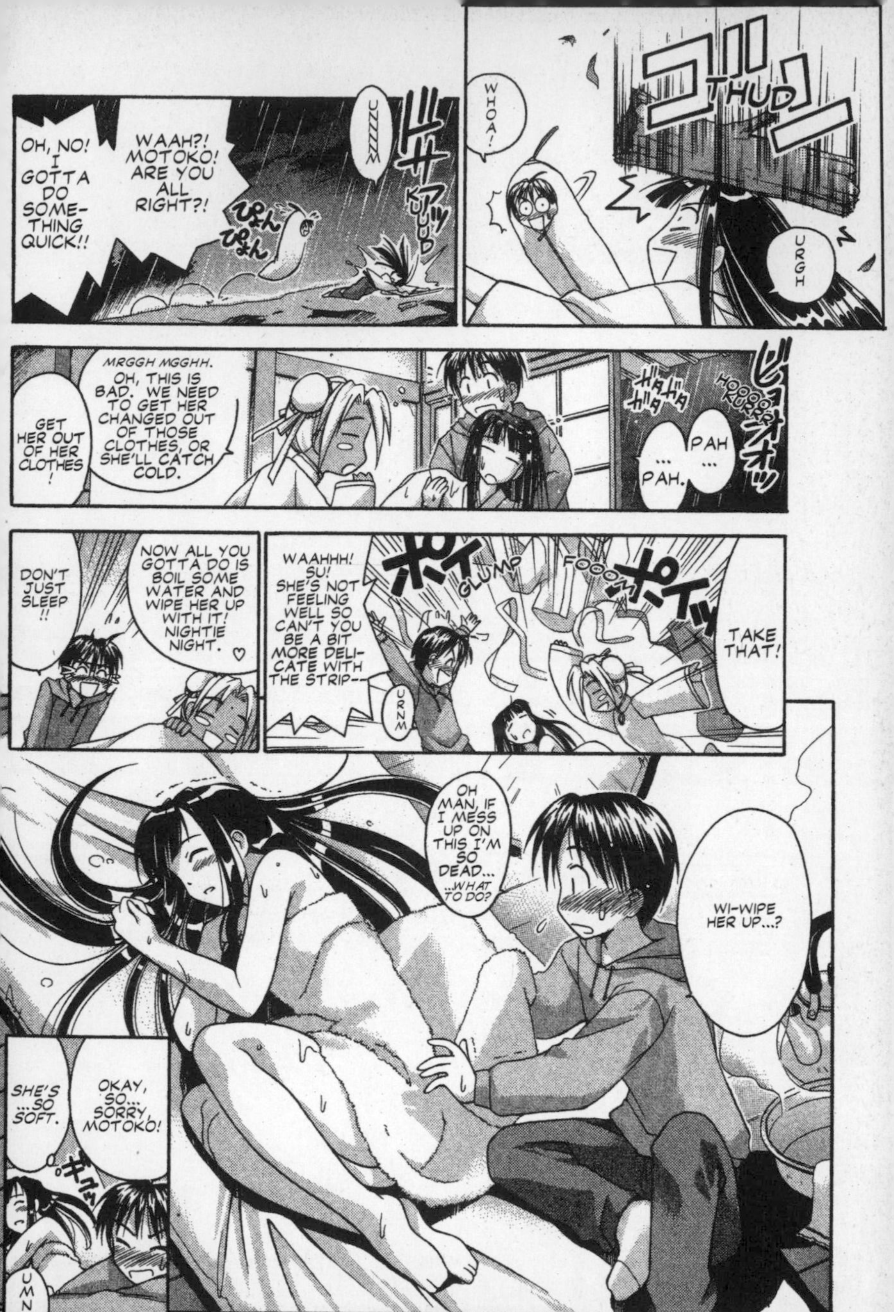
THUD
WHOA!
URGH
UNNNM
WAAH?! MOTOKO! ARE YOU ALL RIGHT?!
OH, NO! I GOTTA DO SOME-THING QUICK!!
PAH... PAH.
MRGGH MGGHH.
OH, THIS IS BAD. WE NEED TO GET HER CHANGED OUT OF THOSE CLOTHES, OR SHE'LL CATCH COLD.
GET HER OUT OF HER CLOTHES!
TAKE THAT!
GLUMP
WAAHHH! SU! SHE'S NOT FEELING WELL SO CAN'T YOU BE A BIT MORE DELI-CATE WITH THE STRIP--
URNM
NOW ALL YOU GOTTA DO IS BOIL SOME WATER AND WIPE HER UP WITH IT! NIGHTIE NIGHT. ♡
DON'T JUST SLEEP!!
WI-WIPE HER UP...?
OH MAN, IF I MESS UP ON THIS I'M SO DEAD... ...WHAT TO DO?
OKAY, SO... SORRY, MOTOKO!
SHE'S ...SO SOFT.
UMNN.

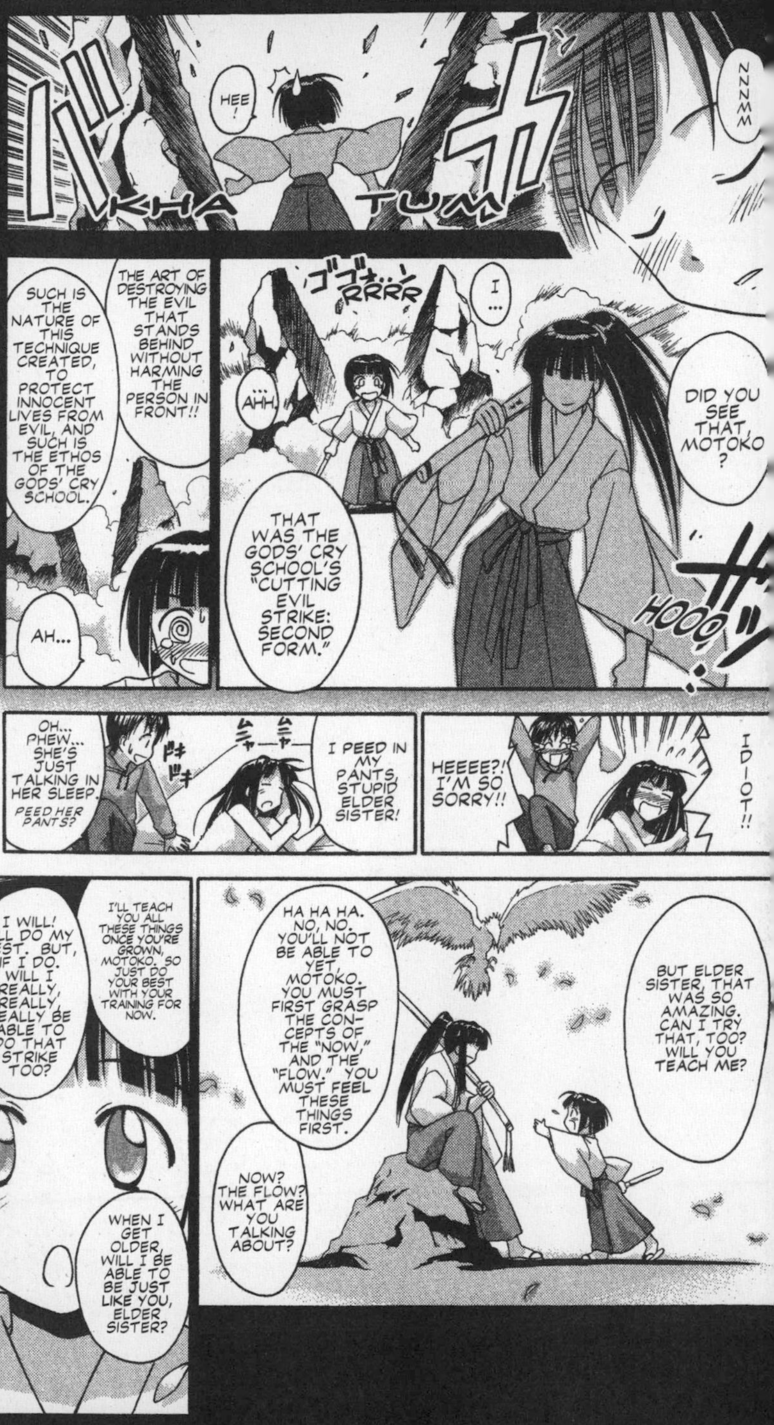
NNNMM
HEE!
KHA TUM
DID YOU SEE THAT, MOTOKO?
I...
RRRR
...AHH.
HOOO
THAT WAS THE GODS' CRY SCHOOL'S "CUTTING EVIL STRIKE: SECOND FORM."
THE ART OF DESTROYING THE EVIL THAT STANDS BEHIND WITHOUT HARMING THE PERSON IN FRONT!!
SUCH IS THE NATURE OF THIS TECHNIQUE CREATED, TO PROTECT INNOCENT LIVES FROM EVIL, AND SUCH IS THE ETHOS OF THE GODS' CRY SCHOOL.
AH...
IDIOT!!
HEEEE?! I'M SO SORRY!!
I PEED IN MY PANTS, STUPID ELDER SISTER!
OH... PHEW... SHE'S JUST TALKING IN HER SLEEP.
PEED HER PANTS?
BUT ELDER SISTER, THAT WAS SO AMAZING. CAN I TRY THAT, TOO? WILL YOU TEACH ME?
HA HA HA. NO, NO. YOU'LL NOT BE ABLE TO YET, MOTOKO. YOU MUST FIRST GRASP THE CONCEPTS OF THE "NOW," AND THE "FLOW." YOU MUST FEEL THESE THINGS FIRST.
NOW? THE FLOW? WHAT ARE YOU TALKING ABOUT?
I'LL TEACH YOU ALL THESE THINGS ONCE YOU'RE GROWN, MOTOKO. SO JUST DO YOUR BEST WITH YOUR TRAINING FOR NOW.
I WILL! I'LL DO MY BEST. BUT, IF I DO. WILL I REALLY, REALLY BE ABLE TO DO THAT STRIKE TOO?
WHEN I GET OLDER, WILL I BE ABLE TO BE JUST LIKE YOU, ELDER SISTER?

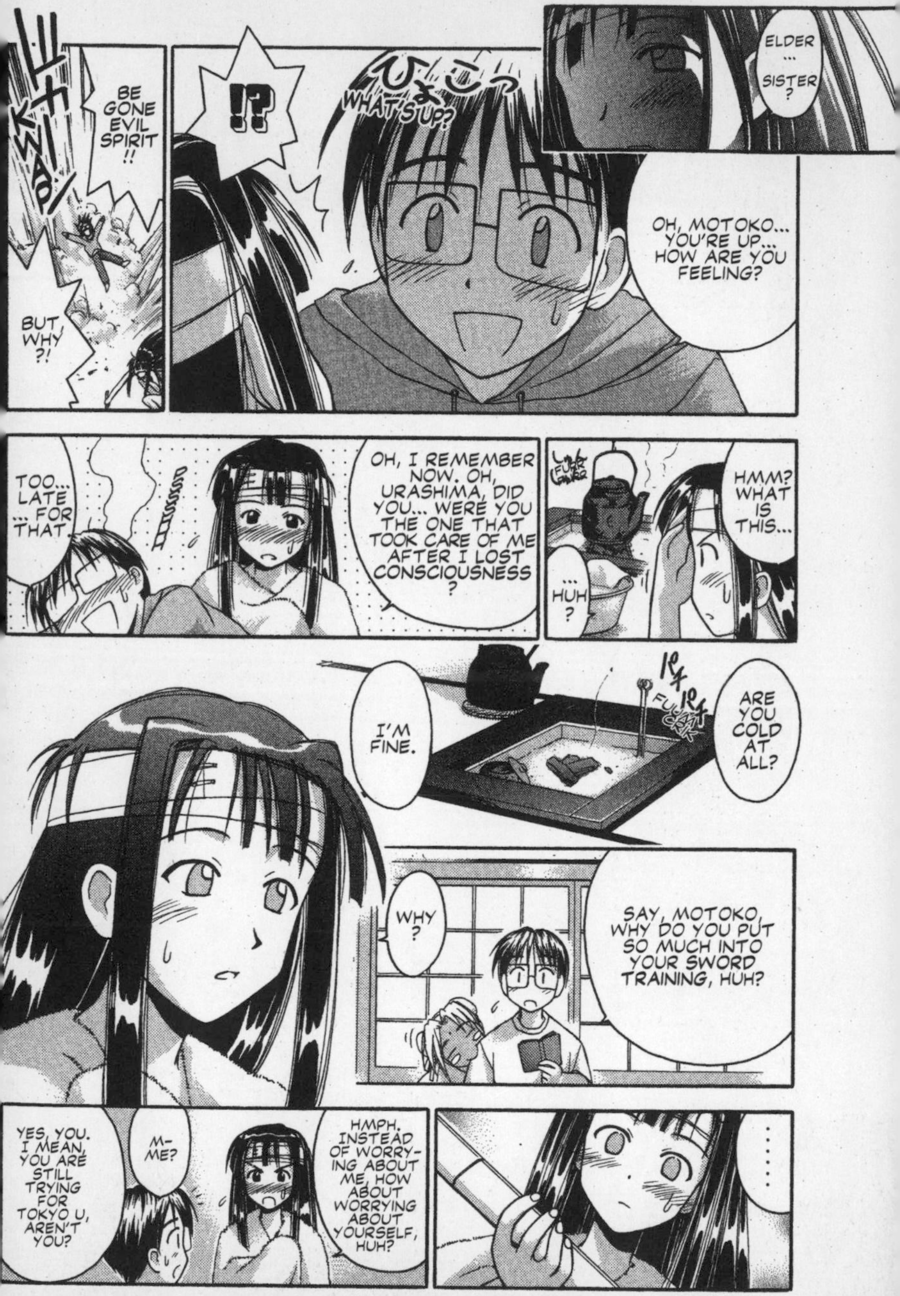
ELDER ... SISTER?
WHAT'S UP?
OH, MOTOKO... YOU'RE UP... HOW ARE YOU FEELING?
!?
BE GONE EVIL SPIRIT!!
WAP
BUT, WHY?!
HMM? WHAT IS THIS...
...HUH?
OH, I REMEMBER NOW. OH, URASHIMA, DID YOU... WERE YOU THE ONE THAT TOOK CARE OF ME AFTER I LOST CONSCIOUSNESS?
TOO... LATE ... FOR THAT.
ARE YOU COLD AT ALL?
I'M FINE.
SAY, MOTOKO, WHY DO YOU PUT SO MUCH INTO YOUR SWORD TRAINING, HUH?
WHY?
......
HMPH. INSTEAD OF WORRYING ABOUT ME, HOW ABOUT WORRYING ABOUT YOURSELF, HUH?
M-ME?
YES, YOU. I MEAN, YOU ARE STILL TRYING FOR TOKYO U, AREN'T YOU?

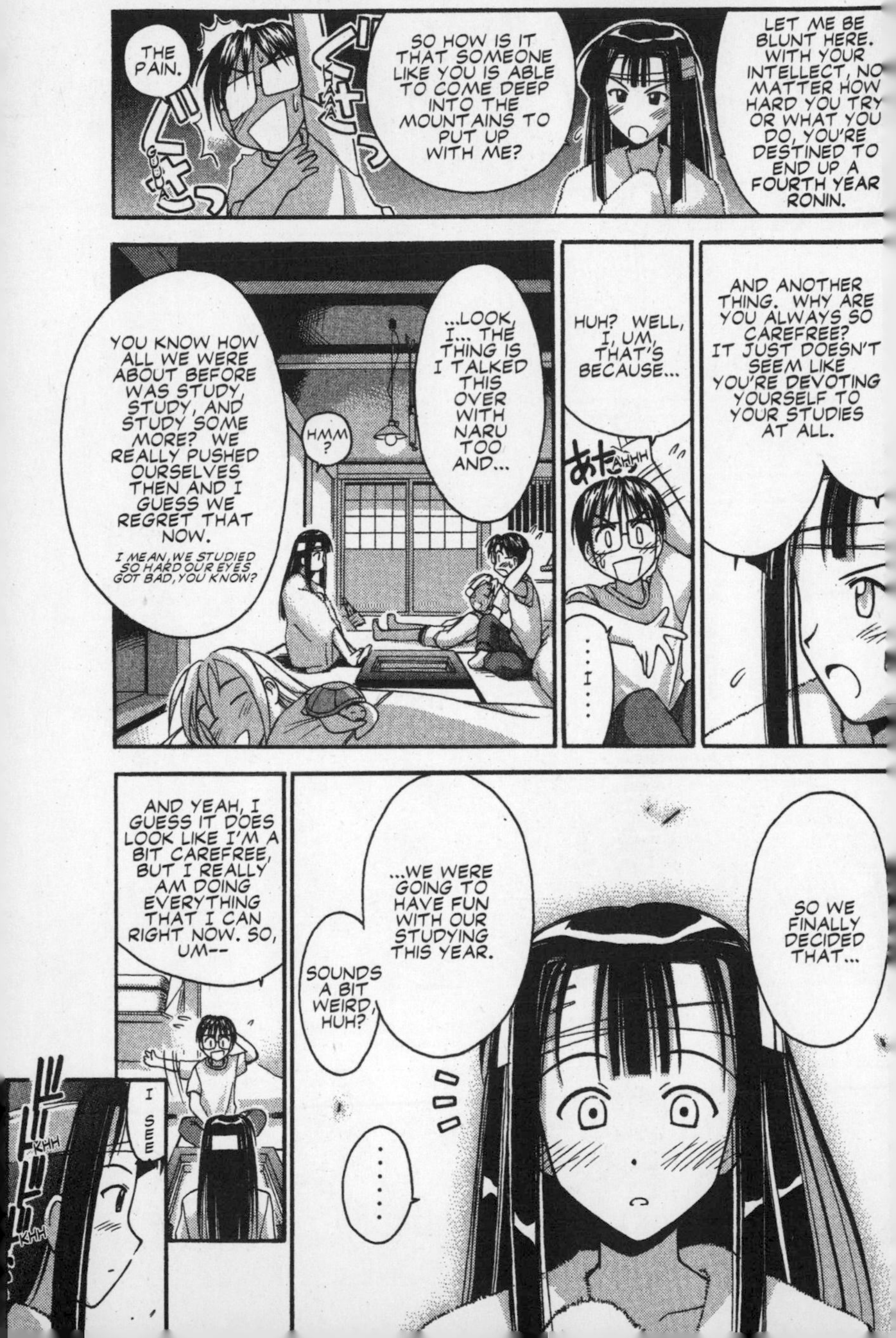
LET ME BE BLUNT HERE. WITH YOUR INTELLECT, NO MATTER HOW HARD YOU TRY OR WHAT YOU DO, YOU'RE DESTINED TO END UP A FOURTH YEAR RONIN.
SO HOW IS IT THAT SOMEONE LIKE YOU IS ABLE TO COME DEEP INTO THE MOUNTAINS TO PUT UP WITH ME?
THE PAIN.
AND ANOTHER THING. WHY ARE YOU ALWAYS SO CAREFREE? IT JUST DOESN'T SEEM LIKE YOU'RE DEVOTING YOURSELF TO YOUR STUDIES AT ALL.
HUH? WELL, I, UM, THAT'S BECAUSE...
....I....
...LOOK, I... THE THING IS I TALKED THIS OVER WITH NARU TOO AND...
HMM?
YOU KNOW HOW ALL WE WERE ABOUT BEFORE WAS STUDY, STUDY, AND STUDY SOME MORE? WE REALLY PUSHED OURSELVES THEN AND I GUESS WE REGRET THAT NOW.
I MEAN, WE STUDIED SO HARD OUR EYES GOT BAD, YOU KNOW?
SO WE FINALLY DECIDED THAT...
...WE WERE GOING TO HAVE FUN WITH OUR STUDYING THIS YEAR.
SOUNDS A BIT WEIRD, HUH?
......
AND YEAH, I GUESS IT DOES LOOK LIKE I'M A BIT CAREFREE, BUT I REALLY AM DOING EVERYTHING THAT I CAN RIGHT NOW. SO, UM--
I SEE.
KHH
KHH

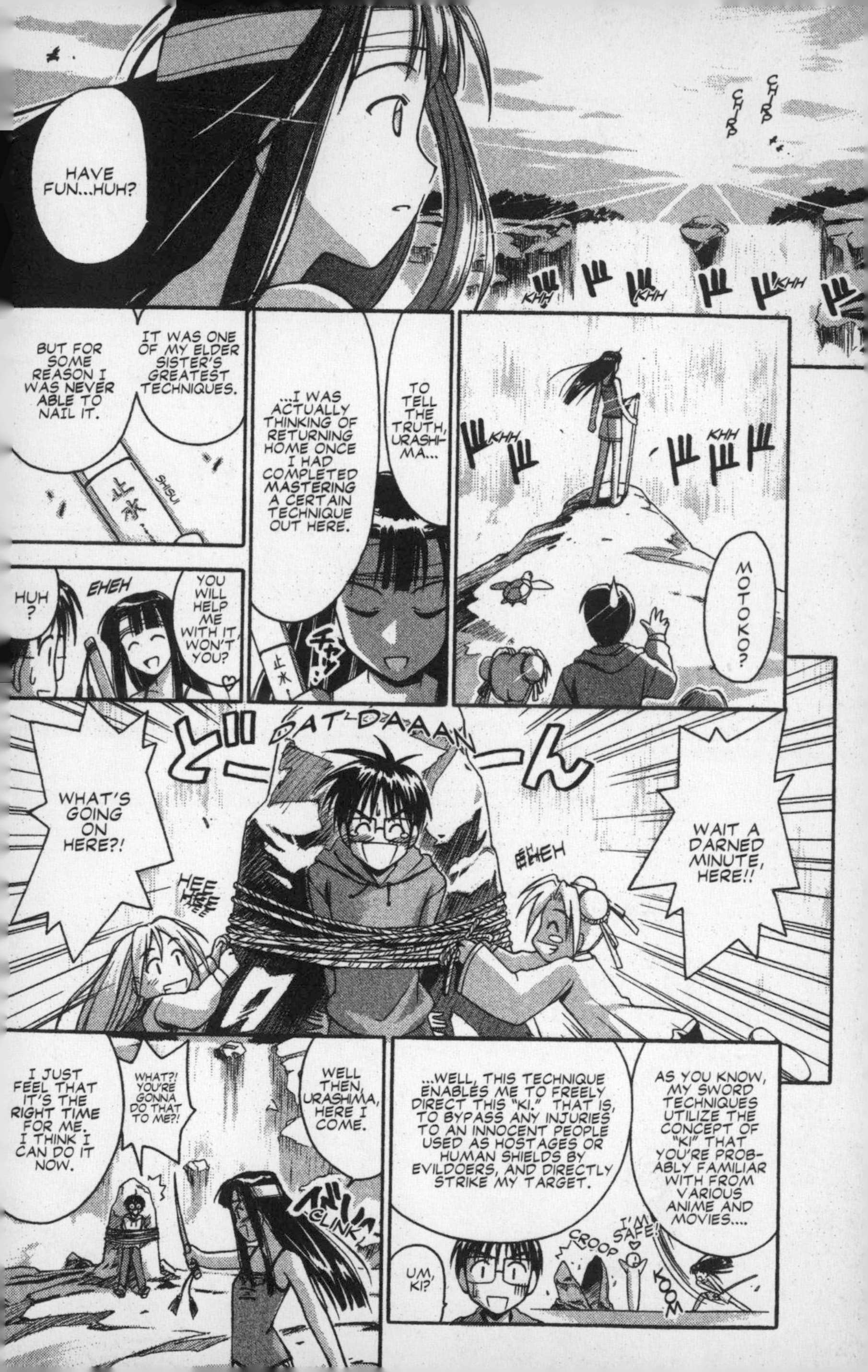
CHIRP
CHIRP
KHH
KHH
KHH
HAVE FUN...HUH?
KHH
KHH
MOTOKO?
TO TELL THE TRUTH, URASHIMA...
...I WAS ACTUALLY THINKING OF RETURNING HOME ONCE I HAD COMPLETED MASTERING A CERTAIN TECHNIQUE OUT HERE.
IT WAS ONE OF MY ELDER SISTER'S GREATEST TECHNIQUES.
BUT FOR SOME REASON I WAS NEVER ABLE TO NAIL IT.
SHISUI
YOU WILL HELP ME WITH IT, WON'T YOU?
EHEH
HUH?
WAIT A DARNED MINUTE, HERE!!
EHEH
DAT-DAAAN
HEE HEE
WHAT'S GOING ON HERE?!
AS YOU KNOW, MY SWORD TECHNIQUES UTILIZE THE CONCEPT OF "KI" THAT YOU'RE PROBABLY FAMILIAR WITH FROM VARIOUS ANIME AND MOVIES....
...WELL, THIS TECHNIQUE ENABLES ME TO FREELY DIRECT THIS "KI." THAT IS, TO BYPASS ANY INJURIES TO AN INNOCENT PEOPLE USED AS HOSTAGES OR HUMAN SHIELDS BY EVILDOERS, AND DIRECTLY STRIKE MY TARGET.
I'M SAFE!
CROOP
KOOM
UM, KI?
WELL THEN, URASHIMA, HERE I COME.
WHAT?! YOU'RE GONNA DO THAT TO ME?!
I JUST FEEL THAT IT'S THE RIGHT TIME FOR ME. I THINK I CAN DO IT NOW.
CLINK

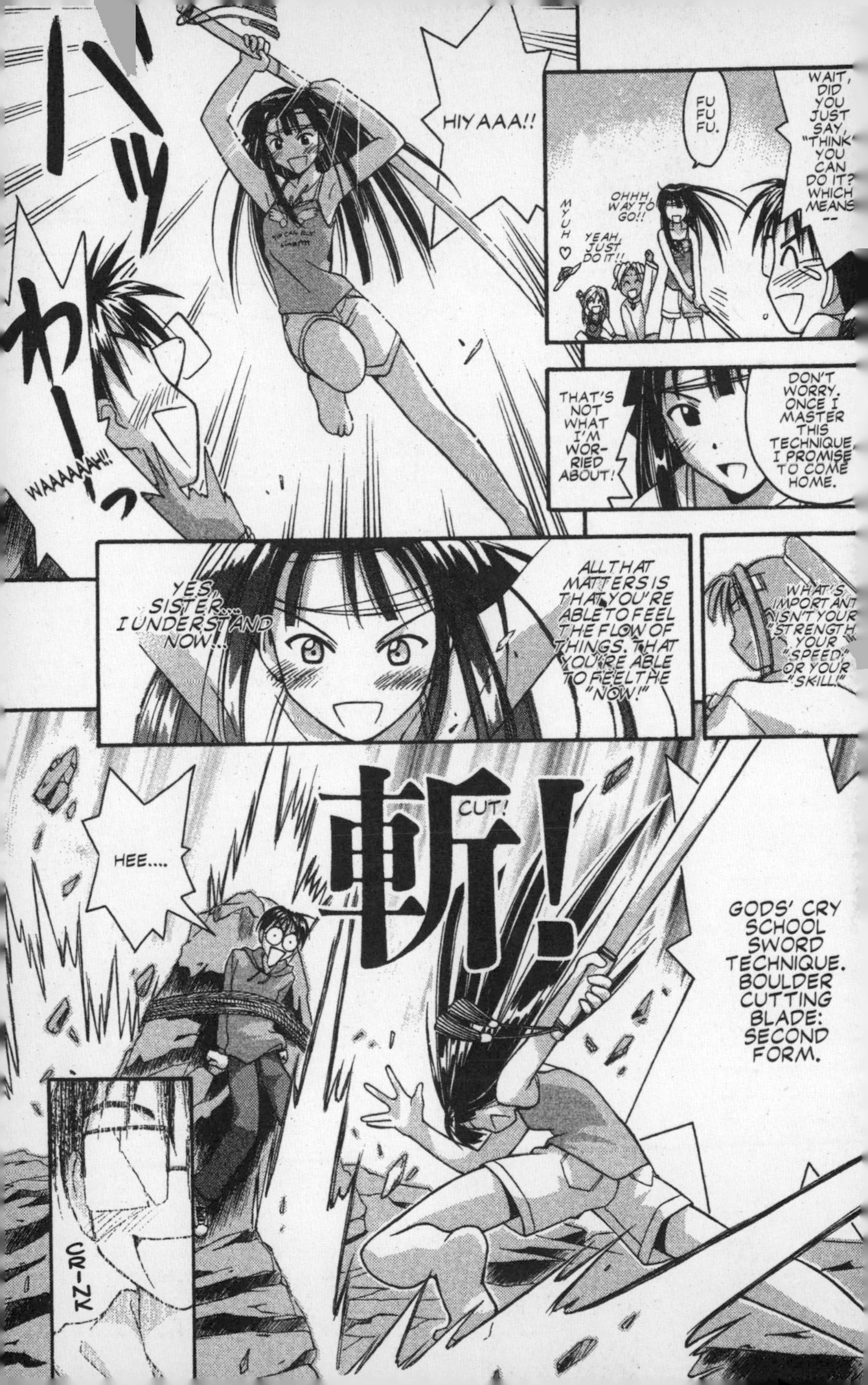

WAIT, DID YOU JUST SAY, "THINK YOU CAN DO IT?" WHICH MEANS--
FU FU FU.
OHHH, WAY TO GO!!
YEAH, JUST DO IT!!
MYUH ♡
DON'T WORRY. ONCE I MASTER THIS TECHNIQUE, I PROMISE TO COME HOME.
THAT'S NOT WHAT I'M WOR-RIED ABOUT!
ハッ
HIYAAA!!
わーーっ
WAAAAAAH!!
WHAT'S IMPORTANT ISN'T YOUR "STRENGTH," YOUR "SPEED," OR YOUR "SKILL."
ALL THAT MATTERS IS THAT YOU'RE ABLE TO FEEL THE FLOW OF THINGS. THAT YOU'RE ABLE TO FEEL THE "NOW!"
YES, SISTER.... I UNDERSTAND NOW...
GODS' CRY SCHOOL SWORD TECHNIQUE. BOULDER CUTTING BLADE: SECOND FORM.
斬!
CUT!
HEE....
CR-NK

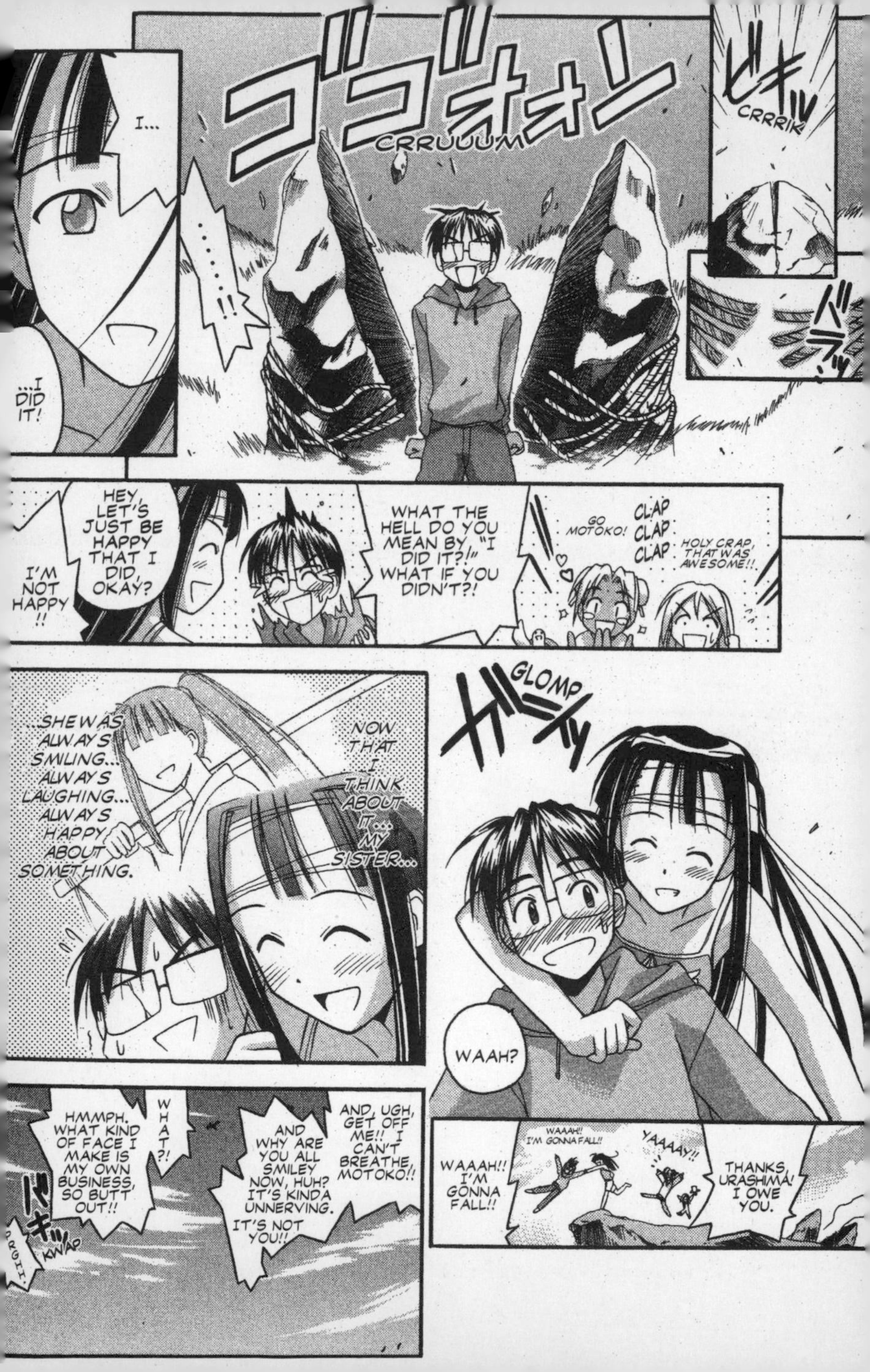
CRRRIK
ゴゴオォン
CRRUUUM
I...
...!!
...I DID IT!
HOLY CRAP, THAT WAS AWESOME!!
CLAP CLAP CLAP
GO MOTOKO!
WHAT THE HELL DO YOU MEAN BY "I DID IT?!" WHAT IF YOU DIDN'T?!
HEY, LET'S JUST BE HAPPY THAT I DID, OKAY?
I'M NOT HAPPY!!
GLOMP
WAAH?
NOW THAT I THINK ABOUT IT... MY SISTER...
...SHE WAS ALWAYS SMILING... ALWAYS LAUGHING... ALWAYS HAPPY ABOUT SOMETHING.
THANKS, URASHIMA! I OWE YOU.
YAAAAY!!
WAAAH!! I'M GONNA FALL!!
WAAAH!! I'M GONNA FALL!!
AND, UGH, GET OFF ME!! I CAN'T BREATHE, MOTOKO!!
AND WHY ARE YOU ALL SMILEY NOW, HUH? IT'S KINDA UNNERVING.
IT'S NOT YOU!!
WHAT?!
HMMPH. WHAT KIND OF FACE I MAKE IS MY OWN BUSINESS, SO BUTT OUT!!
KWAP
ARGH!!

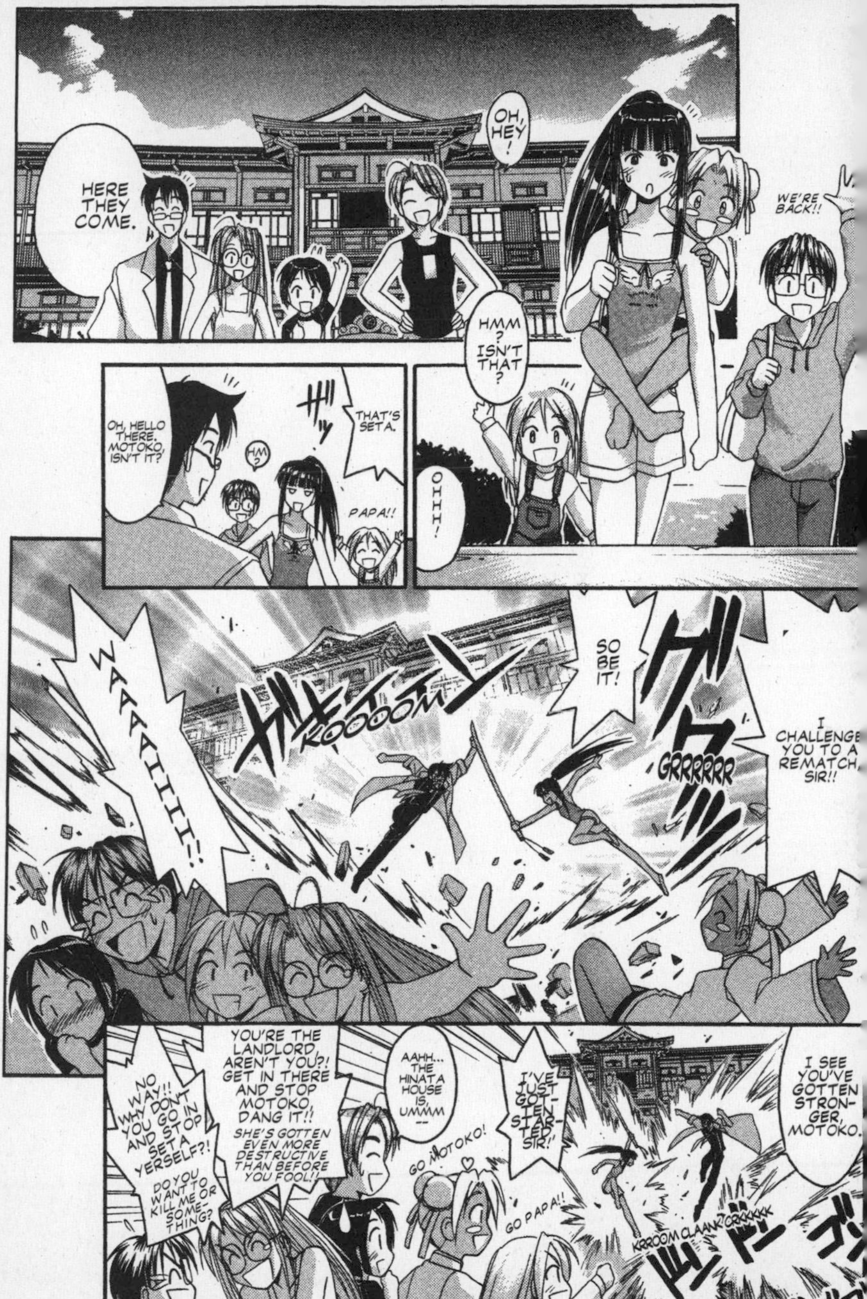
WE'RE BACK!!
OH, HEY!
HERE THEY COME.
HMM? ISN'T THAT?
OHHH!
THAT'S SETA.
PAPA!!
HM?
OH, HELLO THERE, MOTOKO, ISN'T IT?
I CHALLENGE YOU TO A REMATCH, SIR!!
GRRRRRR
SO BE IT!
KROOOOM
WAAAAIIIIII!!
I SEE YOU'VE GOTTEN STRONGER, MOTOKO.
I'VE JUST GOTTEN STARTED, SIR!
KRROOM CLAANK CRKKKKK
GRRRRRR
AAHH... THE HINATA HOUSE IS, UMMM--
GO MOTOKO!
GO PAPA!!
YOU'RE THE LANDLORD, AREN'T YOU?! GET IN THERE AND STOP MOTOKO, DANG IT!!
SHE'S GOTTEN EVEN MORE DESTRUCTIVE THAN BEFORE YOU FOOL!!
NO WAY!! WHY DON'T YOU GO IN AND STOP SETA YERSELF?!
DO YOU WANT TO KILL ME OR SOMETHING?

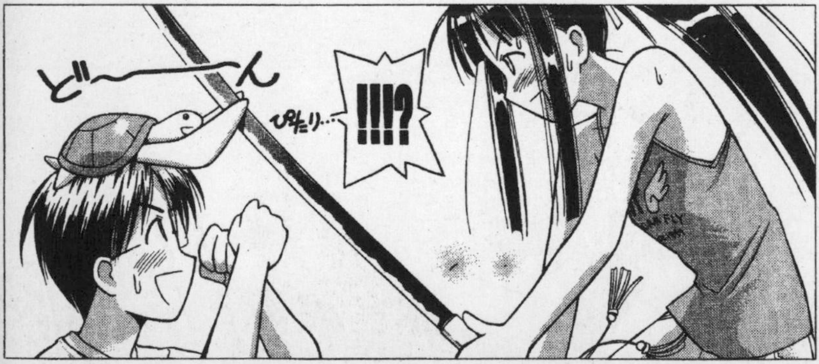
!!!?
ぴたり…
ど〜〜〜ん

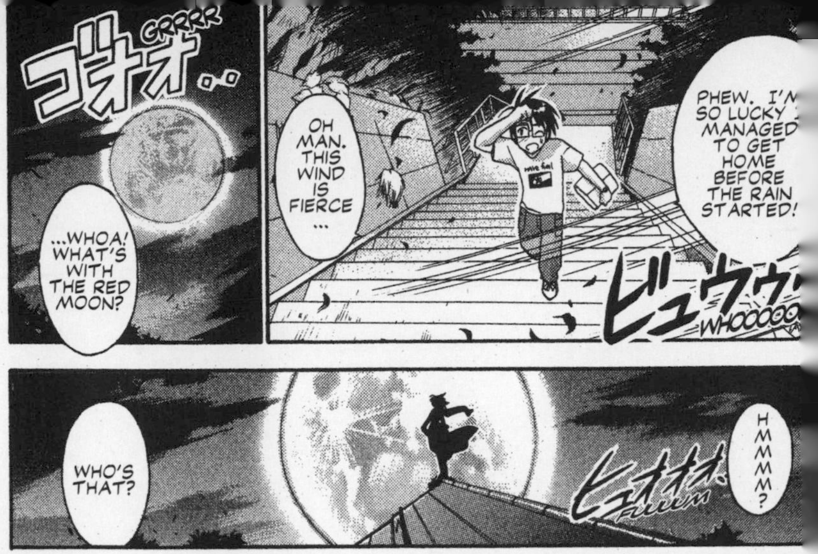
PHEW. I'M SO LUCKY I MANAGED TO GET HOME BEFORE THE RAIN STARTED!
OH MAN. THIS WIND IS FIERCE...
ビュウウ
WHOOOOO
ゴオオ
GRRRR
...WHOA! WHAT'S WITH THE RED MOON?
HMMMM?
ヒュオオオ
WHO'S THAT?

Love Hina

HINATA.41

The Secret of the Mysterious Girl! ♡

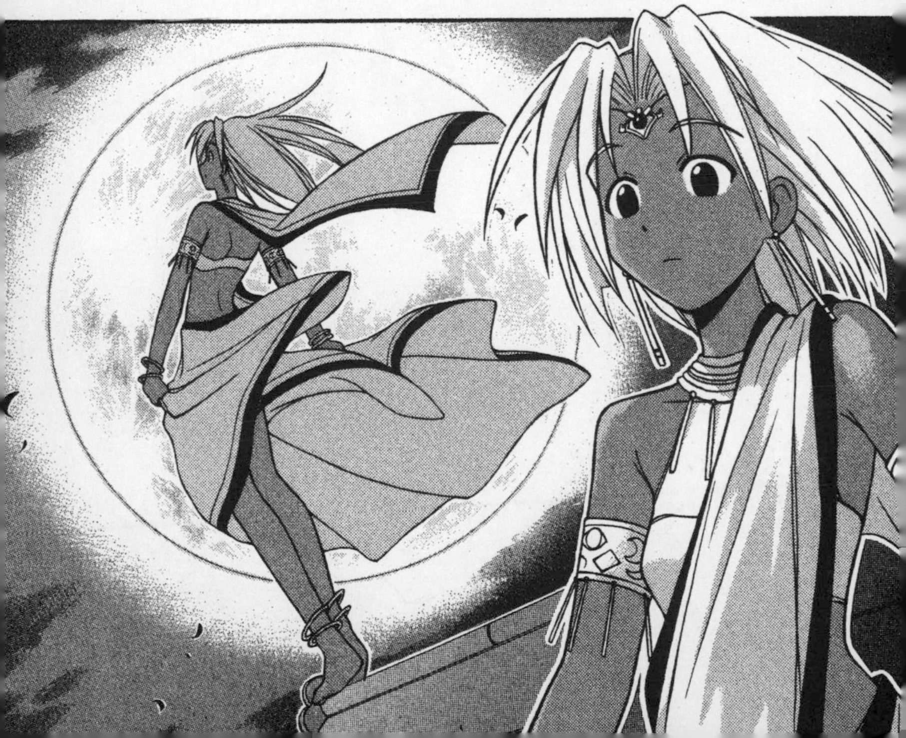

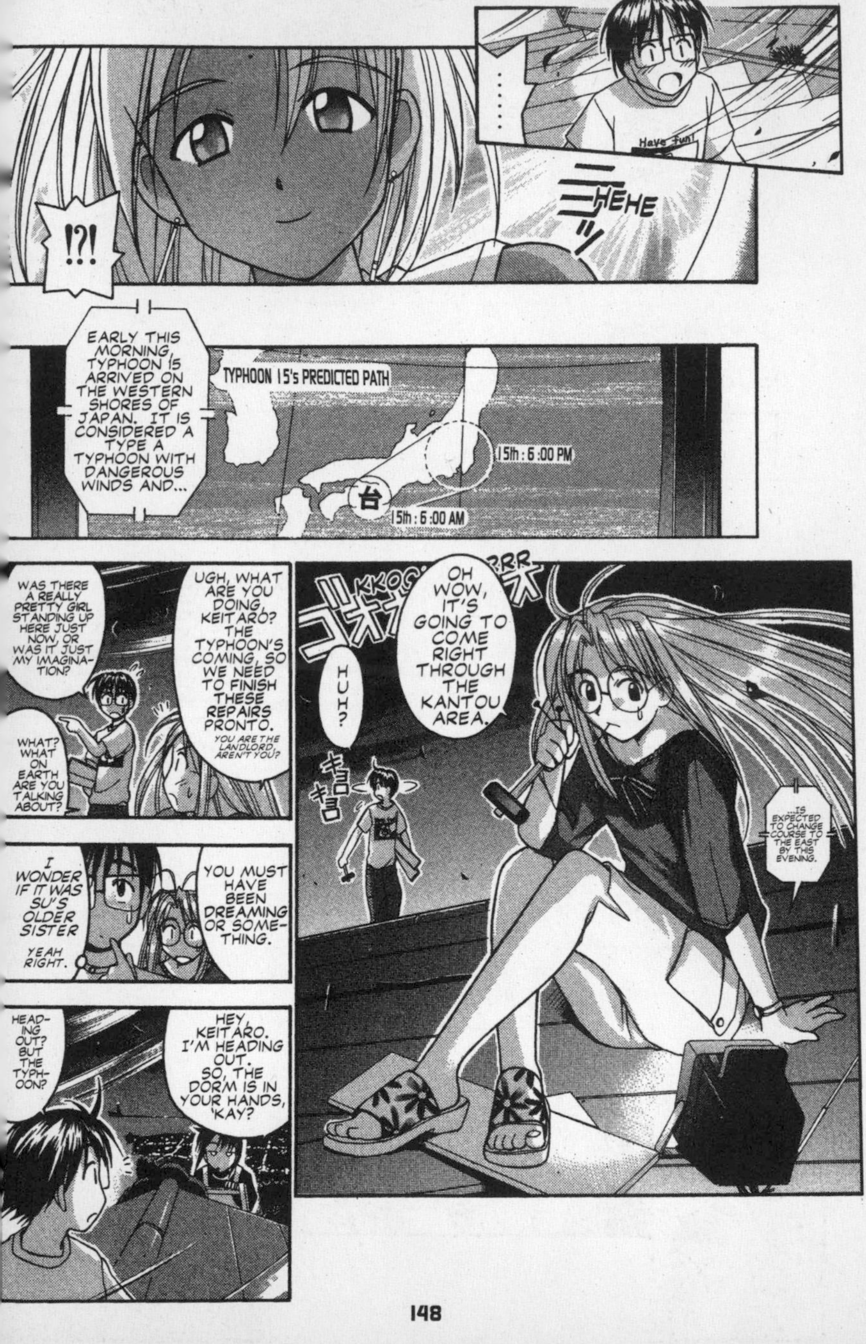

......
HEHE
!?!
EARLY THIS MORNING, TYPHOON 15 ARRIVED ON THE WESTERN SHORES OF JAPAN. IT IS CONSIDERED A TYPE A TYPHOON WITH DANGEROUS WINDS AND...
TYPHOON 15's PREDICTED PATH
15th : 6:00 PM
台
15th : 6:00 AM
...IS EXPECTED TO CHANGE COURSE TO THE EAST BY THIS EVENING.
KKOOSRRR
OH WOW, IT'S GOING TO COME RIGHT THROUGH THE KANTOU AREA.
HUH?
UGH, WHAT ARE YOU DOING, KEITARO? THE TYPHOON'S COMING, SO WE NEED TO FINISH THESE REPAIRS PRONTO.
YOU ARE THE LANDLORD, AREN'T YOU?
WAS THERE A REALLY PRETTY GIRL STANDING UP HERE JUST NOW, OR WAS IT JUST MY IMAGINATION?
WHAT? WHAT ON EARTH ARE YOU TALKING ABOUT?
YOU MUST HAVE BEEN DREAMING OR SOMETHING.
I WONDER IF IT WAS SU'S OLDER SISTER
YEAH RIGHT.
HEY, KEITARO. I'M HEADING OUT. SO, THE DORM IS IN YOUR HANDS, 'KAY?
HEADING OUT? BUT THE TYPHOON?

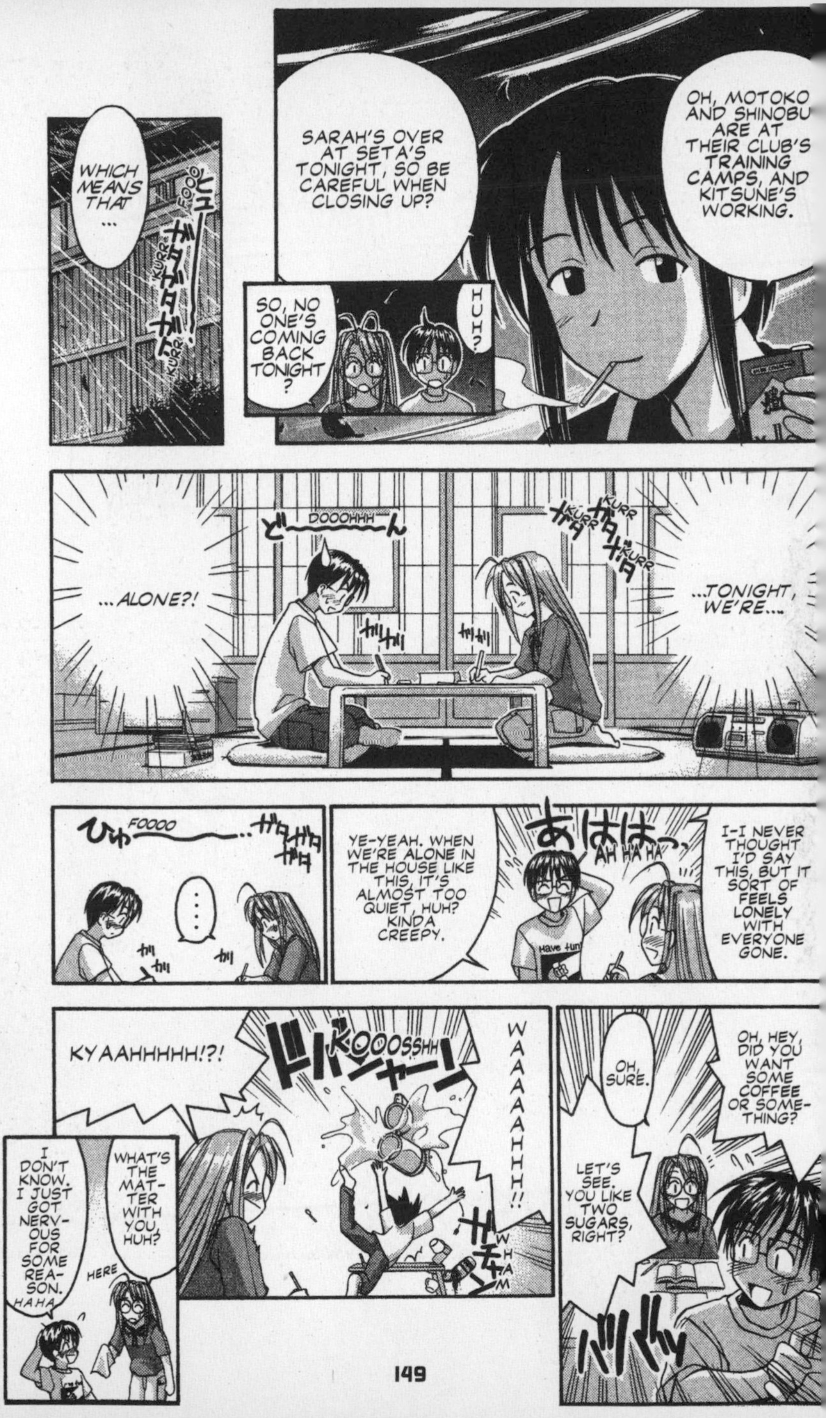
OH, MOTOKO AND SHINOBU ARE AT THEIR CLUB'S TRAINING CAMPS, AND KITSUNE'S WORKING.
SARAH'S OVER AT SETA'S TONIGHT, SO BE CAREFUL WHEN CLOSING UP?
HUH?
SO, NO ONE'S COMING BACK TONIGHT?
ヒュー FOOO
ガタガタガト KURR KURR
WHICH MEANS THAT ...
...TONIGHT, WE'RE...
ガタガタガタ KURR KURR KURR
どーーーん DOOOHHH
...ALONE?!
I-I NEVER THOUGHT I'D SAY THIS, BUT IT SORT OF FEELS LONELY WITH EVERYONE GONE.
あははっ AH HA HA
YE-YEAH. WHEN WE'RE ALONE IN THE HOUSE LIKE THIS, IT'S ALMOST TOO QUIET, HUH? KINDA CREEPY.
ひゅーー FOOOO
ガタガタガタ
...
OH, HEY, DID YOU WANT SOME COFFEE OR SOMETHING?
OH, SURE.
LET'S SEE. YOU LIKE TWO SUGARS, RIGHT?
WAAAAAAAHHH!!
ドバシャーー KOOOSSHH
KYAAHHHHH!?!
ガチャーン WHAM
WHAT'S THE MATTER WITH YOU, HUH?
I DON'T KNOW. I JUST GOT NERVOUS FOR SOME REASON.
HAHA
HERE

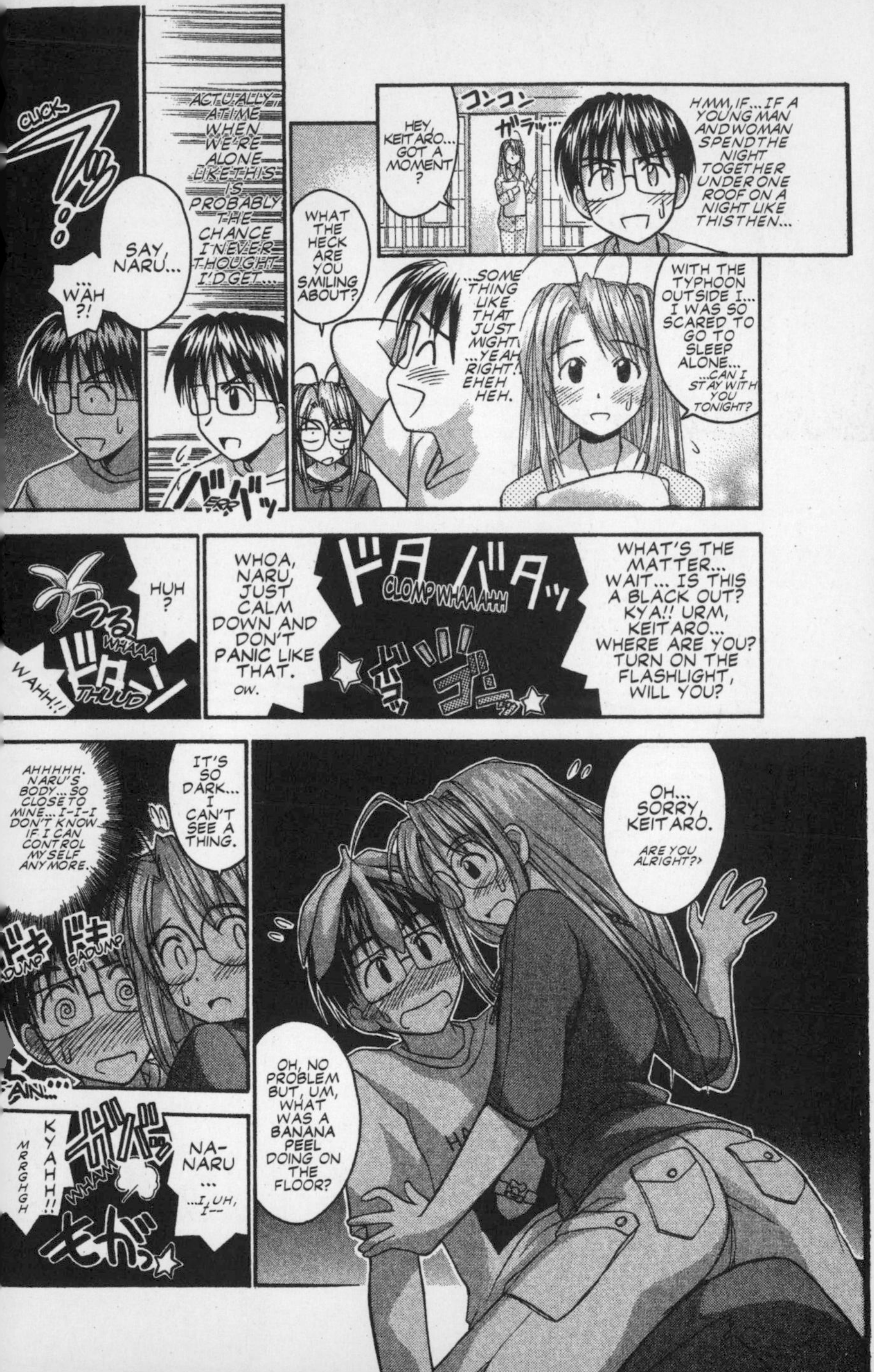
HMM, IF... IF A YOUNG MAN AND WOMAN SPEND THE NIGHT TOGETHER UNDER ONE ROOF ON A NIGHT LIKE THIS THEN...
HEY, KEITARO... GOT A MOMENT?
WITH THE TYPHOON OUTSIDE I... I WAS SO SCARED TO GO TO SLEEP ALONE... ...CAN I STAY WITH YOU TONIGHT?
...SOMETHING LIKE THAT JUST MIGHT ...YEAH RIGHT! EHEH HEH.
WHAT THE HECK ARE YOU SMILING ABOUT?
ACTUALLY A TIME WHEN WE'RE ALONE LIKE THIS IS PROBABLY THE CHANCE I NEVER THOUGHT I'D GET...
SAY, NARU...
CLICK
...WAH?!
WHAT'S THE MATTER... WAIT... IS THIS A BLACK OUT? KYA!! URM, KEITARO... WHERE ARE YOU? TURN ON THE FLASHLIGHT, WILL YOU?
CLOMP WHAAAHH
WHOA, NARU, JUST CALM DOWN AND DON'T PANIC LIKE THAT.
OW.
HUH?
WHAAA
THUD
WAHH!!
OH... SORRY, KEITARO.
ARE YOU ALRIGHT?
OH, NO PROBLEM BUT, UM, WHAT WAS A BANANA PEEL DOING ON THE FLOOR?
IT'S SO DARK... I CAN'T SEE A THING.
AHHHHH. NARU'S BODY... SO CLOSE TO MINE... I-I-I DON'T KNOW IF I CAN CONTROL MYSELF ANYMORE.
BADUMP
BADUMP
NA-NARU... ...I, UH, I--
WHAM
KYAHH!!
MRRGHGH

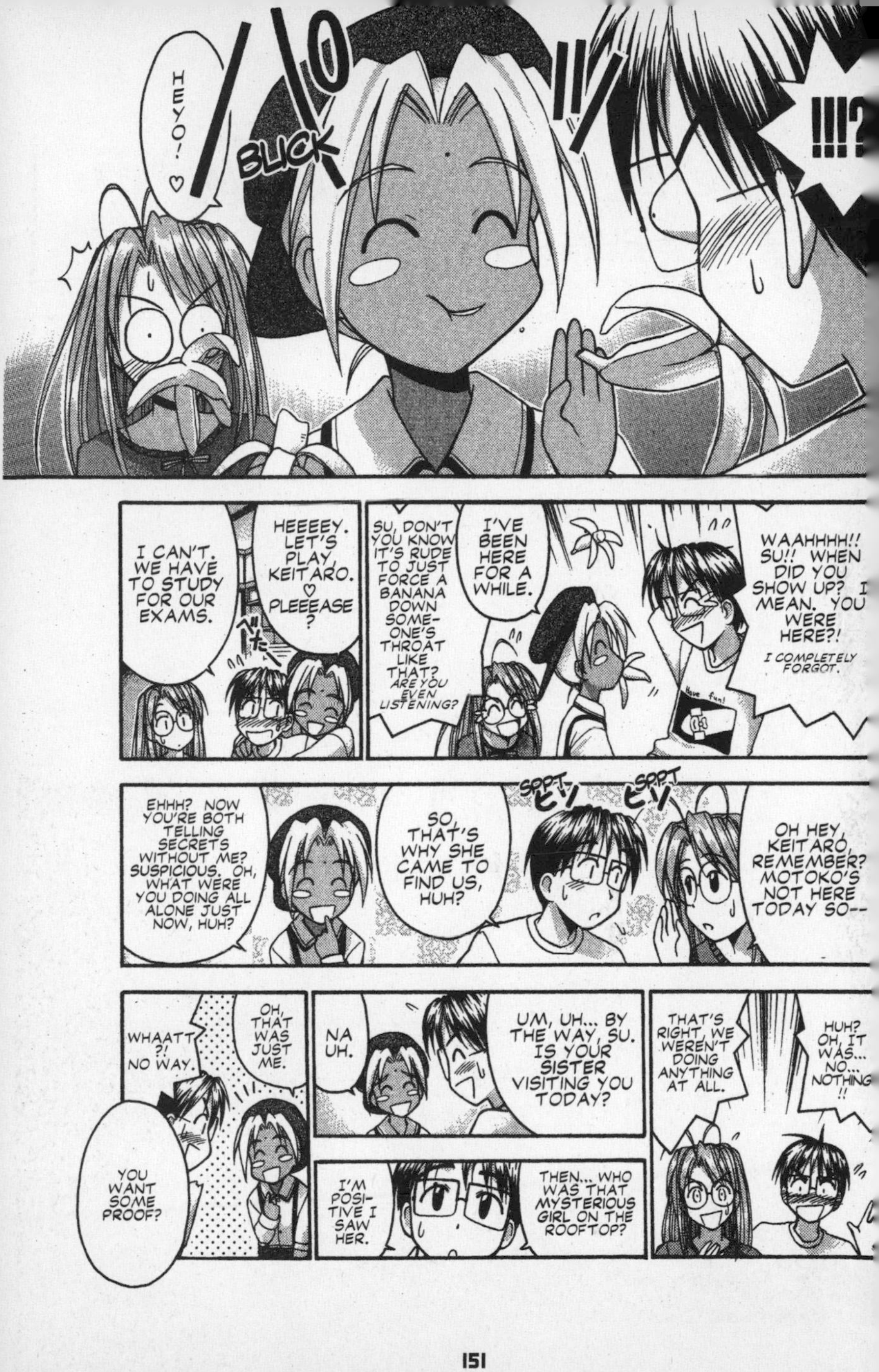
!!!?
BLICK
HEYO! ♡
WAAHHHH!! SU!! WHEN DID YOU SHOW UP? I MEAN. YOU WERE HERE?!
I COMPLETELY FORGOT.
I'VE BEEN HERE FOR A WHILE.
SU, DON'T YOU KNOW IT'S RUDE TO JUST FORCE A BANANA DOWN SOME-ONE'S THROAT LIKE THAT? ARE YOU EVEN LISTENING?
HEEEEY. LET'S PLAY, KEITARO. ♡ PLEEEASE?
I CAN'T. WE HAVE TO STUDY FOR OUR EXAMS.
OH HEY, KEITARO, REMEMBER? MOTOKO'S NOT HERE TODAY SO--
SPPT
SPPT
SO, THAT'S WHY SHE CAME TO FIND US, HUH?
EHHH? NOW YOU'RE BOTH TELLING SECRETS WITHOUT ME? SUSPICIOUS. OH, WHAT WERE YOU DOING ALL ALONE JUST NOW, HUH?
HUH? OH, IT WAS... NO... NOTHING!!
THAT'S RIGHT, WE WEREN'T DOING ANYTHING AT ALL.
UM, UH... BY THE WAY, SU. IS YOUR SISTER VISITING YOU TODAY?
NA UH.
THEN... WHO WAS THAT MYSTERIOUS GIRL ON THE ROOFTOP?
I'M POSI-TIVE I SAW HER.
OH, THAT WAS JUST ME.
WHAATT?! NO WAY.
YOU WANT SOME PROOF?

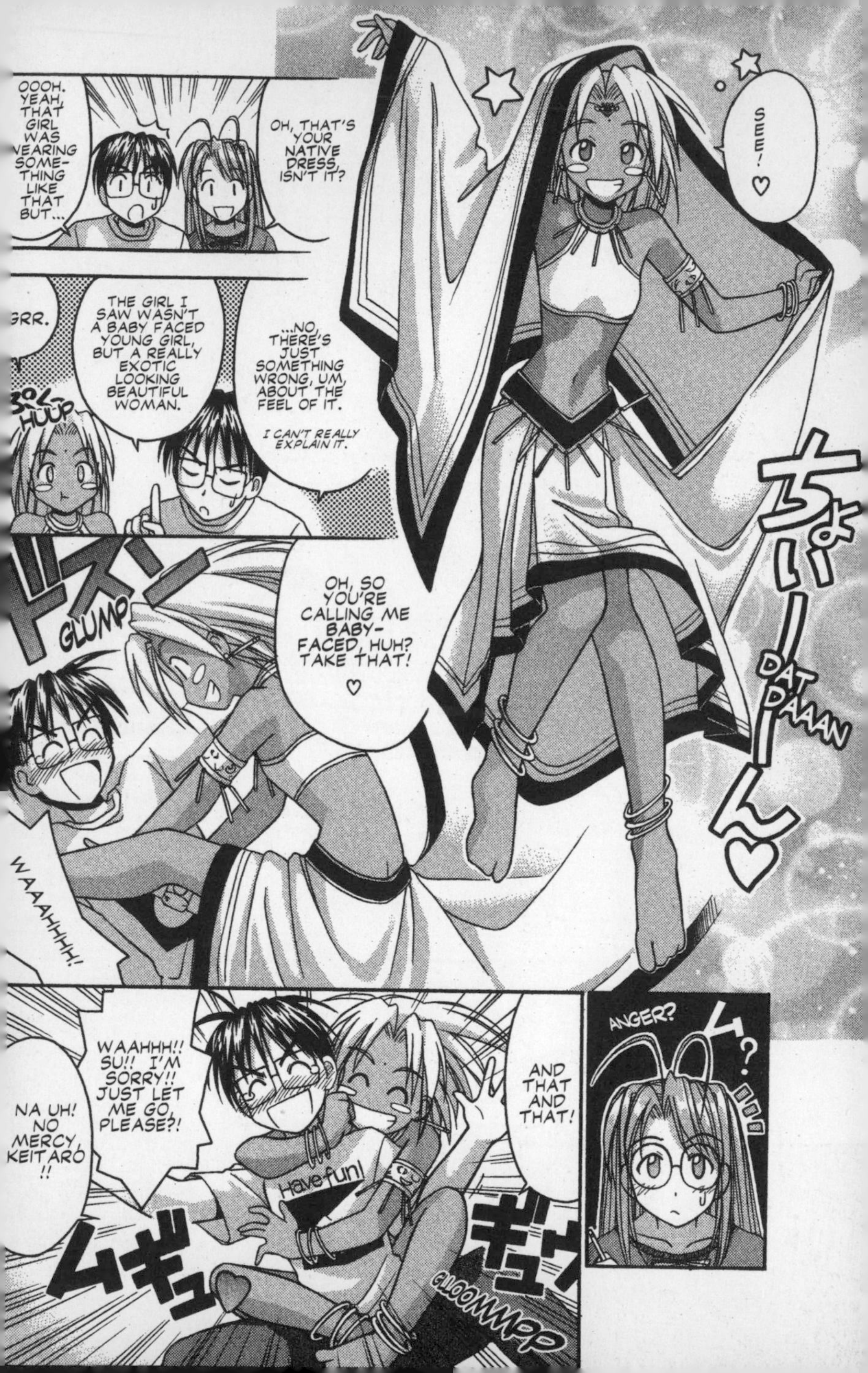
SEE! ♥
ちょいーん♥
DAT DAAAN
OH, THAT'S YOUR NATIVE DRESS, ISN'T IT?
OOOH. YEAH, THAT GIRL WAS WEARING SOME-THING LIKE THAT BUT...
...NO, THERE'S JUST SOMETHING WRONG, UM, ABOUT THE FEEL OF IT.
I CAN'T REALLY EXPLAIN IT.
THE GIRL I SAW WASN'T A BABY FACED YOUNG GIRL, BUT A REALLY EXOTIC LOOKING BEAUTIFUL WOMAN.
GRR.
HUUP
OH, SO YOU'RE CALLING ME BABY-FACED, HUH? TAKE THAT! ♥
GLUMP
WAAAHHHH!
ANGER?
AND THAT AND THAT!
WAAHHH!! SU!! I'M SORRY!! JUST LET ME GO, PLEASE?!
NA UH! NO MERCY, KEITARO!!
Have fun!
ムギュ
GLOOMMPP

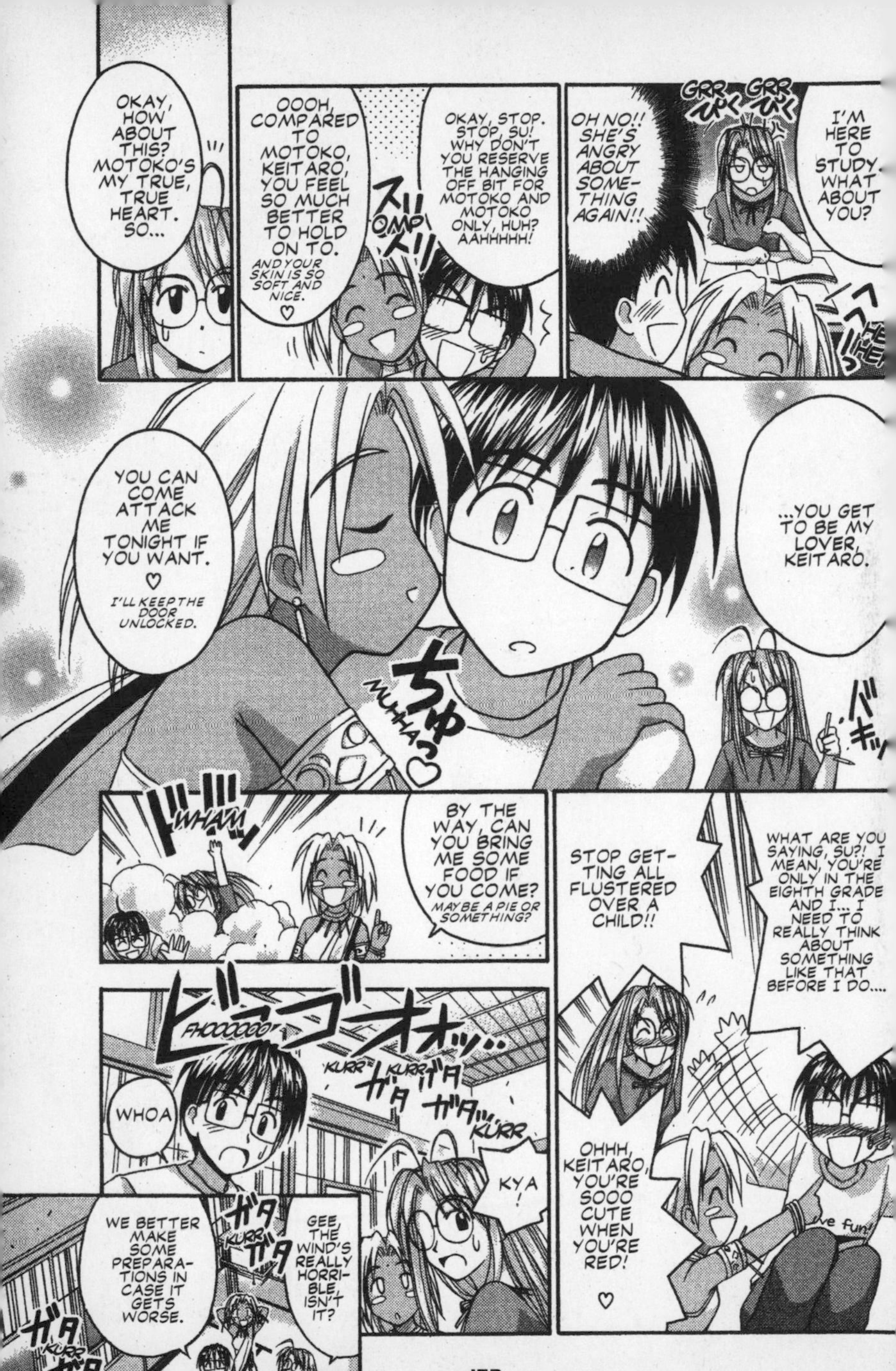
I'M HERE TO STUDY. WHAT ABOUT YOU?
HEH HEH
GRR GRR
OH NO!! SHE'S ANGRY ABOUT SOME-THING AGAIN!!
OKAY, STOP. STOP, SU! WHY DON'T YOU RESERVE THE HANGING OFF BIT FOR MOTOKO AND MOTOKO ONLY, HUH? AAHHHHH!
OOOH, COMPARED TO MOTOKO, KEITARO, YOU FEEL SO MUCH BETTER TO HOLD ON TO.
AND YOUR SKIN IS SO SOFT AND NICE. ♡
OMP
OKAY, HOW ABOUT THIS? MOTOKO'S MY TRUE, TRUE HEART. SO...
...YOU GET TO BE MY LOVER, KEITARO.
YOU CAN COME ATTACK ME TONIGHT IF YOU WANT. ♡
I'LL KEEP THE DOOR UNLOCKED.
ちゅっ
MUHHA ♡
WHAT ARE YOU SAYING, SU?! I MEAN, YOU'RE ONLY IN THE EIGHTH GRADE AND I... I NEED TO REALLY THINK ABOUT SOMETHING LIKE THAT BEFORE I DO....
STOP GET-TING ALL FLUSTERED OVER A CHILD!!
OHHH, KEITARO, YOU'RE SOOO CUTE WHEN YOU'RE RED! ♡
BY THE WAY, CAN YOU BRING ME SOME FOOD IF YOU COME?
MAYBE A PIE OR SOMETHING?
WHAM
FHOOOOOO
KURR KURR KURR
WHOA
KYA!
GEE, THE WIND'S REALLY HORRI-BLE, ISN'T IT?
WE BETTER MAKE SOME PREPARA-TIONS IN CASE IT GETS WORSE.
KURR
KURR

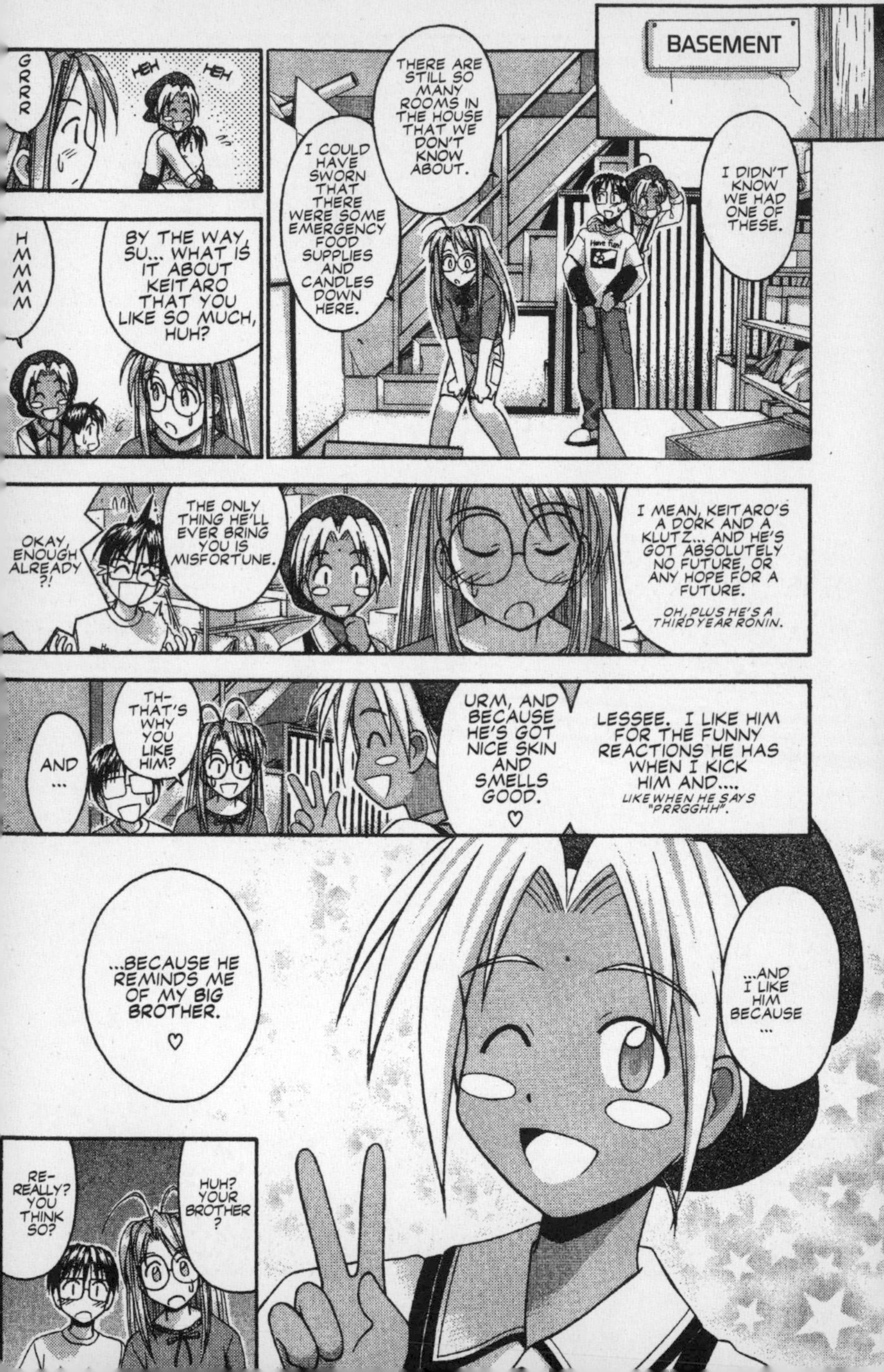
BASEMENT
I DIDN'T KNOW WE HAD ONE OF THESE.
THERE ARE STILL SO MANY ROOMS IN THE HOUSE THAT WE DON'T KNOW ABOUT.
I COULD HAVE SWORN THAT THERE WERE SOME EMERGENCY FOOD SUPPLIES AND CANDLES DOWN HERE.
HEH HEH
GRRR
BY THE WAY, SU... WHAT IS IT ABOUT KEITARO THAT YOU LIKE SO MUCH, HUH?
HMMMMM
I MEAN, KEITARO'S A DORK AND A KLUTZ... AND HE'S GOT ABSOLUTELY NO FUTURE, OR ANY HOPE FOR A FUTURE.
OH, PLUS HE'S A THIRD YEAR RONIN.
THE ONLY THING HE'LL EVER BRING YOU IS MISFORTUNE.
OKAY, ENOUGH ALREADY ?!
LESSEE. I LIKE HIM FOR THE FUNNY REACTIONS HE HAS WHEN I KICK HIM AND....
LIKE WHEN HE SAYS "PRRGGHH".
URM, AND BECAUSE HE'S GOT NICE SKIN AND SMELLS GOOD. ♡
TH-THAT'S WHY YOU LIKE HIM?
AND ...
...AND I LIKE HIM BECAUSE ...
...BECAUSE HE REMINDS ME OF MY BIG BROTHER. ♡
HUH? YOUR BROTHER ?
RE-REALLY? YOU THINK SO?

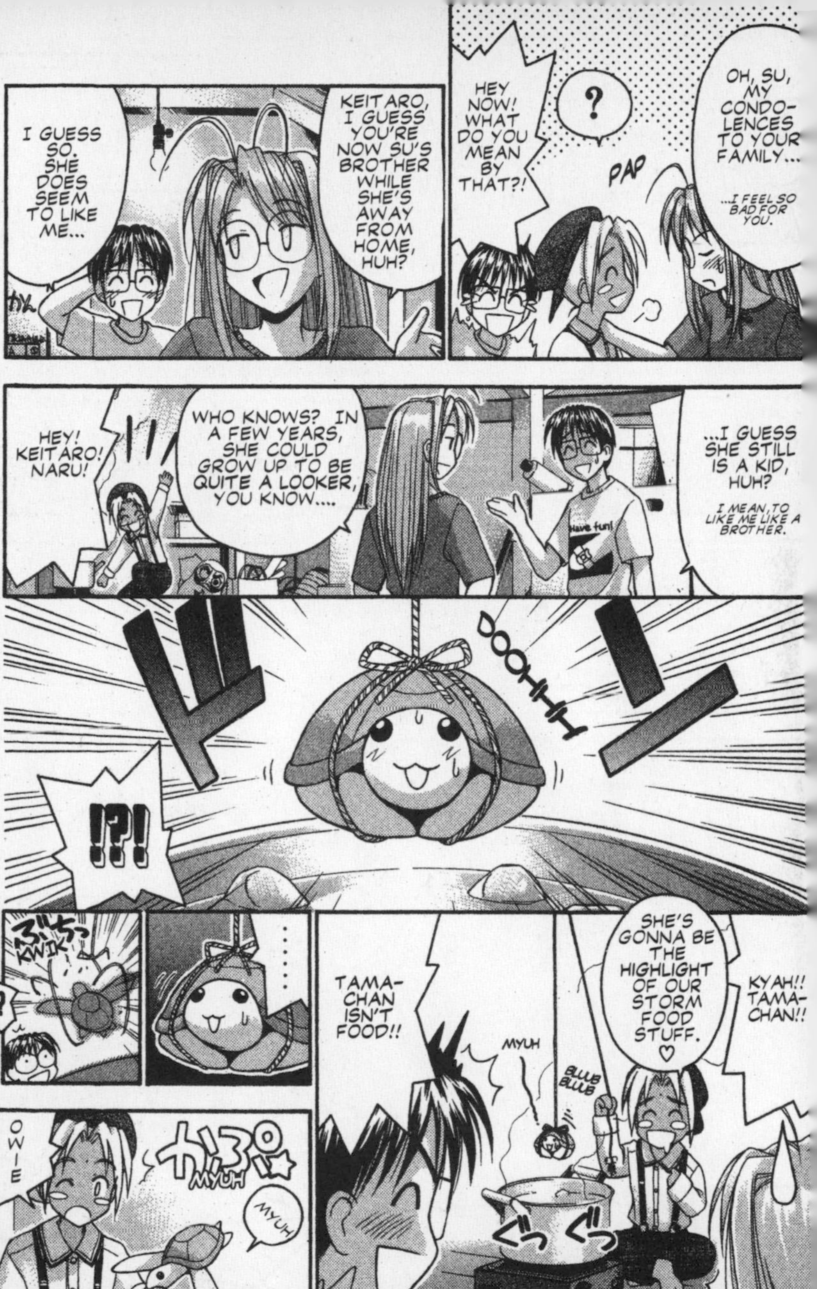
OH, SU, MY CONDOLENCES TO YOUR FAMILY...
...I FEEL SO BAD FOR YOU.
?
PAP
HEY NOW! WHAT DO YOU MEAN BY THAT?!
KEITARO, I GUESS YOU'RE NOW SU'S BROTHER WHILE SHE'S AWAY FROM HOME, HUH?
I GUESS SO. SHE DOES SEEM TO LIKE ME...
...I GUESS SHE STILL IS A KID, HUH?
I MEAN, TO LIKE ME LIKE A BROTHER.
Have fun!
WHO KNOWS? IN A FEW YEARS, SHE COULD GROW UP TO BE QUITE A LOOKER, YOU KNOW....
HEY! KEITARO! NARU!
DOOHHHH
!?!
KYAH!! TAMA-CHAN!!
SHE'S GONNA BE THE HIGHLIGHT OF OUR STORM FOOD STUFF. ♡
BLUB BLUB
MYUH
TAMA-CHAN ISN'T FOOD!!
......
KWIK
!?
MYUH
MYUH
OWIE

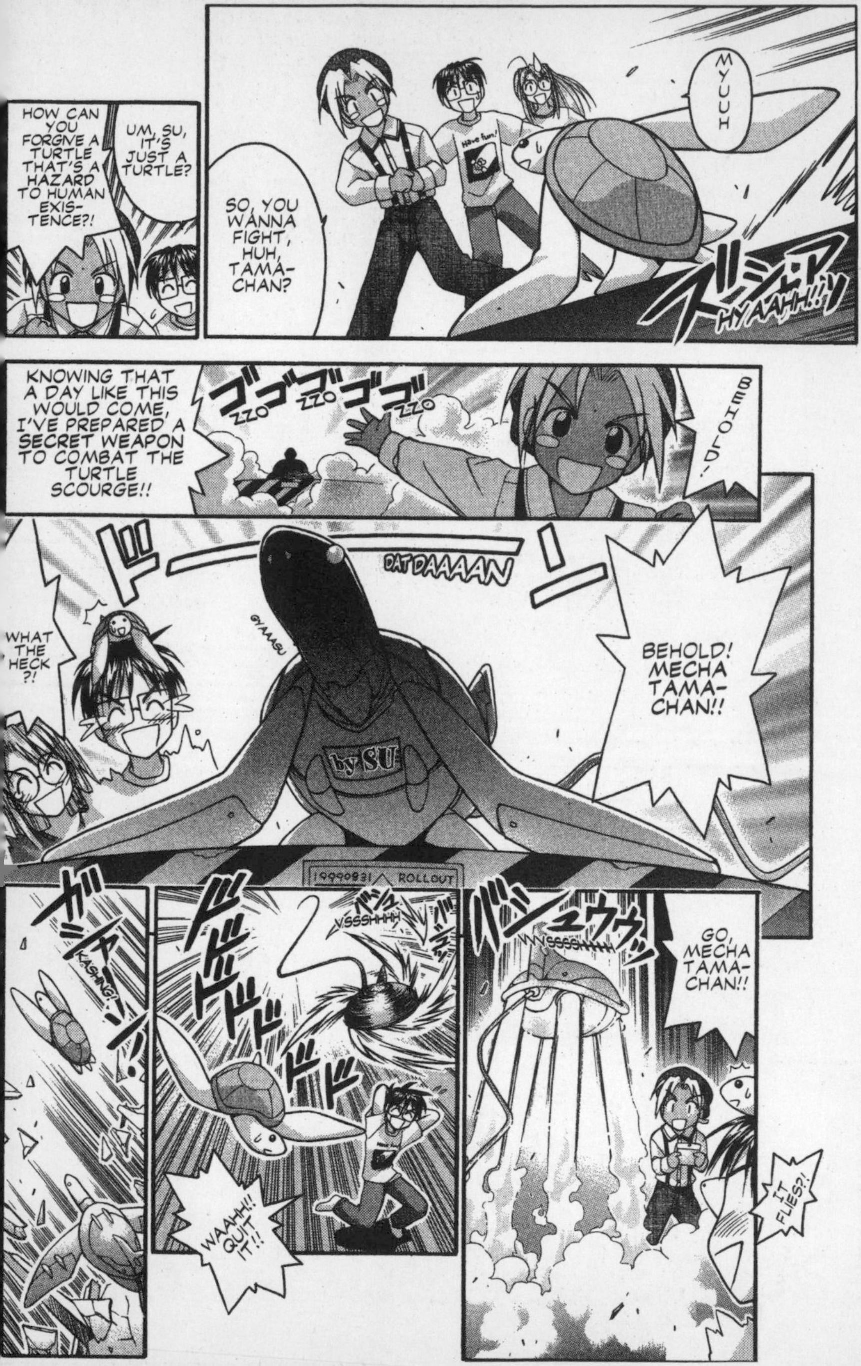
MYUUH
SO, YOU WANNA FIGHT, HUH, TAMA-CHAN?
HYAAHH!!
HOW CAN YOU FORGIVE A TURTLE THAT'S A HAZARD TO HUMAN EXIS-TENCE?!
UM, SU, IT'S JUST A TURTLE?
BEHOLD!
ZZO ZZO ZZO
KNOWING THAT A DAY LIKE THIS WOULD COME, I'VE PREPARED A SECRET WEAPON TO COMBAT THE TURTLE SCOURGE!!
DATDAAAAN
BEHOLD! MECHA TAMA-CHAN!!
by SU
WHAT THE HECK ?!
19990831 ROLLOUT
GO, MECHA TAMA-CHAN!!
SSSSHHHH
IT FLIES?!
VSSSHHHH
WAAHH!! QUIT IT!!
KASHING!

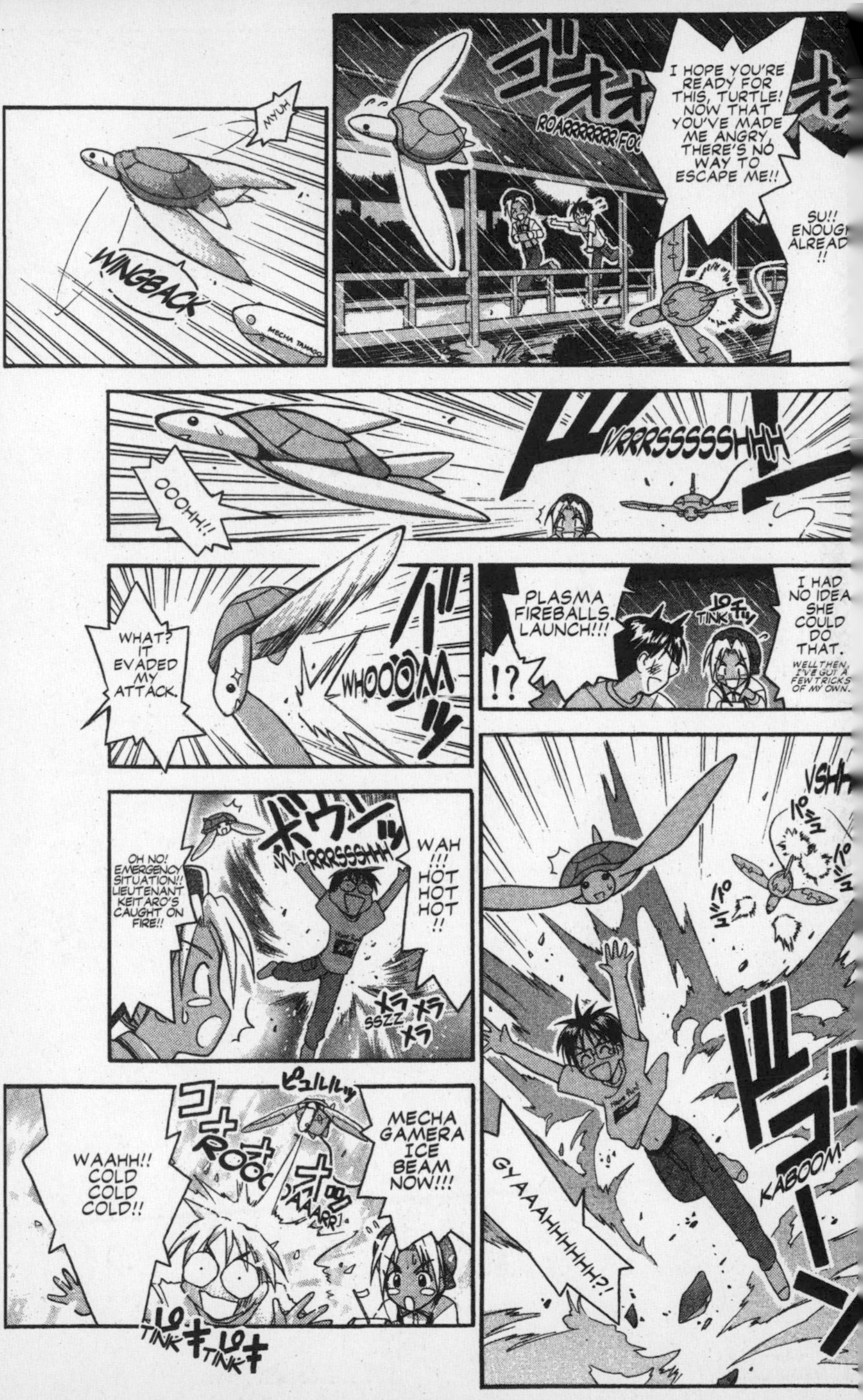

ROARRRRRRR FOO
I HOPE YOU'RE READY FOR THIS, TURTLE! NOW THAT YOU'VE MADE ME ANGRY, THERE'S NO WAY TO ESCAPE ME!!
SU!! ENOUGH ALREAD !!
MYUH
WINGBACK
MECHA TAMAGO
VRRRSSSSSSHHH
OOOHH!!
I HAD NO IDEA SHE COULD DO THAT.
WELL THEN, I'VE GOT A FEW TRICKS OF MY OWN.
TINK
PLASMA FIREBALLS. LAUNCH!!!
!?
WHOOOOM
WHAT? IT EVADED MY ATTACK.
VSHH
KABOOM
GYAAAHHHHH?!
WAH!!! HOT HOT HOT!!
VVARRRSSSHHH
OH NO! EMERGENCY SITUATION!! LIEUTENANT KEITARO'S CAUGHT ON FIRE!!
SSZZ
MECHA GAMERA ICE BEAM NOW!!!
ROOOAAAARR
WAAHH!! COLD COLD COLD!!
TINK TINK

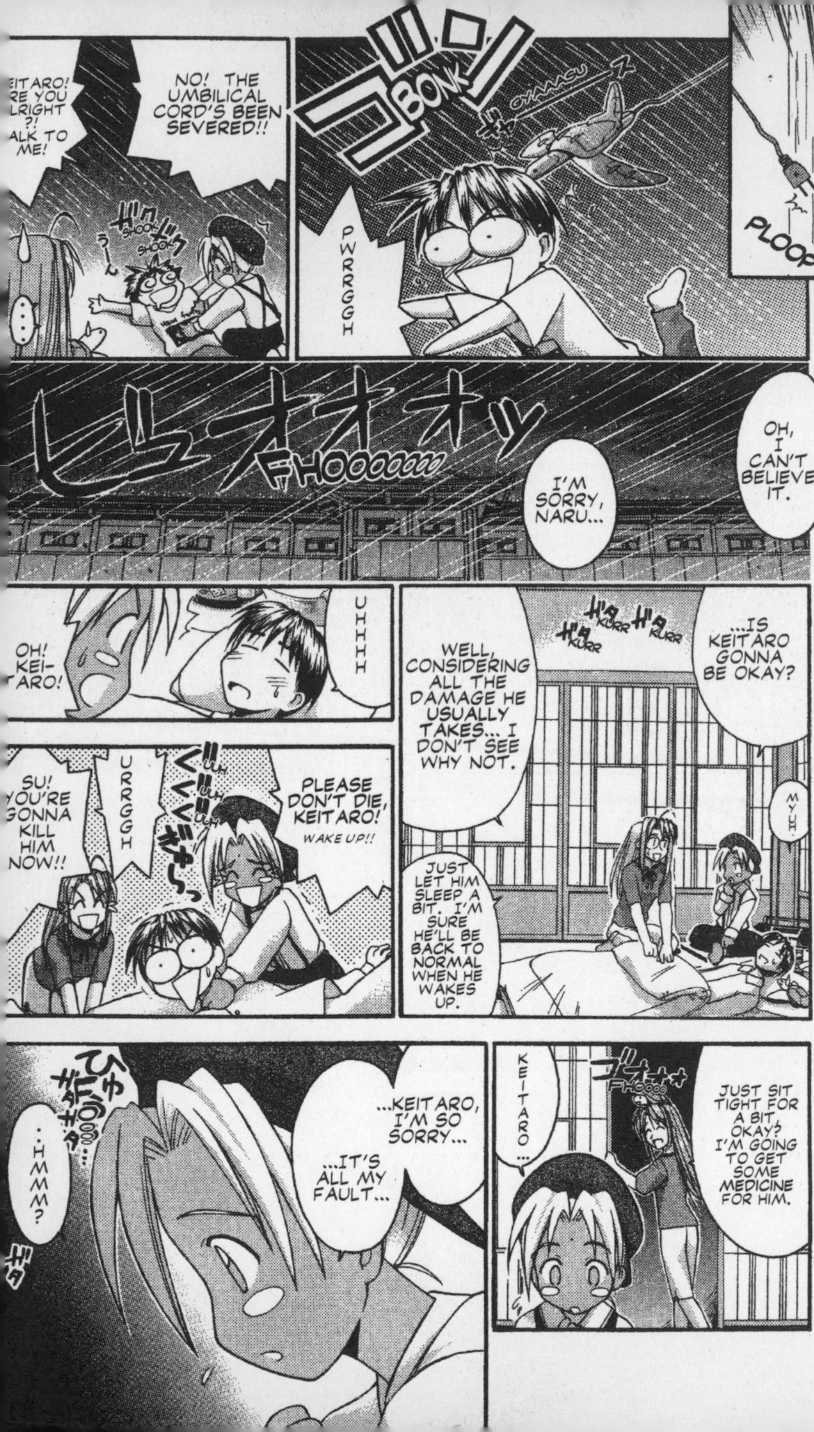
PLOOP
BONK
PWRRGGH
NO! THE UMBILICAL CORD'S BEEN SEVERED!!
EITARO! RE YOU LRIGHT ?! ALK TO ME!
SHOOK SHOOK
...
OH, I CAN'T BELIEVE IT.
I'M SORRY, NARU...
FHOOOOOOO
...IS KEITARO GONNA BE OKAY?
KURR KURR KURR
WELL, CONSIDERING ALL THE DAMAGE HE USUALLY TAKES... I DON'T SEE WHY NOT.
MYUH.
JUST LET HIM SLEEP A BIT. I'M SURE HE'LL BE BACK TO NORMAL WHEN HE WAKES UP.
UHHHH
OH! KEI-TARO!
PLEASE DON'T DIE, KEITARO!
WAKE UP!!
URRGGH
SU! YOU'RE GONNA KILL HIM NOW!!
JUST SIT TIGHT FOR A BIT, OKAY? I'M GOING TO GET SOME MEDICINE FOR HIM.
FHOOOO
KEITARO...
...KEITARO, I'M SO SORRY...
...IT'S ALL MY FAULT...
..HMMM?

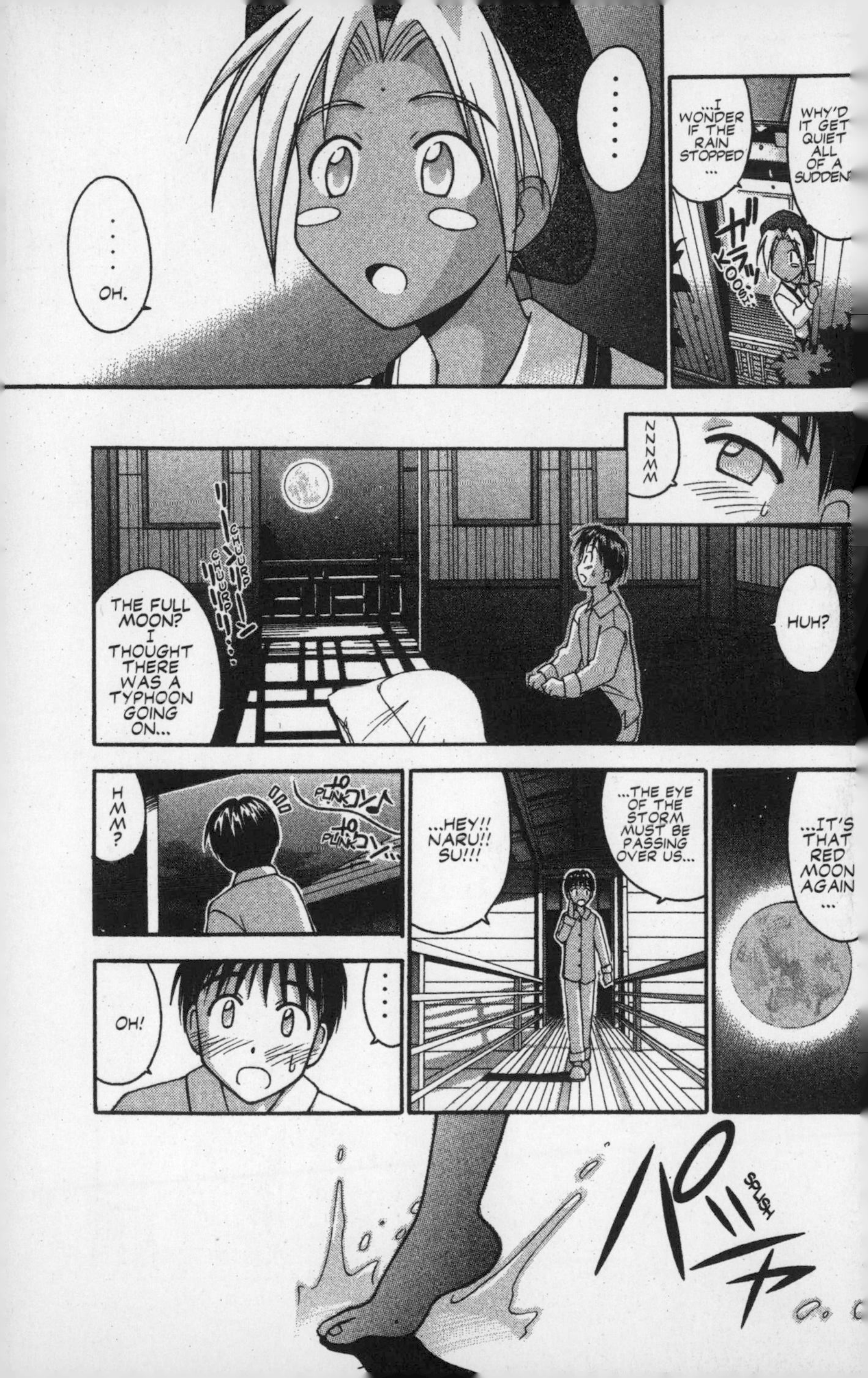
WHY'D IT GET QUIET ALL OF A SUDDEN?
...I WONDER IF THE RAIN STOPPED ...
ガラッ KOOSH!
......
...... OH.
NNNMM
HUH?
THE FULL MOON? I THOUGHT THERE WAS A TYPHOON GOING ON...
CHUURP
CHUURP
...IT'S THAT RED MOON AGAIN ...
...THE EYE OF THE STORM MUST BE PASSING OVER US...
...HEY!! NARU!! SU!!!
HMM?
PLINK
PLINK
....
OH!
SPLISH

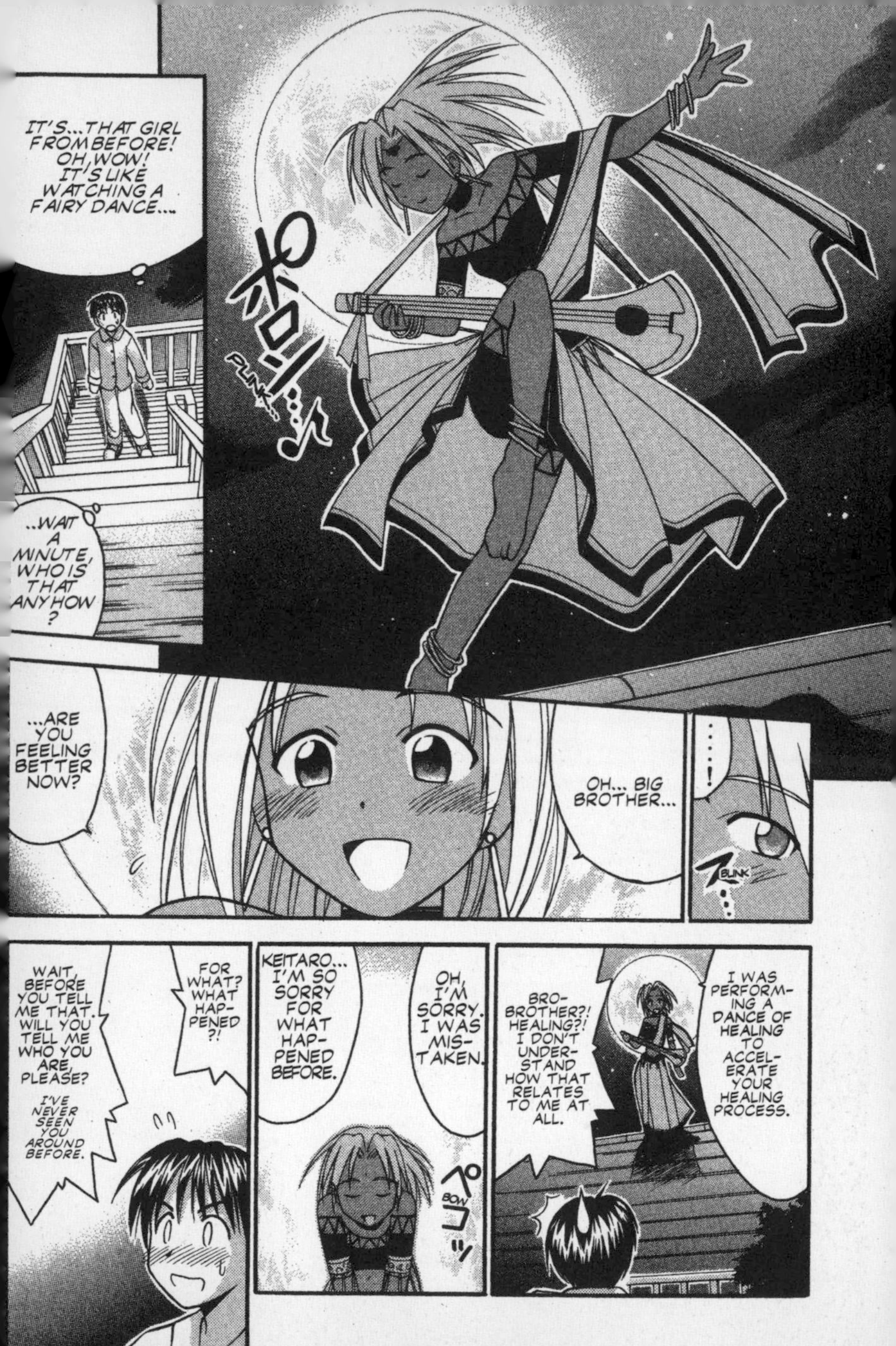
ポロン
PLINK...
IT'S...THAT GIRL FROM BEFORE! OH, WOW! IT'S LIKE WATCHING A FAIRY DANCE...
...WAIT A MINUTE, WHO IS THAT ANYHOW?
...!
BLINK
OH... BIG BROTHER...
...ARE YOU FEELING BETTER NOW?
I WAS PERFORMING A DANCE OF HEALING TO ACCELERATE YOUR HEALING PROCESS.
BRO-BROTHER?! HEALING?! I DON'T UNDERSTAND HOW THAT RELATES TO ME AT ALL.
OH, I'M SORRY. I WAS MISTAKEN.
KEITARO... I'M SO SORRY FOR WHAT HAPPENED BEFORE.
ペコッ
BOW
FOR WHAT? WHAT HAPPENED?!
WAIT, BEFORE YOU TELL ME THAT. WILL YOU TELL ME WHO YOU ARE, PLEASE?
I'VE NEVER SEEN YOU AROUND BEFORE.

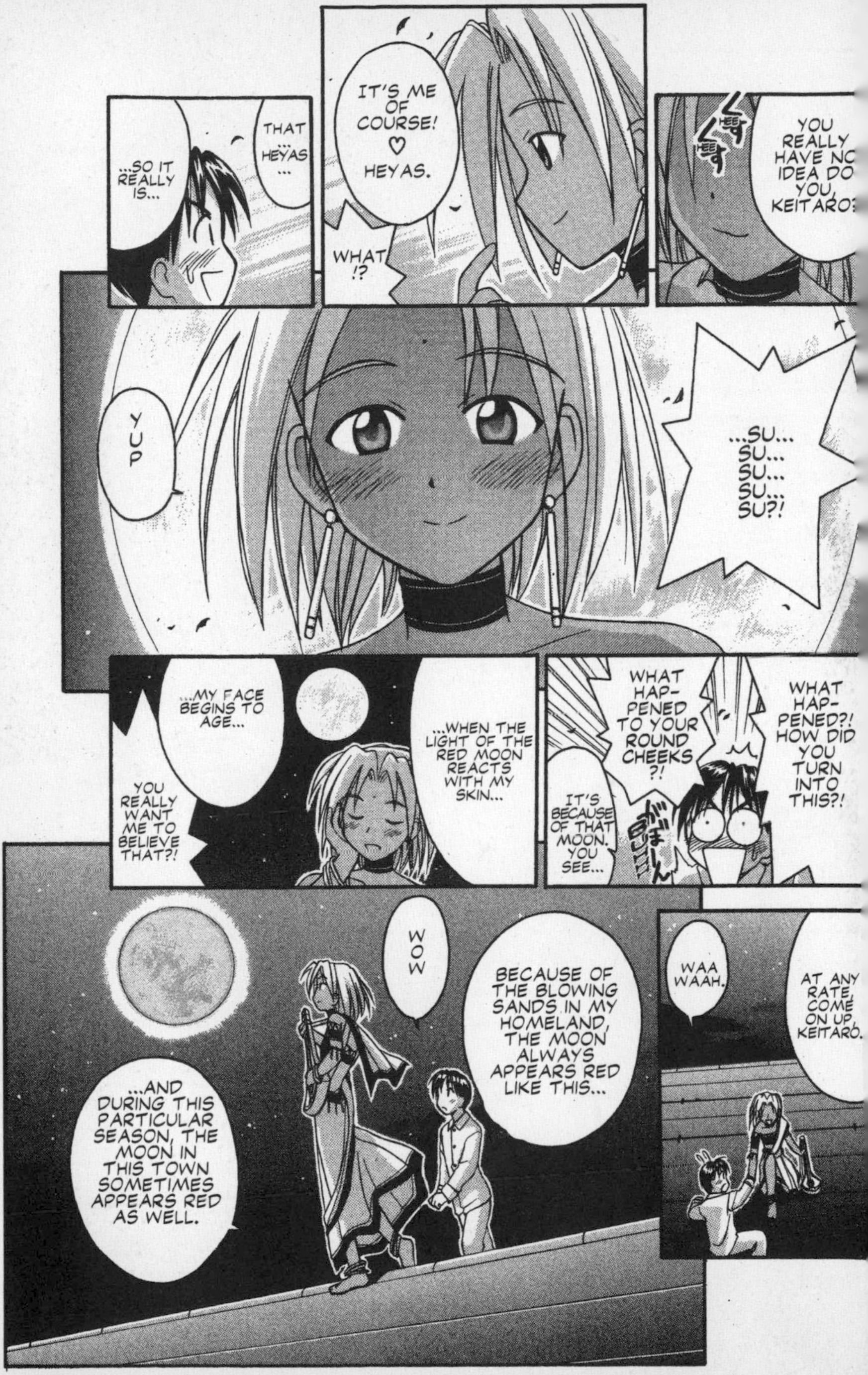
HEE HEE
YOU REALLY HAVE NO IDEA DO YOU, KEITARO?
IT'S ME OF COURSE! ♡ HEYAS.
WHAT !?
THAT ... HEYAS ...
...SO IT REALLY IS...
...SU... SU... SU... SU... SU?!
YUP
WHAT HAP-PENED?! HOW DID YOU TURN INTO THIS?!
WHAT HAP-PENED TO YOUR ROUND CHEEKS ?!
IT'S BECAUSE OF THAT MOON, YOU SEE...
...WHEN THE LIGHT OF THE RED MOON REACTS WITH MY SKIN...
...MY FACE BEGINS TO AGE...
YOU REALLY WANT ME TO BELIEVE THAT?!
AT ANY RATE, COME ON UP, KEITARO.
WAA WAAH.
BECAUSE OF THE BLOWING SANDS IN MY HOMELAND, THE MOON ALWAYS APPEARS RED LIKE THIS...
WOW
...AND DURING THIS PARTICULAR SEASON, THE MOON IN THIS TOWN SOMETIMES APPEARS RED AS WELL.

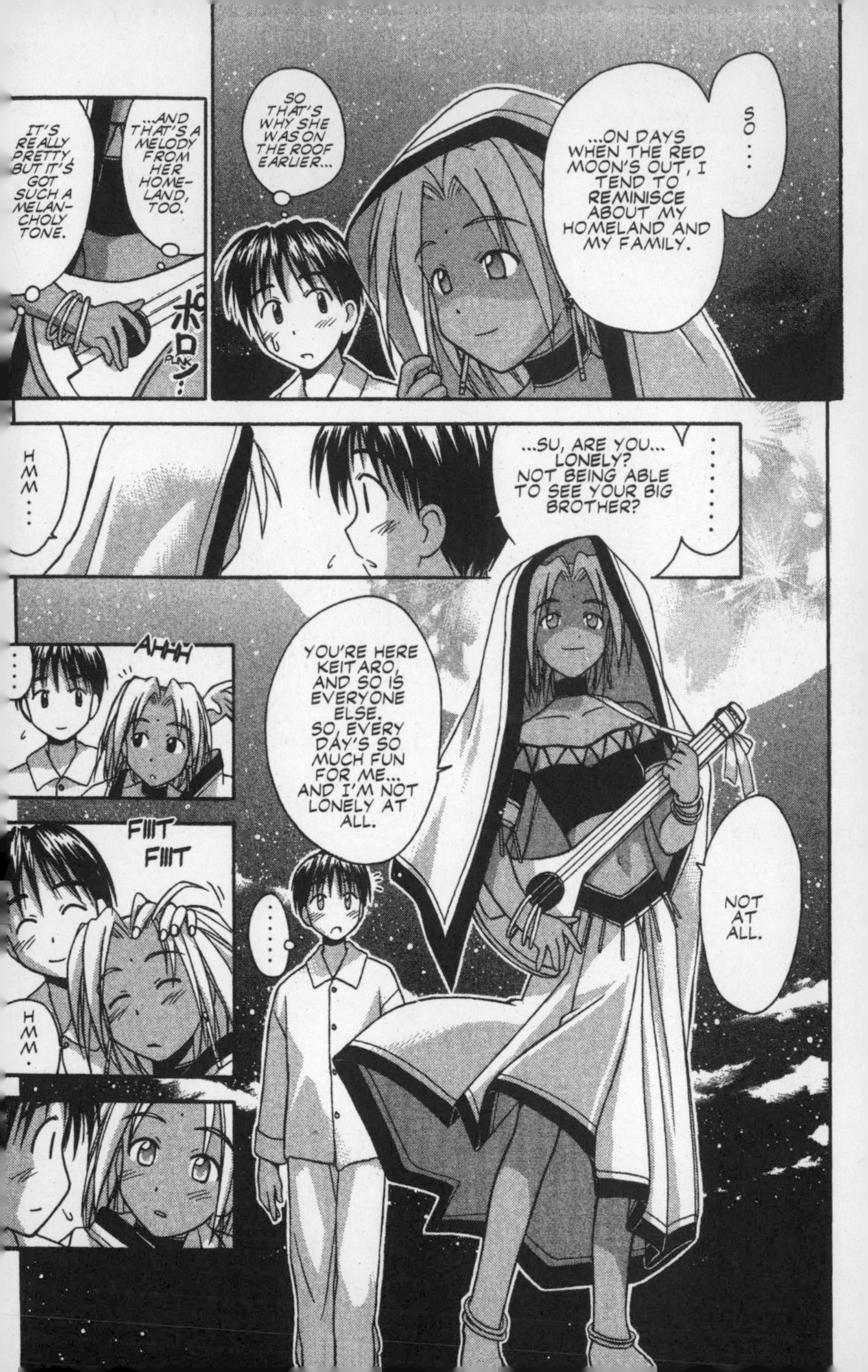

SO...
...ON DAYS WHEN THE RED MOON'S OUT, I TEND TO REMINISCE ABOUT MY HOMELAND AND MY FAMILY.
SO THAT'S WHY SHE WAS ON THE ROOF EARLIER...
...AND THAT'S A MELODY FROM HER HOMELAND, TOO.
IT'S REALLY PRETTY, BUT IT'S GOT SUCH A MELANCHOLY TONE.
PLINK
......
...SU, ARE YOU... LONELY? NOT BEING ABLE TO SEE YOUR BIG BROTHER?
HMM....
NOT AT ALL.
YOU'RE HERE KEITARO, AND SO IS EVERYONE ELSE. SO, EVERY DAY'S SO MUCH FUN FOR ME... AND I'M NOT LONELY AT ALL.
......
AHHH
...
FIIIT
FIIIT
HMM.

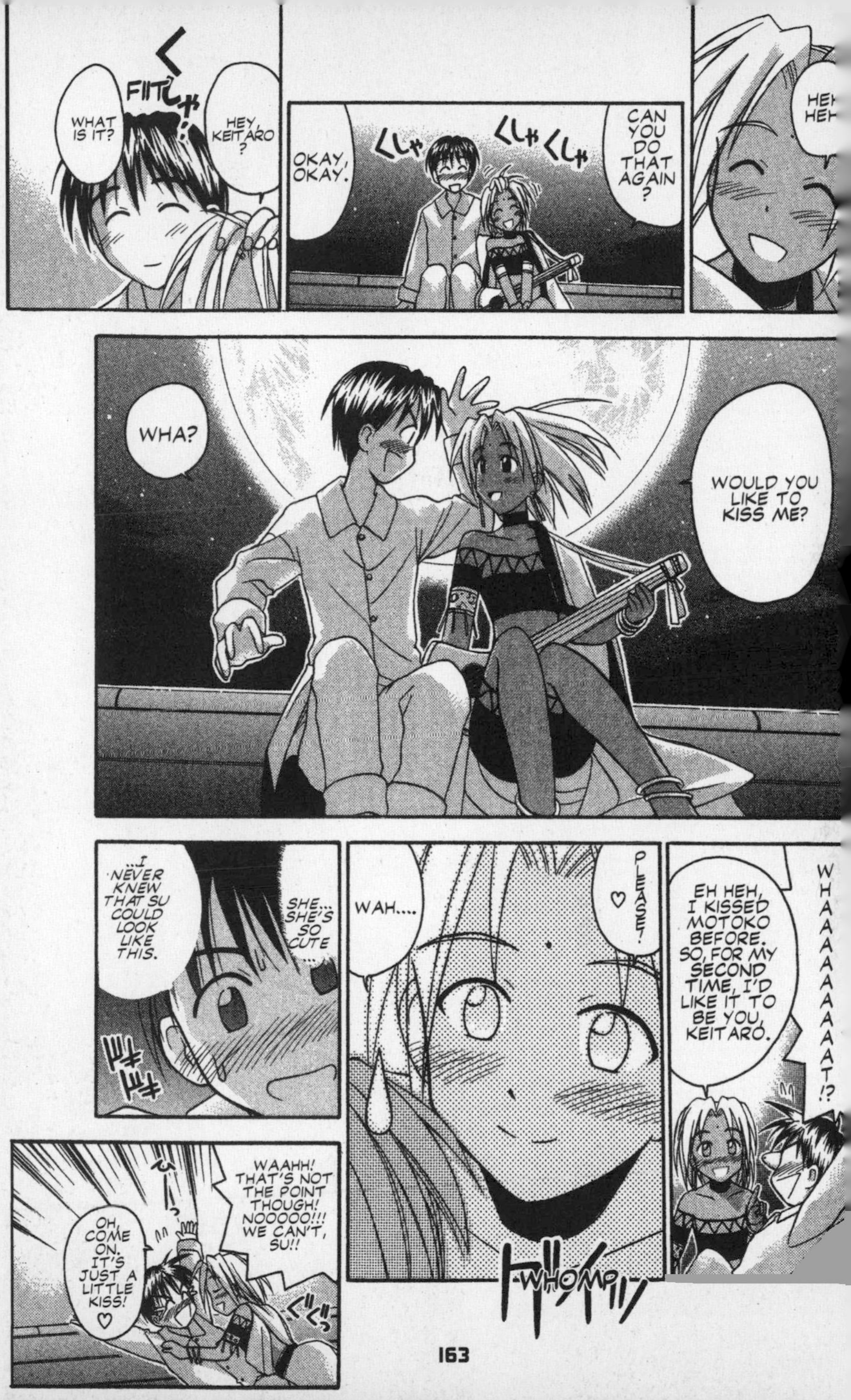
HEH HEH
CAN YOU DO THAT AGAIN?
くしゃ くしゃ
くしゃ
OKAY, OKAY.
HEY, KEITARO?
く
FIIT しゃ
WHAT IS IT?
WOULD YOU LIKE TO KISS ME?
WHA?
WHAAAAAAAAAAAT!?
EH HEH, I KISSED MOTOKO BEFORE. SO, FOR MY SECOND TIME, I'D LIKE IT TO BE YOU, KEITARO.
PLEASE! ♡
WAH....
SHE... SHE'S SO CUTE...
...I NEVER KNEW THAT SU COULD LOOK LIKE THIS.
WHOMP
WAAHH! THAT'S NOT THE POINT THOUGH! NOOOOO!!! WE CAN'T, SU!!
OH, COME ON. IT'S JUST A LITTLE KISS! ♡

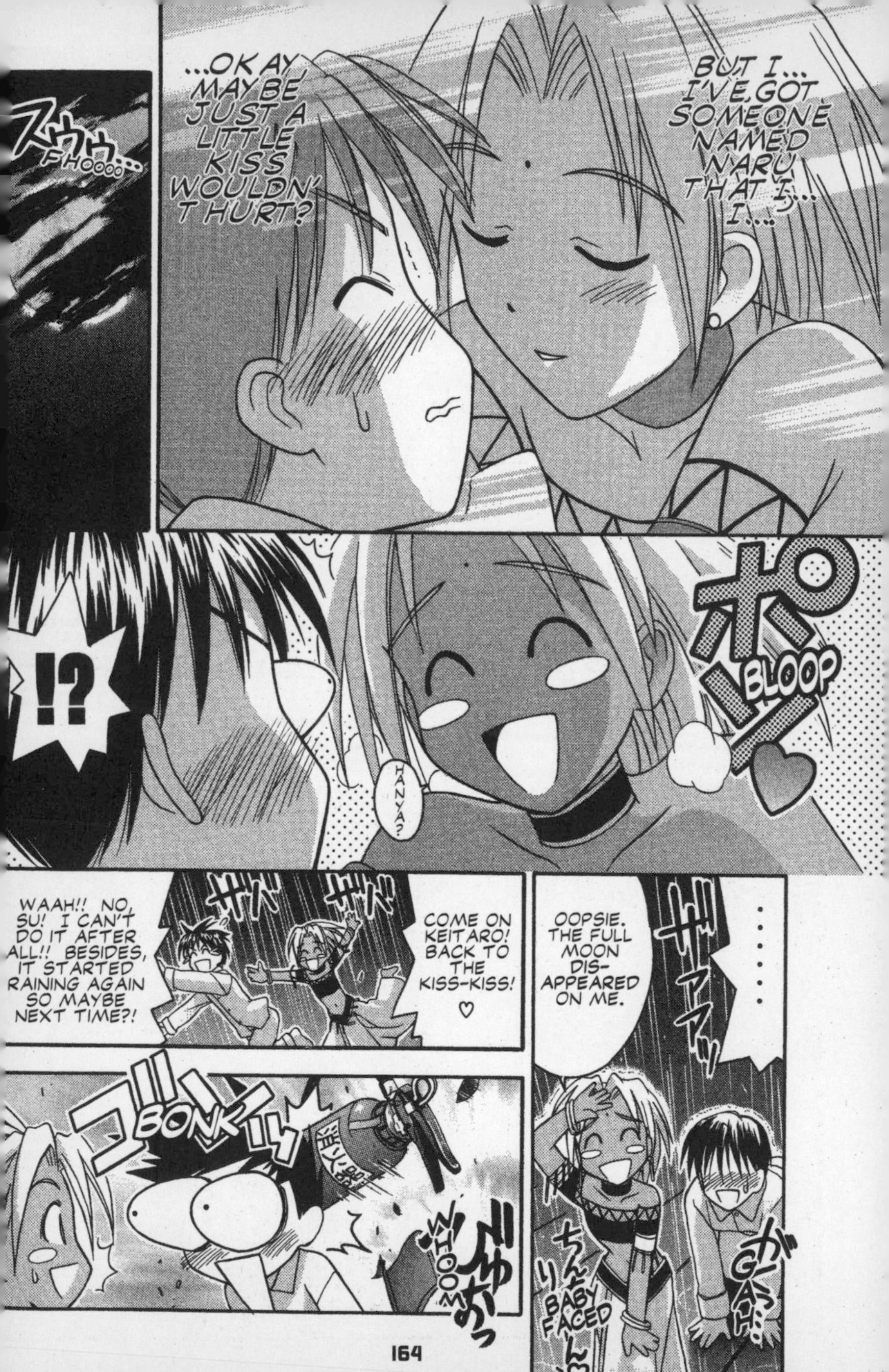
BUT I... I'VE GOT SOMEONE NAMED NARU THAT I... I...
...OKAY MAYBE JUST A LITTLE KISS WOULDN'T HURT?
スゥウ...
FHOOOO...
ポン
BLOOP
HANYA?
!?
......
ザァアッ
OOPSIE. THE FULL MOON DIS-APPEARED ON ME.
がーん
GAAH...
ちんまり
BABY FACED
ザバ ザバ
COME ON KEITARO! BACK TO THE KISS-KISS! ♡
WAAH!! NO, SU! I CAN'T DO IT AFTER ALL!! BESIDES, IT STARTED RAINING AGAIN SO MAYBE NEXT TIME?!
ゴツ
BONK
消火器
ぎゅおっ
WHOOM

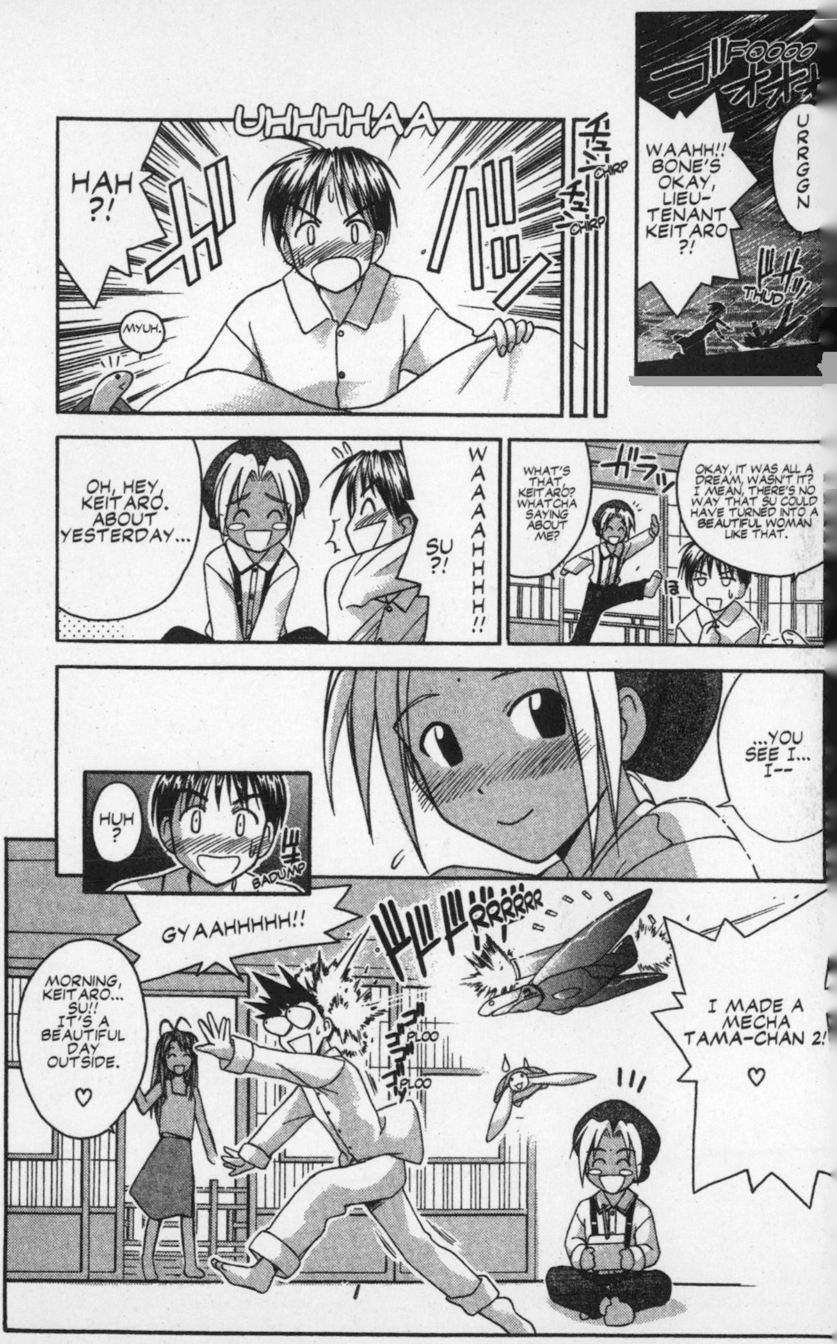

FOOOO
URRGGN
WAAHH!! BONE'S OKAY, LIEUTENANT KEITARO ?!
THUD
UHHHHAA
CHIRP
CHIRP
HAH ?!
MYUH.
OKAY, IT WAS ALL A DREAM, WASN'T IT? I MEAN, THERE'S NO WAY THAT SU COULD HAVE TURNED INTO A BEAUTIFUL WOMAN LIKE THAT.
WHAT'S THAT, KEITARO? WHATCHA SAYING ABOUT ME?
WAAAAAHHHH!!
SU ?!
OH, HEY, KEITARO. ABOUT YESTERDAY...
...YOU SEE I... I--
HUH ?
BADUMP
I MADE A MECHA TAMA-CHAN 2! ♡
RRRRRR
GYAAHHHHH!!
PLOO
PLOO
MORNING, KEITARO... SU!! IT'S A BEAUTIFUL DAY OUTSIDE. ♡

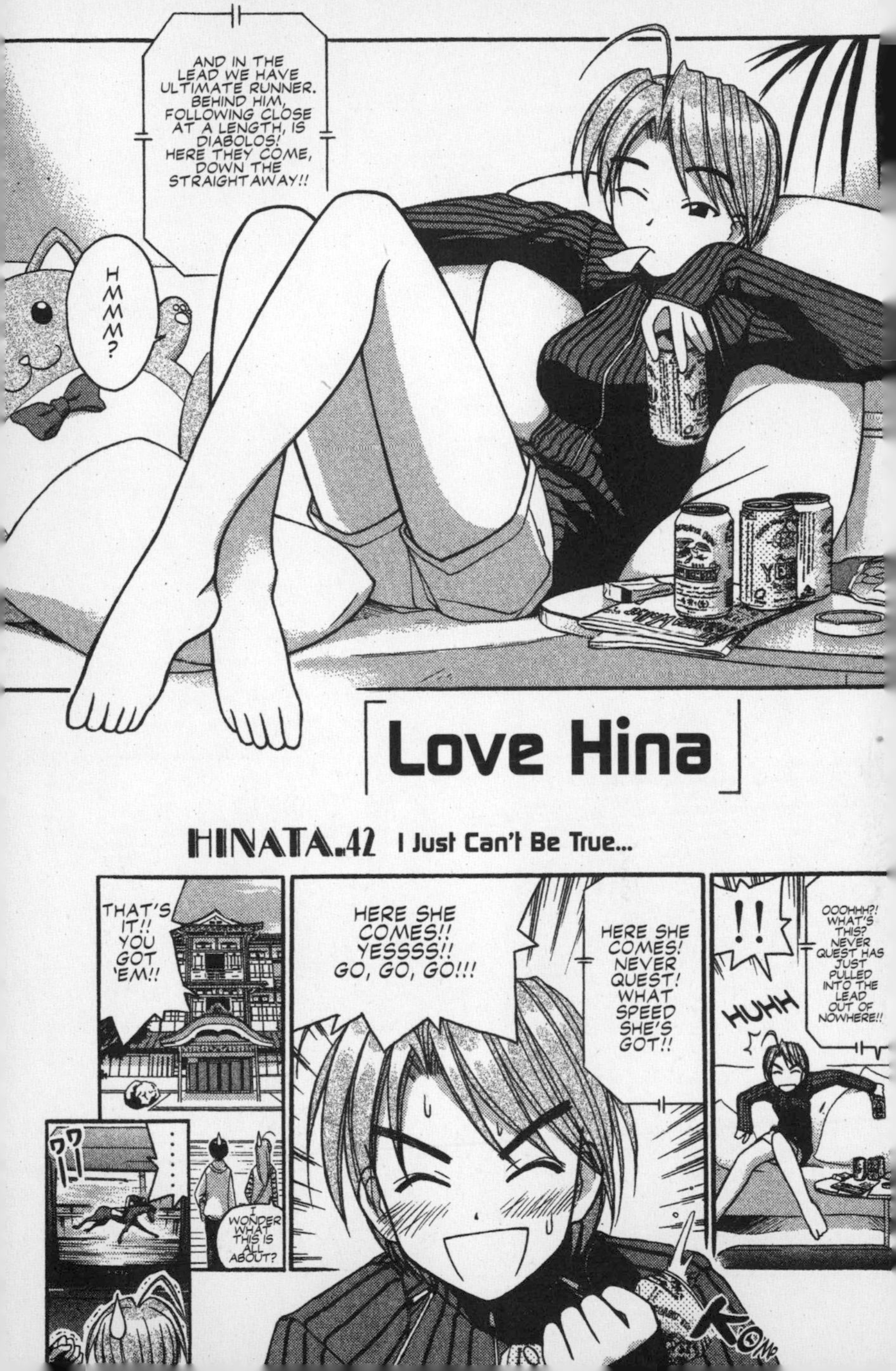
AND IN THE LEAD WE HAVE ULTIMATE RUNNER. BEHIND HIM, FOLLOWING CLOSE AT A LENGTH, IS DIABOLOS! HERE THEY COME, DOWN THE STRAIGHTAWAY!!
HMMMM?
Love Hina
HINATA.42 I Just Can't Be True...
!!
OOOHHH?! WHAT'S THIS? NEVER QUEST HAS JUST PULLED INTO THE LEAD OUT OF NOWHERE!!
HUHH
HERE SHE COMES! NEVER QUEST! WHAT SPEED SHE'S GOT!!
HERE SHE COMES!! YESSSS!! GO, GO, GO!!!
THAT'S IT!! YOU GOT 'EM!!
......
I WONDER WHAT THIS IS ALL ABOUT?

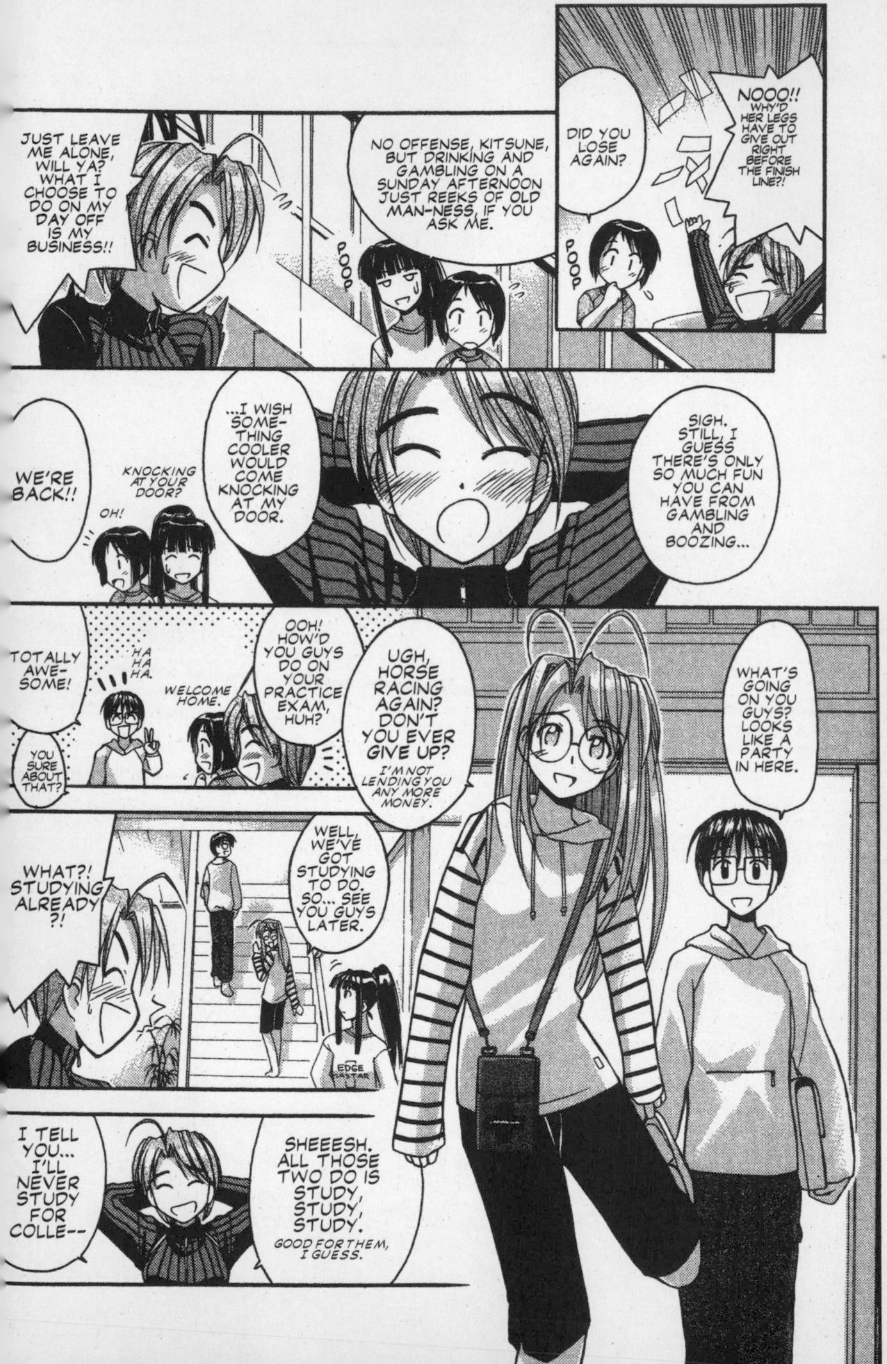
NOOO!! WHY'D HER LEGS HAVE TO GIVE OUT RIGHT BEFORE THE FINISH LINE?!
DID YOU LOSE AGAIN?
POOP
NO OFFENSE, KITSUNE, BUT DRINKING AND GAMBLING ON A SUNDAY AFTERNOON JUST REEKS OF OLD MAN-NESS, IF YOU ASK ME.
POOP
JUST LEAVE ME ALONE, WILL YA? WHAT I CHOOSE TO DO ON MY DAY OFF IS MY BUSINESS!!
SIGH. STILL, I GUESS THERE'S ONLY SO MUCH FUN YOU CAN HAVE FROM GAMBLING AND BOOZING...
...I WISH SOME-THING COOLER WOULD COME KNOCKING AT MY DOOR.
KNOCKING AT YOUR DOOR?
OH!
WE'RE BACK!!
WHAT'S GOING ON YOU GUYS? LOOKS LIKE A PARTY IN HERE.
UGH, HORSE RACING AGAIN? DON'T YOU EVER GIVE UP?
I'M NOT LENDING YOU ANY MORE MONEY.
OOH! HOW'D YOU GUYS DO ON YOUR PRACTICE EXAM, HUH?
WELCOME HOME.
HA HA HA.
TOTALLY AWE-SOME!
YOU SURE ABOUT THAT?
WELL, WE'VE GOT STUDYING TO DO. SO... SEE YOU GUYS LATER.
WHAT?! STUDYING ALREADY?!
SHEEESH. ALL THOSE TWO DO IS STUDY, STUDY, STUDY.
GOOD FOR THEM, I GUESS.
I TELL YOU... I'LL NEVER STUDY FOR COLLE--

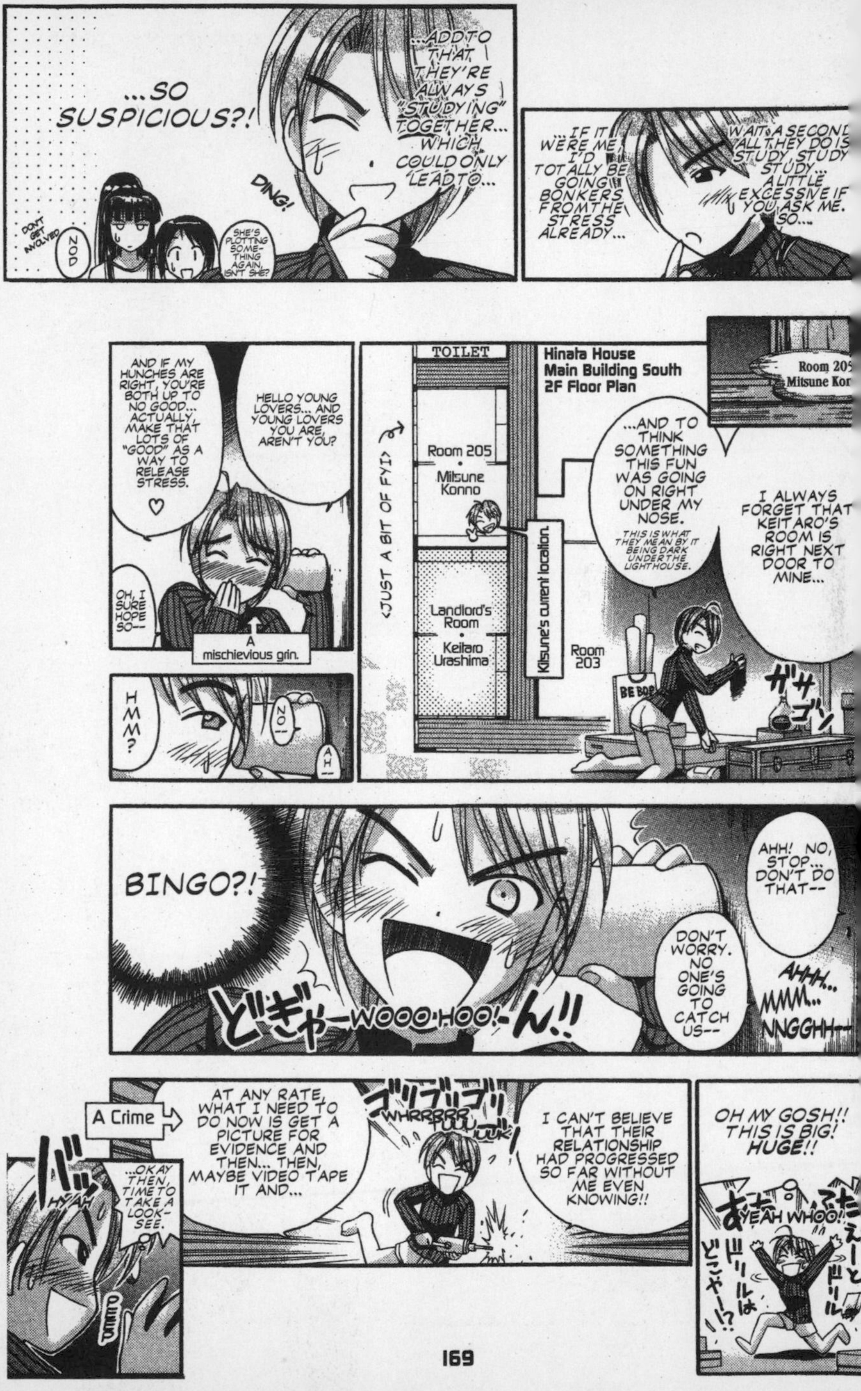
WAIT A SECOND... ALL THEY DO IS STUDY, STUDY, STUDY... A LITTLE EXCESSIVE IF YOU ASK ME. SO...
IF IT WERE ME, I'D TOTALLY BE GOING BONKERS FROM THE STRESS ALREADY...
...ADD TO THAT, THEY'RE ALWAYS "STUDYING" TOGETHER... WHICH COULD ONLY LEAD TO...
DING!
...SO SUSPICIOUS?!
SHE'S PLOTTING SOMETHING AGAIN, ISN'T SHE?
NOD
DON'T GET INVOLVED
I ALWAYS FORGET THAT KEITARO'S ROOM IS RIGHT NEXT DOOR TO MINE...
...AND TO THINK SOMETHING THIS FUN WAS GOING ON RIGHT UNDER MY NOSE.
THIS IS WHAT THEY MEAN BY IT BEING DARK UNDER THE LIGHTHOUSE.
Hinata House Main Building South 2F Floor Plan
TOILET
Room 205 • Mitsune Konno
Landlord's Room • Keitaro Urashima
Room 203
Kitsune's current location.
<JUST A BIT OF FYI>
ガサゴソ
HELLO YOUNG LOVERS... AND YOUNG LOVERS YOU ARE, AREN'T YOU?
AND IF MY HUNCHES ARE RIGHT, YOU'RE BOTH UP TO NO GOOD... ACTUALLY, MAKE THAT LOTS OF "GOOD" AS A WAY TO RELEASE STRESS. ♡
OH, I SURE HOPE SO--
A mischievious grin.
NO--
AH--
HMM?
AHH! NO, STOP... DON'T DO THAT--
DON'T WORRY. NO ONE'S GOING TO CATCH US--
AHHH... MMM... NNGGHH--
BINGO?!
どぎゃ-WOOO HOO!-ん!!
OH MY GOSH!! THIS IS BIG! HUGE!!
YEAH WHOO!
I CAN'T BELIEVE THAT THEIR RELATIONSHIP HAD PROGRESSED SO FAR WITHOUT ME EVEN KNOWING!!
WHRRRRR TUUUUK!
AT ANY RATE, WHAT I NEED TO DO NOW IS GET A PICTURE FOR EVIDENCE AND THEN... THEN, MAYBE VIDEO TAPE IT AND...
A Crime
...OKAY THEN, TIME TO TAKE A LOOK-SEE.
HYAH

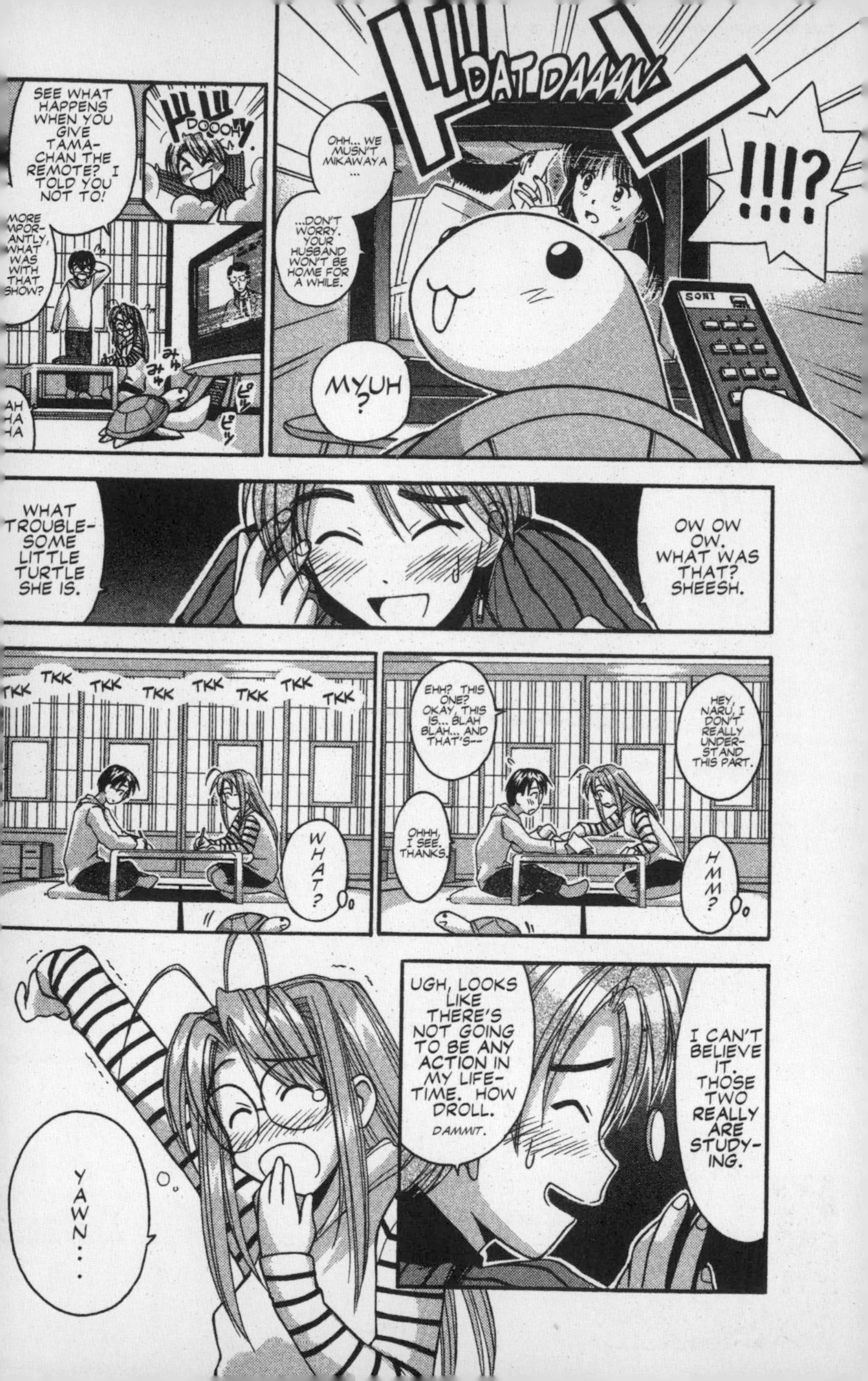
DAT DAAAN
!!!?
OHH... WE MUSN'T MIKAWAYA ...
...DON'T WORRY. YOUR HUSBAND WON'T BE HOME FOR A WHILE.
MYUH ?
SEE WHAT HAPPENS WHEN YOU GIVE TAMA-CHAN THE REMOTE? I TOLD YOU NOT TO!
MORE IMPORTANTLY, WHAT WAS WITH THAT SHOW?
AH HA HA
OW OW OW. WHAT WAS THAT? SHEESH.
WHAT TROUBLE-SOME LITTLE TURTLE SHE IS.
HEY, NARU, I DON'T REALLY UNDER-STAND THIS PART.
EHH? THIS ONE? OKAY, THIS IS... BLAH BLAH... AND THAT'S--
OHHH, I SEE. THANKS.
HMM?
TKK TKK TKK TKK TKK TKK TKK TKK
WHAT?
I CAN'T BELIEVE IT. THOSE TWO REALLY ARE STUDY-ING.
UGH, LOOKS LIKE THERE'S NOT GOING TO BE ANY ACTION IN MY LIFE-TIME. HOW DROLL.
DAMMIT.
YAWN...

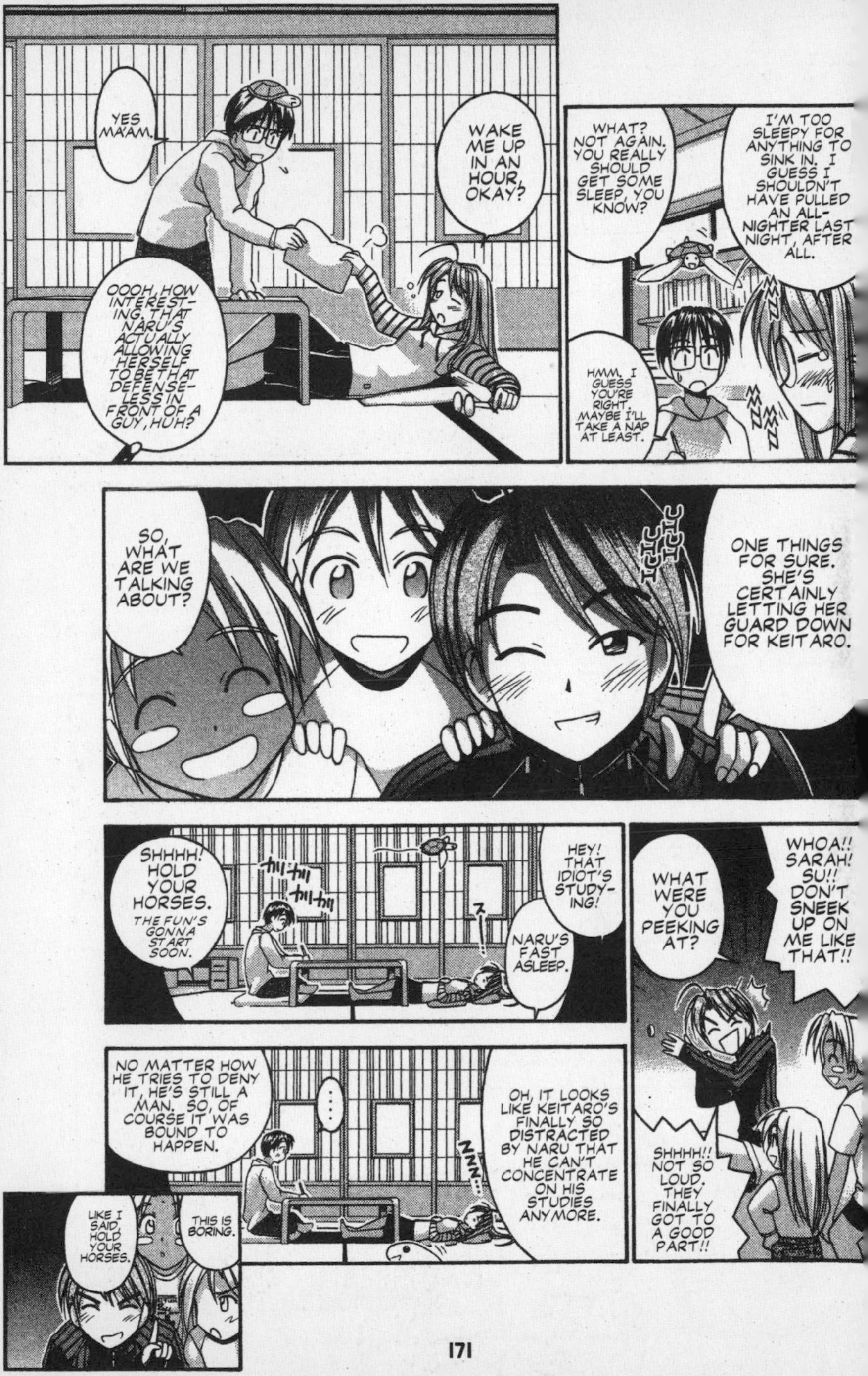
I'M TOO SLEEPY FOR ANYTHING TO SINK IN. I GUESS I SHOULDN'T HAVE PULLED AN ALL-NIGHTER LAST NIGHT, AFTER ALL.
WHAT? NOT AGAIN. YOU REALLY SHOULD GET SOME SLEEP, YOU KNOW?
MNN MNN
HMM. I GUESS YOU'RE RIGHT. MAYBE I'LL TAKE A NAP AT LEAST.
MNN MNN
WAKE ME UP IN AN HOUR, OKAY?
YES MA'AM.
OOOH, HOW INTERESTING THAT NARU'S ACTUALLY ALLOWING HERSELF TO BE THAT DEFENSELESS IN FRONT OF A GUY, HUH?
ONE THINGS FOR SURE. SHE'S CERTAINLY LETTING HER GUARD DOWN FOR KEITARO.
SO, WHAT ARE WE TALKING ABOUT?
WHOA!! SARAH! SU!! DON'T SNEEK UP ON ME LIKE THAT!!
WHAT WERE YOU PEEKING AT?
SHHHH!! NOT SO LOUD. THEY FINALLY GOT TO A GOOD PART!!
HEY! THAT IDIOT'S STUDYING!
NARU'S FAST ASLEEP.
SHHHH! HOLD YOUR HORSES. THE FUN'S GONNA START SOON.
OH, IT LOOKS LIKE KEITARO'S FINALLY SO DISTRACTED BY NARU THAT HE CAN'T CONCENTRATE ON HIS STUDIES ANYMORE.
ZZZ...
.....
NO MATTER HOW HE TRIES TO DENY IT, HE'S STILL A MAN. SO, OF COURSE IT WAS BOUND TO HAPPEN.
THIS IS BORING.
LIKE I SAID, HOLD YOUR HORSES.

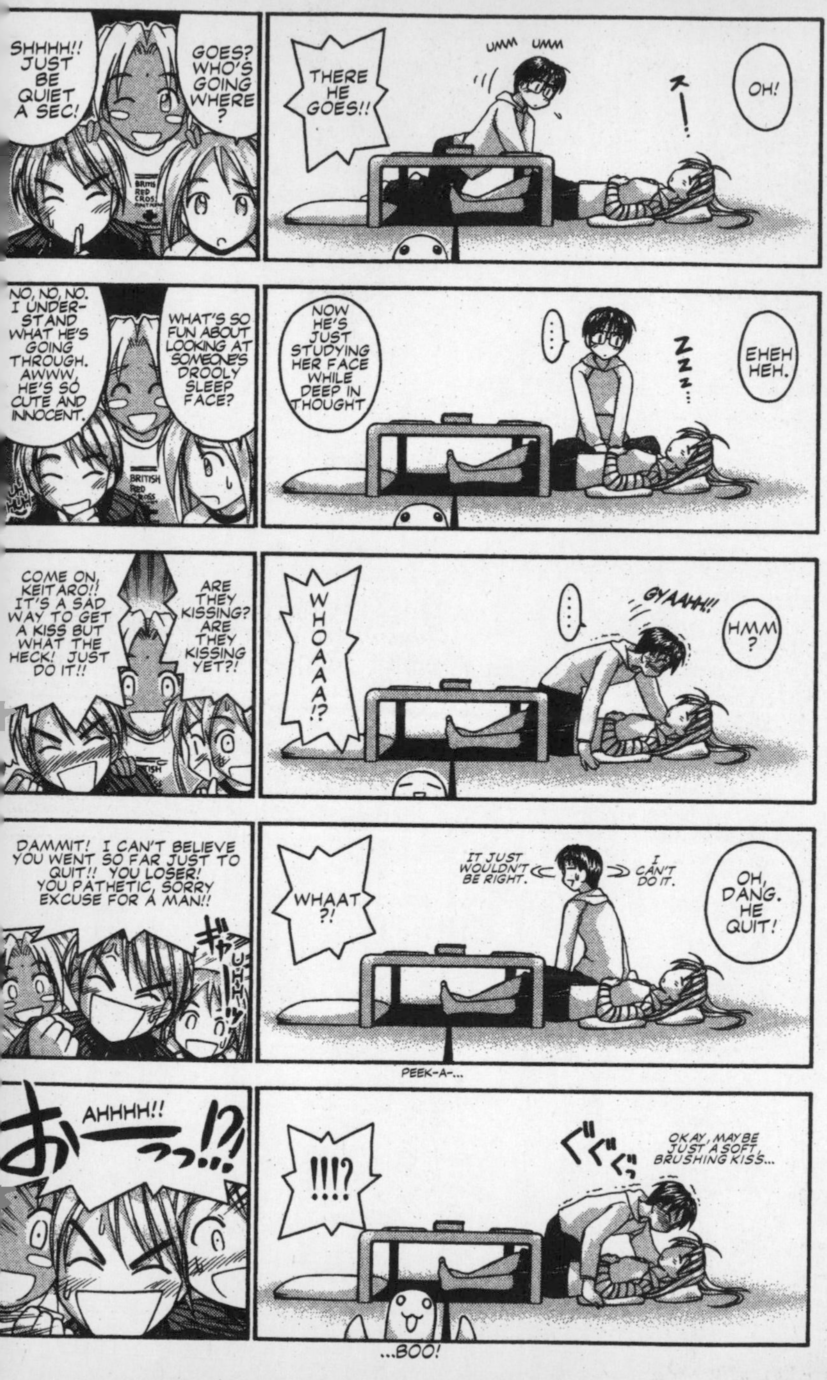

OH!
スー!
UMM UMM
THERE HE GOES!!
GOES? WHO'S GOING WHERE?
SHHHH!! JUST BE QUIET A SEC!
EHEH HEH.
ZZZ...
...
NOW HE'S JUST STUDYING HER FACE WHILE DEEP IN THOUGHT
WHAT'S SO FUN ABOUT LOOKING AT SOMEONE'S DROOLY SLEEP FACE?
NO, NO, NO. I UNDERSTAND WHAT HE'S GOING THROUGH. AWWW, HE'S SO CUTE AND INNOCENT.
BRITISH RED CROSS
HMM?
GYAAHH!!
...
WHOAAAA!?
ARE THEY KISSING? ARE THEY KISSING YET?!
COME ON, KEITARO!! IT'S A SAD WAY TO GET A KISS BUT WHAT THE HECK! JUST DO IT!!
OH, DANG. HE QUIT!
I CAN'T DO IT.
IT JUST WOULDN'T BE RIGHT.
WHAAT?!
DAMMIT! I CAN'T BELIEVE YOU WENT SO FAR JUST TO QUIT!! YOU LOSER! YOU PATHETIC, SORRY EXCUSE FOR A MAN!!
ギャ
PEEK-A-...
OKAY, MAYBE JUST A SOFT, BRUSHING KISS...
ぐぐぐっ
!!!?
AHHHH!!
おーっっ!?!
...BOO!

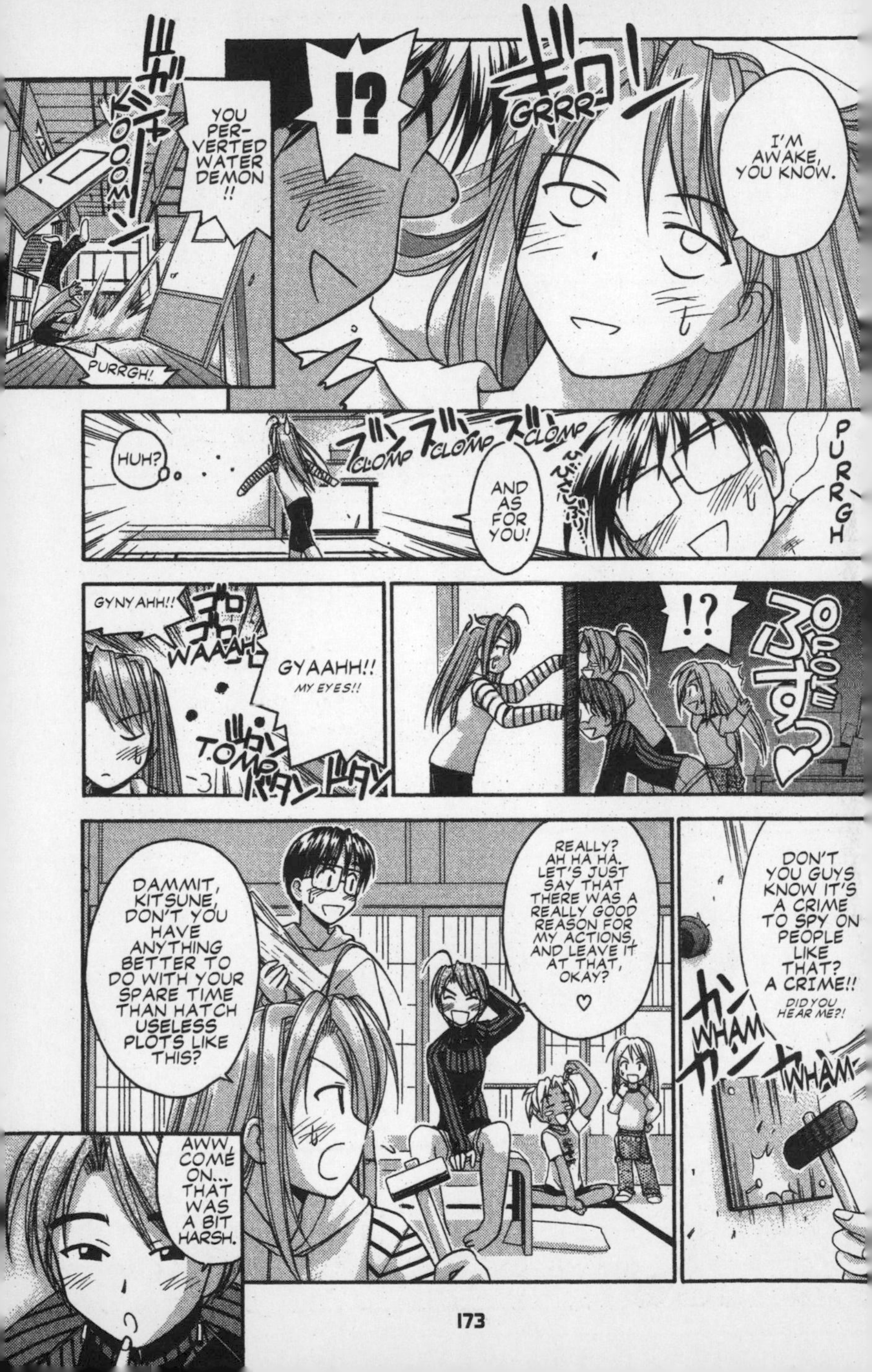
I'M AWAKE, YOU KNOW.
GRRR
!?
YOU PER-VERTED WATER DEMON!!
KOOOOM
PURRGH!
PURRGH
AND AS FOR YOU!
CLOMP
CLOMP
CLOMP
HUH?
!?
GYAAHH!! MY EYES!!
GYNYAHH!!
WAAAH
TOMP
DON'T YOU GUYS KNOW IT'S A CRIME TO SPY ON PEOPLE LIKE THAT? A CRIME!! DID YOU HEAR ME?!
WHAM
WHAM
REALLY? AH HA HA. LET'S JUST SAY THAT THERE WAS A REALLY GOOD REASON FOR MY ACTIONS, AND LEAVE IT AT THAT, OKAY? ♡
DAMMIT, KITSUNE, DON'T YOU HAVE ANYTHING BETTER TO DO WITH YOUR SPARE TIME THAN HATCH USELESS PLOTS LIKE THIS?
AWW, COME ON... THAT WAS A BIT HARSH.

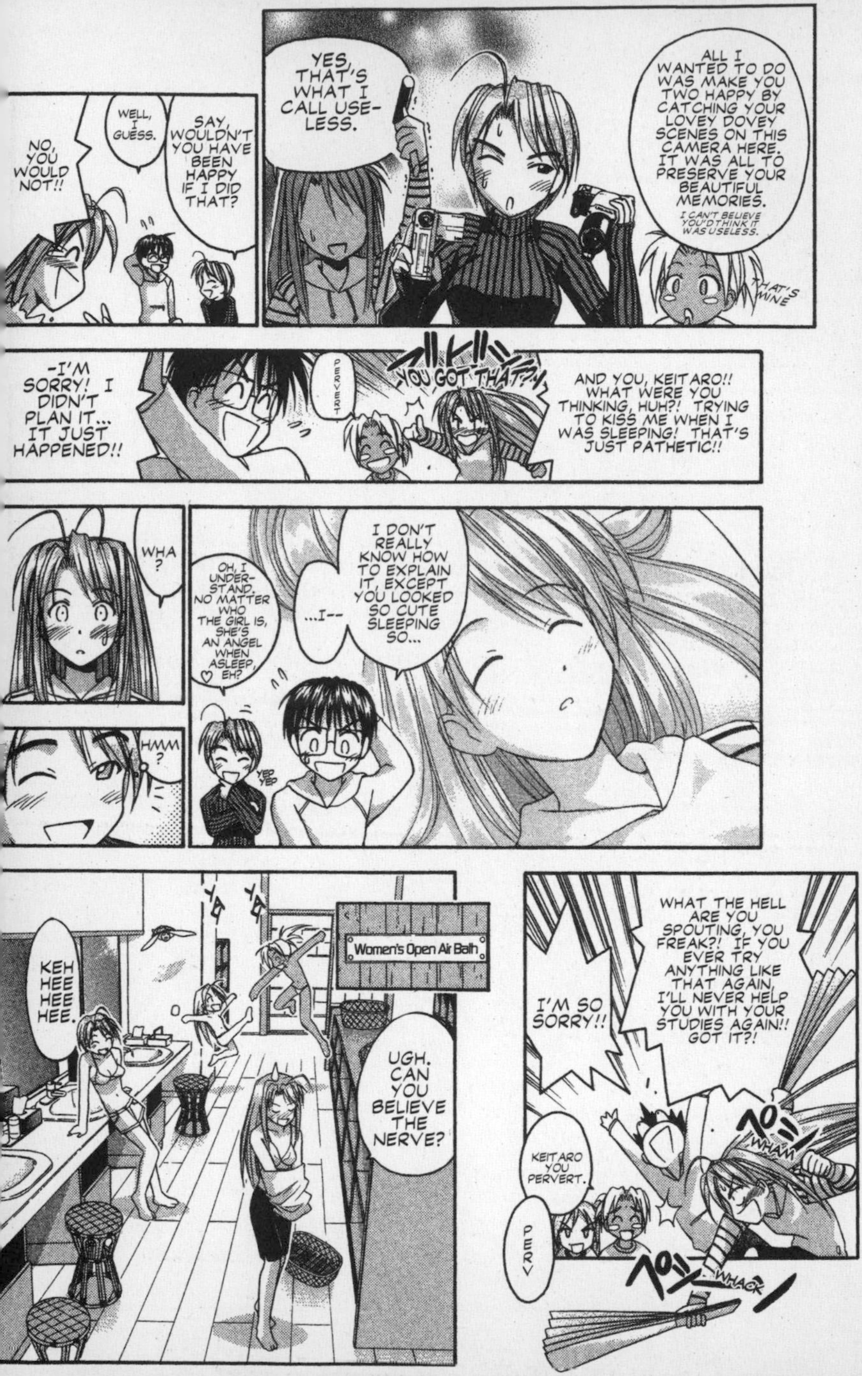
ALL I WANTED TO DO WAS MAKE YOU TWO HAPPY BY CATCHING YOUR LOVEY DOVEY SCENES ON THIS CAMERA HERE. IT WAS ALL TO PRESERVE YOUR BEAUTIFUL MEMORIES.
I CAN'T BELIEVE YOU'D THINK IT WAS USELESS.
YES, THAT'S WHAT I CALL USE-LESS.
THAT'S MINE
SAY, WOULDN'T YOU HAVE BEEN HAPPY IF I DID THAT?
WELL, I GUESS.
NO, YOU WOULD NOT!!
AND YOU, KEITARO!! WHAT WERE YOU THINKING, HUH?! TRYING TO KISS ME WHEN I WAS SLEEPING! THAT'S JUST PATHETIC!!
YOU GOT THAT?!
PERVERT
-I'M SORRY! I DIDN'T PLAN IT... IT JUST HAPPENED!!
I DON'T REALLY KNOW HOW TO EXPLAIN IT, EXCEPT YOU LOOKED SO CUTE SLEEPING SO...
...I--
OH, I UNDER-STAND. NO MATTER WHO THE GIRL IS, SHE'S AN ANGEL WHEN ASLEEP, EH? ♡
YEP YEP
WHA?
HMM?
WHAT THE HELL ARE YOU SPOUTING, YOU FREAK?! IF YOU EVER TRY ANYTHING LIKE THAT AGAIN, I'LL NEVER HELP YOU WITH YOUR STUDIES AGAIN!! GOT IT?!
I'M SO SORRY!!
WHAM
KEITARO YOU PERVERT.
PERV
WHACK
Women's Open Air Bath
UGH. CAN YOU BELIEVE THE NERVE?
KEH HEE HEE HEE.

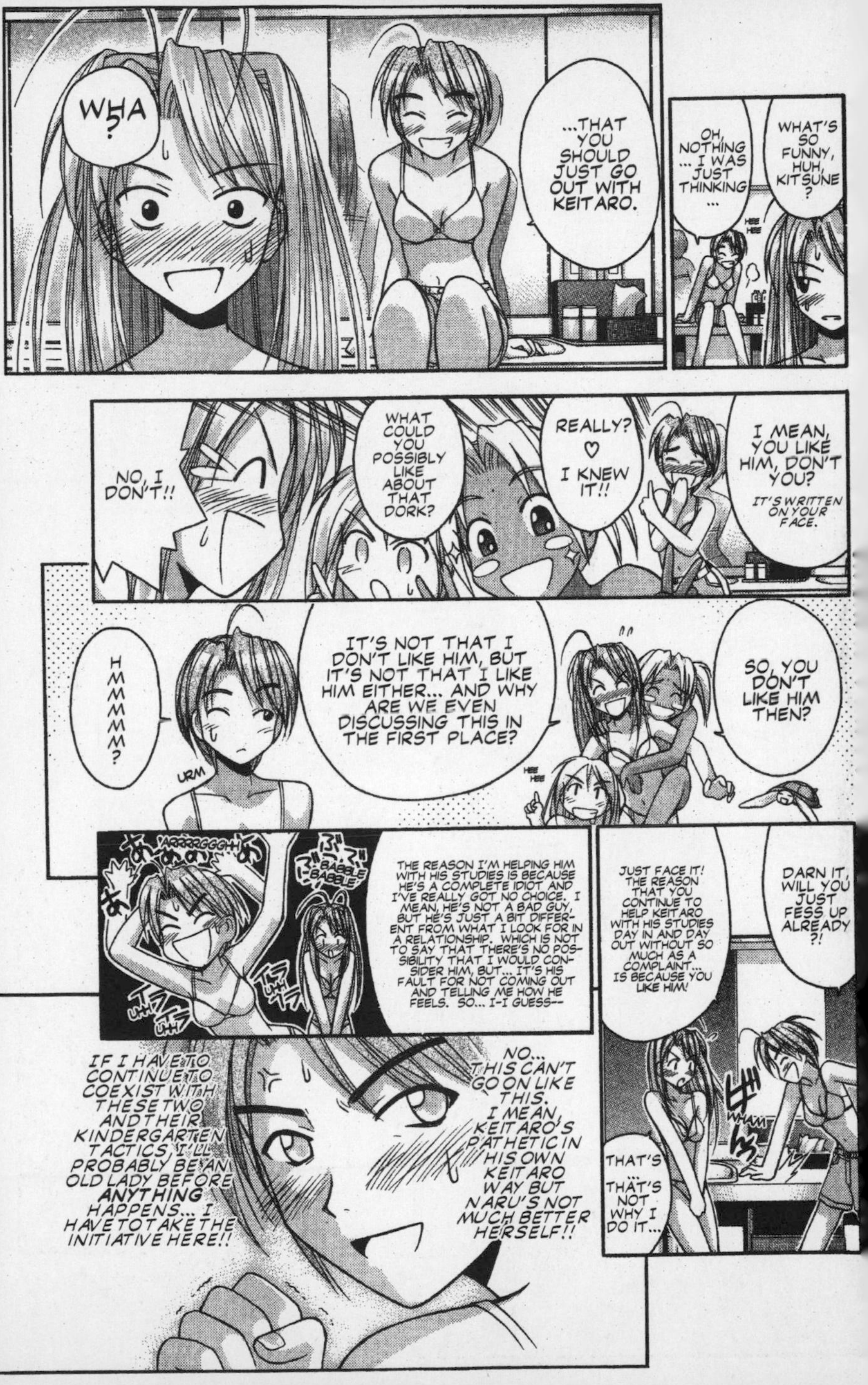
WHAT'S SO FUNNY, HUH, KITSUNE?
OH, NOTHING ... I WAS JUST THINKING ...
HEE HEE
...THAT YOU SHOULD JUST GO OUT WITH KEITARO.
WHA?
I MEAN, YOU LIKE HIM, DON'T YOU?
IT'S WRITTEN ON YOUR FACE.
REALLY? ♡ I KNEW IT!!
WHAT COULD YOU POSSIBLY LIKE ABOUT THAT DORK?
NO, I DON'T!!
SO, YOU DON'T LIKE HIM THEN?
HEE HEE
IT'S NOT THAT I DON'T LIKE HIM, BUT IT'S NOT THAT I LIKE HIM EITHER... AND WHY ARE WE EVEN DISCUSSING THIS IN THE FIRST PLACE?
HMMMMM?
URM
DARN IT, WILL YOU JUST FESS UP ALREADY?!
JUST FACE IT! THE REASON THAT YOU CONTINUE TO HELP KEITARO WITH HIS STUDIES DAY IN AND DAY OUT WITHOUT SO MUCH AS A COMPLAINT... IS BECAUSE YOU LIKE HIM!
WHAM
THAT'S ... THAT'S NOT WHY I DO IT...
THE REASON I'M HELPING HIM WITH HIS STUDIES IS BECAUSE HE'S A COMPLETE IDIOT AND I'VE REALLY GOT NO CHOICE. I MEAN, HE'S NOT A BAD GUY, BUT HE'S JUST A BIT DIFFERENT FROM WHAT I LOOK FOR IN A RELATIONSHIP. WHICH IS NOT TO SAY THAT THERE'S NO POSSIBILITY THAT I WOULD CONSIDER HIM, BUT... IT'S HIS FAULT FOR NOT COMING OUT AND TELLING ME HOW HE FEELS. SO... I-I GUESS--
ARRRRGGGH
BABBLE BABBLE
UHH UHH
NO... THIS CAN'T GO ON LIKE THIS. I MEAN, KEITARO'S PATHETIC IN HIS OWN KEITARO WAY BUT NARU'S NOT MUCH BETTER HERSELF!!
IF I HAVE TO CONTINUE TO COEXIST WITH THESE TWO AND THEIR KINDERGARTEN TACTICS, I'LL PROBABLY BE AN OLD LADY BEFORE ANYTHING HAPPENS... I HAVE TO TAKE THE INITIATIVE HERE!!

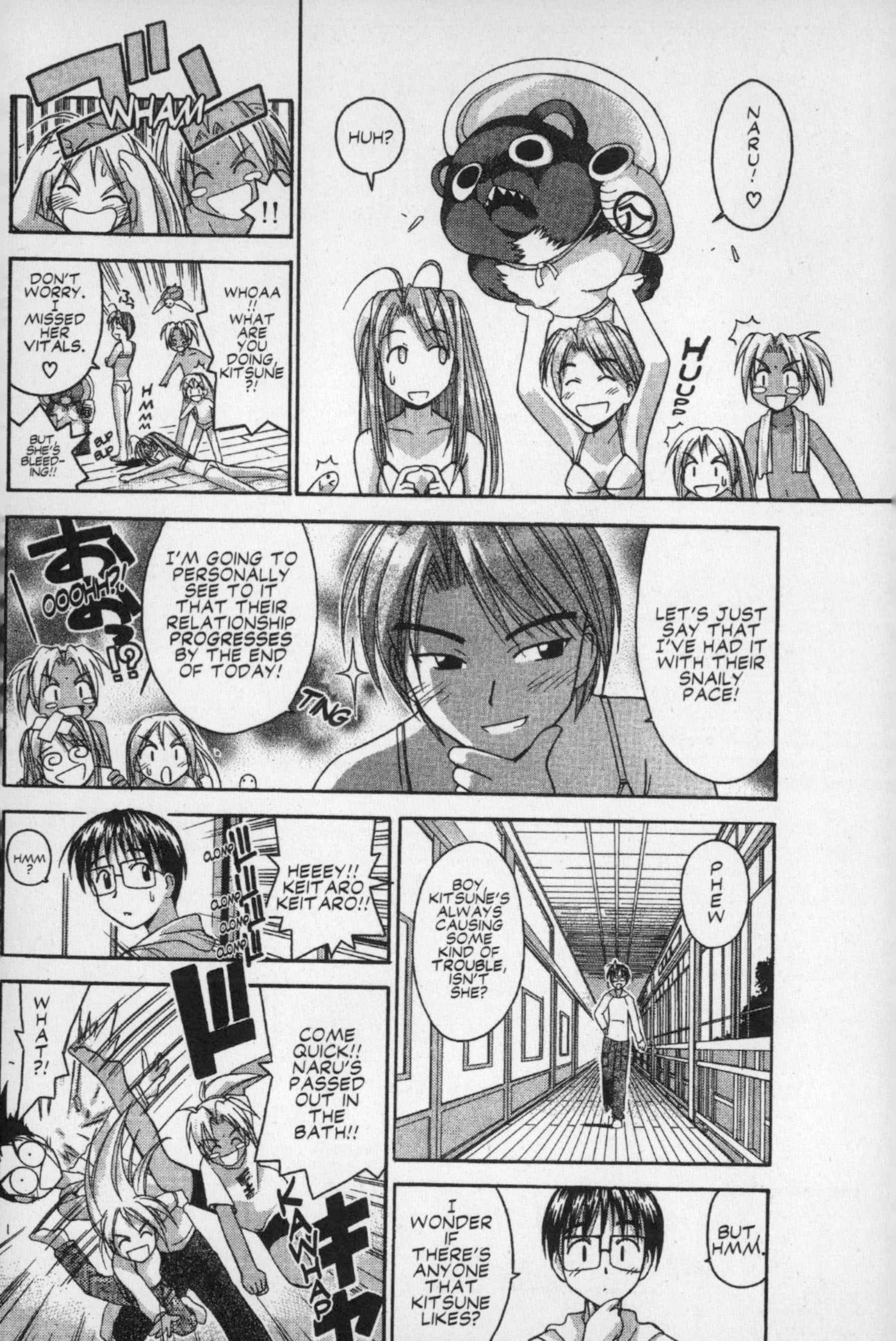
NARU! ♡
HUH?
HUUPP
WHAM
!!
WHOAA!! WHAT ARE YOU DOING, KITSUNE?!
HMMM
DON'T WORRY. I MISSED HER VITALS. ♡
BUP BUP
BUT, SHE'S BLEEDING!!
LET'S JUST SAY THAT I'VE HAD IT WITH THEIR SNAILY PACE!
TING
I'M GOING TO PERSONALLY SEE TO IT THAT THEIR RELATIONSHIP PROGRESSES BY THE END OF TODAY!
OOOHH?!
PHEW
BOY KITSUNE'S ALWAYS CAUSING SOME KIND OF TROUBLE, ISN'T SHE?
BUT HMM.
I WONDER IF THERE'S ANYONE THAT KITSUNE LIKES?
HEEEY!! KEITARO KEITARO!!
CLOMP CLOMP CLOMP CLOMP
HMM?
COME QUICK!! NARU'S PASSED OUT IN THE BATH!!
KAWHAP
WHAT?!

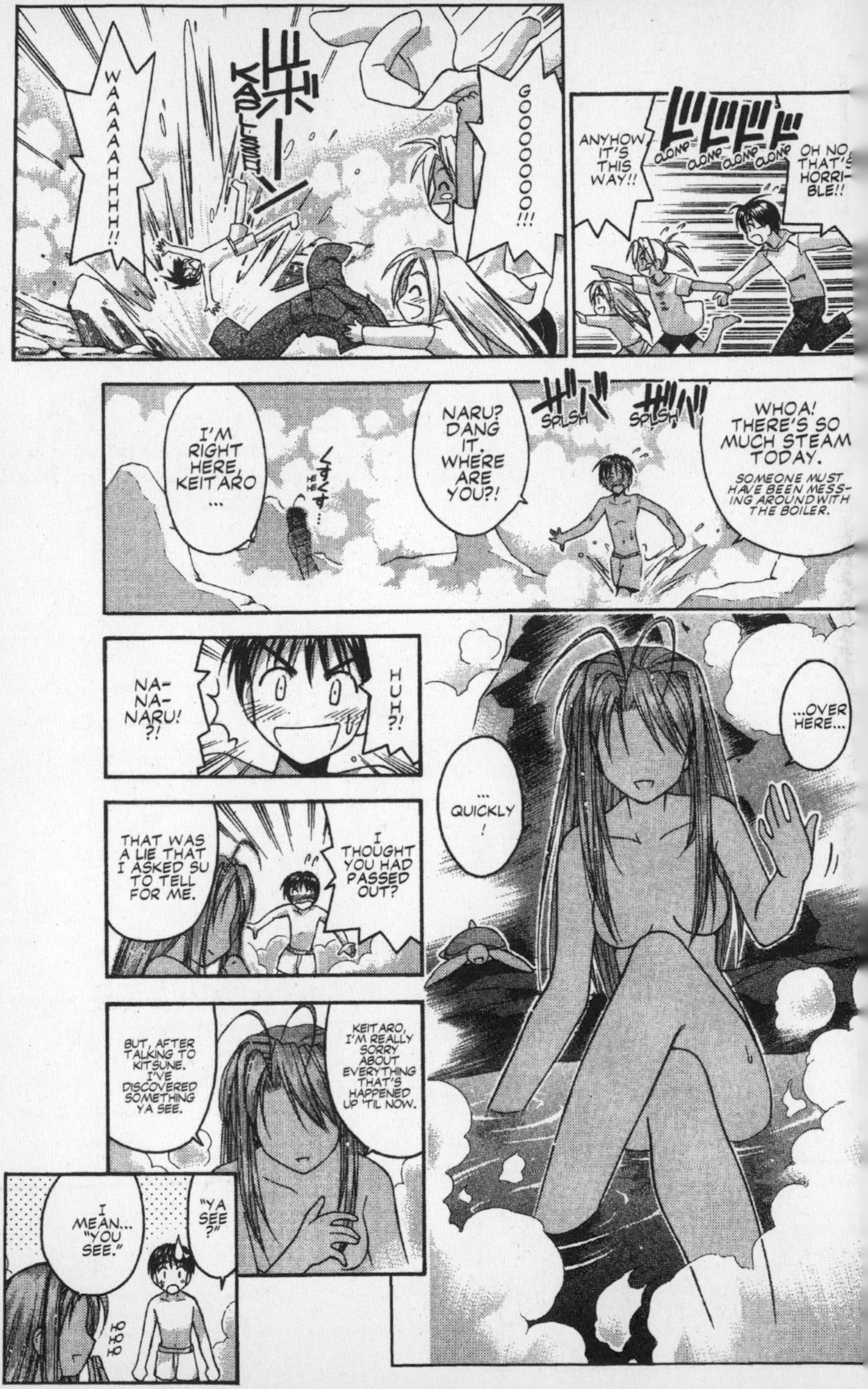
OH NO THAT'S HORRI-BLE!!
CLOMP CLOMP CLOMP CLOMP
ANYHOW IT'S THIS WAY!!
GOOOOOOO!!!
WAAAAAAHHHH!!
WHOA! THERE'S SO MUCH STEAM TODAY.
SOMEONE MUST HAVE BEEN MESSING AROUND WITH THE BOILER.
SPLSH SPLSH
NARU? DANG IT. WHERE ARE YOU?!
I'M RIGHT HERE, KEITARO ...
...OVER HERE...
... QUICKLY !
HUH?!
NA-NA-NARU! ?!
I THOUGHT YOU HAD PASSED OUT?
THAT WAS A LIE THAT I ASKED SU TO TELL FOR ME.
KEITARO, I'M REALLY SORRY ABOUT EVERYTHING THAT'S HAPPENED UP 'TIL NOW.
BUT, AFTER TALKING TO KITSUNE. I'VE DISCOVERED SOMETHING YA SEE.
"YA SEE?"
I MEAN... "YOU SEE."

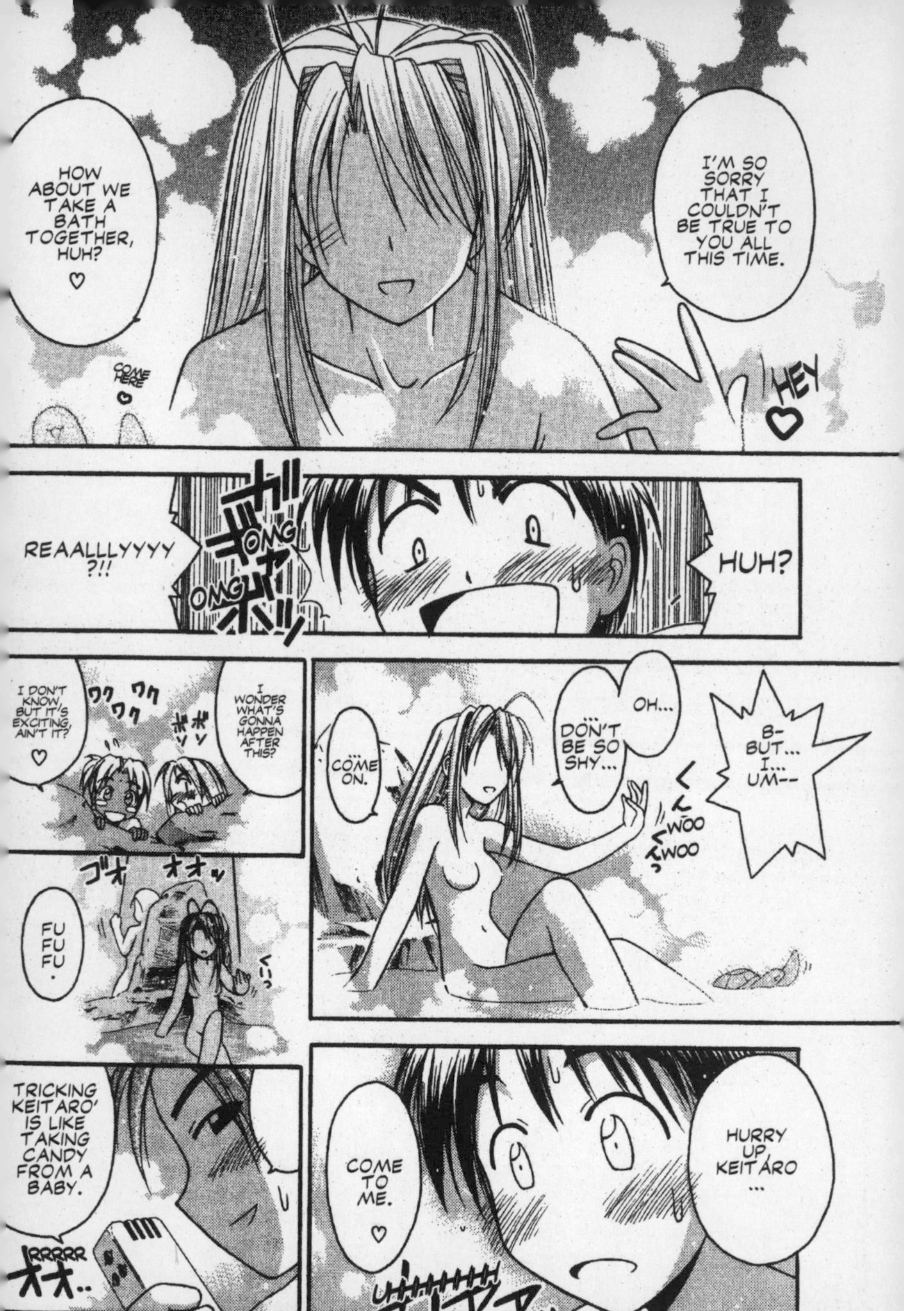
I'M SO SORRY THAT I COULDN'T BE TRUE TO YOU ALL THIS TIME.
HEY ♡
HOW ABOUT WE TAKE A BATH TOGETHER, HUH? ♡
COME HERE ♡
HUH?
OMG OMG
REAALLLYYYY ?!!
B-BUT... I... UM--
WOO WOO
OH... DON'T BE SO SHY...
...COME ON.
I WONDER WHAT'S GONNA HAPPEN AFTER THIS?
I DON'T KNOW, BUT IT'S EXCITING, AIN'T IT? ♡
FU FU FU.
HURRY UP, KEITARO ...
COME TO ME. ♡
TRICKING KEITARO' IS LIKE TAKING CANDY FROM A BABY.
RRRRRR

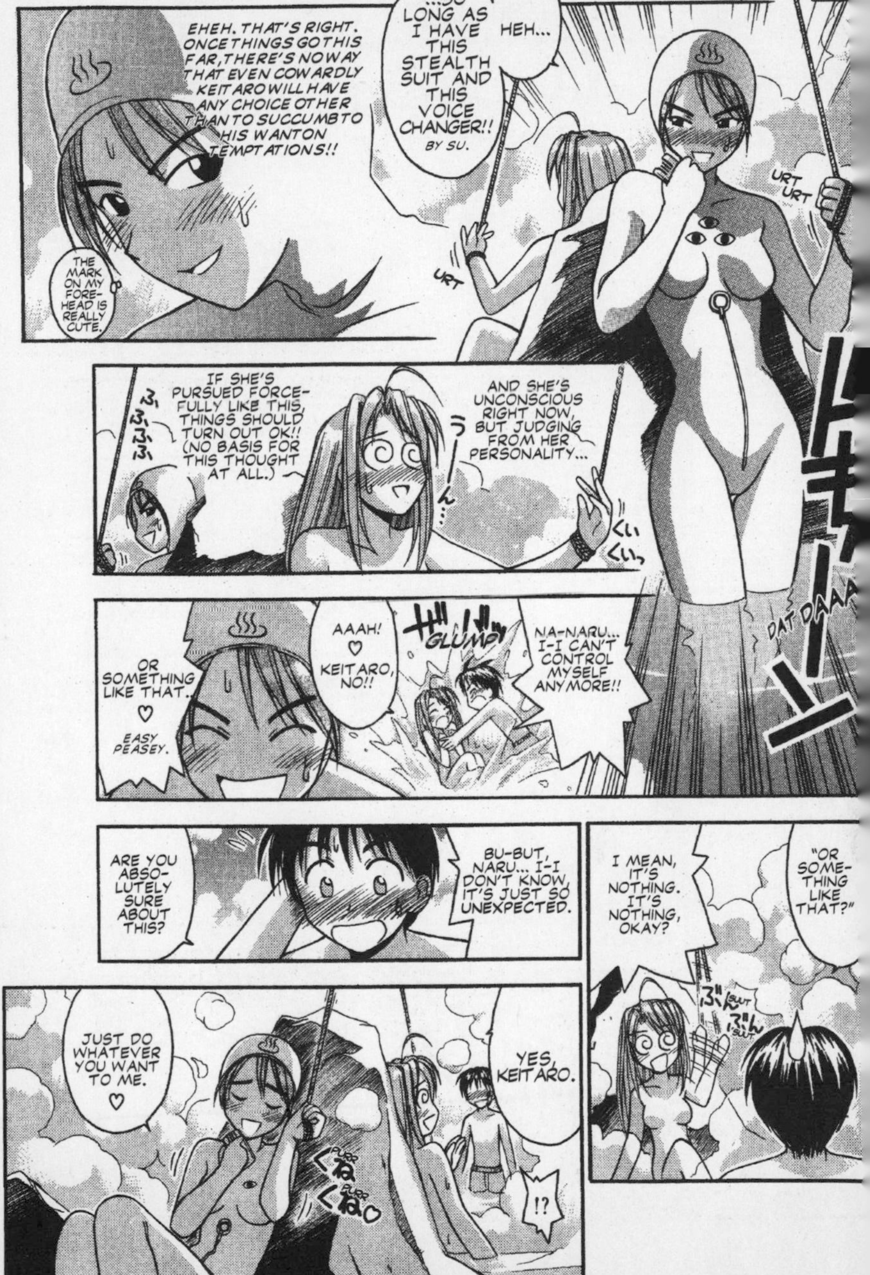
...SO LONG AS I HAVE THIS STEALTH SUIT AND THIS VOICE CHANGER!!
BY SU.
HEH...
URT URT
URT
ドキーン
DAT DAAA
EHEH. THAT'S RIGHT. ONCE THINGS GO THIS FAR, THERE'S NO WAY THAT EVEN COWARDLY KEITARO WILL HAVE ANY CHOICE OTHER THAN TO SUCCUMB TO HIS WANTON TEMPTATIONS!!
THE MARK ON MY FOREHEAD IS REALLY CUTE.
AND SHE'S UNCONSCIOUS RIGHT NOW, BUT JUDGING FROM HER PERSONALITY...
くいくいっ
う~ん...
IF SHE'S PURSUED FORCEFULLY LIKE THIS, THINGS SHOULD TURN OUT OK!! (NO BASIS FOR THIS THOUGHT AT ALL.)
ふふふふ
NA-NARU... I-I CAN'T CONTROL MYSELF ANYMORE!!
ガバッ
GLUMP
AAAH! ♡ KEITARO, NO!!
OR SOMETHING LIKE THAT.. ♡
EASY PEASEY.
"OR SOMETHING LIKE THAT?"
I MEAN, IT'S NOTHING. IT'S NOTHING, OKAY?
ぶん SUIT
ぶん SUIT
BU-BUT, NARU... I-I DON'T KNOW, IT'S JUST SO UNEXPECTED.
ARE YOU ABSOLUTELY SURE ABOUT THIS?
YES, KEITARO.
!?
くね PURR
くね PURR ♡
JUST DO WHATEVER YOU WANT TO ME. ♡

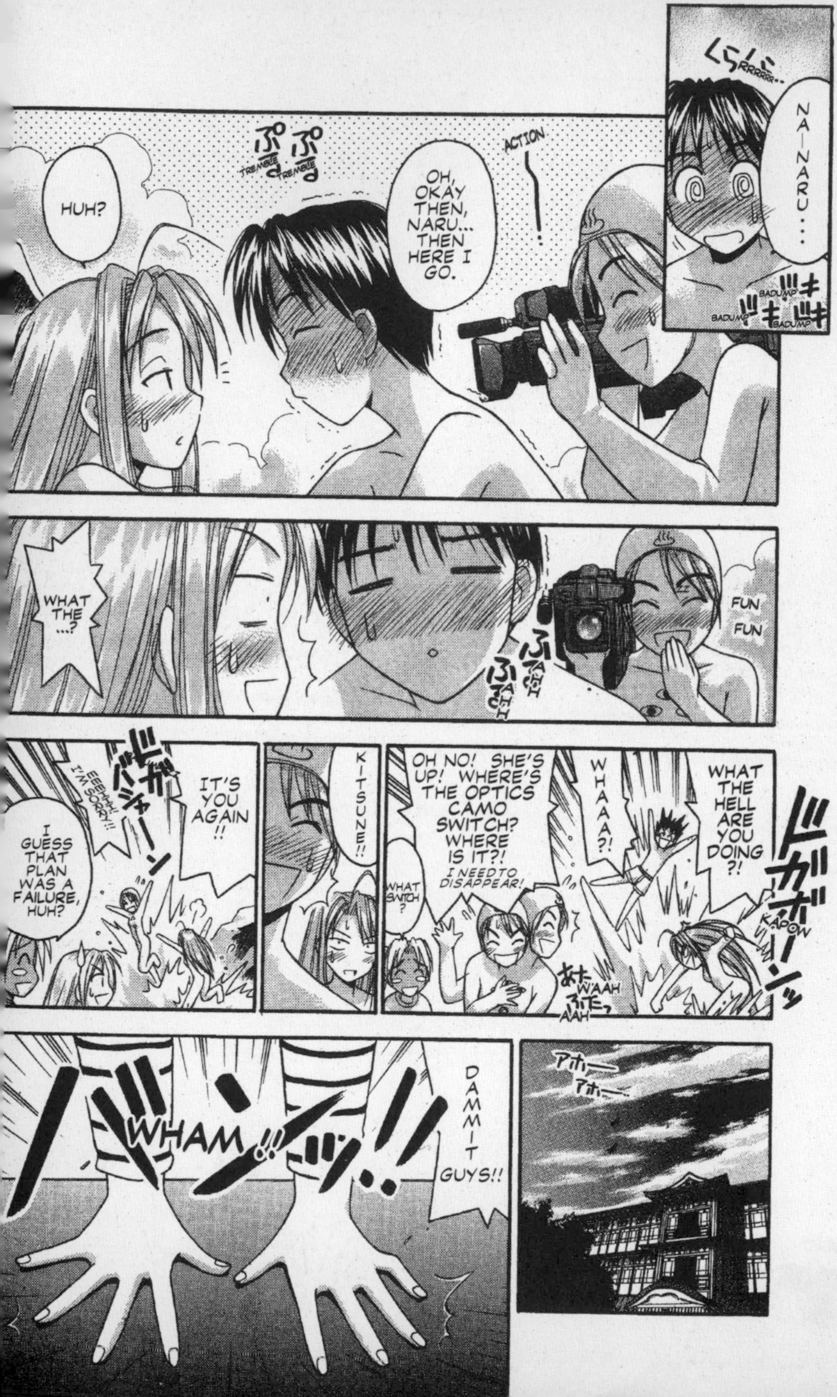

くらくら RRRRRR...
NAI-NARU...
BADUMP BADUMP BADUMP
ACTION
OH, OKAY THEN, NARU... THEN HERE I GO.
TREMBLE TREMBLE
HUH?
FUN FUN
FUAHH FUAHH
WHAT THE ...?
KAPOW
WHAT THE HELL ARE YOU DOING?!
WHAAAA?!
OH NO! SHE'S UP! WHERE'S THE OPTICS CAMO SWITCH? WHERE IS IT?!
I NEED TO DISAPPEAR!
WHAT SWITCH?
WAAH AAH
KITSUNE!!
IT'S YOU AGAIN!!
EEEIII! I'M SORRY!!
I GUESS THAT PLAN WAS A FAILURE, HUH?
アホー アホー
DAMMIT GUYS!!
WHAM!!

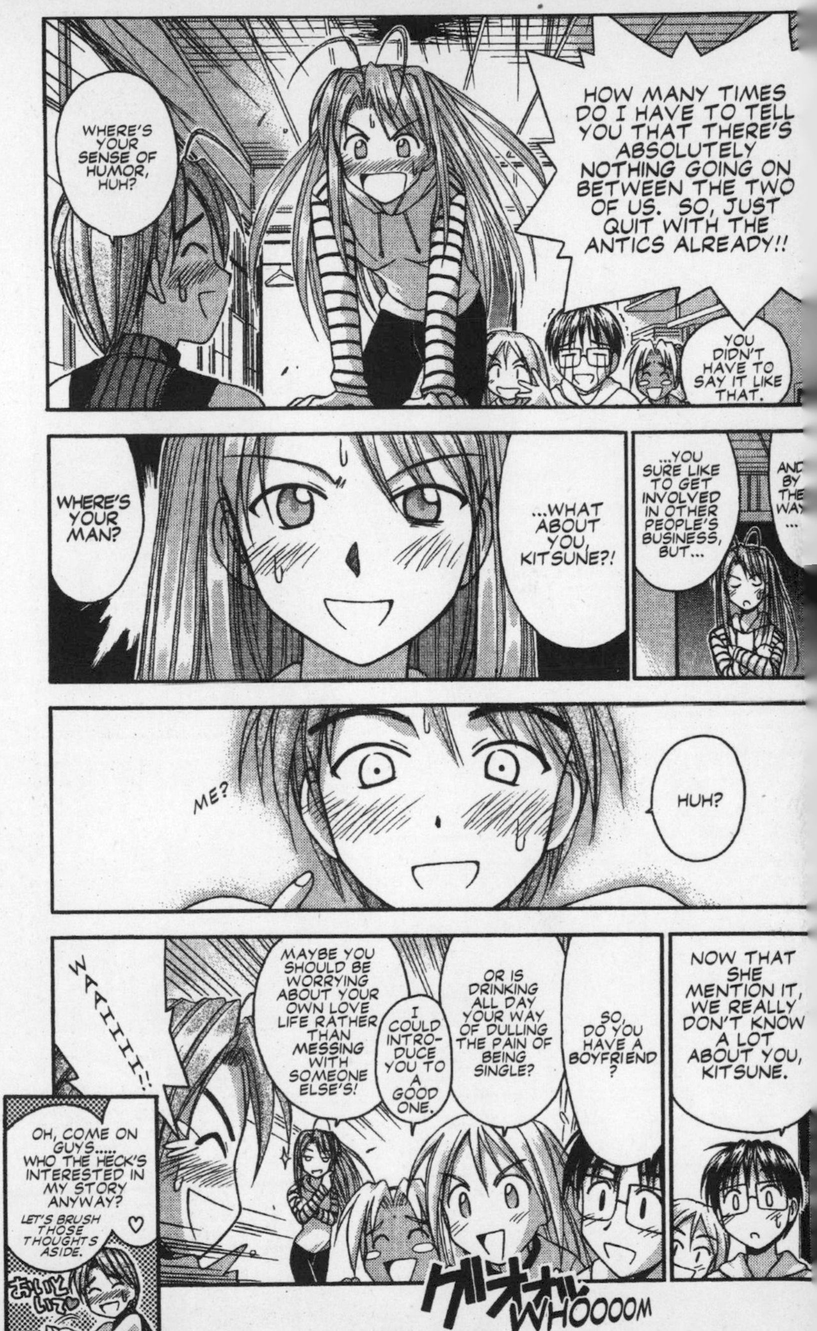
HOW MANY TIMES DO I HAVE TO TELL YOU THAT THERE'S ABSOLUTELY NOTHING GOING ON BETWEEN THE TWO OF US. SO, JUST QUIT WITH THE ANTICS ALREADY!!
WHERE'S YOUR SENSE OF HUMOR, HUH?
YOU DIDN'T HAVE TO SAY IT LIKE THAT.
AND BY THE WAY ...
...YOU SURE LIKE TO GET INVOLVED IN OTHER PEOPLE'S BUSINESS, BUT...
...WHAT ABOUT YOU, KITSUNE?!
WHERE'S YOUR MAN?
HUH?
ME?
NOW THAT SHE MENTION IT, WE REALLY DON'T KNOW A LOT ABOUT YOU, KITSUNE.
SO, DO YOU HAVE A BOYFRIEND?
OR IS DRINKING ALL DAY YOUR WAY OF DULLING THE PAIN OF BEING SINGLE?
I COULD INTRODUCE YOU TO A GOOD ONE.
MAYBE YOU SHOULD BE WORRYING ABOUT YOUR OWN LOVE LIFE RATHER THAN MESSING WITH SOMEONE ELSE'S!
WAAIIII!!
WHOOOOM
OH, COME ON GUYS..... WHO THE HECK'S INTERESTED IN MY STORY ANYWAY?
LET'S BRUSH THOSE THOUGHTS ASIDE. ♡
おいといて

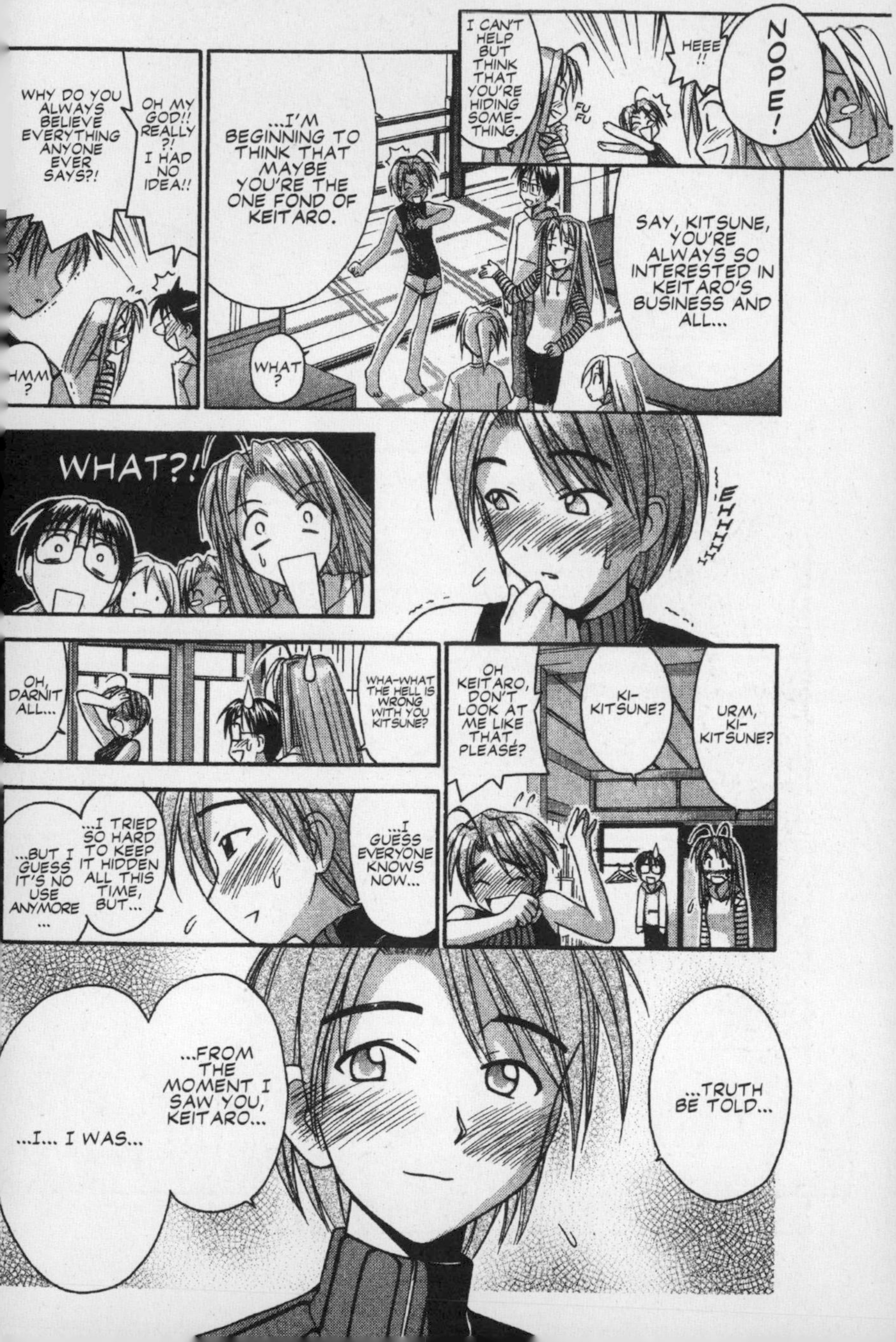
NOPE!
HEEE!!
I CAN'T HELP BUT THINK THAT YOU'RE HIDING SOME-THING.
FU FU
SAY, KITSUNE, YOU'RE ALWAYS SO INTERESTED IN KEITARO'S BUSINESS AND ALL...
...I'M BEGINNING TO THINK THAT MAYBE YOU'RE THE ONE FOND OF KEITARO.
WHAT?
OH MY GOD!! REALLY?! I HAD NO IDEA!!
WHY DO YOU ALWAYS BELIEVE EVERYTHING ANYONE EVER SAYS?!
HMM?
EHHHHH
WHAT?!
URM, KI-KITSUNE?
KI-KITSUNE?
OH KEITARO, DON'T LOOK AT ME LIKE THAT, PLEASE?
WHA-WHAT THE HELL IS WRONG WITH YOU KITSUNE?
OH, DARNIT ALL...
...I GUESS EVERYONE KNOWS NOW...
...I TRIED SO HARD TO KEEP IT HIDDEN ALL THIS TIME, BUT...
...BUT I GUESS IT'S NO USE ANYMORE...
...TRUTH BE TOLD...
...FROM THE MOMENT I SAW YOU, KEITARO...
...I... I WAS...

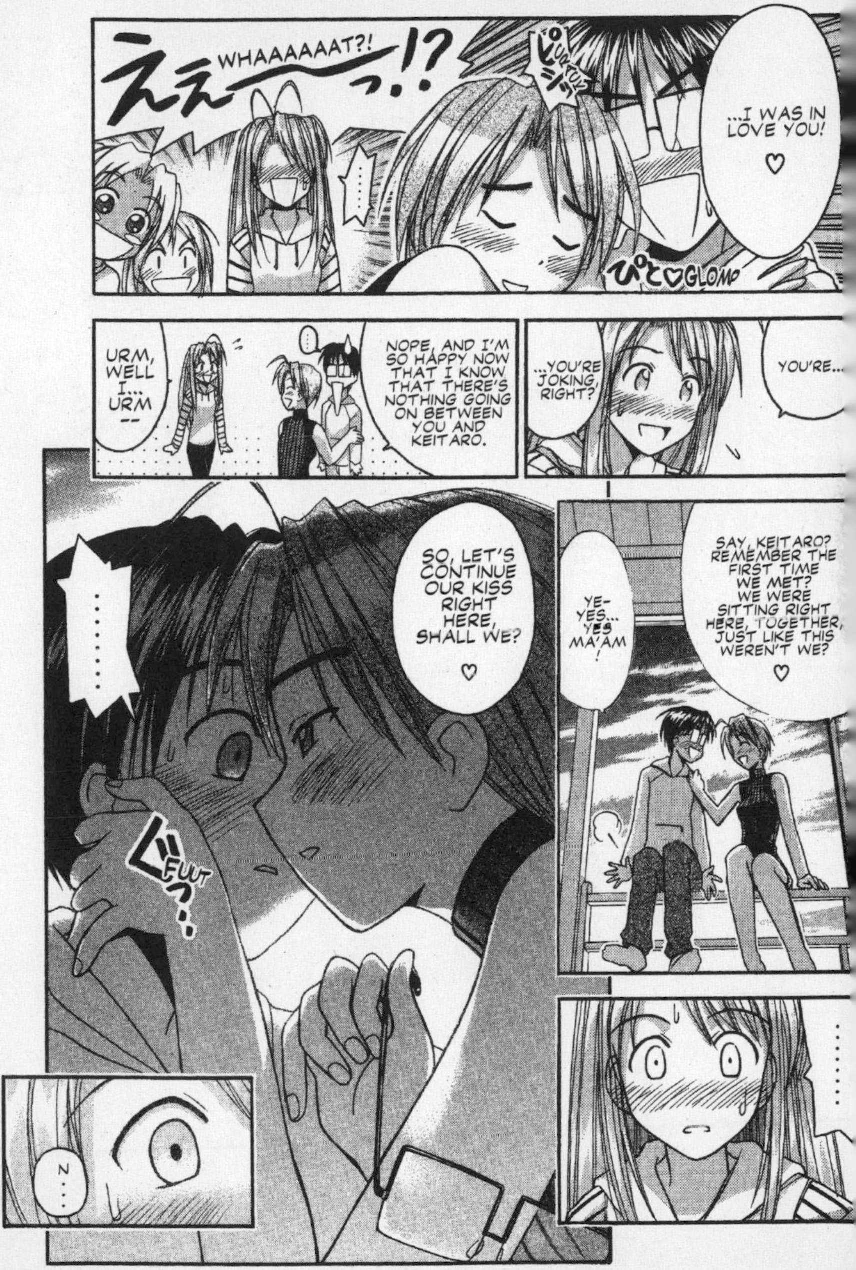
...I WAS IN LOVE YOU! ♡
GLOMP
ええーっ!?
WHAAAAAAT?!
YOU'RE...
...YOU'RE JOKING, RIGHT?
NOPE, AND I'M SO HAPPY NOW THAT I KNOW THAT THERE'S NOTHING GOING ON BETWEEN YOU AND KEITARO.
URM, WELL I... URM --
SAY, KEITARO? REMEMBER THE FIRST TIME WE MET? WE WERE SITTING RIGHT HERE, TOGETHER, JUST LIKE THIS WEREN'T WE? ♡
YE-YES... YES MA'AM!
SO, LET'S CONTINUE OUR KISS RIGHT HERE, SHALL WE? ♡
FUUT
N....

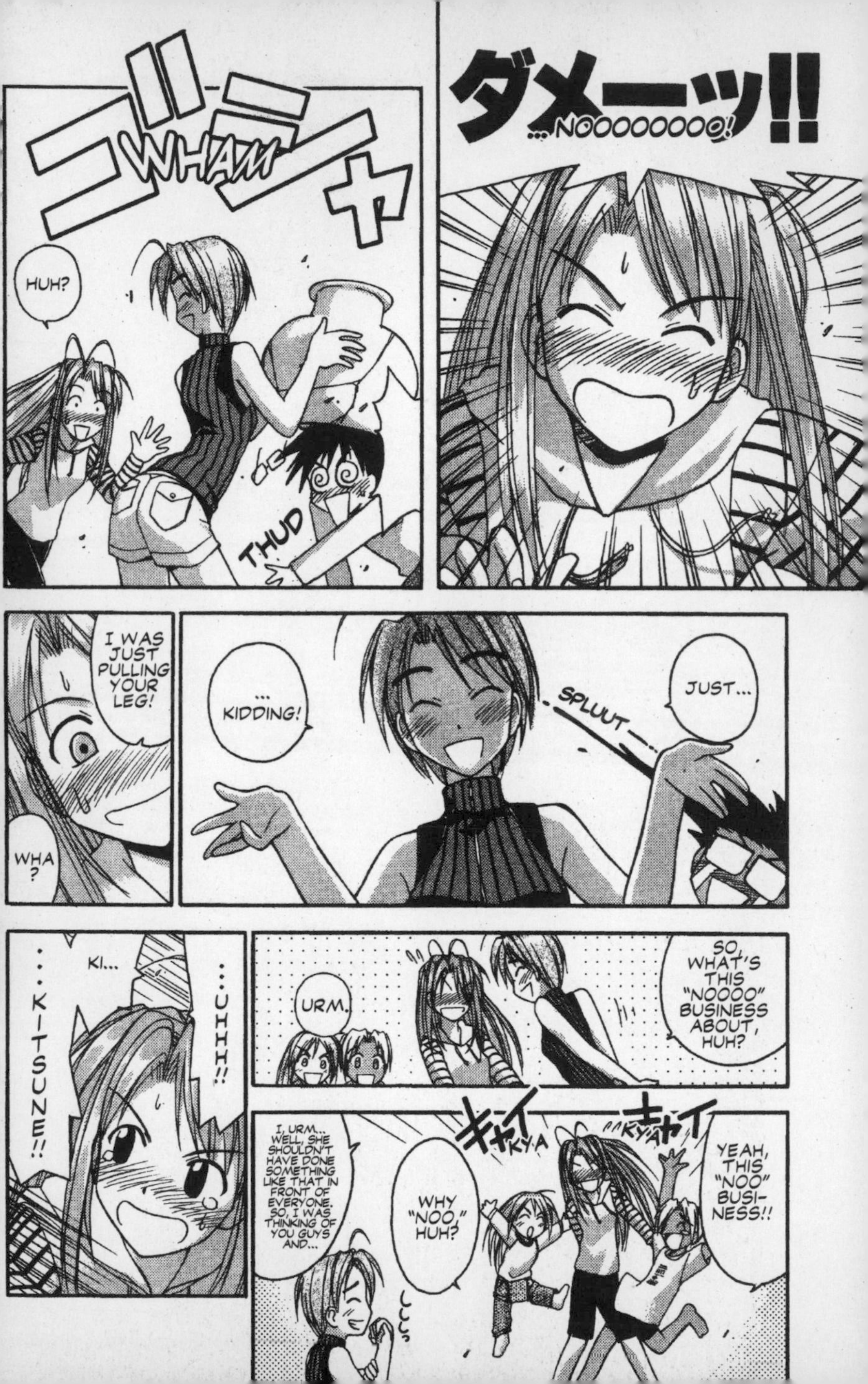
ダメーッ!!
...NOOOOOOOO!
WHAM
HUH?
THUD
JUST...
SPLUUT
... KIDDING!
I WAS JUST PULLING YOUR LEG!
WHA?
SO, WHAT'S THIS "NOOOO" BUSINESS ABOUT, HUH?
URM.
キャイ
KYA
キャイ
KYA
YEAH, THIS "NOO" BUSI-NESS!!
WHY "NOO," HUH?
I, URM... WELL, SHE SHOULDN'T HAVE DONE SOMETHING LIKE THAT IN FRONT OF EVERYONE. SO, I WAS THINKING OF YOU GUYS AND...
...UHHH!!
KI...
...KITSUNE!!

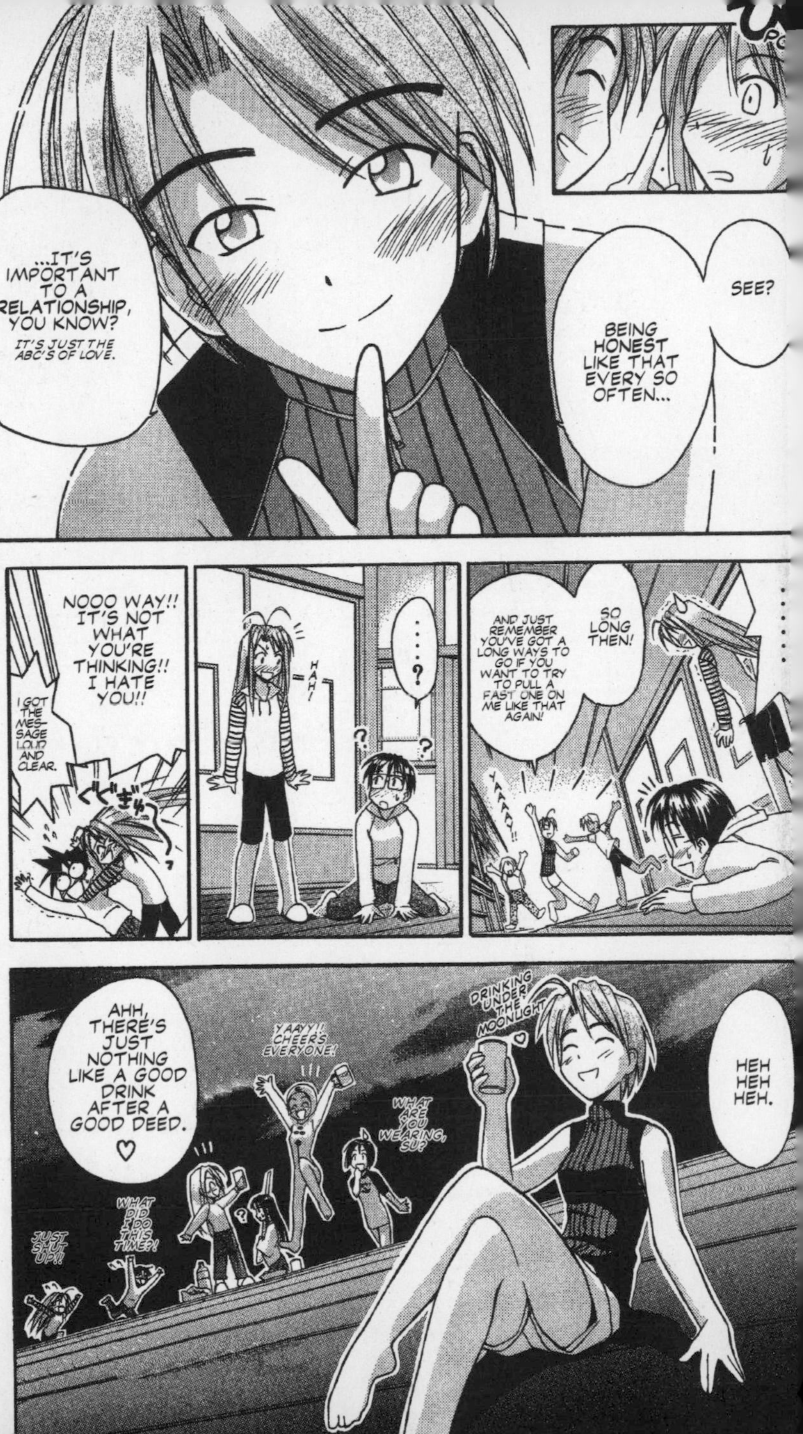
SEE?
BEING HONEST LIKE THAT EVERY SO OFTEN...
...IT'S IMPORTANT TO A RELATIONSHIP, YOU KNOW?
IT'S JUST THE ABC'S OF LOVE.
SO LONG THEN!
AND JUST REMEMBER YOU'VE GOT A LONG WAYS TO GO IF YOU WANT TO TRY TO PULL A FAST ONE ON ME LIKE THAT AGAIN!
YAAAAY!!
...?
HAH!
NOOO WAY!! IT'S NOT WHAT YOU'RE THINKING!! I HATE YOU!!
I GOT THE MES-SAGE LOUD AND CLEAR.
HEH HEH HEH.
DRINKING UNDER THE MOONLIGHT ♡
AHH, THERE'S JUST NOTHING LIKE A GOOD DRINK AFTER A GOOD DEED. ♡
YAAYY!! CHEERS EVERYONE!
WHAT ARE YOU WEARING, SU?
WHAT DID I DO THIS TIME?!
JUST SHUT UP!!

STAFF

Ken Akamatsu
Takashi Takemoto
Kenichi Nakamura
Takaaki Miyahara
Masaki Ohyama
Yumiko Shinohara

EDITOR

Noboru Ohno
Tomoyuki Shiratsuchi
Yasushi Yamanaka

KC Editor

Mitsuei Ishii

Love Hina

Preview for Volume Six

A year has passed since Keitaro arrived at Hinata House and things seem to be finally looking up - he obtains two tickets to go to a new amusement park and then scores a decent grade on his last practice college entrance exam. And there's no better way to celebrate his improved score than to ask his cute housemate/study partner/romantic interest, the tempestuous Naru, to the amusement park as thanks for all of her tutoring. Keitaro intends for the outing to be solely a gesture of thanks, yet nosy roommates quickly come to more wicked conclusions about the status of their relationship. But, despite declarations to the contrary, Naru may be beginning to see Keitaro in another light!

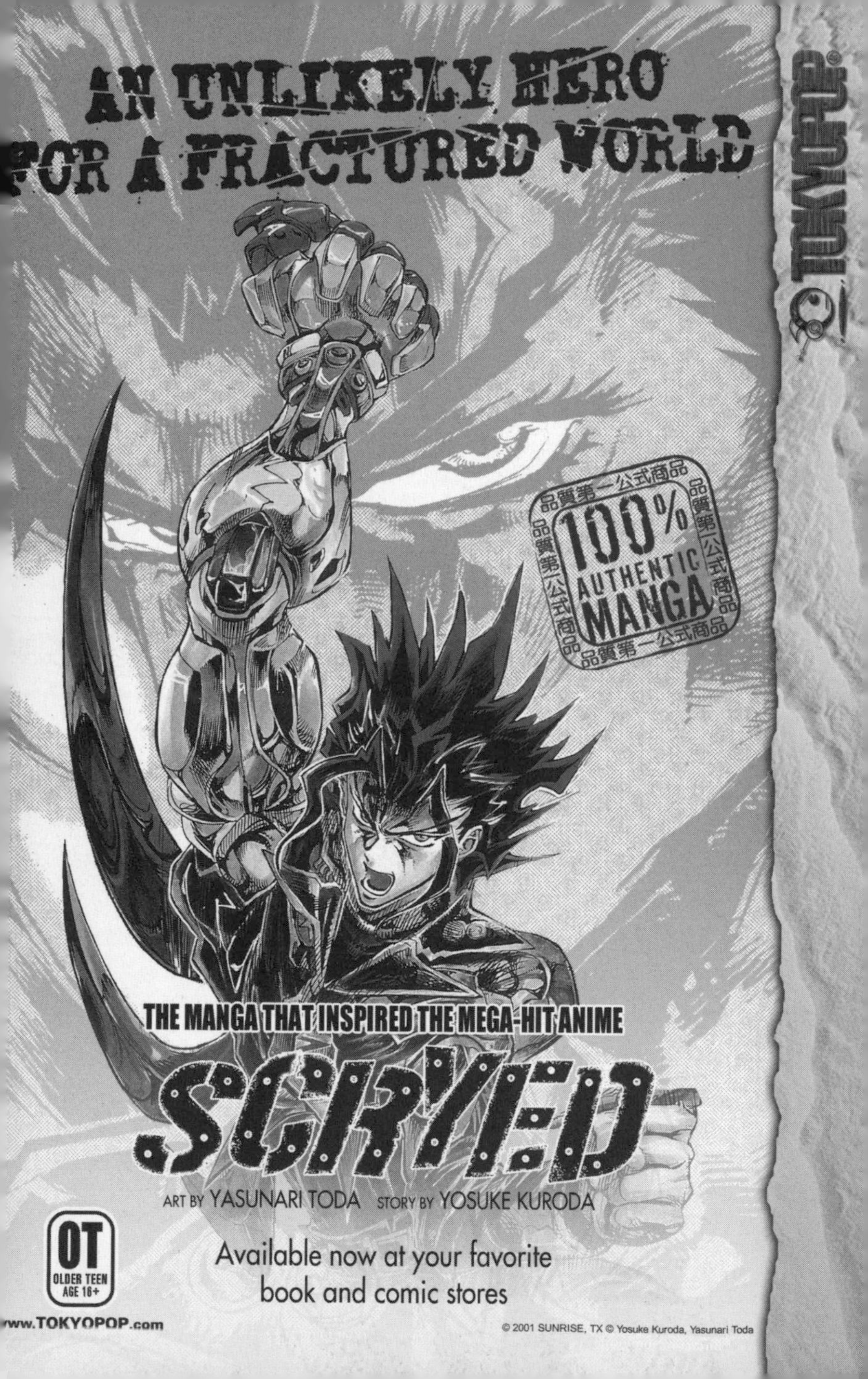
AN UNLIKELY HERO
FOR A FRACTURED WORLD
TOKYOPOP®
品質第一公式商品
100% AUTHENTIC MANGA
THE MANGA THAT INSPIRED THE MEGA-HIT ANIME
SCRYED
ART BY YASUNARI TODA STORY BY YOSUKE KURODA
OT OLDER TEEN AGE 16+
Available now at your favorite
book and comic stores
www.TOKYOPOP.com
© 2001 SUNRISE, TX © Yosuke Kuroda, Yasunari Toda

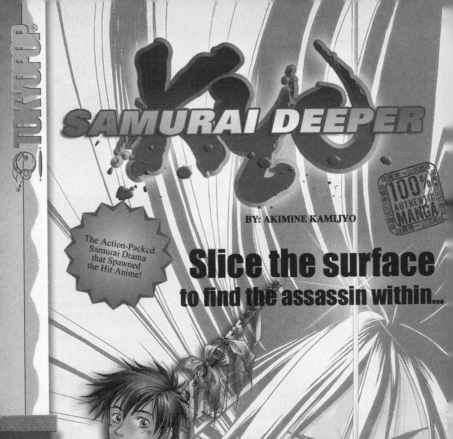

STOP!

This is the back of the book.
You wouldn't want to spoil a great ending!

This book is printed "manga-style," in the authentic Japanese right-to-left format. Since none of the artwork has been flipped or altered, readers get to experience the story just as the creator intended. You've been asking for it, so TOKYOPOP® delivered: authentic, hot-off-the-press, and far more fun!

DIRECTIONS

If this is your first time reading manga-style, here's a quick guide to help you understand how it works.

It's easy... just start in the top right panel and follow the numbers. Have fun, and look for more 100% authentic manga from TOKYOPOP®!